The Integral Advaitism
of
Sri Aurobindo

The
Integral Advaitism
of
Sri Aurobindo

RAM SHANKAR MISRA

MOTILAL BANARSIDASS PUBLISHERS
PRIVATE LIMITED • DELHI

First Edition : Delhi, 1998

© MOTILAL BANARSIDASS PUBLISHER PRIVATE LIMITED
All Rights Reserved

ISBN: 81-208-1329-4

Also available at :

MOTILAL BANARSIDASS

41 U.A. Bungalow Road, Jawahar Nagar, Delhi 110 007
8, Mahalaxmi Chamber, Warden Road, Mumbai 400 026
120 Royapettah High Road, Mylapore, Chennai 600 004
Sanas Plaza, Subhash Nagar, Pune 411 002
16 St. Mark's Road, Bangalore 560 001
8 Camac Street, Calcutta 700 017
Ashok Rajpath, Patna 800 004
Chowk, Varanasi 221 001

PRINTED IN INDIA
BY JAINENDRA PRAKASH JAIN AT SHRI JAINENDRA PRESS,
A-45 NARAINA, PHASE I, NEW DELHI 110 028
AND PUBLISHED BY NARENDRA PRAKASH JAIN FOR
MOTILAL BANARSIDASS PUBLISHERS PRIVATE LIMITED,
BUNGALOW ROAD, NEW DELHI 110 007

To
The Sacred Memory
of
My Revered Teacher
Pandit Batuk Nath Sharma

PREFACE

Sri Aurobindo occupies a pre-eminent place among the philosophers and thinkers of modern India. He has produced monumental works on The *Veda*, The *Bhagavadgītā* and on *Yoga* and has presented the philosophy of the *Upaniṣads* in a new light and in all its integrality and depth. He has made a reinterpretation of the ancient Vedic and Vedāntic thought and has given a new orientation and, in some respects, a higher dimension to it. He is the only Indian philosopher of the present era who has developed a full-fledged system of the philosophy of the Vedānta. In this respect he belongs to the rank of the great philosophers and founders of the schools of the Vedānta like Ācārya Śaṅkara and Ācārya Rāmānuja. His system of the Vedānta is called Integral Advaitism and it is developed with great thoroughness, profundity and originality in his *magnum opus The Life Divine*.

The Integral Advaitism of Sri Aurobindo has certain distinctive features which distinguish it clearly from the other great systems of the Vedānta, namely, Advaita, Viśiṣṭādvaita etc. A most distinctive feature of Sri Aurobindo's Integral View of Reality or his Integral Advaitism is that he has established it on the basis of higher reason or logic which he significantly calls the Logic of the Infinite. Sri Aurobindo has shown with great clarity and thoroughness that reason which operates on the basis of the Laws of Formal Logic, namely, Identity, Contradiction etc., is merely abstract and analytic in character and it cannot adequately determine the nature of the Absolute or Brahman and its relationship with man and the world in all its integrality and depth.The abstract and formal reason has to deny the reality of one or the other aspect of the Absolute in order to make it consistent with the laws of formal logic, which are empty of content and do not present a picture of reality. Sri Aurobindo has brought this truth into clear focus that the *a priori* and unconditional application of the laws of formal logic, namely, Identity, Contradiction and Excluded Middle to propositions which express the nature of Reality is logically unwarranted and unjustified. The *a priori* application of these laws is permissible in the field of mathematics and deductive sciences and not in respect of propositions which refer to Reality, empirical or transcendent. The nature of the Absolute can be determined in an adequate and comprehensive way only by a higher reason or logic which makes an application of the laws of Identity, Contradiction etc. in the light of experience and pays equal attention to self-consistency in reasoning as well as to truth. Sri Aurobindo has shown in an effective way and on strong rational grounds the inadequacy and shortcomings of dialectical reasoning and has provided ample evidence for the acceptance and application of higher reason or the logic of the Infinite to ascertain and comprehend the nature of the supreme Reality or the Absolute. This constitutes, in our view, a most notable and fundamental contribution of Sri Aurobindo to Metaphysics and, specially, to the Vedānta, which is essentially based on the *Vedas* and the *Upaniṣads* and has unfailingly derived life, light and inspiration from them down the ages. The concept of the Logic of the Infinite has provided strong rational foundation to Sri Aurobindo's Integral Advaitism.

Sri Aurobindo has also developed and expounded the concept of Integral knowledge. It gives an all-embracing view of Reality, of Reality as a whole, and does not create any wedge between its fundamental poises or aspects, namely, Impersonal and Personal, Being and Becoming, Subject and Object, One and Many etc. In this respect, it is absolutely free from the limitations which constitute an essential feature of other sources of knowledge, namely, sense experience, reason and intuition. The Integral Knowledge, according to Sri Aurobindo, is inherent in the integral Reality; it constitutes an essential feature of our own spiritual consciousness. So it has not to be created, invented or learned by man. It has simply to be discovered or uncovered by our own spiritual endeavour. As this knowledge is already there in our eternal and immutable Self, Ātman, so it lies within our reach and can be realised by us, if by our spiritual effort we are able to remove the veil of ignorance, avidyā that hides it from us. Sri Aurobindo does admit that man conditioned by finitude does not possess the capacity to have an all-embracing and integral vision of Reality. But he can realise the truth of Integral Knowledge and can be in its possession if he awakens himself to it even in his surface consciousness. This awakening will enable him to have an integral comprehension of Reality at the rational level on the basis of the logic of the Infinite. The Integral Knowledge is not a construction or creation of mind and is not speculative in character. It is a fact of our spiritual consciousness and experience. So man can realise its truth and have an integral view of Reality at the rational level if he becomes deeply aware of it even in his surface consciousness. The Logic of the Infinite can be freed from the charge of being merely speculative in character, if it is shown to operate on the sound foundation of Integral Knowledge which, according to Sri Aurobindo, is the very stuff of our own spiritual consciousness. It is not something that has not been realised by man so far. In his great work *On The Veda*, Sri Aurobindo has clearly stated that the ancient seers and the enlightened Āryans had made an ascent to that supreme level of spiritual consciousness where they were in possession of Integral Knowledge and had direct and immediate experience of Integral Reality. "That ascension has already been effected by the Ancients, the human forefathers, and the spirits of these great Ancestors still assist their offspring; for the new dawns repeat the old and lean forward in light to join the dawns of the future. Kanwa, Kutsa, Atri, Kakshiwan, Gotama, Shunashepa have become types of certain spiritual victories which tend to be constantly repeated in the experience of humanity. The seven sages, the Aṅgīrasas, are waiting still and always, ready to chant the word, to rend the cavern, to find the lost herds, to recover the hidden sun."[1]

Thus it is clear that Sri Aurobindo's conception of Integral Reality and of Integral Knowledge is not merely speculative in character. It is directly based on the supreme spiritual experiences of the ancient seers which are revealed and expounded in the hymns of The *Veda* and in the philosophical and religious thought of the *Upaniṣads*. The concept of Integral Knowledge enables reason to free itself from its abstract, analytic and formal character and comprehend Reality in all its integrality and depth. Thus the concept of Integral Knowledge constitutes another most distinctive feature of Sri Aurobindo's Integral View of Reality or his Integral Advaitism. It provides a solid epistemological foundation to his Integral Advaitism. Thus we find

---

1. *On The Veda*, 1956, p. 438.

that Sri Aurobindo has developed his system of the Vedānta on the solid foundations of logic and epistemology. He has achieved admirable success in bridging the gap between ontology, epistemology and logic, as we shall see in the course of the present work.

Sri Aurobindo's system differs in a somewhat radical way from the other systems of the Vedānta in respect of his conception of the destiny of man. Unlike other systems, he does not consider liberation of Spirit, Ātman as the supreme end of human life. He envisages the possibility of the liberation of the whole personality of man, of man as a whole, of his Self or Ātman, as well as of his body-mind organism. The attainment of this supreme goal of life is not possible for man in the present state of his existence. But it will be realised by him, when in the course of cosmic evolution, man transcends his finitude in an absolute way and rises to the state of supramental consciousness and being. This ascent of man to the highest state of spiritual existence will be possible, when there is a descent of supramental consciousness and force in man and the rest of creation in the course of cosmic evolution. The descent of this divine power in man will effect an entire transformation of his personality and not only his self, but his body-mind organism also will attain freedom from finitude, time and death. This constitutes the supreme goal of man's life according to Sri Aurobindo.

Sri Aurobindo's theory of individual and cosmic evolution and his conception of the destiny of man do constitute novel and notable features of his philosophy. But the ascent of man and the world to a higher divine or supramental status and the transformation of man into superman or gnostic being may be conceived as a future possibility. This view provides new meaning to man's life in the world and opens immense possibilities before him, individually and collectively. But it cannot be treated as constituting an essential feature or an inseparable part of Sri Aurobindo's Integral Advaitism. The Integral Advaitism of Sri Aurobindo stands on its own ground on the solid foundations of Integral Knowledge and the Logic of the Infinite. Any view of history, whether it is conceived as moving in a straight line or in a cyclic order, cannot make any difference to it.

In the present work, an attempt has been made to present Sri Aurobindo's philosophy in a critical, comparative and systematic way. Sri Aurobindo's thought has been compared with that of some Indian and Western systems in an objective and critical manner. A most notable feature of his system is that it presents a meeting of the extremes. Absolutism is here reconciled, on the one hand, with theism and, on the other, with modern evolutionism. In the same way, there is a meeting of the Vedāntic and Tāntric thought in his system. His philosophy combines in itself the best elements of Indian and Western thought, both ancient and modern. Sri Aurobindo has reinterpreted and recreated Indian religious and philosophical thought and the modern Western idea of evolution to an extent seldom excelled before. His conception of the Absolute, of the Logic of the Infinite and his theory of evolution provide an ample evidence of it. This fact gives Sri Aurobindo a unique place in the history of philosophy, Indian and Western. It has to be noted that though Sri Aurobindo's system presents a meeting of the extremes, yet it is not a syncretism. It does not make any facile attempt to reconcile the irreconcilable ideas or the opposite currents of thought at their own level. It reconciles them in a rational way at a higher level of unity where the opposites are shown to meet. It is amply illustrated in Sri Aurobindo's discussions on the Absolute and evolution.

The present work was first published long back in 1957 by the Banaras Hindu University. It has been out of print for a considerably long period, though it has been in demand all along by the students and teachers interested and engaged in the study, research and teaching of Sri Aurobindo's philosophy in the Indian Universities. It is now being republished by the renowned publishers Motilal Banarsidass.

In the present edition of the book, I have modified and developed considerably the second chapter entitled, 'The Logic of the Infinite' in view of its great importance for Sri Aurobindo's Integral Advaitism. I have particularly made a critical analysis and evaluation of Hegel's Logic and the Mādhyamika dialectic, as a clear idea of their merits and shortcomings enables one to have an adequate understanding and appreciation of the necessity and justification of the Logic of the Infinite. I have also added a few pages to the third chapter of the book entitled, 'The Absolute as Existence'. It has been done with a view to show the inadequacy of the theories which conceive Becoming as the absolute Reality and deny the reality of pure Being, *Sat*. No change or modification has been made in the rest of the book.

I remember at this moment with deep love and gratitude my revered teacher, late Professor Batuk Nath Sharma, who awakened in me a keen desire in my early age to learn and appreciate the deeper truths of Philosophy and Religion and the mystery of holy life. His sacred memory has always been a source of hope and solace to me in my moments of distress and despair. It is in token of my deep love, gratitude and devotion to my saintly preceptor that I have dedicated this book to him.

I also remember with sincere gratitude late Professor S.K. Maitra under whom I enjoyed the privilege in my early life to do higher study and research in the philosophy of Sri Aurobindo. The manuscript of the present work was first prepared during that period under the supervision and guidance of this renowned authority on Sri Aurobindo's philosophy.

I extend my grateful thanks to Shri J.P. Jain, Director, Motilal Banarsidass Publishers Private Limited, who has readily consented to publish the book, thus providing me with the opportunity to make some sound and significant improvement in it, as has been pointed out above. I also thank Shri N.P. Jain for his important suggestions in respect of the revision of the book.

I feel happy to express my indebtedness to my old students and to scholars of India and abroad with whom I had meaningful discussions from time to time on living philosophical and religious issues and was greatly benefited by them; they helped me in giving a definite shape and direction to my thought.

Varanasi   R.S. Misra

ABBREVIATIONS

CONTENTS

Part II—The Absolute

Prakṛti.

Part III—Creation or Descent

Part IV—Evolution or Ascent

PART I

INTRODUCTION

CHAPTER I

GENERAL PRINCIPLES

(A) *Integral Advaitism: Its Meaning and Significance*

The word *Advaitism* is generally associated with the celebrated system of Śaṅkara. As Indian Philosophy is generally associated in the West with the Vedānta, so in India, Advaitism is associated with the system of Śaṅkara. Advaitism is invariably taken to mean the doctrine which establishes the oneness of the supreme Reality or Brahman by denying the reality of the world. To Śaṅkara and the Śaṅkarites, the denial of the reality of the world is the essential prerequisite of arriving at the advaitic standpoint. Brahman and the world are regarded by them as opposed to and contradictory of each other. Brahman is the knower, while the world is the object of knowledge. The former is pure consciousness while the latter is unconscious. The former is unlimited, while the latter has got spatio-temporal limitations. The former is changeless, while the latter is subject to change and mutation. The former is immortal, while the latter is subject to death and destruction. The former is independent and self-existent, while the latter enjoys merely a dependent existence. In this way, Brahman and the world are regarded by Śaṅkara and the Śaṅkarites as so much opposed to, and contradictory of each other that they find no way of making any synthesis or reconciliation between them. And their failure to establish any relationship between Brahman and the world leads them to deny the reality of the latter altogether. Though Śaṅkara regards the world as real from the empirical standpoint, yet he denies its reality from the metaphysical or transcendental standpoint, as we will show in detail in a subsequent chapter, while comparing Sri Aurobindo's conception of the Absolute with that of Śaṅkara.

Now, if we admit the reality of the world along with that of Brahman, then there will be two alternatives open to us. The world may be regarded either as independent of Brahman and a separate reality altogether or dependent on it and as an integral part of it. If the first alternative is admitted, then it will lead to an inevitable dualism of the Sāṅkhyan type. But dualism does not solve the problem of reality. It makes it rather insoluble. "The dualistic realism," says Dr. Radhakrishnan, "is the result of a false metaphysics".[1] "If we assume the essential unrelatedness of subject and object, it would be impossible to pass from the one to the other. The unity of the two terms is the presupposition of their difference. It is simply due to our avidyā, our ignorance or want of reflection on the nature and conditions of experience, that we fail to recognise the ultimate oneness of subject and object. It is quite true that the dualistic conception of mind and object is natural to our minds, but a little reflection tells us that if the two are independent we require a *tertium quid* to connect the two. The moment we realise the utter unsatisfactoriness of this *tertium quid* hypothesis, we are left with the view that the two are aspects of one ultimate consciousness, which is the basis of all knowledge as well as existence."[2] Thus our reason is constrained to reject ultimately the dualistic standpoint and posit the fundamental reality of the Absolute or Brahman lying behind the subjective and the objective orders of existence and constituting their essence. Now if the second alternative is accepted and the world is regarded as dependent on Brahman and as an integral part of it, then it cannot, according to the Śaṅkarites, fail to affect its unity. The world being subject to change and destruction will affect the immutable and imperishable nature of Brahman. In the same way the finitude of the world will put a serious limitation upon the infinity of Brahman. To regard the world as an integral part of Brahman will be to introduce spatio-temporal limitations in it which will inevitably reduce Brahman to the level of the finite. Thus to regard the world as an integral part of Brahman is, according to Śaṅkara and his followers, self-contradictory. They

1. *Indian Philosophy*, Vol. II, p. 320.
2. *Ibid.*, p. 328.

make a critical examination of all the categories such as cause-effect, substance-attribute etc., that are advanced by the theistic systems of the Vedānta to determine the relationship between Brahman and the world and show their self-contradictory nature. The only way of escape from this self-contradiction, according to them, consists in the denial of the reality of the world. Thus Śankara and the Śankarites contend that the unity of Brahman can remain unaffected and the advaitic standpoint can be maintained only if the world is ultimately regarded as unreal. Now, it is this contention of Śankara and his followers that is seriously challenged by Sri Aurobindo. He holds that Advaitism can be established even while admitting the reality of the world. The contradictions that seem to exist between Brahman and the world seem to be irreconcilable only to the finite or abstract reason. Our reason finds itself baffled by these contradictions and is unable to solve them due to the fact that it takes a very narrow and abstract view of the different terms and categories. These contradictions, according to Sri Aurobindo, can be solved by a higher and more plastic reason which gives a deeper and a wider meaning to the categories. Thus the higher reason reconciles the so-called opposites or contradictories, such as One and Many, Being and Becoming, Infinite and Finite, Knowledge and Ignorance and so on, by giving a deeper and wider meaning to them, as we will show in a subsequent chapter. The contradictions, Sri Aurobindo argues, do not exist, in fact, in reality but in our limited finite reason or mind. It is because we make an approach to reality through mind that we are confronted with all sorts of irreconcilable contradictions and antinomies. But if we approach reality through the higher reason, called by Sri Aurobindo, the Logic of the Infinite, then we shall be able to reconcile the so-called opposition between Brahman and the world. Then we shall be able to maintain the advaitic standpoint without denying the reality of the world. "The Logic of the Infinite," Dr. Varadachari remarks "involves the understanding of the totality which is not capable of being equated with the sum of finites or the many. Sri Aurobindo points out that the Infinite is not an opposite of the finites understood as the many, nor contradictory to them. The finite is a veiled or concealed or condensed Infinite even as Matter is the concealed Spirit. The negation that we perceive between the finite and the infinite is a phenomenal

description; it is but the expression of the concealed nature or
veiled form of the Infinite."[1]

Sri Aurobindo calls his system *Advaita* for the reason that he
regards Brahman or the Absolute as one and the fundamental
reality. His Advaitism is called *integral* for the reason that it does
not deny the reality of any of the aspects of Existence. It is not
based on the denial of the reality of the world and the individual.
It reconciles all the opposition between Infinite and Finite, One
and Many, Being and Becoming, Indeterminate and Determinate
or *nirguṇa* and *saguṇa* and so on as we will show in a subsequent
chapter. Thus Sri Aurobindo's Integral Advaitism differs from the
Advaitism of Śaṅkara. Whereas the Advaitism of Śaṅkara is based,
as we have stated above, on the denial of the reality of the world,
the Advaitism of Sri Aurobindo does not deny the reality either of
the world or of the individual. The Advaitism of Śaṅkara is abstract
and all-exclusive in nature. But Sri Aurobindo's Advaitism is inte-
gral and all-inclusive. It includes all the aspects of reality in its all-
embracing unity. "The real Monism, the true Advaita," observes Sri
Aurobindo, "is that which admits all things as the one Brahman
and does not seek to bisect its existence into two incompatible
entities, an eternal Truth and an eternal Falsehood, Brahman and
not-Brahman, Self and not-Self, a real Self and an unreal, yet
perpetual Maya. If it be true that the Self alone exists. it must be
also true that all is the Self."[2]

(B) *Integral Advaitism Steers Clear of two Negations—The Materialist Denial and the Refusal of the Ascetic*

Thus the Integral Advaitism of Sri Aurobindo affirms the reality of
the world as well as of the Absolute, of Matter as well as of spirit.
Philosophy, according to Sri Aurobindo, cannot ignore the claims
of either Matter or Spirit. A spiritualistic philosophy that denies the
reality of Matter is as one-sided as a materialistic philosophy that
totally denies the reality of Spirit. So philosophy must steer clear
of the two extremes of materialism ignoring Spirit, and spiritualism
ignoring Matter, or what Sri Aurobindo calls the Materialist Denial
and the Refusal of the Ascetic. Matter and Spirit are, according to

1. Dr. K.C. Varadachari, *A Critique of the Pramāṇas*, Sri Aurobindo Mandir Annual,
   1948, p. 117.
2. *L.D.*, Vol. I, p. 39.

Sri Aurobindo, the lowest and the highest terms of Existence. Matter is nothing but the manifestation of Spirit. Thus we cannot ignore either Matter or Spirit if we have to take an integral and comprehensive view of Reality. "The affirmation of a divine life upon earth and an immortal sense in mortal existence," observes Sri Aurobindo, "can have no base unless we recognise not only eternal Spirit as the inhabitant of this bodily mansion, the wearer of this mutable robe, but accept Matter of which it is made, as a fit and noble material out of which He weaves constantly His garbs, builds recurrently the unending series of His mansions."[1]

In order to guard oneself against a recoil from life, one must perceive behind their appearances the identity between these extreme terms of existence and proclaim in the words of the Upaniṣads that "Matter also is Brahman."[2] Sri Aurobindo contends that Matter and Spirit will not appear in a trenchant opposition if we take into account the intervening grades between them, namely, Life, Mind, Supermind and the grades that link Mind to Supermind. "Otherwise the two must appear as irreconcilable opponents bound together in an unhappy wedlock and their divorce the only reasonable solution."[3] If Spirit and Matter are separated from each other, then one is forced to make a choice between the two. "For both Thought and Life, a choice then becomes imperative. Thought comes to deny the one as an illusion of the imagination or the other as an illusion of the senses; Life comes to fix on the immaterial and flee from itself in a disgust or a self-forgetting ecstasy, or else to deny its own immortality and take its orientation away from God and towards the animal."[4]

Thus the separation of Matter and Spirit from each other and their mutual rejection has not only led to the barrenness of thought but also to the barrenness of life as well. 'The Materialist Denial' and 'The Refusal of the Ascetic' have both done immense harm to humanity but the latter is more perilous in its effect than the former. "The denial of the materialist, although more insistent and immediately successful, more facile in its appeal to the generality of mankind, is yet less enduring, less effective finally than the

1. *L.D.*, Vol. I, p. 7.
2. अन्नं ब्रह्मेति व्यजानात् । 3.2.
3. *L.D.*, Vol. I, p. 8.
4. *Ibid.*, p. 8.

absorbing and perilous refusal of the ascetic."[1] The refusal of the ascetic is "more complete, more final, more perilous in its effects on the individuals or collectivities that hear its potent call to the wilderness". But Sri Aurobindo unhesitatingly admits that both the asceticism and the materialism have rendered great service also to mankind. Asceticism has raised man to the status of the Divine. Without it man might have been forced to roll helplessly in the mud and mire of animal existence. In the same way, the rational-istic materialism of the West has helped us in the sharpening of our intellect and getting rid of superstitious beliefs and irrational dogmas. "For that vast field of evidence and experience which now begins to reopen its gates to us, can only be safely entered when the intellect has been severely trained to a clear austerity; seized on by unripe minds, it lends itself to the most perilous distortion and misleading imagination and actually in the past encrusted a real nucleus of truth with such an accretion of per-verting superstition and irrationalising dogmas that all advance in true knowledge was rendered impossible. It became necessary for a time to make a clean sweep at once of the truth and its disguise in order that the road might be clear for a new departure and a surer advance. The rationalistic tendency of Materialism has done mankind this great service."[2] Thus though Sri Aurobindo admits the debt of materialism for making us, to a great extent, free from superstitious beliefs and irrationalising dogmas and of asceticism for raising to a great extent the tone of life morally and spiritually, yet he considers, as has been stated above, both these views to be partial and one-sided. Leaving apart their practical consequenc-es on the life of mankind, they have even theoretically stood in the way of our having an integral and all-comprehensive view of reality. We have already indicated, in brief, how the Absolutism of Śaṅkara fails to arrive at an integral view of reality on account of its denial of the world. Now we proceed to show how Mate-rialism and Idealism are partial and one-sided in character as they also fail to give us an integral view of reality.

(i) *Materialism: A Partial View of Reality*
Materialism regards matter or physical existence as the fundamen-

1. *L.D.*, Vol. I, p. 11.
2. *Ibid.*, p. 13.

tal reality and life, mind etc. as the products of matter. To it, our sense-experience is the sole means of valid knowledge. Whatever does not come within the purview of our sense-experience cannot be given a passport of reality. But this view of reality and knowledge is obviously partial and one-sided in nature. "If pushed to its extreme," observes Sri Aurobindo, "it would give to a stone or plum-pudding a greater reality and to thought, love, courage, genius, greatness, the human soul and mind facing an obscure and dangerous world and getting mastery over it an inferior dependent reality or even an unsubstantial and evanescent reality".[1] Thus this view ignores the subjective side of our existence altogether. But it may be held that the objective has value only insofar as it is related to a subject. The objective and the subjective are so closely related to each other that one cannot be fully understood without the other. "In fact, subjectivity and objectivity are not independent realities, they depend on each other; they are the Being, through consciousness, looking at itself as subject on the object and the same Being offering itself to its own consciousness as object to the subject."[2] So the subjective and the objective are two necessary aspects of the manifested Reality and of equal value. We cannot deny the truths of the subjective aspect of our existence simply on the ground that they do not come within the range of our sense-experience. Our sense-experience itself depends on the evidence of consciousness. It is consciousness that synthesises the manifold sense impressions and gives unity to them. The outer senses "can bear a reliable evidence only when they refer their version of the object to the consciousness and that consciousness gives a significance to their report, adds to its externality its own internal intuitive interpretation and justifies it by a reasoned adherence; for the evidence of the senses is always by itself imperfect, not altogether reliable and certainly, not final because it is incomplete and constantly subject to error. Indeed we have no means of knowing the objective universe except by our subjective consciousness of which the physical senses themselves are instruments; as the world appears not only to that but in that, so it is to us".[3] Thus it is clear that even our experience of the objective

---

1. *L.D.*, Vol. II, Part II, pp. 432-33.
2. *Ibid.*, p. 433.
3. *Ibid.*, 433-34.

side of existence depends on the unity of consciousness.

Now if we admit the evidence of consciousness in the case of our experience of the physical universe, we cannot logically deny its evidence in the case of the subjective side of existence or of supra-physical objectivities. Sri Aurobindo says, "If we deny reality to the evidence of this universal witness for subjective or for supra-physical objectivities, there is no sufficient reason to concede reality to its evidence for physical objectivities; if the inner or the supra-physical objects of consciousness are unreal, the objective physical universe has also every chance of being unreal. In each case understanding, discrimination, verification are necessary; but the subjective and the supra-physical must have another method of verification than that which we apply successfully to the physical and the external objective."[1] So our sense-experience cannot be the judge of the subjective experiences or of supra-physical domains of existence.

Sri Aurobindo deprecates the habit of man created by the limitations of his physical mind of "believing entirely only in the physical and of doubting or challenging all that does not come into accord with his own experience or his own scope of understanding or square with his own standard or sum of established knowledge".[2] He calls it the ego-centric attitude. "In its extreme, this claim of the individual to be the judge of everything is an egoistic illusion, a superstition of the physical mind, in the mass a gross and vulgar error."[3] It is thought that if one departs from the objective and scientific method of direct observation and experience, one may be led to gross delusion and admit all sorts of subjective phantasy and unverified truth into the realm of knowledge. But the possibility of error and delusion and the introduction of subjective attitude into the pursuit of knowledge is present even in the objective or scientific method. "The probability of error is no reason for refusing to attempt discovery and subjective discovery must be pursued by. a subjective method of enquiry, observation and verification; research into the supra-physical must evolve, accept and test an appropriate means and methods other than those by

1. *L.D.*, Vol. II, Part II, p. 434.
2. *Ibid.*, p. 435.
3. *Ibid.*, p. 435.

which one examines the constituents of physical objects and the processes of Energy in material Nature."[1] Thus it is clear that our physical mind cannot be the judge of our higher experience. As Sri Aurobindo puts it, "The greatest inner discoveries, the experience of self-being, the cosmic consciousness, the inner clam of the liberated spirit, the direct effect of mind upon mind, the knowledge of things by consciousness in direct contact with other consciousness or with its objects, most spiritual experiences of any value, cannot be brought before the tribunal of the common mentality which has no experience of these things and takes its own absence or incapacity of experience as a proof of their invalidity or their non-existence."[2]

Thus it is clear that we can neither regard sense-experience as the sole means of knowledge nor Matter as the fundamental reality. Now matter is said to be a structure of Energy. "It is therefore no longer possible to take Matter as the sole reality."[3] Matter, according to Sri Aurobindo, represents one grade of Existence. Hence it cannot be equated with the whole of reality. Thus Materialism represents a partial and one-sided view of Reality and not an integral view of it. To have an integral and all-embracing view of Reality, one must, according to Sri Aurobindo, take into account the truth of all the aspects of Existence. The solution of the whole problem of Reality cannot be based on an exclusive and one-sided knowledge. We must know "not only what Matter is and what are its processes, but what mind and life are and what are their processes, and one must know also spirit and soul and all that is behind the material surface; only then can we have a knowledge sufficiently integral for a solution of the problem".[4]

Now we proceed to show that Idealism also which is fundamentally opposed to Materialism represents a partial and one-sided view of Reality.

(ii) Idealism: A Partial View of Reality
Idealism holds that everything knowable, every object of experience is in its proper or original nature, a content of consciousness.

---

1. L.D., Vol. II, Part II, p. 436.
2. Ibid., p. 436.
3. Ibid., p. 439.
4. Ibid., p. 439.

It regards consciousness or Mind as the fundamental reality and explains the universe as the expression and embodiment of mind. There are various forms of Idealism such as Subjective Idealism, Objective Idealism, Transcendental Idealism and so on. But here we do not propose to discuss the views of these different forms of Idealism. We shall indicate here in a general way the partial character of the idealistic position.

Sri Aurobindo holds that Mind, whether it is individual or universal cannot be regarded as the creator of the universe. The individual mind suffers from all sorts of limitations and so it is obvious that it cannot be considered as the constitutive stuff of the universe. "It is clear that a Mind of the nature of our surface intelligence can be only a secondary power of existence. For it bears the stamp of incapacity and ignorance as a sign that it is derivative and not the original creative; we see that it does not know or understand the objects it perceives, it has no automatic control of them; it has to acquire a laboriously built knowledge and controlling power. This initial incapacity could not be there if these objects were the Mind's own structures, creations of its self-power."[1] It may be said that the universe is the expression or embodiment of a universal Mind which is possessed of omniscience and omnipotence. But Sri Aurobindo holds that the universe cannot be regarded as an expression of the universal Mind also. If the universal Mind is of the same character as the individual Mind, then it cannot be said to be possessed of omnipotence and omniscience. And if it is different from the individual Mind altogether, then it cannot strictly be called Mind. Mind as we know it, Sri Aurobindo argues, is an ignorance seeking for knowledge; "it is a knower of fractions and worker of divisions striving to arrive at a sum, to piece together a whole—it is not possessed of the essence of things or their totality: a universal Mind of the same character might know the sum of its divisions by force of its universality, but it would still lack the essential knowledge and without the essential knowledge there would be no true integral knowledge. A consciousness possessing the essential and integral knowledge, proceeding from the essence to the whole and from the whole to the parts, would be no longer Mind, but a perfect Truth-Consciousness automatically possessed of inherent self-

1. L.D., Vol. II, Part II, p. 429.

knowledge and world-knowledge".[1] Sri Aurobindo does hold the view that the universe is not independent of consciousness and that it is essentially a creation of consciousness. But the universe is not merely a figment of mind. It is the creation of consciousness which is one with the being of the Divine. Whatever it creates is constituted of the stuff or substance of being and therefore is real. As Sri Aurobindo puts it, "It is true that there is no such thing as an objective reality independent of consciousness; but at the same time there is a truth in objectivity and it is this, that the reality of things resides in something that is within them and is independent of the interpretation our mind gives to them and of the structures it builds upon its observation. These structures constitute the mind's subjective image or figure of the universe, but the universe and its objects are not a mere image or figure. They are in essence creations of consciousness, but of a consciousness that is one with being, whose substance is the substance of Being and whose creations too are of that substance, therefore real. In this view, the world cannot be a purely subjective creation of consciousness; the subjective and the objective truth of things are both real, they are two sides of the same Reality."[2]

In this respect Sri Aurobindo's view differs from that of Subjective Idealism. In Subjective Idealism reality is said to be constituted of subjective experiences, i.e., perceptions and ideas. Existence, according to it, consists in perceiving or being perceived. The objects do not exist apart from the subjects perceiving them. The doctrine of subjective Idealism is expressed in the famous dictum of Berkeley, namely, *Esse est percipi*. It means that to exist is to be perceived. Thus the existence of the objects apart from and independent of the mind is not admitted in subjective idealism. Berkeley cannot be said to be a consistent subjective idealist, for he admits the reality of the self and God, although we have no perceptions or ideas of them. We find the doctrine of Subjective Idealism exemplified in a much more consistent manner in the Yogācāra school of Buddhist philosophy. Sri Aurobindo does not hold that the objects are nothing else than our perceptions and ideas. According to him, in perception, we get an image or figure of the object but we do not produce the object as the subjective

---

1. *L.D.*, Vol. II, Part, II pp. 429-30.
2. *Ibid.*, p. 430.

idealists would have us believe. The being of the object is not exhausted in our perceptions.

In Kant's transcendental Idealism also we find reason regarded as the creator of the universe. According to Kant, we do not see things as they are in themselves but as they appear to us through space, time and categories. So we see the phenomenon and not the noumenon or thing-in-itself. The phenomenon is the product of reason. It does not exist outside of us but in us. So Kant may also be called a subjective idealist in this sense. "Now, while the Aesthetic brings us to the threshold of subjective idealism," Weber rightly remarks, "the Transcendental Logic carries us right into it, in spite of Kant's protests against our confounding him with Berkeley. Not only, he tells us, does reason, as an intuition, constitute, produce or create the phenomenon, but reason, in the form of the understanding, also determines the reciprocal relations of sensible phenomena. Reason makes them *a priori* quantities, qualities, causes and effects, and thus impresses upon them the seal of its legislative power; it is through reason that the things become quantities, qualities, effects and causes, which they are not in themselves. Hence we may say without exaggeration that it is reason which prescribes its laws to the sensible universe; it is reason which makes the cosmos".[1]

Sri Aurobindo does not regard mind as a creator of the universe as the subjective idealists and Kant would have us believe. Mind, according to him, perceives the objects, it provides us with the image or the symbol of the objects but it does not create them. The objects do not exist in the mind but outside and independent of it. It cannot be said to be the creator of the external objects. Our mind is "primarily a percipient and interpreter, secondarily and derivatively a creator. This indeed is the value of all mental subjectivity that it reflects in it some truth of the Being which exists independently of the reflection,—whether that independence presents itself as a physical objectivity or a supra-physical reality perceived by the mind but not perceptible by the physical senses. Mind, then is not the original constructor of the universe: it is an intermediate power valid for certain actualities of being; an agent, an intermediary, it actualises possibilities and has its share in the creation, but the real creatrix is a Consciousness, an Energy inherent

---

1. Weber, Alfred, *History of Philosophy*, p. 450.

in the transcendent and the cosmic Spirit".[1]

Thus Sri Aurobindo does not regard the universe as the creation of mind as the idealists would have us believe. He regards Idealism as well as Materialism as partial and one-sided in nature. He neither regards matter as the creation of mind nor mind as the creation of matter. He does not agree with the views of the materialists and the behaviourists who try to reduce consciousness to a function of the brain. The brain, according to the materialists, secretes thought as the liver secretes bile. But according to Sri Aurobindo, brain is merely an instrument through which consciousness manifests itself, it is not the creator of thought or consciousness. Sri Aurobindo fully upholds the primacy of consciousness. But this consciousness cannot be identified with mind. This is the supreme consciousness which underlies the subjective and the objective orders of existence and constitutes their essence. The whole universe is, according to him, the creation of the supreme Consciousness-Force and not the creation of mind.

Thus, according to Sri Aurobindo, neither mind nor matter can be identified with the ultimate reality. The ultimate reality is Spirit or Brahman which lies at the root of the subjective and the objective orders of existence and constitutes their essence. In this respect he agrees with Śaṅkara who also regards Spirit or Brahman as the fundamental reality. But he considers Śaṅkara's conception of reality as partial and one-sided insofar as it denies the reality of the world, as we have pointed out above. The denial of the reality of the world makes Śaṅkara's Absolutism or Advaitism rather abstract in nature. Sri Aurobindo regards Brahman as the fundamental and ultimate reality but he regards the world as the real manifestation of Brahman, as we have shown above. Reality according to him is integral in nature. It includes all the aspects of existence in it and at the same time it transcends them all.

Now, we proceed to give in brief a general outline of Sri Aurobindo's view of Reality and will show how it reconciles all the so-called contradictory aspects of existence in its all-embracing unity.

(C) Sri Aurobindo's Integral View of Reality

As has been stated above, Sri Aurobindo regards the Absolute or Brahman as the fundamental reality. In itself the Absolute or

1. *L.D.*, Vol. II, Part II, pp. 431-32.

Brahman is indeterminable and unknowable. It can be determined neither by our affirmations nor by our negations. But it is not a pure indeterminable. It is "not a rigid indeterminable oneness, not an infinity vacant of all that is not a pure self-existence attainable only by the exclusion of the many and the finite, but something which is beyond these definitions, beyond indeed any description either positive or negative. All affirmations and negations are expressive of its aspects and it is through both a supreme affirmation and a supreme negation that we can arrive at the Absolute".[1] In the same way the Absolute is not altogether unknowable. It is unknowable by our finite mind but can be known and realised by the eternal portion of our being or the immortal spiritual principle hidden within us. The Absolute or Brahman manifests itself to our consciousness as Saccidānanda, the triune principle of Existence, Consciousness and Bliss. In its aspect of self-existence, Saccidānanda manifests itself to us in three forms, Self, Conscious Being or Spirit and God or the Divine Being. In other words, it manifests itself as Ātman, Puruṣa and Īśvara. The second aspect of Saccidānanda is that of Consciousness. But this Consciousness is not merely a pure Consciousness but it is also possessed of force. It is not merely Consciousness but is also Consciousness-Force or Cit-Śakti. This Consciousness-Force or Conscious Force is inherent in the Pure Existent. It is the supreme power of the Absolute or Saccidānanda. It represents the power aspect of Saccidānanda. So it is inseparable from Him and in whatever form He exists, the Consciousness-Force also exists in an inalienable and inseparable union with Him. As Saccidānanda in its aspect of self-existence manifests to our consciousness in three forms, so Consciousness-Force also assumes three forms corresponding to it. These three forms of Conscious Force are called Māyā, Prakṛti and Śakti and they correspond to three aspects of Existence—Ātman, Puruṣa and Īśvara respectively. Thus Ātman-Māyā, Puruṣa-Prakṛti and Īśvara-Śakti go together.

There is another fundamental aspect of Saccidānanda, called Bliss. It is the fundamental and basic principle of all existence. It is for bliss and out of bliss that Saccidānanda manifests the cosmos. As Consciousness is inherent and involved in the whole of existence, so Bliss is also present in all the aspects of existence and

---

1. *L.D.*, Vol. II, Part II, p. 419.

consciousness. Our Psychic being or Soul is the eternal and im-
mortal portion of the principle of Bliss. The presence of pain and
evil does not, according to Sri Aurobindo, contradict the univer-
sality of Bliss, as we will show in a subsequent chapter. They are
only a mode of manifestation of Bliss. As Sri Aurobindo beautifully
puts it in *Savitri* :

"Bliss is the secret stuff of all that lives,
Even pain and grief are garbs of world-delight,
That hides behind thy sorrow and thy cry."[1]

At a higher state of evolution, pain and evil will lose their
essential character and will turn into the principle of Bliss. So Bliss
is the inherent characteristic of all existence, of every finite being
and of all cosmos. But it is present there at present in a latent
manner. It is not able to manifest itself overtly at present on account
of ignorance and inconscience. But it is destined to manifest itself
overtly in the individual and the cosmos when the supramental
descent takes place and the evolution proceeds further through
knowledge, as we will show in a subsequent chapter.

The next principle that we have to consider is the Supermind.
Supermind is not something different from Saccidānanda. It is the
creative aspect of Saccidānanda. It is Saccidānanda itself in its
aspect of creator. It is through the Supermind that Saccidānanda
manifests the universe out of its indivisible unity. The Supermind
is not only the principle of knowledge but the principle of will
also. Sri Aurobindo calls it Truth-Consciousness or Real-Idea. It is
an intermediary principle between Saccidānanda and the world. It
is the Supermind which reconciles the opposition between Brah-
man and the world, as we will show in a subsequent chapter. The
Integral Advaitism of Sri Aurobindo is based on the supramental
principle.

.Saccidānanda has to take a plunge into ignorance in order to
manifest the world. The Consciousness-Force of Saccidānanda as-
sumes the form of ignorance in order to manifest itself in spatio-
temporal limitations. Thus, ignorance is a self-limited and self-
concentrated form of Saccidānanda. It is not something opposed
to knowledge. Ignorance exists neither in the indivisible unity of

1. *Savitri*, Part II, Book VI, Canto 11, First Complete Ed., 1951, p. 98.

Saccidānanda nor in the Supermind, nor in the divine soul. It manifests itself in the plane of mind. Thus it cannot be called an original and independent principle. So the principle of ignorance being a self-limited and self-concentrated form of Saccidānanda cannot affect its unity. The Consciousness-Force of the Absolute assumes the form of Ignorance out of its own free-will. Hence the principle of Ignorance cannot affect the advaitic position of Sri Aurobindo. The Integral Advaitism of Sri Aurobindo is neither affected by the emergence of pain and evil nor by ignorance, as we will show in detail in the subsequent chapters.

The Absolute manifests the spatio-temporal world, as has been stated above, through ignorance. The world of mind, life and matter seems to be diametrically opposed to the Absolute. Mind suffers from ignorance, imperfection and limitation. Life is characterised by death, desire and incapacity. Matter has the characteristics of division, inertia and inconscience. Thus mind, life and matter seem to be totally opposed to the Absolute or Saccidānanda. But the opposition is, according to Sri Aurobindo, merely apparent and not real. It is the Absolute or Brahman which has put itself in the forms of mind, life and matter through ignorance. So mind, life and matter being the self-limited and self-concentrated forms of Saccidānanda cannot put a limitation upon it. They cannot contradict its absoluteness. Moreover, mind, life and matter suffer from imperfection, limitation, division etc. at the present stage. But these do not constitute their permanent characteristics. They are destined to get rid of these imperfect characteristics in the course of evolution. Thus it is clear that the Integral Advaitism of Sri Aurobindo cannot be said to be affected by the emergence of the world of mind, life and matter. All the principles that seem to be opposed to or contradictory of the Absolute will, according to Sri Aurobindo, cease to appear so during the course of evolution. Matter, Life and Mind seem to be opposed to the Absolute due to the fact that the Absolute has not manifested itself fully in them. They are destined to make an ascent to the status of Spirit and manifest fully its light and power in the course of evolution.

The evolution of the principles of matter, life and mind into the status of Spirit is possible on account of the involution of Spirit into them. The double process of involution and evolution explains the whole of the cosmic working and order. According to Sri Aurobindo, the higher principle evolves out of the lower simply because it is already present in the lower in a latent manner. Unlike Alexander, Sri Aurobindo does not regard space-time as the primordial stuff out of which all existents are made. Space-time matrix represents the lowest level of existence in Alexander's philosophy. But as everything evolves out of it, it becomes the Absolute for Alexander. "It is greater than all existent finites or infinites because it is their parent. But it has not as space-time their wealth of qualities, and being elementary is so far less than they are".[1] Alexander is not quite logical in explaining the higher principles in terms of a lower order of existence. As Dr. Radhakrishnan remarks, "Alexander is not quite consistent when he says that every existent is 'expressible without residue' in terms of a lower order of existence. That would make his philosophy crudely naturalistic, and quite opposed to the 'emergence' view which he accepts."[2] Sri Aurobindo does not commit the inconsistency of explaining the higher principle in terms of a lower one. As Langley puts it, "According to Aurobindo, the higher emerges from the lower because it is eternally present in the lower. It is a logical contradiction to assume that physical energy, which is inconscient and blind, is the exclusive source of consciousness, or even of life. To make this assumption is to derive consciousness and the immense possibilities inherent in conscious being, from accidental concatenations of physical constituents: in other words, to accept the conclusion that consciousness has no adequate ground. This is certainly not so reasonable as to assume that the higher modes of being are eternally immanent in the lower and that in this immanence rests the power for the possible ascent."[3]

According to Sri Aurobindo, the lower principles are the subordinate forms of the higher principles. Mind, Life and Matter are the subordinate forms of Supermind, Consciousness-Force and Existence respectively. Similarly, the psychic entity or soul is the projection of Bliss. Thus our existence, according to Sri Aurobindo, "is a sort of refraction of the divine existence in inverted order of ascent and descent, thus ranged:

1. Alexander, *Space, Time and Deity*, i, p. 342.
2. Radhakrishnan, *An Idealist View of Life*, pp. 322-23.
3. G.H. Langley, *Sri Aurobindo*, pp. 37-38.

Existence	Matter
Consciousness-Force	Life
Bliss	Psyche
Supermind	Mind"[1]

"The Divine descends from pure existence through the play of Consciousness-Force and Bliss and the creative medium of Supermind into cosmic being; we ascend from Matter through a developing life, soul and mind and the illuminating medium of supermind towards the divine being."[2] In the course of evolution "mind can recover its divine light in the all-comprehending supermind, the soul realise its divine self in the all-possessing all-blissful Ananda, life repossess its divine power in the play of omnipotent Conscious-Force and Matter open to its divine liberty as a form of the divine Existence".[3]

The process of evolution is a triple one, which may be called a widening, heightening and integration. First of all, there is a widening of the field which provides scope for the operation of each principle as it emerges, secondly, there is an ascent from the lower grade to the higher grade, and thirdly, there is a descent of the higher principle into the lower grades and a lifting up and transformation of all the lower grades to a higher status. This is called integration. It means that when a higher principle emerges, it makes a descent into all the lower grades and causes a transformation of their essential character and makes them work to a considerable extent in accordance with the higher principle or law of being. For example, when the principle of mind evolves, it makes a descent into life and matter and transforms them in such a way that life and matter become different after the emergence of mind from what they were prior to its emergence. Thus the principle of integration occupies a very important place in Sri Aurobindo's conception of evolution. The lower principles in this view are not rejected at the appearance of the higher principles. All the lower principles have to rise to the status of the Spirit. This is possible on account of the principle of integration. All the lower principles are to be raised to the status of the Spirit and integrated

1. *L.D.* Vol. I, p. 333.
2. *Ibid.*, p. 333.
3. *Ibid.*, p. 333.

and harmonised in an all-embracing unity. This is the meaning of the integral view. Thus the Integral Advaitism of Sri Aurobindo does not reject the lower principles like matter, life and mind but it views them as the different forms and grades of the Absolute. So, by the triple process of widening, heightening and integration, evolution proceeds from Matter to Mind. This is cosmic evolution. But there is, according to Sri Aurobindo, the evolution of the individual soul also. This takes place through rebirth. The problem of the evolution of the individual soul is linked with the problem of rebirth. Sri Aurobindo argues that the belief in rebirth is based on the sound foundations of reason, as the whole question of evolution of the individual soul depends on it, as we will show in a subsequent chapter.

Evolution, according to Sri Aurobindo, has up till now proceeded through four stages, namely, Matter, Life, Psyche and Mind. Now the evolution of the world has to proceed to the supramental status. The next step in evolution will therefore be the descent of the Supermind and the emergence of the divine man or gnostic being. But evolution has to undergo a triple transformation before the emergence of the gnostic being takes place. The triple transformation consists of a psychic, a spiritual and a supramental transformation. As Sri Aurobindo puts it, "There must first be the psychic change, the conversion of our whole present nature into a soul-instrumentation; on that or along with that, there must be the spiritual change, the descent of a higher Light, Knowledge, Power, Force, Bliss, Purity into the whole being, even into the lowest recesses of the life and body, even into the darkness of our subconscience, last, there must supervene the supramental transformation—there must take place as the crowning movement the ascent into the supermind and the transforming descent of the supramental consciousness into our entire being and nature."[1]

The aim of evolution, according to Sri Aurobindo, is not only the liberation of the spirit but the integral transformation of nature also. The principles of mind, life and matter have also to be liberated along with the liberation of the spirit. The perfect liberation of the spirit and nature takes place in the personality of the gnostic being. But the process of evolution does not stop with the emer-

---

1. *L.D.*, Vol. II, Part II, p. 729.

gence of the gnostic being. Even after the supramental descent, evolution will continue not through ignorance as previously, but through knowledge. It reaches its culmination when Saccidānanda ultimately manifests itself in the earth-consciousness. Not until then is the destiny of man completely fulfilled, but the process of his divinisation begins with the emergence of the Supermind.

The gnostic being becomes one with the whole of Reality, with all the orders or aspects of existence and consciousness. He enjoys an integral knowledge and comprehensive vision of the whole of cosmic and supra-cosmic reality. It is the gnostic being who enjoys an integral knowledge of reality. He does not bisect Existence into real and unreal, truth and falsehood, etc. Sri Aurobindo aims at having an integral view of reality. His Integral Advaitism is all-inclusive. It includes, as has been stated above, all the various and so-called contradictory aspects of Reality in its all-embracing unity.

But this integral view of reality can be attained only by an integral knowledge and not by any kind of partial knowledge. Now let us consider what this integral knowledge is and how it will enable us to have an integral view of reality.

(D) *Integral Knowledge: Its Nature and Significance*

"The Integral Knowledge," says Sri Aurobindo, "is something that is already there in the integral Reality: It is not a new or still non-existent thing that has to be created, acquired, learned, invented or built up by the mind; it must rather be discovered or uncovered, it is a Truth that is self-revealed to a spiritual endeavour: for it is there veiled in our deeper and greater self; it is the very stuff of our own spiritual consciousness, and it is by awaking to it even in our surface self that we have to possess it. There is an integral self-knowledge that we have to recover and because the world-self also is our self, an integral world-knowledge".[1] Thus it is clear that the integral knowledge is not of the nature of our sense-experience or mind. It is supramental in nature. It is the knowledge possessed by the divine Being himself. Man is not at present in possession of this knowledge. But he is, according to Sri Aurobindo, destined to attain it during the course of evolution when he will rise to the supramental status. The integral knowledge takes an all-embracing view of all the aspects of Existence or Reality. It does

---

1. *L.D.*, Vol. II, Part II, pp. 415-16.

not raise a permanent barrier between Spirit and Matter, Self and not-Self, etc. "An integral spiritual consciousness carries in it a knowledge of all the terms of being; it links the highest to the lowest through all the mediating terms and achieves an indivisible whole. At the highest summit of things it opens to the reality, ineffable because superconscient to all but its own self-awareness of the Absolute. At the lowest end of our being it perceives the Inconscience from which our evolution begins; but at the same time it is aware of the One and the All self-involved in those depths, it unveils the secret Consciousness in the Inconscience. Interpretative, revelatory, moving between these two extremes; its vision discovers the manifestation of the One in the Many, the identity of the Infinite in the disparity of things finite, the presence of the timeless Eternal in eternal Time; it is this seeing that illumines for it the meaning of the universe".[1] "This consciousness", further observes Sri Aurobindo "does not abolish the universe; it takes it up and transforms it by giving to it its hidden significance. It does not abolish the individual existence; it transforms the individual being and nature by revealing to them their true significance and enabling them to overcome their separateness from the Divine Reality and the Divine Nature".[2]

Thus the integral knowledge remains free from all kinds of partisanship, isolationism and one-sidedness. It considers neither the materialistic view nor the abstract spiritualistic view nor any other views falling between these two extremes as representing the essential truth of the whole of reality. All these views represent different aspects of reality and not the whole of it. Sri Aurobindo does not base his system on any one source of knowledge, whether it is the sense-experience or reason or intuition. These different sources of knowledge, whether taken singly or jointly cannot, according to him, give us an integral and all-embracing view of reality. The real and integral knowledge of reality can be attained only when one attains the supramental consciousness during the course of evolution. Unlike the materialists, the empiricists and the positivists, Sri Aurobindo does not assert that all human knowledge is derived from sense-experience. Sense-experience is undoubtedly

---

1. *L.D.*, Vol. II, Part II, p. 416.
2. *Ibid.*, p. 416.

a source of knowledge. But it does not constitute the whole of human knowledge. One cannot arrive at universal and necessary knowledge simply on the basis of sense-experience.

Similarly, unlike the Rationalists, Sri Aurobindo does not hold that reason is the only source of philosophic knowledge. Reason alone, according to the Rationalists, gives us certain and universal knowledge. Reason has innate in it self-evident and necessary principles. They are *a priori* principles lying implicit in the human mind from the very birth and prior to all experience. Thus philosophy, according to the rationalists, must start from such self-evident and *a priori* principles and arrive at other truths, which logically and necessarily follow from them. We find the best and most successful demonstration of the rationalistic method in the system of Spinoza. But the difficulty with reason is that it is not able to give us a direct knowledge of Reality. It is experience alone that gives us the direct knowledge of things or objects of the world. Reason can only give us the abstract principles or the abstract view of reality. It cannot give us the knowledge of concrete things without the aid of sense-experience.

Thus both these views, that of the empiricists and of the rationalists, seem to be one-sided. This one-sidedness of the views of the empiricists and of the rationalists has been best shown by Kant. Kant holds that both reason and sense-experience are necessary for arriving at a correct knowledge. Reason provides us with the form and experience with the matter of knowledge. From experience we get the knowledge of particular objects. But our sense-experience cannot give us the knowledge of relations. We cannot show any necessary relation between two objects simply on the basis of sense-experience. Sense-experience can give us the knowledge of A and B. But it cannot show any necessary relation existing between A and B. This can be done only by reason. It is reason alone which can give us the universal and necessary knowledge. The combination of sense-experience and reason is able to give us only the knowledge of the phenomena and not of the transcendent reality. All knowledge is, according to Kant, confined to phenomena and does not extend to noumena. Sri Aurobindo agrees with Kant in holding, as we shall show in detail in the next chapter, that reality cannot be realised by mind or mental categories. But he does not assert that mind along with the senses is the only source of knowledge. There are, according to him, higher sources of knowledge attainable by man which can give us a real and integral view of reality. Unlike Kant, Hegel does not regard reason as necessarily tied down to the apron-strings of sense-experience. Reason, according to him, not only knows reality but is also one with reality. The categories of reason in Hegel are not only the subjective forms through which our thought develops and seeks to know the world but they are also the constitutive principles of nature and reality. We shall deal with Hegel's conception of thought and reality in a subsequent chapter. Here it will suffice to know that the dialectical method of Hegel does not go beyond reason. But reason, according to Sri Aurobindo, cannot be the ultimate principle of reality. We cannot characterise reality by any of the principles known to the human consciousness at the present stage. Though reason normally forms the highest stage of man's consciousness at present, yet it does not mean that human consciousness is forever condemned to remain confined to the principle of reason. The merit of Hegel is that he identifies consciousness with reality. But the defect in his view is that by consciousness he means thought or reason. Thought by itself cannot represent the true nature of reality as such. Even the synthetic and dynamic thought of Hegel cannot explain adequately the world-process, much less can it be the creative principle of the world, as we will show in a subsequent chapter.

So the intellect by itself cannot give us either the knowledge of the world or of the transcendent Reality. For the knowledge of objects of the world it has to depend on sense-experience. Similarly, for a knowledge of the transcendent Reality, it has to depend on a higher source of knowledge, called in the Vedānta intuition. Intellect can give us only a conceptual knowledge of Reality and not a direct realisation of it. But intuition gives us an immediate awareness of Reality.

Intuition forms the bedrock of the Vedānta. The Vedānta has always held fast to intuition. The great founders of the classical systems of the Vedānta like Śaṅkara, Rāmānuja, Bhāskara, Nimbārka, Madhva and others have recognised intuition as the highest source of knowledge. The western philosophers like Bradley, Bergson and others also regard intuition as the supreme source of knowledge. But to Sri Aurobindo, even intuition is not the highest or the supreme source of knowledge. He admits that intuition, as viewed by the different Vedāntic systems and some other systems, does take us to the Transcendent. But intuition does not give us the integral and all-embracing view of Reality. The different systems of the Vedānta, for example, arrive at totally different views of reality in spite of their recognition of intuition as the highest and the real source of knowledge.

Śaṅkara's intuition leads him to an affirmation of *nirguṇa* Brahman as the ultimate Reality, while Rāmānuja's intuition gives the supreme place to *saguṇa* Brahman. It means that the intuitional knowledge is not altogether free from the limitations of mind or intellect. Intuition also, like mind, comes to regard *nirguṇa* and *saguṇa* Brahman as opposed to each other and not as the complementary aspects of Reality. Thus intuition is dominated by mind and fails to give us an integral view of Reality.

Reality, Sri Aurobindo argues, can be realised fully and integrally only by means of integral knowledge and not by any other means of knowledge, such as, sense-experience, reason and intuition. The sense-experience, reason and intuition present us only the partial aspects of Reality. Thus the different systems based on these partial sources of knowledge are necessarily partial in character. Only the integral knowledge, as has been stated above, can give us an integral and all-embracing view of Reality. The integral knowledge is possessed by the Supermind. Man also can attain this knowledge when he rises to the status of the Supermind during the course of evolution and turns into a gnostic being. The integral knowledge does not deny altogether the valid truths presented to us by the other sources of knowledge. But it does make us realise their partial character and seeks to get rid of their imperfections and limitations. "The integral knowledge admits the valid truths of all views of existence, valid in their own field, but it seeks to get rid of their limitations and negations and to harmonise and reconcile these partial truths in a larger truth which fulfils all the many sides of our being in the one omnipresent Existence."[1] Thus the Integral Advaitism of Sri Aurobindo is based on integral knowledge. It is integral knowledge that provides a clue to the understanding of his Integral Advaitism.

The integral knowledge of the supreme Reality or the Absolute cannot be attained by man by means of his abstract and analytic

---

1. *L.D.*, Vol. II, Part II, p. 455.

reason which operates on the basis of the laws of Formal Logic, namely, Identity, Contradiction etc. It can be attained by him on the basis of his higher reason or, what Sri Aurobindo significantly calls, The Logic of the Infinite.

So now we proceed to discuss Sri Aurobindo's view of the nature and significance of The Logic of the Infinite.

CHAPTER II

THE LOGIC OF THE INFINITE

The Logic of the Infinite, as the name suggests, is the logic of the divine or the supreme Being. It is a reason which lies inherent in the consciousness of the divine Being. The Divine acts in accordance with its own law or reason, called The Logic of the Infinite. But the nature and working of this higher reason or logic can be realised by man only if he attains the supramental consciousness. But the human reason can have a conceptual or logical grasp of the nature and function of the Logic of the Infinite also. Ordinarily the working of the Logic of the Infinite appears as magic to the human reason. But the more the human reason succeeds in getting rid of its abstract nature, the more it is able to have a conceptual grasp of the nature and working of the higher logic. But before trying to understand the meaning and the significance of the higher logic or the logic of the Infinite, it is better for us to have a comprehensive grasp of the working of the lower reason or the logic of the finite. It is by comparing and contrasting with the logic of the finite that we can have a clear grasp of the Logic of the Infinite. It is through the lower reason that we are to make an approach to the higher reason.

With this end in view, we now proceed to discuss the three main systems of Logic—Formal Logic, Kantian Logic and Hegelian Logic. Here we will show what place reason occupies in these different systems and how far it is able to solve the fundamental problems of philosophy. It will also be a sort of a genetic study of reason as it will show the development and evolution of reason from the abstract and analytic to the concrete and synthetic state.

And finally it will show how reason attains its perfect development and culmination in the higher reason or what Sri Aurobindo calls the Logic of the Infinite and how it reconciles all the oppositions and contradictions that appear irreconcilable and baffling to human thought.

(A) *Formal Logic: Its Nature and Significance*

Formal logic is based on the discursive and abstract reason. It formulates some general principles or laws and all its reasoning is based on them. From certain general premises, it deduces certain conclusions in accordance with these fundamental principles. Its real aim is to see that these principles, e.g. the *Law of Identity,* the *Law of Contradiction,* the *Law of Excluded Middle* etc. are not violated in the process of our reasoning. Thus its aim is self-consistency in our thought. It does not care if its reasoning tallies with the facts of the world or not. The Cartesian system, for example, is based on Formal logic. The system of Spinoza, based on the geometrical method, represents Formal logic in its perfection. Here we have the definition of substance at the top and from it the rest of Spinoza's philosophy is derived purely deductively. But Spinoza has not been able to reconcile his doctrine of Being or Substance with the doctrine of attributes and modes. He has not been able to show how *natura naturata* follows from *natura naturans.* Thus Spinoza is not able to resolve simply on the basis of Formal logic, the contradiction between the Absolute and the relative, as we will show subsequently.

(I) *The Three Laws of Formal Logic: Their Nature and Scope*

The three laws of Formal Logic, namely, the Law of Identity, the Law of Contradiction and the Law of Excluded Middle are conceived as universally true. They are formal in nature and express the most general nature of things. This is true of all logical principles. These principles in their full generality cannot be proved, though they are required in every proof. When these principles are disregarded, our thoughts and words are reduced to confusion and gibberish.[1]

---

1. Cohen and Nagel, *An Introduction to Logic And Scientific Method,* p. 187.

(i) Tautologies and Contradictions

The Law of Identity and the Law of Excluded Middle are, according to modern logicians, tautologies. They are necessarily true. Wittgenstein holds that the propositions of logic are tautologies. Necessary truths are all tautologies. Propositions which are found to be true under all possible assignments of truth-values to their constituents are, according to him, tautologies. Being tautologies, the truths of Logic are completely empty. The propositions of Logic say nothing. A tautology is, according to Wittgenstein, empty and says nothing simply because it is true under all conditions, no matter what reality is like.[1] A non-empty proposition describes a certain situation. It describes some fact. But a tautology does not describe any situation at all. It does not assert anything about any situation or fact. If it did so, it might turn out to be false and in that case, it could not be a tautology. The situation which a proposition describes is its sense. Since a tautology describes no situation, it may be said that it lacks sense. But it does not mean that a tautology is non-sensical.[2] Tautologies are not non-sensical. Wittgenstein conceives them as part of the symbolism, just as 'O' is part of the symbolism of arithmatic.

A tautology represents one extreme of propositions. There is the other extreme of propositions called contradictions. Contradiction is necessarily false. A self-contradictory statement is always false. Contradiction is false under all circumstances or conditions. As a tautology is always true, contradiction is always false. Like a tautology, contradiction describes no fact or situation. So it also lacks sense. Wittgenstein observes: Neither a contradiction nor a tautology is a picture of reality. We can know a priori that the one is true and the other is false.

A proposition, says Wittgenstein, is a truth-function of elementary propositions.[3] "When the truth or falsity of a complex statement can be determined solely from the truth and falsity of its constituent statements, it is called a truth-function of its constituent statements. Thus 'he is old and he is tired' is a truth-function of 'he is old' and 'he is tired'....."[4] Urmson observes: Logicians have

---

1. George Pitcher, The Philosophy of Wittgenstein.
2. Ibid., pp. 109-10.
3. Tractatus, 5(1).
4. Urmson, J.O., Philosophical Analysis, p. 9.

no means within their discipline of determining the truth or falsity of these truth-functions which may be true or may be false; therefore as logicians they have little interest in them.[1] But the logicians are, according to him, specially interested in two other sorts of truth-functions, namely, Tautologies and Contradictions. He observes: Truth-functions which are true for all possibilities of truth and falsehood of their constituents are called tautologies. Truth-functions which are false, irrespective of the truth or falsehood of their constituents, are called contradictories. The main interest of truth-functions for the formal logician is to spot out which of them are tautologies and to devise ways of proving whether any given function however complicated is a tautology.[2]

(ii) *Descriptive Propositions*
Apart from tautologies and contradictions, there is another class of propositions which are called Descriptive Propositions. These propositions describe definite situation and assert that some particular situation exists or does not exist. The truth-value of the descriptive propositions cannot be determined *a priori*. In this respect they are unlike tautologies and contradictions whose truth-value can be known *a priori*. Whether a descriptive proposition is true or false can be known only from experience. The truth of the proposition 'It is raining' can be ascertained only from experience, as it describes a certain situation or fact. Thus the descriptive propositions owe their validity to empirical verification.

The propositions of Logic are independent of experience and so they do not owe their validity to empirical verification. A.J. Ayer observes: "The contention of Mill's which we reject is that the propositions of logic and mathematics have the same status as empirical hypotheses; that their validity is determined in the same way. We maintain that they are independent of experience in the sense that they do not owe their validity to empirical verification. We may come to discover them through an inductive process; but once we have apprehended them we see that they are necessarily true, that they hold good for every conceivable instance. And this serves to distinguish them from empirical generalisations. For we know that a proposition whose validity depends upon experience

1. Urmson, J.O., *Philsophical Analysis*, p. 9.
2. *Ibid.*, p. 10.

cannot be seen to be necessarily and universally true."[1] The truths of logic and mathematics are analytic propositions or tautologies. Unlike descriptive or synthetic propositions, the analytic propositions are devoid of factual content. They do not make any assertion about the empirical world. Ayer vindicates the empiricist claim that there can be no *a priori* knowledge of reality. "For we show that the truths of pure reason, the propositions which we know to be valid independently of all experience, are so only in virtue of their lack of factual content. To say that a proposition is true *a priori* is to say that it is a tautology. And tautologies, though they may serve to guide us in our empirical search for knowledge, do not in themselves contain any information about any matter of fact."[2]

(II) *The Three Laws: Their Defence by Modern Logicians*

Some great philosophers and thinkers of the modern era have made strong criticism of the three principles, namely, Identity, Contradiction and Excluded Middle, as they are understood and interpreted by the exponents of Formal Logic. The most trenchant criticism in this respect has been made by Hegel, as we shall see subsequently. But the modern logicians have presented a strong defence of these principles or laws of Formal Logic. The objections of the critics are, according to them, based on misunderstanding or confusion. They have made ceaseless attempts to provide evidence for their view by making a critical analysis and evaluation of these principles.

The principle of Identity asserts that 'if any statement or proposition is true, it is true. The principle signifies that a thing is perfectly identical with itself. It retains its essential nature at all times and places and in the midst of change. Things are subject to change, but the law expresses the unalterable or fixed nature of things. According to this law, if a term is used in one sense, it has to be used in that sense throughout the same argument. Logic is essentially concerned with propositions and not with things. I.M. Copi observes: "The Principle of Identity" has been criticised on the grounds that things change. But Logic deals only with propositions which do not change. Those statements whose truth-values change

1. *Language, Truth and Logic*, p. 75.
2. *Ibid.*, p. 87.

with time are elliptical or incomplete expressions of propositions which do not change and it is the latter with which logic deals. When we confine our attention to complete or non-elliptical statements, the Principle of Identity is perfectly true and unobjectionable.[1] Cohen and Nagel observe: "The Principle of Identity does not deny the possibility of change. It does say that anything whatsoever in some definite context and occasion has some determinate character. If the coin has a round shape at this time and from this point of view, then the shape cannot also be not round."[2]

The principle of contradiction asserts that 'No proposition can be both true and false.' It means that two contradictory qualities cannot be affirmed of the same thing at the same time. A proposition in which two contradictory qualities are affirmed of the same thing at the same time and in the same sense is necessarily false. This law has been subjected to criticism on the ground that there are situations where contradictory forces or two forces opposed to each other are seen at work. But the formal logicians do not accept this contention of the critics. Copi observes: The Principle of Contradiction has been criticised by Hegelians, General Semanticists and Marxists on the grounds that there are situations in which contradictory or conflicting forces are at work. That there are situations containing conflicting forces must be admitted: this is as true in the realm of mechanics as in the social and economic spheres. But it is a loose and inconvenient terminology to call these forces 'contradictory'. The heat applied to a contained gas, which tends to make it expand, and the container, which tends to keep it from expanding, may be described as conflicting with each other, but neither is the negation or denial or contradictory of the other. When understood in the sense in which it is intended the Principle of Contradiction is unobjectionable and perfectly true.[3]

The Principle of Excluded Middle asserts that 'Any proposition must be either true or false.' According to this principle, two contradictory qualities cannot both be false of one and the same thing at the same time and in the same sense. If one of them turns out to be false, the other must be true of it. There is no possibility of any middle course or third alternative. Two contradictory terms

---

1. *Introduction to Logic*, Third Edition, p. 245.
2. *Op. cit.*
3. *Op. cit.*, p. 245.

are exhaustive as well as exclusive. The Principle of Excluded Middle, says Copi, has been the object of more attacks than either of the other principles. These attacks are based on a confusion between contradictory and contrary terms. Two contrary terms predicated of a thing at the same time and in the same sense may both be false. The denial or negation of either of them does not lead to the affirmation of the other. They cannot both be true, but they can both be false. Two statements, for example, 'this is white' and 'this is black', if they refer to the same thing cannot both be true, but they can both be false. They are contrary, not contradictory. The negation or contradictory of "this is white" is "this is not-white" and one of these statements must be true—if the word "white" is used in precisely the same sense in both statements. When restricted to statements containing completely unambiguous and perfectly precise terms, the Principle of Excluded Middle also is perfectly true.[1]

Thus the three fundamental principles or laws of Logic discussed above are shown by the exponents of Formal Logic to be unobjectionable and perfectly true. The conformity to these principles is necessary for all valid reasoning. They constitute the universal and necessary conditions of all valid reasoning, whatever the matter may be. These principles are indispensable for securing formal truth. In any valid inference, the conclusion follows with logical necessity from the premises. The conclusion gives only formal truth. In formal reasoning the premises are taken for granted. Formal logic is not concerned with the question whether the premises are true in fact. It is only concerned with the question whether the conclusion necessarily follows or not from the given premises. If either of the given propositions be materially false, the conclusion cannot be materially true. In formal reasoning, a conclusion may be formally true, but materially false. Cohen and Nagel observe: Formal logic deals with the possible relations (in regard to truth and falsity) between propositions, no matter what their subject-matter. This gives the *necessary* conditions for valid inference and enables us to eliminate false reasoning, but that is not *sufficient* to establish any material or factual truth in any particular field. Formal logic shows that any such propositions must be true if certain others are so. The categorical assertion that our premises

---

1. Copi, *op. cit.*, pp. 245-46.

are actually true cannot be a matter of logic alone without making the latter identical with all knowledge. Logic then is involved in all reasoned knowledge but is not the whole of it.[1] The fundamental task of logic is the study of those objective relations between propositions which condition the validity of inference by which we pass from premises to conclusions.[2]

A valid argument relating to descriptive propositions cannot violate the laws of logic. If it is said, "The table is red," one cannot at the same time and in the same sense say, "The table is not-red." Both the statements cannot be true. One of them must be false. Thus the laws of Identity, Contradiction and Excluded Middle condition all our valid reasoning. The conformity to these principles is a pre-condition for all valid arguments whether they deal with analytic propositions or with descriptive propositions. In this respect these fundamental principles of logic condition existence. If a proposition which describes a certain situation is true, its contradictory cannot be held as true at the same time. Thus this proposition puts a limitation on that particular situation or fact and leaves no scope for something else to be true at the same time and in the same sense. It is in this sense that these fundamental laws of logic condition existence. Cohen and Nagel observe: Every significant proposition, if true, limits the subject-matter, and prohibits something else to be true. In this sense, and only in this sense, do logical principles condition existence.[3] The principles of logic do not condition the existence of objects or facts. But they do condition the propositions which express them. The logical principles determine the use of language. Blyth observes: In formal logic we are primarily concerned with the logical function of language and only indirectly with the informative and practical functions. This function of language is governed by the principles of Logic. One cannot abandon them without contradicting oneself.

It has to be noted that the formal logic by itself cannot determine the material truth of any statement. The material truth of the premises can be known only through sense experience or some other non-deductive source of knowledge. This fact shows the

---

1. *Op. cit.*, p. 191.
2. *Ibid.*, p. 110.
3. *Ibid.*, p. 187.

limitations to the use of the principles of logic.

(III) *Principles of Logic: Their Limitations*

The principles of logic only determine the validity of an argument and not the truth value of the premises. Blyth observes: To prove the truth or falsity of some statement by reference to other statements we must start with a knowledge of the truth value of those statements. This indicates a very important limitation to the use of logic. The argument by itself does not prove that the premises are true. To prove the premises we should have to show that they are implied by other premises known to be true. But even if we construct a chain of arguments, the premises with which we start the chain cannot be proved by that chain. In short, by the use of formal deductive logic alone we cannot prove the material truth of a single existential statement. Thus to prove the material truth of any statements at all, we must have some way of determining the truth of some initial premises without resort to formal deductive logic.[1]

From the above discussion it is clear that by the application of the principles of logic, we can prove only the formal truth of statements and not their material truth. In a syllogism, the material truth of conclusion depends on that of the premises. If either of the premises be false, the conclusion must be false. Formal logic, as we have seen above, cannot determine the truth value of the premises. So it is clear that the principles of logic, namely, Identity, Contradiction etc., can be applied in an *a priori* and unconditional way to prove the truth of analytic propositions. They cannot be used in the same manner to prove the truth of descriptive propositions or non-analytic propositions. We may take, for example, the Principle of Contradiction. It asserts that two qualities which are contradictory cannot be affirmed of the same thing at the same time and in the same sense. But this principle does not tell us what qualities are really contradictory or discrepant. As Bradley puts it: "there is no logical principle which will tell us what qualities are really discrepant".[2] This indicates, as Blyth has pointed out, a very important limitation to the use of logic. It also shows that there is a clear gap between logic and reality. An *a priori* and

---

1. Blyth, John W., *A Modern Introduction to Logic*, p. 379.
2. *The Principles of Logic*, Vol. I, p. 146.

unconditional application of the principles of logic to statements which express the nature of reality is, thus, logically inadmissible.

Formal logic has its own advantages. As Blyth puts it. The most important advantages of Formal logic are found in the proof of the truth or falsity of one statement by reference to other statements and the systematic organisation of knowledge. If we know that some statements are true we may prove the truth of any statement strictly implied by them. Falsity of a statement may be determined in the same way.[1] In this respect, Formal Logic can be used with great profit.

But Formal Logic can also be misused. Its chief misuse lies in the *a priori* and unconditional application of its fundamental laws to statements which refer to the objects of the world or to reality. There is a decisive gap, as has been pointed above, between logic and reality. The laws of logic are not laws of nature or of reality. They do not govern the world of matter, life and mind. So their *a priori* and unconditional application to statements which refer to the objects of the world or trans-empirical reality is not logically justified. Blyth says: Modern developments in logic have made it clear that there is no necessary connection between a formal system of logic and the entities to which we try to apply a system.[2] He also says that 'it is no longer plausible to assume that the so-called laws of any one system of logic are identical with the laws of all relational thought and the laws of things'. It is quite possible that certain relations between objects in experience may not conform to the order of some logical system. But on that very basis it cannot be said that those relations are unintelligible or false. A system of logic may be developed which may explain those relations between objects in experience in an intelligible and rational way. Our inability to explain those relations on the basis of the principles of Formal logic simply shows the limitations of this system of logic. It does not in any way show that the order found in nature or reality is itself unintelligible, unreal or false.

Leibniz shows clear awareness of the limitations of the principles of formal logic. He holds that the real world cannot be brought under and measured by the scales of the laws of Formal Logic. Therefore, he introduces another principle, namely, the

1. *Op. cit.*
2. *Ibid.*, p. 166.

Principle of Sufficient Reason to understand the nature of the real world. All the important spheres of human life, social, moral, religious etc., are placed by him under the domain of the *Principle of Sufficient Reason*. But Leibniz calls the truths that are governed by the principle of contradiction *necessary truths,* and those governed by the Principle of Sufficient Reason *contingent truths.* Necessary truths follow with logical certainty. They are eternal and unalterable. Thus they fall under the logical law of contradiction; their opposite is unthinkable. But the necessary truths are really abstract. They are the truths which belong to the domain of mathematics. When we come to the practical world, we do not find any necessity involved there. We have to find some sufficient reason to understand the world of practical life and experience. Thus it is clear that Leibniz has not been able to extricate himself wholly from the sway of the Formal logic, as he calls the truths governed by the principle of contradiction necessary truths; but he has given us a glimpse into another logic governed by the *Principle of Sufficient Reason,* which is applicable to human life and the world.

(B) *Kantian Logic: Its Nature and Significance*

When we come to Kant, we find a more vigorous and bold attempt on the part of thought to free itself from the hold of Formal logic. Kant does not want to rest satisfied with the attainment of mere self-consistency in thought. His aim is to know the real. Hence he formulates the fundamental problem of the *Critique* thus: How are *synthetic judgments a priori* possible?

There are analytic judgments and synthetic judgments. The former do not give us any new knowledge. They merely analyse an idea without adding anything new to it. Take, for example, the judgment, bodies are extended. The predicate 'extended' does not add anything to the subject that is not already contained in it. This judgment does not in any way increase our knowledge. If, on the other hand it is said, the earth is a planet, it is a synthetic judgment. Here a new predicate is joined to the subject as the idea of the planet cannot be said to be an inseparable part of the idea of earth. Thus synthetic judgments increase, enrich and extend our knowledge, which is not the case with analytic judgments.

But a judgment, Kant argues, should not only be synthetic but should also be *a priori.* It must possess the characteristics of universality and necessity. It should not be true in some cases only but in all cases. To say that "it is warm" is undoubtedly a synthetic judgment, but it is accidental and contingent. It has no universality and necessity about it. But if it is said "Heat expands bodies," it is a synthetic judgment which will hold good for all time.

But the idea of universality and necessity is not given in our experience. In this respect Hume is perfectly right in denying the validity of cause-effect relationship etc. But if the idea of universality and necessity cannot be derived from experience, it does not mean that it is merely a figment of imagination or due to habitual association between things. These universal relationships, like cause-effect etc., are rooted in our reason. The synthetic *a priori* judgments are the joint products of our sensibility and reason. Our senses provide us with the sensations or matter of knowledge, while our reason supplies the different forms or categories which give unity to the bundle of sensations. Finally, we have the ego which gives unity to our sense-experience as well as to our categories. This unity of the ego is called by Kant, the synthetic unity of apperception.

In this way, Kant reconciles the opposition between Empiricism and Rationalism. Both these views, according to him, are partial. For the attainment of real knowledge, both the sources of knowledge—sense-experience and reason are necessary and indispensable. Without experience, our knowledge will be merely formal and analytic and without reason it will be accidental and contingent. This idea is expressed in the famous dictum of Kant that "concepts without percepts are empty and percepts without concepts are blind".

Thus it is clear that the real problem of Kant is to substitute a logic of reality or a logic of objects in place of formal logic. Really speaking, Kant has given us, as he himself says, a logic of objects, as reality, meaning, the thing-in-itself, is for Kant outside the scope of logic. *A priori* synthetic judgments really mark a fundamental change in the logical outlook. Now thought does not rest content with the analysis of a proposition in accordance with the laws of Formal logic. It wants to know the real. The new logic which Kant gives us in place of Formal logic is called by him transcendental logic. It is not, like Formal logic, the logic of mere self-consistency. It is the logic of experience. Here thought joins itself with the objective world to attain fruitful and objective knowledge. Thought now no more remains a spectator of the world-play but plays an active role in it. The objective world is seen to be dependent on thought not only for experience but also for its very existence. An object is an object only in relation to a subject. To know an object we have not only to relate it to other objects but also to the subject—the perceiver. Unity of experience is not possible without reference to the unity of self-consciousness. This unity of self-consciousness Kant calls "the transcendental unity of apperception". "No knowledge whatever," Kant observes, "no unity and connection of objects is possible for us, apart from that unity of consciousness which is prior to all data of perception and without relation to which no consciousness of objects is possible. This original, unchangeable consciousness I call transcendental apperception."

Now the problem is, does Kant succeed in uniting together the two apparently opposed aspects of experience, the subject and the object, reason and sensibility? Does reason attain real power of synthesis in Kant's system? Does it get rid of all traces of formalism? The answer is a definite 'no'. The object in Kant's view is not integrally related to the subject, for an essential condition of it is that it must be presented to the subject by our sensibility which has only an external connection with the understanding. Self-consciousness by itself does not possess any content. It is nothing but the bare logical condition of all knowledge. As Cohen expressly puts it, "The 'I' can only be looked upon as a capacity, as the transcendental condition of the possibility of the logical judgment." Self-consciousness, therefore, derives its content from objective knowledge i.e. sensibility. The result is, as Norman Kemp Smith says, "there can be no such thing as a pure self-consciousness, that is, a consciousness in which the self is aware of itself and of nothing but itself". Self in Kant's view, is aware of itself only insofar as it is conscious of the objective world. Self-consciousness is a mediated consciousness. It is mediated by the consciousness of the objects. In itself the Self or the Ego is devoid of all content or object. It cannot give us the knowledge of the objects unless it joins hands, as has been stated above, with sensibility.

Thus the self, according to Kant, is a *subject* and not a *substance*. It is the logical and *a priori* condition of all knowledge and is itself not an object of knowledge. It is the ground of all categories and hence cannot be an object of any category. Thus Kant observes in the *Critique of Pure Reason* that the Ego "is so completely empty of all content that it cannot be called even a conception, but merely a consciousness that accompanies all conceptions. This 'I' or 'he' or 'it', this thing that thinks is nothing but the idea of a transcendental subject of thought=X, which is known only through the thoughts that are its predicates, and which apart from them, cannot be conceived at all. We turn round and round it in a perpetual circle, for we can make no judgment about it without making use of the idea of it in our judgment. Nor can this inconvenience be avoided, for consciousness in itself is not so much the distinct idea of a particular object as a general form of all the ideas through which knowledge of objects is to be obtained, and indeed the only form of which I can say, that without it I can think nothing whatever".[1]

In his criticism of rational psychology Kant points out that the mistake of Descartes lay in his ignoring the distinction between the self as a *subject* and the self as a *substance*. The *Cogito ergo sum* of Descartes is a classical example of the fallacy of regarding the self as a substance. From the 'cogito' or 'I think', nothing can be said about the content of the self. The 'I think' is merely the logical condition which makes consciousness possible, but it can give no content to consciousness.

Thus it is clear that consciousness in its real nature is, according to Kant, analytic and not synthetic. It attains the power of synthesis only when it unites with the sensibility in order to gain objective knowledge. Thus all the synthetic power of self depends upon sensibility. It does not constitute, as has been stated above, the essential nature of self. This is a great tragedy in Kantian system. Kant is not able to bridge the gulf between sensibility and reason. Sensibility is an extraneous element to self and reason. Without it, reason cannot attain objective knowledge. If it tries to do so, it is involved in irreconcilable antinomies or contradictions, as Kant explicitly shows in the Transcendental Dialectic. Thus the poor reason in Kant's system remains always at the mercy of sensibility for the attainment of concreteness and richness. But if divorced from sensibility, it is reduced to a bare abstract identity. It then presents itself as a mere consciousness devoid of all contents. So

---

1. Watson's *Selections from Kant*, p. 148.

Kant ultimately fails to give us a view of reason which bridges the yawning gulf between the subject and the object. Thought in Kant is still very much analytic. It has ultimately failed to attain concreteness and the true power of synthesis on account of its utter dependence upon sensibility. It is confronted on all sides by irreconcilable contradictions. It finds itself unable to solve the contradiction between subject and object, reason and sensibility, phenomena and noumena etc.

(C) *Hegelian Logic: Its Nature and Significance*

In Hegel we find thought rising to a higher stage of synthesis. Hegel does not consider contradictions or antinomies as irreconcilable in nature. If thought is confronted with contradictions and antinomies, it is also, according to Hegel, possessed of the power to overcome them. Thought is dynamic and not static. It is possessed of the power to manifest itself in its opposite, to become other than what it is and to overcome the contradiction between itself and its 'other' or 'opposite'. Thus every thought has three moments—*thesis* or the assertion of itself, *antithesis* or the assertion of its opposite, and *synthesis* or the reconciliation of the contradiction or opposition between itself and its opposite. Now this synthesis again becomes a thesis and is confronted with an antithesis and is again reconciled by a new synthesis, which in its turn will again become a thesis and so on till we reach the Absolute Idea itself, which is the final goal and the real nature of thought. Thus thought starts in its triumphant march from the category of *Being* and reconciles all the contradictions and oppositions that fall on its way till it reaches the highest stage of synthesis or concreteness, the *Absolute Idea*.

This is the moving principle in Hegelian Logic; a contradiction is reconciled in a unity, is again confronted by a new contradiction only to be reconciled in a higher unity, and this process continues until all the contradictions are resolved in a final unity. "It has been hitherto one of the rooted prejudices of logic and a commonly accepted belief," says Hegel, "that the contradiction is not so essential or so inherent a characteristic (in thought and existence) as the identity. Yet in comparison with it the identity is, in truth, but the characteristic of what is simply and directly perceived, of lifeless existence. The contradiction, however, is the source of all movement, and life, only insofar as it contains a contradiction can anything have movement, power and effect".

Hegel regards contradiction as inherent in reality. It does not mean that reality fails to reconcile all contradictions in it but that it has got the power to become other than what it is and also to overcome the opposition, as has been stated above. Thus the power of involving and overcoming all opposition is the characteristic of reality. Where this power is lacking we have to take it as an abstraction and not as a reality. "The true and positive meaning of the antinomies" says Hegel, "is this that every actual thing involves a co-existence of opposed elements".[1]

This statement of Hegel throws a direct challenge to formal logic. It gives a crushing blow to its cherished and fundamental conceptions. It challenges the absolute validity of its fundamental laws.

(I) *The Laws of Logic: Hegel*

Hegel has made a critical analysis and evaluation of the principles or laws of logic and has made a serious attempt to deduce their implications. His interpretation of the fundamental principles of logic, namely, Identity, Contradiction etc., differs in a radical way from that of formal logic.

(i) *The Law of Identity*

Hegel observes: "In its positive expression $A = A$, this law is nothing more than empty tautology. It has therefore rightly been observed that this law of Thought is without content and leads no further. Those therefore are stranded upon empty Identity who take it to be a truth in itself, and are in the habit of repeating that Identity is not variety, but that Identity and Variety are different. They do not see that they are themselves here saying that Identity is *different*, for they say that Identity is different from variety, and since this must at the same time be admitted to be the nature of Identity, their assertion implies that Identity has the quality of being different not externally but in its very nature."[2] Hegel has made here a very significant observation. The concept of Identity

1. *Logic*, Wallace's Translation, Vol. II, p. 100.
2. Hegel's *Science of Logic*, Vol. II, translated by W.H. Johnson and L.G. Struthers, pp. 39-40.

if closely and critically examined is found to imply the concept of difference. Difference is not only externally related to Identity but it constitutes its essential nature. The Formal Logic conceives the principles of Identity, Contradiction etc., as universally true. But this truth is merely abstract and formal. This truth, according to Hegel, is also incomplete. It does not reveal the full implications of the principle of identity and other logical principles. As Hegel puts it, "But further, since they cling to this rigid Identity which has its opposite in variety, they do not see that they are thereby making it into a one-sided determinateness, which has no truth. It is admitted that the Law of Identity expresses only a one-sided determinateness, that it contains only formal truth, which is abstract and incomplete. But this correct judgment immediately implies that truth is complete only in the union of Identity with Variety, and therefore consists only in this unity."[1] Identity, apart from variety, cannot be conceived as representing the full truth either of the concepts of thought or of the objects of the world. The formal logicians show no awareness of the full implications of the Law of Identity. They have taken notice of the criticism that a thing is not only identical with itself but it also undergoes change. Their answer to this criticism is, as we have shown above, that logic is not concerned with the phenomenon of change. It is concerned only with the propositions which do not change. But Hegel's criticism goes deeper. He has shown that Identity in its very nature implies difference. The very idea of Identity is characterised by the idea of difference, as Identity cannot be understood and apprehended apart from variety. Hegel does not, in fact, question the truth of the Principle of Identity itself. He questions the inadequate and one-sided interpretation of this Law that has been made by the Formal Logicians and others.

(ii) *The Law of Contradiction*

Hegel gives an original interpretation of the Law of Contradiction as well. With great dexterity and thoroughness, he deduces the implications of this Law. Hegel observes: "But it has been a fundamental prejudice of hitherto existing logic and of ordinary imagination that Contradiction is a determination having less essence

---

1. Hegel's *Science of Logic*, Vol. II, translated by W.H. Johnson and L.G. Struthers p. 40.

and immanence than identity; but indeed, if there were any question of rank, and the two determinations had to be fixed as separate, Contradiction would have to be taken as the profounder and more fully essential. For as opposed to it Identity is only the determination of the simple immediate, or of dead Being, while Contradiction is the root of all movement and life, and it is only insofar as it contains a contradiction that anything moves and has impulse and activity."[1] Contradiction, says Hegel, "is the Negative in its essential determination, the principle of all self-movement, which consists of nothing but an exhibition of Contradiction".

According to Formal Logic, all that is contradictory is false. Any entity or concept which involves contradiction is false or unreal; it is to be negated or rejected. But Hegel's view of contradiction is altogether different. Abstract self-identity, according to him, has no life. Something has life only insofar as it contains contradiction. What is called positive is in itself also negativity; it causes the positive to pass outside itself and to change. A living unity contains contradiction within itself and also overcomes it. "But if an existent something cannot in its positive determination also encroach on its negative, cannot hold fast the one in the other and contain Contradiction within itself, then it is not living unity, or Ground, but perishes in Contradiction."[2]

Contradiction is revealed in the determinations of relations. As Hegel puts it: "The most trivial examples—above and below, right and left, father and son, and so on without end—all contain contradiction in one term. That *is* above which *is* not below; 'above' is determined only as not being 'below' and conversely: one determination implies its opposite. Father is the other of son, and son of father, and each exists only as this other of the other; and also the one determination exists only in relation to the other...." Contradiction reveals itself in other kinds of relations as well. The categories of thought, namely, cause and effect, substance and attribute, universal and particular etc.—all are fraught with contradiction. But it does not mean that they can be characterised as unreal or false.

Edward Caird has given a most penetrating account of the Law of Contradiction. He says, "When Aristotle laid down the Law of

1. *Op. cit.*, pp. 66-67.
2. *Ibid.*, p. 68.

Contradiction as the highest law of thought, and opposed it to the Heraclitean principle of universal flux, he argued that, unless distinction is maintained,—unless things are definitely what they are, and are kept to this definition, knowledge and thought become impossible."[1] Caird contends that it is certainly one necessary aspect of truth. Thought is always "distinction, determination, the marking off of one thing from another". "But thought is not only distinction, it is at the same time relation. If it marks off one thing from another, it at the same time connects one thing with another."[2] "If therefore, the law of contradiction be taken as asserting the self-identity of things or thoughts in a sense that excludes their community—in other words, if it be not taken as limited by another law which asserts the relativity of things or thoughts distinguished—it involves a false abstraction. A half-truth is necessarily distorted into a falsehood when taken as a whole truth. An absolute distinction by its very nature would be self-contradictory, for it would cut off all connection between the things it distinguished. It would annihilate the relation implied in the distinction, and so it would annihilate the distinction itself."[3] So the knowledge of distinction is not enough. We have not to judge things in their isolation but in relation to other things. We have to find out the principle of unity underlying the different and so-called opposite things. We can attain the real knowledge of things only when we grasp the fundamental principle of unity lying behind them and constituting their essence.

Thus the realisation of the principle of unity running through the world of multiplicity is the main work of reason. Reason becomes more and more concrete and integral as it links together all the manifold objects of the world by the one fundamental principle of unity. But this is not enough. Reason has to find unity not only between objects of the world, but also between subject and object or between itself and the world. The real knowledge of the object, as Kant has shown, cannot be attained simply by linking or relating it with other objects and by ignoring the existence of the subject altogether. To take away the subject is to reduce the object to nothing. As Radhakrishnan puts it, "Without the self,

---

1. *Hegel* (Blackwood's *Philosophical Classics*), p. 134.
2. *Ibid.*, p. 135.
3. *Ibid.*, p. 135.

there can be no knowledge, no art, no morality. Objects out of relation to a self are non-existent. From the subject are all objects, and the subject itself is not a thing among other things."¹ Thus reason attains concreteness and integrality only when it bridges the gulf existing between the subjective and the objective orders of existence. It is formal and abstract so far as it considers the object to be fundamentally different from and opposed to the subject. To the formal and abstract reason the subject and the object are contradictory to each other. But to the concrete and integral reason, the subject and object are not contradictory to each other; they are the complementary aspects of the same reality. We find reason attaining this high status in the philosophy of Hegel.

(D) *Hegel's View of Thought and Being as Identical*
There is a famous statement of Hegel that Thought and Being are identical. The .whole of Hegelian philosophy is based on this statement. Thought is, according to Hegel, the universal principle which lies at the root of the subjective and objective orders of existence and guides their working. It is not only constituted of our internal mental states but it is also the constitutive principle of the world of objects. But in Nature or in objective existence, thought is present in an unconscious and latent form. It does not manifest itself outwardly in things. The categories of thought are not only the different forms through which we look at the world but they are the constitutive stuff of the world and reveal the history of the world-process. As Hegel observes, "To speak of thought or objective thought as the heart and soul of the world, may seem to be ascribing consciousness to the things of nature. We feel a certain repugnance against making thought the inward function of things, especially as we speak of thought as marking the divergence of man from nature. It would be necessary, therefore, if we use the term thought at all, to speak of nature as the system of unconscious thought, or, to use Schiller's expression, a petrified intelligence. And in order to prevent misconception, thought-form or thought-type should be substituted for the ambiguous term thought."² He says further, "If thought is the consti-

---

1. *Indian Philosophy*, Vol. I, p. 154.
2. *Logic (Encyclopaedia of the Philosophical Sciences)*, Wallace's Translation, p. 46.

tutive substance of external things, it is also the universal substance of what is spiritual. In all human perception thought is present; so too thought is the universal in all the acts of conception and recollection; in short, in every mental activity, in willing, wishing and the like. All these faculties are only further specialisations of thought. When it is presented in this light, thought has a different part to play from what it has if we speak of a faculty of thought, one among a crowd of other faculties such as perception, conception and will, with which it stands on the same level. When it is seen to be the true universal of all that nature and mind contain, it extends its scope far beyond all these, and becomes the basis of everything."[1]

Thus it is clear from these statements of Hegel that thought is the constitutive principle of all the subjective and objective orders of existence. Thought, according to Hegel, is the all-inclusive unity, the unity within which all distinctions, including the distinction of the knower and the known fall. Hegel does not deny the reality of matter. To say that matter is ultimately nothing but thought is not to deny the reality of matter. All that Hegel means is this that what is called material is ultimately spiritual in nature without ceasing to be material. Matter is merely one aspect or poise of reality. But the materialist takes it for the whole of reality. Here lies the fundamental difference between the materialist view of matter and the Hegelian view. It is because Hegel sets a logic of the real,[2] as Dr. S.K. Maitra puts it, over against Formal logic that he has been able to reconcile the opposition between Spirit and Matter, Subject and Object, Thought and Sensibility, One and Many etc. Kant held that an object has no meaning unless it is related to the self. But object remained a foreign element in Kant's philosophy. But in Hegel object becomes an integral part of the subject. To say that existence means existence for self, says Caird, "implies not merely that there is a relation between consciousness on one side and existence on the other (in which case the relation would exist not for the conscious being himself, but for someone else), but it implies also that consciousness transcends the dualism between itself and its object. It means, in short, that though, within

---

1. Logic (Encyclopaedia of the Philosophical Sciences), Wallace's Translation, p. 46.
2. The Logic of the Real (Proceedings of the Second Indian Philosophical Congress, 1926).

certain limits, we oppose the subject to the object, the conscious-
ness to that of which it is conscious, yet that from a higher point
of view this antagonism is within consciousness; or to put it from
the other side, that consciousness, as such, overreaches the divi-
sion between itself and its object. And the same reasoning must
be applied to all the contrasts which in the system of Kant spring
out of this fundamental opposition—the contrasts of necessity and
freedom, of nature and spirit, of phenomenal and noumenal".[1] The
subject in Kant's view is pure consciousness, while in Hegel it is
self-conscious. "Self-consciousness," says Caird, "is the standing
enigma for those who would separate identity and difference; for
it is not merely that in one aspect of it, self-consciousness is a
duality, and in another aspect a unity; duality and unity are so
inseparably blended in it, that neither has any meaning without
the other. Or to put it still more definitely, the self exists as one
self only as it opposes itself as object, to itself, as subject, and
immediately denies and transcends that opposition".[2] Thus Hegel
shows the real nature and significance of the conception of self-
consciousness and categories. Consciousness, according to Hegel,
is not an empty universal but an all-inclusive principle. In the same
way the categories are not merely empty frames which receive
their contents from without. They are substantial forms which give
themselves their own content and constitute the different stages
of the eternal process.

Thus it is clear that Hegel's Conception of Thought is quite
different from what is ordinarily understood by it. Ordinarily,
thought is understood as analytic and abstract. But Hegel regards
it, as has been shown above, as concrete, synthetic and also dynamic.
Thought as analytic and static cannot reconcile the oppositions or
contradictions. But thought as synthetic and dynamic cannot lead
us, as we have shown above, to accept the laws of Formal logic
as absolute. The analytic thought does not realise the fundamental
principle of unity lying behind the world-process and constituting
its essence. But thought as synthetic and concrete is based on this
very principle and is one with it. To analytic thought the relation
between cause and effect, substance and attribute, and subject and
object is merely external, but to synthetic thought it is internal. All

---

1. *Hegel*, p. 123.
2. *Ibid.*, p. 149.

differences and so-called oppositions are to synthetic thought within a whole and are the self-expressions of that whole. It is this synthetic thought which in Hegel's system is seen to conquer all oppositions and contradictions. All the functions of mind, all the operations of nature can be understood only in relation to this thought and not apart from it.

(I) *Bradley's Criticism of Hegel's Thought*

In the light of the above discussion, let us now examine Bradley's criticism of Hegel's thought. Bradley holds that thought and reality cannot be identical. So far as this statement is concerned, many other great philosophers, including Sri Aurobindo, will agree with Bradley without any reservation. They will admit Bradley's view that Reality is more than thought. But here we have to see whether Bradley is justified in criticising Hegel's view of thought. Thought in Bradley's view is relational and discursive. It is full of self-contradictions. But the reality is a suprarelational whole which overcomes all the so-called contradictions and oppositions. Thought being relational and discursive fails to grasp the nature of reality which is suprarelational. In order to know reality, thought, according to Bradley, must commit suicide. From this standpoint, Bradley makes a trenchant criticism of Hegel's conception of Thought and its identification with reality. According to him, thought by itself cannot explain our sense-experience. He says, "Let us assume that existence is no longer different from truth, and let us see where this takes us. It takes us straight to thought's suicide. A system of content is going to swallow up our reality but in our reality we have the fact of sensible experience, immediate presentation with its colouring of pleasure and pain. Now I presume there is no question of conjuring this fact away; but how is it to be exhibited as an element in a system of thought content, is a problem not soluble. Thought is relational and discursive, and if it ceases to be this it commits suicide, and yet if it remains thus how does it contain immediate presentation?"[1] He says further, "Let us suppose the impossible accomplished; let us imagine a harmonious system of ideal contents united by relations, and reflecting itself in self-conscious harmony. This is to be reality, all reality, and

---

1. *Appearance and Reality* (2nd Edition, revised), p. 170.

there is nothing outside it. The delights and pains of the flesh, the agonies and raptures of the soul, these are fragmentary meteors fallen from thought's harmonious system. But these burning experiences—how in any sense can they be mere pieces of thought's heaven? For, if the fall is real, there is a world outside thought's region, and if the fall is apparent, then human error itself is not included there. Heaven, in brief, must either not be heaven, or else not all reality. Without a metaphor, feeling belongs to perfect thought, or it does not. If it does not, there is at once a side of existence beyond thought. But if it does belong, then thought is different from thought discursive and relational."[1]

From these explicit statements of Bradley, it is clear that he looks upon the world of sense and feeling as different from and incompatible with the world of thought. But Bradley's statements are based on a gross misunderstanding of Hegel's position. To Bradley, as has been stated above, the term thought means relational and discursive thought. If it is so, then the sense-experience will certainly fall apart from thought. In this respect Hegel has nothing to say against Bradley. The analytic and discursive thought according to Hegel also cannot give us the fundamental unity and cannot explain sensuous experience. Our sense-experience, our feelings, desires, will, emotions etc. cannot be explained by the analytic and discursive thought. But this is not, according to Hegel, the real nature of thought. In Hegel's system, "Thought as the subject of knowledge is the correlative of, and therefore opposed to, the object of knowledge. But this correlatively and opposition implies a unity which transcends the opposition. It is with thought as the ultimate unity—the Absolute, that Hegel identifies Reality and, not with it as the mere subject of knowledge."[2] Thought in its dialectical march reaches a higher stage where it gains in richness and concreteness and is able to synthesise all the disparate elements of our experience in an all-embracing unity. No aspect of experience, Hegel argues, can lie outside and apart from this synthetic and all-unifying principle. Bradley has, in fact, nothing to say against this synthetic and concrete thought. All his weighty criticisms are hurled against the nature of thought as abstract, analytic, relational and discursive. The abstract, analytic and discursive thought is individual

1. *Appearance and Reality* (2nd Edition, revised), pp. 170-71.
2. *Neo-Hegelianism*, p. 472.

while the synthetic, concrete thought is universal in nature. In the individual mind we find the principle of thought or cognition only as an aspect of our total consciousness. Conation and affection cannot be reduced to thought. But Hegel does not look upon this thought as the constitutive stuff of mind and nature. So Bradley has no logical justification to hurl vehement criticisms against Hegel's conception of the unity of Thought and Being, taking thought as merely analytic and discursive in nature. Bradley thinks that a principle can be called thought only if it is relational and discursive in nature. But this is merely a difference in terminology. We shall show in a later chapter in our discussion of Bradley's conception of the Absolute that what Bradley calls intuition is not very much different from Hegel's thought. Both can be represented by the principle of identity-in-difference.

(II) *Hegel's Thought is Intuition: Mure's View*

Hegel's conception of Thought has led some scholars to say that what Hegel calls thought is not merely thought but also intuition. Mure in his book *An Introduction to Hegel* raises this important problem. Hegel's thought, he argues, is not merely thought but also intuition. Let us quote at length Mure's statement in order to understand what he really means by saying that Hegel's thought is not merely thought but also intuition. He says, "We have seen that Hegel restores to thought the intuitive factor in knowledge, the moment of immediate existence and individuality, which Kant had confined at least in respect of human knowing, to passive sensibility. In thus denying the Kantian divorce between thinking and knowing, in thus giving a far more real meaning to that activity which Kant had continued to attribute to thought emasculated of its intuitional moment, Hegel in a sense returns to a position common to all Kant's greatest predecessors. In different forms the conception of intuitive thought is present equally in Aristotle and in Descartes, Spinoza and Leibniz. But none of these thinkers had, in Hegel's view, clearly grasped either (a) the general nature of intuition or (b) its relation to discursion within the nature of thought itself....As against these modern thinkers Hegel saw in the religious view of the world a form of experience less complete than philosophy. His conception of thought as intuitive is an effort to expand the Aristotelian *nous* and to surpass both the view of thought as illuminant and the idea of it as creative. At least in

Aristotle and Descartes intuition tends to become wholly severed from discursion. We seem to be presented with a number of self-evident truths whose connection with the consequences supposed to follow from them thus becomes inexplicable. We are confronted with a dilemma: either inference is tautologous *petitio principii* or it is an inconsequent leap to a fresh intuition. Hegel's conception of thought as dialectical is an attempt to solve this dilemma. His hope is to show that it arises from conceiving two moments of unity in abstract separation. Thought is intuitive, but so far merely immediate. It is discursive, but this discursus is its own activity of self-mediation. Moreover, this mediation is a self-development towards new immediacy in which mediation enriches, a progress and yet a return upon itself. The whole activity, verbally expressed as if it were three temporary phases, is real only in the union of the first and the second moment in the third."[1]

From this long statement it is clear that Mure calls Hegel's thought intuitive for the reason that it bridges the gulf between sensibility and reason, between subject and object and between spirit and matter. Hegel's thought has undoubtedly got an intuitive element in it. Much of what goes by the name of intuition has been incorporated by Hegel in his conception of Thought. His Thought is, as we have shown in the foregoing pages, a pliant thought. So there is a good deal of intuitive element in Hegel's Thought though he would not admit it. Hegel in fact was a born foe of intuitionism. By intuition he meant some infra-rational principle and not something which transcends reason. The strength of Hegelian dialectic lies in the fact that he has incorporated much of the real essence of intuition. Hegel would not have been able to resolve contradictions had he not incorporated intuition in his Thought. Thought as thought, that is, as a mere abstract and discursive principle, is not possessed of the power to overcome contradictions. But it is able to overcome all obstructions in the form of contradictions simply for the reason that it becomes more than mere thought. It becomes a kind of intuition.

(E) *Transition from Hegelian Logic to the Logic of the Infinite*
Now the problem is, does Thought attain its highest status in Hegel's system? Can it really be identified with reality as Hegel

---

1. *An Introduction to Hegel*, pp. 114-15.

would have us believe? The answer is certainly in the negative. Hegel was not wholly successful in giving a fair interpretation of the reality. We find a lingering trace of formal logic in his system also. Hegel's gradation of categories in a hierarchical form puts a serious limitation on reality. It makes it rather a rigid and closed system. The main defect of the Formal logic is that it tries to circumscribe reality within the span of its own laws. Hegel also tries to confine reality within the limits of mental categories. Reality cannot be expected to work in accordance with the mental laws or categories however meaningful, pregnant and all-embracing they might be. In Hegelian system thought is conceived as proceeding along a fixed line. It is a uni-linear development of thought. But a uni-linear development of thought, however subtle it may be, cannot express adequately the process of the Eternal. So we cannot ultimately identify thought with reality as Hegel would have us believe.

Hegel has not been able to explain the world-process by his conception of reality. "The facts of experience will not adapt themselves as mere examples to any readymade logical schema. If at all it is to stand a critical investigation, what is given in experience must be taken as given, as handed to us; and then the rational connection of this that is so given must be referred to analysis. The speculative idea can be expected at best—and only for the scientific arrangement of the given material—to afford but a regulative."[1] Hegel makes an *a priori* generalisation of the historical process. So he twists the facts of history in order to make them fit into the grooves of his logic. As Schwegler puts it, "Another point of view which contradicts Hegel's conception is this: the historical development is almost always different from the logical. Historically, for example, the origin of the state was the desire for protection from violence and fraud; while logically, on the other hand we are to find it not in natural anarchy but in the idea of justice." Thus it is not possible to make *a priori* speculation of the historical process. The historical process is sure to elude the grasp of our reason and logic. "History marches often in serpentine lines, often apparently in retreat. Philosophy especially, has not infrequently resigned some wide and fruitful territory, in order to turn

---

1. Schwegler, *Handbook of the History of Philosophy*, p. 3.

back on some narrow strip of land, if only all the more to turn this latter into account..... Here reign no unalterable, regularly recurrent laws of nature; history, as the domain of free-will, will only in the last of days reveal itself as a work of reason."[1]

The next thing is that though Hegel claims to have reconciled all the contradictions, yet we find his Thought has not been able to attain this lofty goal. Hegel's Absolute is the Absolute of Thought. Now the Absolute as Absolute must exist by and for itself. It must not depend on anything else for its existence. But in Hegel's system we do not find the Absolute to be so. There is a relation of mutual dependence between the Absolute and the world. If the world cannot exist apart from the Absolute, the Absolute also cannot maintain its concreteness and integrity apart from the world. The Absolute Idea cannot maintain its existence apart from all other categories. The difference between the Absolute Idea and all other categories is simply this that what remains implicit in the latter becomes perfectly explicit in the former. While the relation between thought and objects remains more or less external in other categories, it becomes internal in the Absolute Idea. But the Absolute Idea does depend on these internal relations. We cannot conceive in Hegel's view a differenceless, relationless Absolute. Such an Absolute, according to him, is a mere abstract identity. Here Hegel commits an error of judgment. To say that the Absolute is a concrete reality which includes all the differences within it is one thing; and to say that the Absolute cannot be conceived apart from the differences is a different thing altogether. The first statement will mean that the Absolute is an all-embracing principle and forms the constitutive stuff of the universe and that we cannot understand the universe apart from the Absolute. So far Hegel is perfectly right. But he is wrong in saying that we cannot conceive a relationless, differenceless, transcendent Absolute. It will mean that we cannot conceive the Absolute apart from the universe. This will result in our admitting a relation of mutual dependence between the Absolute and the world. This relation of mutual dependence between the Absolute and the world affects its absoluteness. Relations are necessary in the case of finite objects and not in the case of the Absolute. The principle of relationship which holds

---

1. Schwegler, *Handbook of the History of Philosophy*, p. 3.

good in the case of finite objects cannot in the same manner hold good of the Absolute. An object will be reduced to an abstraction if it is taken in isolation. An object unrelated to any other thing is nothing. It requires a genus and a differentia to reveal its real nature. But the same cannot be said of the Absolute. Hegel thinks that as an object is reduced to an abstraction if taken in isolation, in the same way the Absolute also would become a mere abstract identity, an empty nothing if considered in itself, in its immediacy, apart from the world. Under this very misapprehension Hegel makes a rather baseless criticism of the Vedāntic view of Brahman. The abstract Absolute is, according to this view, "what the Indian names Brahma when, externally motionless and no less internally emotionless, looking years long only to the tip of his own nose, he says within himself just, om, om, om, or perhaps just nothing at all. This dull void consciousness, conceived as consciousness, is Being".[1] To say that the Absolute is a differenceless, transcendent reality does not mean that it is an abstract identity. It means, as Sri Aurobindo has clearly shown, that it is not bound or limited by the relations and differences. The perfect transcendence of the Absolute shows its complete freedom from the limitations by its own determinations. Thus a relationless, differenceless transcendent Absolute does not mean an abstract identity; on the other hand it represents reality in its most concrete and essential aspect. The differences at this stage do not remain as differences in the Absolute but they become one with It. The Absolute can only be Absolute when it is both transcendent and immanent. Hegel unfortunately has shown only the immanent character of the Absolute. But there also he has signally failed because he has not been able to explain the world-process with the help of the Absolute. The conception of a differenceless, supra-relational transcendent Absolute is found in the philosophy of Śaṅkara. But Śaṅkara goes to the other extreme. While Hegel denies the reality of an indeterminate, differenceless and supra-relational Absolute, Śaṅkara denies, as we shall show in detail in a later chapter, the ultimate reality of the concrete universal. But Sri Aurobindo adopts a middle course. He tries to steer clear of the extremes of Hegel and Śaṅkara. To have an integral view of the Absolute one must, according to

---

1. J.H. Stirling, *The Secret of Hegel*, p. 223.

him, take into account the supra-relational as well as the relational aspects of the Absolute. Against Hegel, Sri Aurobindo maintains that we cannot know the Absolute truly and essentially unless we know it also in its differenceless and transcendent status; and against Śaṅkara, he maintains that though the differenceless and supra-relational status of the Absolute is the highest, the purest and the essential status, yet it does not present the Absolute in its integrality. The integral view of the Absolute is possible only when we take into account both its immanent and its transcendent character. Thus the realisation of the Absolute does not necessitate the denial of the world. The "knowledge of distinctions arrives at its greatest truth and effective use when we arrive at the deeper knowledge of that which reconciles distinctions in the unity behind all variations. That deeper knowledge does not deprive the other and more superficial of effectivity nor convict it of vanity".[1] "We cannot conclude from our ultimate material discovery," further observes Sri Aurobindo, "that there is no original substance or Matter, only energy manifesting substance or manifesting as substance—that diamond and pearl are non-existent, unreal, only true to the illusion of our senses of perception and action, that the one substance, energy or motion is the sole eternal truth and therefore the best or only rational use of our science would be to dissolve diamond and pearl and everything else that we can dissolve into this one eternal and original reality and get done with their forms and properties forever".[2] So our knowledge of Brahman as the eternal and fundamental reality does not necessitate our rejection of the world or denial of its reality. The Integral Advaitism of Sri Aurobindo looks at Reality not only in its essential but in its integral aspect. It not only takes into account the essential, differenceless and transcendent aspect of Reality but also its dynamic aspect—its universal and individual aspects. "There is an essentiality of things, a commonalty of things, an individuality of things; the commonalty and individuality are true and eternal powers of the essentiality: that transcends them both, but the three together and not one by itself are the eternal terms of existence."[3] "Each thing is the Absolute, all are that One, but in these three terms

1. *L.D.*, Vol. II, Part I, p. 105.
2. *Ibid.*, pp. 105-06.
3. *Ibid.*, p. 106.

always the Absolute makes its statement of its developed self-existence. We are not, because of the essential unity, compelled to say that all God's various actions and workings are vain, worthless, unreal, phenomenal, illusory, and that the best and only rational or super-rational use we can make of our knowledge is to get away from them, dissolve our cosmic and individual existence into the essential being and get rid of all becoming as a futility forever."[1]

(F) Logic of the Infinite: Its Nature and Significance

So we have to judge each thing in all its three aspects—the individual, the universal and the transcendent. We can realise fully the truth of the individual when we relate it to the universal and the transcendent. In the same way we can understand the nature of the Transcendent fully when we relate it with its universal and individual aspects. Sri Aurobindo does not deny the fact that we can have an exclusive realisation of the Transcendent, as has been stated above. But he does affirm that the exclusive realisation of the Transcendent enables us to know the reality in its essential aspect and not in its integral aspect. The realisation of the essential aspect of Reality is, according to him, a fundamental but partial realisation and not a total and integral realisation of it. The truth of the Transcendent is grasped fully when it is realised not only in its essential and indeterminate aspect but also in its dynamic and determinate aspect; when it is seen manifesting itself in the forms of the individual and cosmic existence. As Sri Aurobindo observes, "The Infinite is at once an essentiality, a boundless totality and a multitude; all these have to be known in order to know truly the Infinite. To see the parts alone and the totality not at all or only as a sum of the parts is a knowledge but also at the same time an ignorance; to see the totality alone and ignore the parts is also a knowledge and at the same time an ignorance, for a part may be greater than the whole because it belongs to the transcendence; to see the essence alone because it takes us back straight towards the transcendence and negate the totality and the parts is a penultimate knowledge but here too there is a capital ignorance A whole knowledge must be there and the reason must become

---

plastic enough to look at all sides, all aspects and seek through them for that in which they are one."[1] So we can understand the full significance of these fundamental truths not by our finite reason but by a higher and more plastic reason called the logic of the Infinite. The Logic of the Infinite, as the name suggests, is the logic of reality and not of the finite reason or mind. It is based on reality, expresses its real nature and does not obey the dictates of dividing mind. It does not mean that Sri Aurobindo denies the truth and validity of the laws of identity and contradiction altogether. All he denies, in fact, is their absolute validity. Like Hegel, he also does not consider them as ultimately and unconditionally true. The laws of identity and contradiction are conditioned by the law of rela-tion. If in some sense it becomes necessary to study a thing by isolating it from other things, in some other sense, it is also nec-essary to study it in relation to other things. So the laws of identity and contradiction cannot be applied unconditionally to the things of the world or Reality. As Kant determines the limits of knowl-edge, in the same way Sri Aurobindo and Hegel determine the limits of the laws of identity and contradiction. No earthly law, whether it is material, vital or mental can be regarded as ultimately and unconditionally valid, according to Sri Aurobindo, on account of its inability to reveal the real and integral nature of Reality. All earthly laws are abstract. An abstract law, according to Hegel, is that which cannot grasp the concrete whole. Mind only grasps certain aspects. The antinomies of pure reason of Kant have shown the limits of mental approach. They are an eye-opener for all times as showing the limits of mental categories. The Absolute in Sri Aurobindo's view cannot be determined by any of our mental categories. If the Absolute or Reality cannot be grasped by mind, how can its nature be judged in the light of the laws of identity and contradiction? How can those who regard the Absolute as unknowable by mind, say that it cannot be both indeterminate and determinate simultaneously as it involves self-contradiction, when they profess to know nothing about it? Do we not here impose the mental laws—the laws of identity and contradiction on the Absolute? Is it not itself self-contradictory to assert that the Abso-lute cannot be grasped by mind or reason and at the same time

---

1. *L.D.*, Vol. II, Part I, pp. 44-45.

try to determine its nature by the scales of mental laws—the laws of identity and contradiction? If the Absolute transcends nature, how can its nature be determined by natural laws—material, vital or mental? Even if the laws of identity and contradiction were equally and unconditionally true of the whole of Nature—material, vital and mental, how can they be considered as ultimately and unconditionally true of the Absolute? It may be that the human mind cannot logically conceive of a thing as possessing contradictory characters. But it will only prove the fact that mind as mind cannot violate its own laws or transcend its own limitations. But it does not in any way prove the fact that a supra-logical or supra-rational consciousness is also bound to conceive or perceive things in accordance with the natural laws or the laws of thought. It does not prove the fact that the Absolute or Reality itself cannot have the aspects which appear contradictory to the human mind. We can say that we as mental or rational beings cannot conceive the Absolute as both indeterminate and determinate simultaneously as it involves self-contradiction. But we have no justification in saying that the Absolute cannot be possessed of indeterminate and determinate aspects simultaneously in its real nature. Our inability or incapacity to think or comprehend the Absolute in its integral aspect—as possessed of the so-called contradictory aspects—does not prove the inability or incapacity of the Absolute to be possessed of those aspects. It is as dogmatic and self-contradictory to assert from the standpoint of mind that the Absolute is both indeterminate and determinate, the One and the Many, as it is to assert that the Absolute cannot be both indeterminate and determinate, the One and the Many simultaneously. Mind is by nature not fit to say what the Absolute can or cannot be. It has no rational or logical justification to dictate terms to the Absolute. The Absolute manifests itself in accordance with its own Law, the divine Law and not in accordance with the laws of nature—the mental, vital and material laws.

Sri Aurobindo admits that the relationship between the indeterminate and determinate, One and Many etc., cannot be grasped by our normal or finite reason. These fundamental aspects elude the grasp of thought. But he does not argue that if one aspect of the Absolute is regarded as true, fundamental and ultimate, the other must be regarded as unreal or false or as a mere abstraction. The mystery of Reality and its process is revealed according to him not in the plane of mind but in the higher planes of consciousness. Thus it is quite clear that we cannot make any judgment regarding Reality on the basis of mental laws. We cannot call any aspect of Reality unreal or illusory in order to make it consistent with our laws of thought. Instead of sacrificing Reality or any aspect of it at the altar of mind or mental laws, we have to sacrifice mind at the altar of Reality. "The self-existent" observes Sri Aurobindo, "is the Infinite and its way of being and of action must be the way of the Infinite, but our consciousness is limited, our reason built upon things finite: it is irrational to suppose that a finite consciousness and reason can be a measure of the Infinite; this smallness cannot judge that immensity, this poverty bound to a limited use of its scanty means cannot conceive the opulent management of those riches; an ignorant half-knowledge cannot follow the motions of an All-knowledge".[1] Our reasoning is based on our experience of the operations of the physical nature in its material, vital and mental aspects. It formulates certain laws on the basis of its limited and imperfect observation and experience. It seeks to make these laws general and universal and whatever contradicts these laws, it regards as irrational, false and inexplicable. "But there are different orders of the reality, and the conceptions, measures, standards suitable to one need not be applicable to another order. Our physical being is built first upon an aggregate of infinitesimals, electrons, atoms, molecules, cells; but the law of action of these infinitesimals does not explain all the physical working even of human body, much less can they cover all the law and process of action of man's supra-physical parts, his life and mind movements and soul movements."[2] The same is true in the case of life and mind. The laws and working of life cannot explain the operations and laws of mind. In the same way, the laws and working of mind cannot explain what is beyond mind. Our mind or reason finds it difficult to deal with even what is below mind, nor to speak of what lies above it. Life is "infrarational and we find that our intellectual reason applying itself to life is constantly forcing upon it a control, a measure, an artificial pro-crustean rule that either succeeds in killing or petrifying life or constrains it into rigid forms and conventions that lame and imprison its capacity

---

1. *L.D.*, Vol. II, Part I, p. 40.
2. *Ibid.*, p. 40.

or ends by a bungle, a revolt of life, a decay or disruption of the systems and superstructures built upon it by our intelligence. An instinct, an intuition is needed which the intellect has not at its command and does not always listen to when it comes in of itself to help the mental working".[1] "But still more difficult must it be for our reason," further observes Sri Aurobindo, "to understand and deal with the supra-rational; the supra-rational is the realm of the spirit, and in the largeness, subtlety, profundity, complexity of its movement the reason is lost; here intuition and inner experience alone are the guide, or, if there is any other, it is that of which intuition is only a sharp edge, an intense projected ray—the final enlightenment must come from the supramental Truth-consciousness, from a supramental vision and knowledge".[2]

But it must not be thought that the infinite consciousness works arbitrarily. Its ways of thought and action have their own definite and well-established laws. It must not therefore be supposed that the being and the action of the Infinite are a kind of magic having no rationality in them. In all its workings and operations, the Infinite has undeniably a reason, but that reason is something much higher, much greater than our normal reason. It is not mental or intellectual reason but a spiritual and supramental reason. So the being and action of the Infinite are not void of all reason, but are based on the more fundamental spiritual and supramental reason. According to Sri Aurobindo, "there is a logic in it, because there are relations and connections infallibly seen and executed".[3] He further makes a most significant and profound remark that "what is magic to our finite reason is the logic of the Infinite".[4] "It is a greater reason, a greater logic because it is more vast, subtle, complex in its operations; it comprehends all the data which our observation fails to seize, it deduces from them results which neither our deduction nor induction can anticipate, because our conclusions and inferences have a meagre foundation and are fallible and brittle".[5]

Though Sri Aurobindo does not give supreme importance to reason, does not consider it the sole and most reliable means of

1. *L.D.*, Vol. II, Part I, p. 41.
2. *Ibid.*, pp. 41-42.
3. *Ibid.*, p. 42.
4. *Ibid.*, p. 42.
5. *Ibid.*, p. 42.

knowledge, yet he does not minimise the importance of reason in its own sphere. He is definitely of opinion that so long as we are centred in the domain of mind and have reason as our highest and fundamental means of knowledge, we should not and must not give preference to any other means of knowledge in its place. It is not in any way safe to accept an undeveloped and indistinct intuition in its place. But he at the same time spares no pains in emphasising the fact that we are not to turn a deaf ear to the higher and potent calls of the Infinite. Our reason should be large and plastic enough to admit the truth and significance of the supreme Reality and its working or process. "It is not indeed possible, so long as we are compelled to use reason as our main support, for it to abdicate altogether in favour of an undeveloped or half-organised intuition; but it is imperative on us in a consideration of the Infinite and its being and action to enforce on our reason an utmost plasticity and open it to an awareness of the larger states and possibilities of that which we are striving to consider. It will not do to apply our limited and limiting conclusions to That which is illimitable."[1]

So it is clear that Sri Aurobindo is not against the use of reason as such to understand the nature of Reality but against the abstract and formal reason. He hurls a staggering blow at the abstract and formal reason which acts like a Procrustean bed and cuts the integral Reality into fragments. It is only our abstract reason which fails to comprehend the truth of Reality. Our reason can be made more comprehensive, plastic and synthetic enough to have a fair idea of the Reality and its process. It is possible only when reason tries to take into account the nature of experience and does not remain confined merely in examining the validity and invalidity of its own concepts. Our mind or reason cannot have in immediate realisation of Reality; but it can have a conceptual knowledge of it. In its search after reality, it is constrained to posit an Absolute lying behind and constituting the essence of the world of objects. The Absolute is unknowable to our reason in the sense that it cannot have a direct and immediate knowledge or experience of it. It is not unknowable in the sense that reason cannot even conceive of its existence. In the same way the process or working

---

1. *L.D.*, Vol. II, Part I, p. 44.

of the Absolute is unknowable to our reason in the sense that it cannot have a direct or immediate experience of it. It is not unknowable in the sense that it can in no way even conceive of it. Our mind has the experience of the world of diversity. It also posits the existence of the Absolute behind this world of diversity. It conceives that the world of diversity is dependent on the Absolute and has its origin in it otherwise it will lead to dualism. But it does not know how the world-process can come out of the Absolute. That is incomprehensible to it. But the world-process remains absolutely incomprehensible to it so long as it tries to understand it strictly in accordance with the laws of thought. But the moment it tries to examine its concepts in the light of experience, it finds that Reality and the world-process are not so contradictory to each other as they apparently seem to be. The working of the logic of the Infinite can be understood by our reason if it gets rid of its abstract attitude, as has been stated above, by taking into account the facts of experience. The logic of the Infinite is neither a postulate of dogmatic reason nor of a blind religious faith. It can be understood as well as justified by our plastic, synthetic and comprehensive reason. If it were altogether inconceivable by our human reason, then the latter would not have been able to understand or comprehend anything regarding the nature and working of the former. Then the reason would have had an attitude either of scepticism or agnosticism or blind faith towards it. It would have either denied the reality of the logic of the Infinite altogether or would have confessed its inability or incapacity to know it even if it did exist, or would have placed it in an exalted position far above the humdrum of the mundane world and considered it a sacrilege on our part to try to probe into its mysteries. The sceptic and the agnostic attitude would put a brake upon the human endeavour to know Reality and its process and consequently would confine us within the limits of the phenomena. The religious attitude of blind faith would question the validity of our philosophic quest or reasoning of the super-sensible and supra-rational reality itself. To say that human reason must not try to examine rationally the nature of Reality and its process is to deny the utility and the validity of philosophising itself. It will mean a denial of all philosophy.

It is to steer clear of both these extreme attitudes which lead to fatal consequences that we stand in need of the logic of the

Infinite. We stand in need of a consciousness which has the awareness of reality as well as knows the truth of the world-process. Our human reason may not be able to know Reality and its process but the divine Being cannot be said to be unaware of its being and action. It may be said that there is no process at all. The divine Being does not indulge in action. It does not manifest the world at all. The world is merely a figment of mind. It is mind which conceives process in Reality; but Reality itself is free from all process etc. But the human reason, as has been stated above, has no logical justification to make such dogmatic assertions regarding the being and action of the Infinite. It can only say on the grounds of pure logic that it does not know what the Absolute is in its real nature and what its relation is to the world. We find the world-process carried on in accordance with the fixed and immutable laws so far as our knowledge goes. The world of matter has its own fixed and definite laws; the world of life and mind has its own laws. Now if the world of matter, life and mind has its fixed, definite and inviolable laws, how can it be conceived that the Divine has no law at all? It puts a strain on our thought to think that a perfect chaos reigns in the beginning or the ultimate stage of the world-process. It is difficult to believe that the world-process is merely a figment of human imagination or is a magical creation of irrational divine Māyā. It may be that the divine law may be much more complex than the laws of nature. We do not at present have sufficient knowledge regarding the laws of nature. We have a far more meagre knowledge regarding the laws underlying the working of mind. So there is no wonder if we do not know the ultimate law which lies at the root of the whole cosmic process. But our present inability to know the ultimate law or the divine law does not constrain us to deny its existence altogether. It is the height of dogmatism to assert that the world-process is a freak of someone's imagination and irrational fancy, whether it is human or divine, and has no ultimate law as its guiding star. So man as a rational being is bound to believe in an ultimate, universal and all-pervading law that lies at the root of the cosmic process and guides its destiny. The divine acts in accordance with its own law or logic, called the logic of the Infinite. Sri Aurobindo calls it logic in order to dispel all doubts from our mind regarding its nature. By calling it logic he tries to show that it is not altogether unknowable and incomprehensible by human reason. To quote again his significant and pregnant remark, "there is logic in it, because there are relations and connections infallibly seen and executed: what is magic to our finite reason is the logic of the Infinite".[1] So we can perceive and realise the working of the divine law in accordance with its infallible principles, if we attain the supramental consciousness. The divine working may appear to be an act of magic to our ignorant consciousness but it does not appear as magic to itself. The divine law may be unknown to man at the present stage but on this very ground one cannot say that it is unknowable.

So it is clear that a rational study of the world-process compels us to posit an ultimate law, an inviolable, infallible and all-pervading divine law which lies at the root of the world-process and guides its destiny. We have to posit that the ultimate Reality and the world-process are inseparably related together through the divine law and that there is no yawning chasm between them. Now the only difficulty that remains is, that we have no knowledge or understanding with regard to the nature and working of the divine law. This difficulty can be fully removed only when we attain, as it is our destiny to attain, the supramental consciousness. It is only then that we can have an all-embracing view of Reality and realise the full truth of Sri Aurobindo's integral Advaitism. But prior to that, we as rational beings have the capacity to understand the nature of the being and working of the divine by giving a wider, a more comprehensive and more plastic meaning to our concepts that express Its integral nature. We have to give a wider, a more comprehensive and flexible meaning to the concepts, such as indeterminate and determinate, one and many, immutable and mutable and so on. In this way we can overcome all the so-called contradictions that seriously beset all our rational quest and ascertain the being and action of the divine or supreme Reality. This way of approach is in accordance with the higher reason or the logic of the Infinite as compared to the way of approach made by our finite and abstract reason in accordance with the laws of thought. Thus Sri Aurobindo proves the justification of philosophy, of our rational quest of truth and reality by asserting that our reason can

1. *L.D.*, Vol. II, Part I, p. 42.

conceive the nature of Reality and its process fully and integrally provided it seeks to give a higher, a more comprehensive and a deeper meaning to our concepts which express Its nature. The human reason can have a conceptual knowledge of Reality and its process, if it gets rid of the bondage of its own rigid, abstract and inflexible laws and takes recourse to a higher reason, a higher logic, the logic of the Infinite.

(G) *Logic of the Infinite and Synthesis of Opposites or so-called Contradictories*

"If we look from the viewpoint of a larger more plastic reason," observes Sri Aurobindo, "taking account of the logic of the Infinite, at the difficulties which meet our intelligence when it tries to conceive the Absolute and omnipresent Reality, we shall see that the whole difficulty is verbal and conceptual and not real."[1] Now in the light of the higher reason or the logic of the Infinite, we can reconcile the apparent antagonism that seems to exist between the indeterminable aspect of Reality and the world of determinations. The normal or finite reason considers the indeterminable as devoid of all determinations. Here lies the whole trouble. To say that the Absolute is devoid of all determinations naturally means that it is incapable of manifesting determinations out of itself. So the normal reason is constrained to say that the world of determinations must be a creation of Māyā, must be false or illusory as it can have no connection or relation with the Absolute. But the higher reason or the logic of the Infinite, instead of denying the reality of the world to avoid the contradiction, solves it by giving a deeper meaning to the concept indeterminable. It does not interpret negation in a literal sense. Negation, according to it, is not a sign of non-existence, but on the contrary, it leads to an affirmation of a more positive, fuller and richer existence. The negative assertions are thus not in their essence negative but positive. The indeterminability of the Absolute is not in a true sense negative but positive. These negations really indicate two essential characteristics of the Absolute. Firstly, they reveal the freedom of the Absolute from the limitations by its own determinations. Secondly, the Absolute is said to be free from all external

1. *L.D.*, Vol. II, Part I, p. 46.

determinations, by anything not itself. But as there is no possibility, in fact, of such a not-self coming into existence, the freedom of the Absolute from all external determinations is a foregone conclusion. What we call creation is nothing but the "Being becoming in form and movement what it already is in substance and status."[1] But the indeterminability is emphasised because without that "the Reality would be a fixed eternal determinate or else an indeterminate fixed and bound to a sum of possibilities of determination inherent within it".[2] The freedom of the Absolute from all creation and determination, Sri Aurobindo argues, should not itself be turned into a limitation. It should not deprive the Absolute of the other kind of freedom, the freedom of infinite self-manifestation or self-determination. "Its freedom from all limitation, from any binding by its own creation, cannot be itself turned into a limitation, an absolute incapacity, a denial of all freedom of self-determination; it is this that would be a contradiction, it would be an attempt to define and limit by negation the infinite and illimitable."[3] Determination, according to Spinoza, is negation. But Sri Aurobindo makes also a converse of it. In his view, negation also carries the force of determination if taken in an absolute sense, that is, in the sense of rejection. Negation then becomes as much the cause of limitation as determination. But we cannot limit the Absolute either by our affirmation and determination or by negation. So the meaning of negation and freedom of the Absolute should be understood in an integral and comprehensive sense. If it is a freedom to remain free from all limitations, bondage, divisions etc., it is also equally a freedom to indulge in the infinite cosmic-play without being in any way bound by it. Perhaps it is the sign not of the negation of freedom, but of a greater freedom to be in the world as well as beyond it; to manifest cosmos in its being without infringing in any way its real nature, its infinite transcendence. So no real contradiction enters into the central fact of the two aspects of the Absolute. The indeterminate and determinate or *nirguna* and *saguna* are thus the complementary aspects of the Absolute. It is "only the dual statement of a single

---

1. *L.D.*, Vol. II, Part I, p. 47.
2. *Ibid.*, p. 47.
3. *Ibid.*, p. 47.

inescapable fact by human reason in human language".[1]

Thus, we see that the higher reason or the logic of the Infinite is not baffled by the so-called oppositions or contradictions that seem insoluble to our finite reason. Now by applying this higher reason or the logic of the Infinite, we can solve some other most baffling and apparently contradictory problems such as One and the Many, Silence and Dynamis, Infinite and Finite, and so on. We now proceed to examine the various contradictions. First there is the contradiction between the One and the Many.

(I) One and Many

The Absolute or Brahman has been described in the Upaniṣads as the ground, essence and the constitutive stuff of all existences. It is the one fundamental reality. All the existences are said to be the manifestations of this one fundamental and ultimate reality called the Self, the Ātman or the Absolute. Hence though the Reality or the Absolute is essentially One, it manifests itself as Many. As the Upaniṣad expressly states: He is the one supreme ruler, the soul of all beings; He who makes his one form manifold. Those wise men who see Him as seated within themselves, to them belongs eternal happiness and to none else.[2]

Now, here the problem arises, how can the limited and the relative be the Absolute, how can the manifold beings be the divine Being? To the normal or finite reason, the One and the Many appear to be contradictory to each other. But this contradiction is due to the failure of mind or finite reason to understand the real meaning and implication of the terms One and the Many. In raising this apparent contradiction, the mind or finite reason makes, according to Sri Aurobindo, a double error. It considers this Oneness on mathematical basis. It regards it as a limited finite unit which cannot be other than what it is without losing its essential character. "It is thinking in the terms of the mathematical finite unit which is sole in limitation, the one which is less than two and can become two only by division and fragmentation or by addition and multiplication; but this is an infinite Oneness, it is the essential and infinite Oneness which can contain the hundred and the thousand

---

1. *L.D.*, Vol. II, Part I, p. 47.
2. *Kaṭha* 5.13.

and the million and billion and trillion. Whatever astronomic or more than astronomic figures you heap and multiply, they cannot overpass or exceed that Oneness; for, in the language of the Upaniṣad, it moves not, yet is always far in front when you would pursue and seize it".[1] Hence there is no limitation to the oneness of the Absolute. It can be infinitely many without losing its Oneness. It maintains its unity in the midst of all diversity. It can be said that its Oneness would not be infinite if it were not capable of infinite multiplicity. But it does not mean that the One should be taken as plural or as the sum of the many. This is the second error that the mind or finite reason often makes in conceiving the relationship between the One and the Many. The One can be limited neither by multiplicity nor by plurality nor by finite conceptual Oneness. "Pluralism," observes Sri Aurobindo, "is an error because, though there is the spiritual plurality, the many souls are dependent and interdependent existences; their sum also is not the One nor is it the cosmic totality; they depend on the One and exist by its Oneness; yet the plurality is not unreal, it is the One Soul that dwells as the individual in these many souls and they are eternal in the One and by the one Eternal".[2] Thus we find that there is no inherent opposition between the fundamental terms One and the Many if viewed in the light of the logic of the Infinite. We have to understand these terms in a more plastic and comprehensive manner than we do in our abstract reasoning if we are to grasp their real meaning and significance. It is only then that we can make a proper and satisfactory reconciliation between the apparently contradictory but fundamental statements of the Upaniṣads.

(II) Silence and Dynamis

In the light of the logic of the Infinite, we can reconcile the opposition between the silence or status and dynamis or movement of the Spirit. Some look upon Reality as static, immobile and immutable. There are others who perceive the boundless movement of the Spirit and thus lay emphasis on its dynamic and mobile aspect. Thus Spirit or Reality is regarded by some as Being and by

---

1. *L.D.*, Vol. II, Part I, pp. 49-50.
2. *Ibid.*, p. 50.

others as Becoming. These two aspects are considered as contradictory to each other and thus the affirmation of the one means consequently the denial of the other. But there can be no such opposition to the supramental reason or the logic of the Infinite. The solely silent and static Infinite without an infinite power and energy cannot be regarded, according to Sri Aurobindo, as the ultimate Reality. "A solely silent and static Infinite, an Infinite without an infinite power and dynamis and energy is inadmissible except as the perception of an aspect; a powerless Absolute, an impotent Spirit is unthinkable; an infinite energy must be the dynamis of the Infinite, an all-power must be the potency of the Absolute, an illimitable force must be the force of the Spirit."[1]

The silence, the status, provides the basis for the movement. An eternal, immobile Being is the necessary ground and condition for infinite mobility, infinite movement. It is the silence, stability and immobility of the Spirit that can uphold the great movement and energy of creation. Thus the opposition that is made between these two aspects of Spirit or Reality is only mental and conceptual. In reality the silence and movement of the Spirit are complementary and inseparable. "The silent and the active Brahman are not different and irreconcilable entities, the one denying, the other affirming a cosmic illusion; they are one Brahman in two aspects—positive and negative, and each is necessary to the other. It is out of this Silence that the word which creates the worlds forever proceeds; for the Word expresses that which is self-hidden in the Silence. It is an eternal passivity which makes possible the perfect freedom and omnipotence of an eternal divine activity in innumerable cosmic systems. For the becomings of that activity derive their energies and their illimitable potency of variation and harmony from the impartial support of the immutable Being, its consent to this infinite fecundity of its own dynamic Nature."[2] Thus the Being of the Spirit cannot be essentially separated from its power or force. The Absolute is capable of holding its infinite energy within itself in a state of silence or status or releasing it in infinite movement and action. "The immutable, silent Spirit may hold its infinite energy silent and immobile within it, for it is not bound by its own

---

1. *L.D.*, Vol. II, Part I, pp. 50-51.
2. *Ibid.*, Vol. I, p. 34.

forces, is not their subject or instrument, but it does possess them, does release them, is capable of an eternal and infinite action, does not weary or need to stop, and yet all the time its silent immobility inherent in its action and movement is not for a moment shaken or disturbed or altered by its action and movement; the witness silence of the Spirit is there in the very grain of all the voices and working of Nature."[1] Thus to say that Brahman is active, dynamic and possessed of force does not mean that it is devoid of silence, of status, of freedom from movement. Force is inherent in Brahman and is one with it both in its status as well as in movement. "Force thus inherent in the pure Existent may be at rest or may be in motion. When it is at rest, it nonetheless exists; indeed it is the nature of conscious Force to have this alternative possibility of rest and motion, the first meaning self-concentration and the second, self-diffusion."[2] Becoming is thus nothing but the state of movement and Being of rest of the Absolute. The world comes out of nothing else but the immutable Brahman or the Absolute. As we find it picturesquely stated in the following verse of the Upaniṣad: As the silk-spider without any external help, spreads its threads out of itself and withdraws into itself, as herbs grow on the earth, as the hair grows on the head and body of a living person, so the whole universe comes out of the immutable Brahman.[3] The wide, comprehensive and all-embracing outlook of Upaniṣadic seers does not see any incompatibility between Being and Becoming. The supramental consciousness or the logic of the Infinite also does not find any contradiction or incompatibility between them. "Yet it is now evident that to the Infinite Consciousness both the static and the dynamic are possible; these are two of its statuses and both can be present simultaneously in the universal awareness, the one witnessing the other and supporting it; or the silence and status may be there penetrating the activity or throwing it up like an ocean immobile below, throwing up a mobility of waves on its surface."[4]

---

1. *L.D.*, Vol. II, Part I, p. 51.
2. Dr. S.K. Maitra, *An Int to the Philosophy of Sri Aurobindo*, pp. 15-16.
3. *Muṇḍaka* 1.1.7.
4. *L.D.*, Vol. II, Part I, p. 61.

(III) *Infinite and Finite*

There seems to be no real justification to raise a permanent barrier between the Infinite and the finite also. The finite is nothing but the self-determination of the Infinite under the conditions of Space and Time. "The finite is a frontal aspect and a self-determination of the Infinite; no finite can exist in itself and by itself, it exists by the Infinite and because it is of one essence with the Infinite".[1] By the Infinite is not meant a solely "illimitable self-extension in Space and Time, but something that is also spaceless and timeless, a self-existent Indefinable and Illimitable which can express itself in the infinitesimal as well as in the vast, in a second of time, in a point of space, in a passing circumstance".[2] Brahman, says the Upaniṣad is subtler than the subtlest and greater even than the greatest.[3] By manifesting itself in the insect, Brahman does not become small, nor by manifesting itself in the cosmos it becomes great. "This mighty energy is an equal and impartial mother, samam Brahma, in the great term of the Gita, and its intensity and force of movement is the same in the formation and upholding of a system of suns and the organisation of the life of an ant-hill".[4] So the division between the finite and the Infinite is only apparent and not real.[5] Sri Aurobindo's Integral Advaitism is all-inclusive and all-embracing. It does not raise a wall of separation between the finite and Infinite but includes them both in its embrace. If we look at the concepts finite and Infinite from the point of view of our normal, abstract reason, we are sure to fall inevitably in irreconcilable antinomies and contradictions. But from the point of view of higher reason or the logic of the Infinite, we find the one fundamental substance or Spirit immanent in the manifold objects. "Brahman dwells in all, indivisible, yet as if divided and distributed."[6] From the standpoint of higher reason all the finite objects and beings will not appear as opposed to or different from the Infinite but as the forms or modes of it. The Infinite will be seen as constituting the essence and the stuff of these objects. "When

---

1. *L.D.*, Vol. II, Part I, p. 53.
2. *Ibid.*, p. 53.
3. अणोरणीयान्महतो महीयान् । *Kaṭha*, 1.2.20.
4. *L.D.*, Vol. I, p. 92.
5. *Ibid.*, Vol. II, Part I, p. 53.
6. अविभक्तं च भूतेषु विभक्तमिव च स्थितम् । *B.G.* 13.17.

we see with the inner vision and sense and not with the physical
eye a tree or other object, what we become aware of is an infinite
one Reality constituting the tree or object, pervading its every atom
and molecule, forming them out of itself, building the whole nature,
process of becoming, operation of indwelling energy; all these are
itself, are this infinite, this Reality: we see it extending indivisibly
and uniting all objects so that none is really separate from other
objects."[1]

So the Integral Advaitism of Sri Aurobindo holds that the inte-
gral Reality can be known only by an integral knowledge and not
by any partial and limited consciousness whether it is sensuous,
mental or intuitional. It is only the supramental consciousness that
can have an immediate realisation of all the aspects and grades of
Reality simultaneously. Thus we have to consider each object as
"that Infinite and one in essential being with all other objects that
are also forms and names—powers, numens—of the Infinite".[2]
"This incoercible unity in all divisions and diversities," observes Sri
Aurobindo, "is the mathematics of the Infinite, indicated in a verse
of the Upanishads—This is the complete and That is the complete;
subtract the complete from the complete, the complete is the
remainder".[3] The One does not cease to be One by manifesting
the manifold objects of the world out of it or in it. To say that
Reality is identical does not mean that it is incapable of undergoing
any change at all. "The Identical to our notions is the Immutable;
it is ever the same through eternity, for if it is or becomes subject
to mutation or if it admits of differences, it ceases to be identical;
but what we see everywhere is an infinitely variable fundamental
oneness which seems the very principle of Nature."[4] Thus the
principle of "infinitely variable fundamental oneness" is not only
true of the operations of the Infinite but it seems to be the very
principle of Nature also. "The basic Force is one, but it manifests
from itself innumerable forces; the basic substance is one, but it
develops many different substances and millions of unlike objects;

1. *L.D.*, Vol. II, Part I, p. 53.
2. *Ibid.*, p. 53.
3. *Ibid.*, pp. 53-54.
   पूर्णमदः पूर्णमिदं पूर्णात्पूर्णमुदच्यते ।
   पूर्णस्य पूर्णमादाय पूर्णमेवावशिष्यते ॥
4. *L.D.*, Vol. II, Part I, p. 54.

mind is one but differentiates itself into many mental states, mind-formations, thoughts, percepts differing from each other and entering into harmony or conflict; life is one, but the forms of life are unlike and innumerable; humanity is one in nature, but there are different race types and every individual man is himself and in some way unlike others; Nature insists on tracing lines of difference on the leaves of one tree; she drives differentiation so far that it has been found that the lines on one man's thumb are different from the lines of every other man's thumb so that he can be identified by the differentiation alone—yet fundamentally all men are alike and there is no essential difference."[1] The essence of the Reality remains the same even though it assumes innumerable differences of form, character etc. "Because the self and Spirit in things and beings is one everywhere, therefore Nature can afford this luxury of infinite differentiation: if there were not this secure basis which brings it about that nothing changes yet all changes, all her workings and creations would in this play collapse into disintegration and chaos; there would be nothing to hold her disparate movements and creations together."[2] Thus to the higher reason or logic of the Infinite the immutability of Brahman does not make it incapable of change and differentiation. "The immutability of the Identical does not consist in a monotone of changeless sameness incapable of variation; it consists in an unchangeableness of being which is capable of endless formation of being, but which no differentiation can destroy or impair or minimise."[3] The opposition between the Infinite and the finite or One and many is raised by the finite and abstract reason and not by the higher reason or logic of the Infinite. As Sri Aurobindo observes, "Our surface reason is prone to conclude that the diversity may be unreal, an appearance only, but if we look a little deeper we shall see that a real diversity brings out the real Unity, shows as it were in its utmost capacity, reveals all that it can be and is in itself, delivers from its witness of hue the many tones of colour that are fused together there; Oneness finds itself infinitely in what seems to us to be a falling away from its oneness, but is really an inexhaustible diverse display of unity. This is the

1. *L.D.*, Vol. II, Part I, pp. 54-55.
2. *Ibid.*, p. 55.
3. *Ibid.*, pp. 55-56.

miracle, the Maya of the universe, yet perfectly logical, natural and a matter of course to the self-vision and self-experience of the Infinite."[1]

Thus by taking recourse to the higher reason or logic of the Infinite, Sri Aurobindo has been able to present a satisfactory solution and reconciliation of the most baffling problems of Existence or Reality. His view of the Absolute or Brahman is integral and comprehensive enough to include all the divergent aspects in it and bridge the gulf existing between them. The indeterminate and the determinate, the Being and the Becoming do not appear to him as opposed to and contradictory of each other but as the complementary aspects of the same Reality. Thus Sri Aurobindo maintains his Advaitic position without abrogating the reality of the world. His integral Advaitism affirms, as has been stated above, the reality of Being as well as Becoming. To quote again Sri Aurobindo's statement, "The real Monism, the true Adwaita is that which admits all things as the one Brahman and does not seek to bisect Its existence into two incompatible entities, an eternal Truth and an eternal Falsehood, Brahman and non-Brahman, Self and not-Self, a real self and an unreal-yet perpetual Maya. If it be true that the Self alone exists, it must be also true that all is the Self."[2] Thus we have to recognise the reality of both the pure existence and the world. "The pure existent is then a fact and no mere concept; it is the fundamental reality. But, let us hasten to add, the movement, the energy, the becoming are also a fact, also a reality. The supreme intuition and its corresponding experience may correct the other, may go beyond, may suspend, but do not abolish it. We have therefore two fundamental facts of pure existence and of world-existence, a fact of Being, a fact of Becoming. To deny one or the other is easy; to recognise the facts of consciousness and find out their relation is the true and fruitful wisdom."[3] The Absolute or Brahman is both Being and Becoming as well as is beyond them both. It cannot be rightly characterised simply as Being or simply as Becoming or as a sum of Being and Becoming. Brahman is, as has been stated above, beyond all mental categories. But as we have to make an intellectual approach to the Absolute we are constrained to characterise it as Being and

1. *L.D.*, Vol. II, Part I, p. 56.
2. *L.D.*, Vol. I, p. 39.
3. *Ibid.*, pp. 99-100.

Becoming, as One and Many and so on. But the Absolute cannot be fully expressed by any of our mental categories or by all the mental categories taken together. "Stability and movement, we must remember, are only our psychological representations of the Absolute even as are oneness and multitude. The Absolute is beyond stability and movement as it is beyond unity and multiplicity. But it takes its eternal poise in the one and the stable and whirls round itself infinitely, inconceivably, securely in the moving and multitudinous."[1] "World-existence," further observes Sri Aurobindo, "is the ecstatic dance of Shiva which multiplies the body of the God numberlessly to the view; it leaves that white existence precisely where and what it was, ever is and ever will be; its sole absolute object is the joy of the dancing".[2]

The Absolute, as has already been stated is indescribable in itself. We cannot describe the Absolute in itself beyond silence and dynamis, unity and multiplicity etc. Hence "we must accept the double fact, admit both Shiva and Kali and seek to know what is this measureless Movement in Time and Space with regard to that timeless and Spaceless pure Existence, one and stable, to which measure and measurelessness are inapplicable.

It is now clear that Sri Aurobindo has given a sound rational foundation to his integral view of Reality on the basis of his higher reason or the Logic of the Infinite. Like Hegel, Sri Aurobindo has given his own interpretation of the laws of Formal Logic, namely, Identity, Contradiction etc. Now we proceed to make a critical analysis and evaluation of these laws in the light of the higher reason or the Logic of the Infinite.

(H) *Logic of The Infinite and The Laws of Contradiction and Excluded Middle*

Sri Aurobindo's Integral Advaitism is based on his conception of the Logic of the Infinite. It provides a strong and sound logical foundation to his system of the Vedānta. The Logic of the Infinite, as we have shown above, does not go against the principles of Formal Logic, namely, Identity, Contradiction and Excluded Middle.

---

1. *L.D.*, Vol. I, p. 100.
2. *Ibid.*, p. 100.

It does not in any way come in conflict with them. But it does show clearly their abstract and formal nature and their limitations in respect of their application to statements or propositions which express the nature of the Absolute or of the things of the world. These abstract, formal and analytic laws need reinterpretation in respect of their application to synthetic or descriptive propositions. The interpretation of these laws made by Formal logicians cannot be treated as universally and unconditionally true. The modern thinkers and writers on Formal Logic have themselves accepted limitations to the use of the principles of Logic, as has been discussed above. Hegel, Bradley and Bosanquet have also shown the inadequacy and one-sided nature of these laws and their failure to explain relations between categories and things of the world. Hegel has made a reinterpretation of these Laws and has bridged to a considerable extent, the gap that exists between logic and reality, as we have pointed out above. Sri Aurobindo also questions the justification of the *a priori* and unconditional application of these laws to relational categories and to statements which refer to reality, empirical and trans-empirical.

(I) *The Law of Contradiction*

The law of contradiction, according to Sri Aurobindo, serves its desired purpose only when it is viewed in the light of and in relation to reality. It is no doubt valid in itself as an abstract principle of thought. But it becomes a source of error if it is abstracted altogether from reality. In that case, it is fit only to deal with abstract concepts and not with fundamental truths of Reality or the things of the world. It is quite free to declare *A* and not-*A* as contradictory to each other, but it cannot put concrete things of the world or fundamental aspects of Reality in place of *A* and not-*A* without paying due regard to their nature. For it cannot be applied with equal force to all the aspects of reality. As Sri Aurobindo observes "That law is necessary to us in order that we may posit partial and practical truths, think out things clearly, decisively and usefully, classify, act, deal with them effectively for particular purposes in our divisions of space, distinctions of form and property, moments of Time. It represents a formal and strongly dynamic truth of existence in its practical workings which is strongest in the most outward term of things, the material, but becomes less and less rigidly binding as we go upward in the scale, mount on

the more subtle rungs of the ladder of being."[1] The law of con-
tradiction can be applied with greater force and reason in the case
of material phenomena and forces. But even there it cannot judge
things or objects in isolation. "The isolation is certainly necessary
for our first knowledge. A diamond is a diamond and a pearl a
pearl, each thing of its own class, existing by its distinction from
all others, each distinguished by its own form and properties. But
each has also properties and elements which are common to both
and others which are common to material things in general. And
in reality each does not exist only by its distinctions, but much
more essentially by that which is common to both; and we get
back to the very basis and enduring truth of all material things only
when we find that all are the same thing, one energy, one sub-
stance or, if you like, one universal motion which throws up,
brings out, combines, realises these different forms, these various
properties, these fixed and harmonised potentialities of its own
being."[2] Sri Aurobindo further observes, "If we stop short at the
knowledge of distinctions, we can deal only with diamond and
pearl as they are, fix their values, uses, varieties, make the best
ordinary use and profit of them; but if we can get to the knowl-
edge of and control of their elements and the common properties
of the class to which they belong, we may arrive at the power of
making either a diamond or pearl at our pleasure: go farther still
and master that which all material things are in their essence and
we may arrive even at the power of transmutation which would
give the greatest possible control of material Nature. Thus the
knowledge of distinctions arrives at its greatest truth and effective
use when we arrive at the deeper knowledge of that which re-
conciles distinctions in the unity behind all variations. That deeper
knowledge does not deprive the other and more superficial of
effectivity nor convict it of vanity."[3] We have to see the truth of
our classifications and distinctions, but also their limits. "All things,
even while different, are yet one." The full truth of distinctions can
be grasped and realised only when one becomes aware of the
unity that lies behind them and where all the distinctions are
reconciled. The distinctions cease to appear as contraries or

---

1. *L.D.*, Vol. II, Part I, p. 104.
2. *Ibid.*, p. 105.
3. *Ibid.*, p. 105.

contradictories when they are viewed in relation to the unity which constitutes their essence and reconciles them all. Sri Aurobindo and Hegel have laid great emphasis on realising this truth which holds good in the realm of relational thought, in practical life and in reality. Distinctions remain irreconciled and the two terms appear as contraries or contradictories, if they are viewed in isolation and their underlying unity is lost sight of. Sri Aurobindo does not deny the validity or utility of the law of contradiction. "The law of contradiction here is only valid insofar as two different and opposite statements cannot be true of the same thing at the same time, in the same field, in the same respect, from the same point of view and for the same practical purpose."[1] In this respect the law of contradiction conditions all our valid reasoning. But this law ceases to yield valid knowledge, if it is applied in an *a priori* and unconditional way to apparently different and opposite statements without taking any notice of the conditions, e.g., time, space, point of view etc., as mentioned above. These factors put a limitation to the use of this law. Sri Aurobindo is also not in favour of ignoring the law of contradiction and making a facile synthesis between different and opposite statements. As he puts it, "The human reason is wrong in attaching a separate and definitive value to each contradiction by itself or getting rid of one by altogether denying the other, but it is right in refusing to accept as final and as the last word the coupling of contradictions which have in no way been reconciled together or else found their source and significance in something beyond their opposition."[2] Sri Aurobindo insists on a judicious application of the law of contradiction and other logical principles which alone can give us valid knowledge of the phenomena and the supreme Reality.

Bradley has also thrown clear light on the nature and implications of the law of contradiction. He observes, "If the principle of Contradiction states a fact, it says no more than that the discrepant is discrepant, that the exclusive, despite all attempts to persuade it, remains incompatible."[3] He further says, "Denial and affirmation of the self-same judgment is wholly inadmissible."[4] So far as this

---

1. *L.D.*, Vol. II, Part I, p. 107.
2. *Ibid.*, p. 109.
3. *The Principles of Logic*, Vol. I, p. 145.
4. *Ibid.*, p. 147.

statement of the principle of contradiction is concerned, no one can have any reason to say anything against it. Our reason has to act in accordance with this law in order to arrive at truth. But the problem is, how are we to apply this law to statements which refer to the things of the world or to reality? How are we to know whether two things or two qualities are contradictory or discrepant or not? The law of contradiction simply says that the two contradictories cannot be true of the same thing at the same time. But it does not tell us what qualities are really contradictory or discrepant. As Bradley puts it, "there is no logical principle which will tell us what qualities are really discrepant".[1]

In order to know this one will have to take recourse to experience. Experience alone can tell us whether the two qualities predicated of a thing are contradictory or not. One has first of all to know the nature of the thing in order to have a clear idea about its qualities and their relationship. Without an adequate knowledge of the subject, one cannot know whether its predicates are contradictory or not. The law of contradiction cannot be applied in the same manner to different kinds of objects and at the different levels of experience. This law is seen to apply in the case of an individual thing and not in the case of a class. If a man is civilised, he cannot be non-civilised at the same time. But if the term 'man' is taken in the sense of the class of men, then the two attributes 'civilised' and 'non-civilised' may both be affirmed simultaneously. It means that the two terms may be characterised as contradictories in one case and not in the other. It clearly shows that there are definite limitations to the use of this law and so its *a priori* and unconditional application to all kinds of statements is logically inadmissible.

The more a 'subject' is taken in a narrow sense, the more it is liable to be involved in contradictions. As Bradley puts it, "Standing contradictions appear where the subject is narrowed artificially, and where diversity in the identity is taken as excluded. A thing cannot be at once in two places if in the 'at once' there is no lapse, nor can one place have two bodies at once if both claim it in their character as extended."[2] Bradley further observes, "And, to speak in general, the more narrowly we take the subject, and the less

---

1. *The Principles of Logic*, Vol. I, p. 146.
2. *Appearance and Reality*, pp. 505-06.

internal ground for diversity it contains, the more it threatens us with standing or insoluble contradictions. But, we may add, so much the more abstractedness and less truth does such a subject possess."[1]

It is this truth that has been generally ignored by the great philosophers with the result that they have often made indiscriminate and unwarranted application of the law of contradiction to determine the nature of the Absolute and the world and their relationship. This wrong application of the law has led many acute thinkers to uphold extreme and arbitrary views concerning the Absolute and the world. So one has to be fully conscious of the strength as well as limitations of this law before applying it to the supreme Reality or the Absolute. Sri Aurobindo has laid great emphasis on this fact. He observes, "In the world as we see it, for our mental consciousness however high we carry it, we find that to every positive there is a negative. But the negative is not a zero—indeed whatever appears to us a zero is packed with force, teeming with power of existence, full of actual or potential contents. Neither does the existence of the negative make its corresponding positive non-existent or an unreality; it only makes the positive an incomplete statement of the truth of things and even, we may say, of the positive's own truth. For the positive and the negative exist not only side by side, but in relation to each other and by each other; they complete and would to the all-view, which a limited mind cannot reach, explain one another. Each by itself is not really known; we only begin to know it in its deeper truth when we can read into it the suggestions of its apparent opposite. It is through such a profounder catholic intuition and not by exclusive logical oppositions that our intelligence ought to approach the Absolute."[2]

The Absolute, according to Sri Aurobindo, can be described in a meaningful and integral way both by affirmation and negation. Negation does not mean rejection. It signifies freedom of the Absolute from limitation by its own determinations. Thus affirmation and negation cannot be considered as opposed to each other or as contradictories. As Sri Aurobindo puts it "The positives of the Absolute are its various statements of itself to our consciousness,

1. *Appearance and Reality*, p. 506.
2. *L.D.*, Vol. II, Part I, p. 102.

its negatives bring in the rest of its absolute positivity by which its limitation to these first statements is denied. We have, to begin with, its large primary relations such as the infinite and the finite, the conditioned and unconditioned, the qualitied and unqualitied; in each pair the negative conceals the whole power of the corresponding positive which is contained in it and emerges from it: there is no real opposition."[1] The play of negative and positive is seen in the lower orders of the relative as well; but the apparently opposed terms of the relative have to be reconciled in order to arrive at the Absolute. The opposition between the terms of the relative should not be taken to the bitter end and they should not be taken as contradictories and rejected. This kind of approach to the Absolute will put a limitation upon it, as it will mean a denial of its freedom of self-determination. The spatio-temporal world finds reason and justification for its existence in the Absolute which is the source and principle of its truth. "Cosmos and individual go back to something in the Absolute which is the true truth of individuality, the true truth of cosmic being and not their denial and conviction of their falsity."[2] Sri Aurobindo makes an interesting observation here. "The Absolute is not a sceptical logician denying the truth of all his own statements and self-expressions, but an existence so utterly and so infinitely positive that no finite positive can be formulated which can exhaust it or bind it down to its definitions."[3]

(II) *The Law of Excluded Middle*

This law rules out the possibility of the rejection of both the alternatives in a statement. If one alternative turns out to be false, the other must be held as true and *vice versa*. It treats the two alternatives or so-called contradictories as both exclusive and exhaustive. Thus this principle leaves no possibility of any middle course or third alternative. But this law also is abstract and formal; it is a tautology. It also cannot be applied in an *a priori* and unconditional way to the propositions which refer to the Absolute or things of the world. It is not possible to know on the basis of

---

1   *L.D.*, Vol. II, Part I, pp. 102-03.
2   *Ibid.*, p. 103.
3   *Ibid.*, pp. 103-04.

this law whether two terms or qualities are really contradictory or not. And without this knowledge, the so-called opposites or contradictories cannot be treated as both exclusive and exhaustive. In this situation, the rejection of one alternative does not necessarily lead to the acceptance of the other. It is not possible to know on the basis of reason or experience whether the two alternatives exhaust the universe of discourse and that no third alternative is possible. In this respect this law also suffers from limitations so far as its application to the world of experience or the Absolute is concerned.

The philosophers have generally been aware of the limitations of the principle of Excluded Middle and so they have not hesitated in violating it in their metaphysical thinking and discussions. We find a clear and most effective violation of this law in the Mādhyamika Dialectic. "The Mādhyamika", observes Dr. Murti, "flagrantly violates this law at every step; we find him cutting down all the alternatives that are, by the canons of formal logic, both exclusive and exhaustive".[1] Kant also violates this law insofar as he formulates the antinomies and rejects both of them, e.g., "the world has a beginning in space and time", and "the world has no such beginning" etc. Hegel also does not accept this law; had he done so, he would have been satisfied with either Being or non-Being instead of seeking their reconciliation in a third category. The Hegelian dialectic also like that of the Mādhyamika violates this law at every step, though there is a radical difference in their dialectical procedure. The Advaita Vedāntins also do not recognise this law as it is evident from their conception of Māyā as neither real nor unreal but indescribable (anirvacanīya). The illusory snake can neither be called *sat* (real) nor *asat* (unreal). It cannot be called unreal or non-existent, because it is an object of experience and it cannot be called real because its experience is cancelled. Hence the rejection of both the alternatives in the case of an illusory snake is logically justified, though it implies the violation of the law of Excluded Middle. Dr. Murti observes, "No logical flaw is involved in not observing the Excluded Middle. If any one wants to vindicate this law, he must not only resolve the antinomies which a dialectic presents, but show that in rejecting

1. T.R.V. Murti. *The Central Philosophy of Buddhism*. p. 146.

one alternative, we do so by covertly accepting its contradictory, or *vice versa.*"[1]

The law of Excluded Middle cannot be applied in an unconditional way even in the case of existent subjects. It may be said, for example, that an ape is neither civilised nor non-civilised. While these two predicates together could not be rejected in the case of a man, they can be rejected in the case of an ape. "The law of Excluded Middle," Dr. Murti rightly observes, "assumes a sort of omniscience and makes capital out of our ignorance. That any two alternatives together exhaust the universe of discourse and that no third is possible cannot be known from the alternatives themselves".[2] This is possible, according to him, "in the case of mathematics and other purely deductive sciences, where we possess a knowledge of the entire field so completely and unerringly. that we can formulate the alternatives exhaustively, and by the negation of the one we can affirm the other, and *vice versa*".[3] But this sort of knowledge is not possible in the world of experience. There the rejection of one alternative does not necessarily lead to the acceptance of its contradictory. So it is clear that the law of Excluded Middle cannot be applied in an unconditional way to statements which refer to the different levels of experience or Reality. It cannot be conceived as competent to determine the nature of Reality. Dr. Murti observes, "The Law of Excluded Middle is for the regulation of thought. But here the question is whether thought itself is competent to grasp reality, and not the internal ordering of thoughts. The law, even if formally valid, is applicable within thought, and has no relevance with regard to the metaphysical problem about the relation of thought to reality."[4]

Here a question arises. Is violation of the law of Excluded Middle permissible in a valid argument or reasoning? Does it not condition the descriptive propositions which describe a certain situation or fact? In the case of descriptive propositions, a conclusion should not only be materially true, but formally true as well. In this respect, the law of Excluded Middle also, like the law of Contradiction, conditions all our valid reasoning. Thought may or may not

1. *Op. cit.,* p. 147.
2. *Ibid.,* p. 147.
3. *Ibid.,* footnote.
4. *Ibid.,* p. 148.

be able to grasp reality. But if it makes any judgment about reality, it has to be governed by its own laws. It cannot yield any valid conclusion if it violates the laws of Contradiction and Excluded Middle. According to the law of Excluded Middle, two contrary terms predicated of a subject may both be false and rejected. But the rejection of two contradictory terms predicated of a subject is not logically permissible even in metaphysical thinking. In this respect the principles of Formal Logic enjoy complete validity. But their limitation is that they cannot tell us what qualities are really contradictory. So their unconditional application to the categories of thought or to descriptive propositions is logically not permissible. It is possible only in the case of analytic propositions and not in the case of synthetic or descriptive propositions. Whether two terms are contradictory or not can be known only on the basis of experience. Unless we have an adequate knowledge of the subject, we cannot say whether the two terms predicated of it are contradictory or not. The examples of illusory snake and ape cited above make this fact absolutely clear. The Advaita Vedānta, in fact, does not violate the law of Excluded Middle, when it negates both the alternatives, namely, *sat* and *asat* in respect of an illusory snake. It only shows the limitation of this law and its inapplicability in the case of illusory objects. There will be a violation of this law if a living snake is characterised as neither *sat* (real) nor *asat* (unreal). The terms *sat* and *asat* taken in themselves are mere abstractions. They derive a definite meaning only when they are viewed in relation to a subject. The law of Excluded Middle also, like the law of Contradiction, cannot be applied in an *a priori* and unconditional way to the different levels of experience and reality. The two alternative terms do not reveal their true nature if they are viewed in isolation or simply in relation to each other. Their nature and relation to each other can be known adequately only when both the terms are viewed in relation to the subject or reality which is their referent.

So it is clear that the laws of Contradiction and Excluded Middle are valid in themselves as abstract principles of thought. But they suffer from obvious limitations in respect of their application to propositions which refer to the different levels of world-experience or Reality. These truths about the implications of the laws of contradiction and Excluded Middle have a great significance so far as our investigation of the nature of the Absolute and its relationship with the world is concerned. A true understanding of the nature of the laws of Logic and conditions of their applicability, specially, of the law of Contradiction, is of utmost importance for comprehending the Absolute in all its integrality and depth. Any confusion in this respect leads to fatal consequences. This phenomenon is clearly witnessed in some metaphysical systems of India and the West. The Mādhyamika Dialectic provides a glaring example of the *a priori* and unconditional application of the law of Contradiction to the categories of thought. It is also witnessed, to a considerable extent, in the dialectic of the Advaita Vedānta as well. The Advaita Vedānta shows full awareness of the limitations of the Law of Excluded Middle. But it seems to be completely oblivious of the limitations of the Law of Contradiction. It applies in an *a priori* and unconditional way the law of Contradiction to the statements of the Upaniṣads which reveal the nature of the Absolute in all its integrality and depth. The result is that it has to deny the reality of one fundamental aspect of the Absolute, of Becoming, in order to make it consistent with the laws of logic.

Now the question is, is it logically justified to apply the law of Contradiction in an unconditional way to the categories whose referent happens to be the Absolute? In the above discussion, it has been shown that the laws of Contradiction and Excluded Middle can be applied to the apparently opposed terms or statements only if the nature of the subject is known. But here the trouble is that the nature of the Absolute is not known. It lies beyond the range of empirical experience and thought. The Absolute is not an object of thought. Thought can give only a speculative idea of the Absolute, but it cannot have a direct knowledge of it. But the Absolute is not altogether unknowable. It can be directly known and experienced at the supra-reflectional or spiritual level. This direct and immediate knowledge of the Absolute revealed to the ancient seers of India in their supramental experiences is embodied in the fundamental and living statements of the Upaniṣads. The Upaniṣads characterise the Absolute as both Being and Becoming. But as these two terms appear to be opposed to each other and involve self-contradiction, the Advaita dialectic negates the reality of Becoming and asserts the reality of pure Being, *Sat.* It is true that Being and Becoming taken by themselves or in relation to each other do involve self-contradiction at the level of thought. But how can one be sure that their apparent opposition or contradiction is not resolved in the all-embracing unity of the Absolute? They may cease to appear as contrary or contradictory, when they are viewed in relation to the unity of the Absolute. Even if *Being* and *Becoming* are conceived as contradictories or contraries, they cannot be simultaneously affirmed of the Absolute only if the latter happens to be an individual or a finite entity like a man or a table. But the Absolute cannot be conceived as an individual or finite entity, as in that case there will be a plurality of the Absolutes which in itself is a self-contradictory concept. If the contradictory terms can be true of a class or a general term, they can as well be true of the Absolute which is the most general and comprehensive of all terms. Moreover, there is every possibility that Being and Becoming may not be contradictories or contraries at all. They may be simply complementary to each other in the case of Absolute as hydrogen and oxygen are complementary in the case of water. Hydrogen and oxygen taken by themselves may appear as incompatible to each other as they are possessed of different properties. But viewed in the light of water, they simply appear as complementary to each other. In the same way, Being and Becoming taken by themselves may appear as incompatible to each other, but viewed in the light of the Absolute, they may as well appear as its complementary aspects. Thus the affimation of Being and Becoming as the complementary poises of the Absolute will not come in conflict with the law of Contradiction. They lose their separate identity and become inseparable in the identity of the Absolute. As Bradley significantly puts it, "Supposing that, in such a case as continuity, we seem to find contradictions united, and *A* to be *b* and not-*b* at once, this may yet be reconciled with the axiom of Contradiction *A*. We say is composed of *b* and not-*b*, for, dissecting *A*, we arrive at these elements and uniting these, we get *A* once more. But the question is, while these elements are in *A*, can they be said, while there, to exist in their fully discrepant character of *b* and not-*b* ? ...But, in the object and within the whole. the truth may be that we never really do have these discrepants. We only have moments which *would* be incompatible if they really were separate, but, conjoined together, have been subdued into something within the character of the whole. If we can so understand the identity of opposites and I am not sure that we may not do so—then the law of Contradiction flourishes untouched. If, in coming into one, the contraries as such no longer exist, then where is the contradiction."[1]

From the above discussion regarding the nature and implications of the laws of Contradiction and Excluded Middle, it is clear that these laws by themselves cannot enable one to ascertain the true meaning of the categories of thought and of the nature of things unless they are viewed in relation to the subject or reality. They can enable thought to attain self-consistency in its inferences and reasoning. But they cannot by themselves help us in ascertaining the truth of things or the real nature of Reality. As J.S. Mill pointedly remarks, "The end aimed at by formal logic, and attained by the observance of its precepts, is not truth, but consistency. It has been seen that this is the only direct purpose of the rules of syllogism, the intention and effect of which is simply to keep our inferences or conclusions in complete consistency with our general formulae or directions for drawing them."[2] An inference or conclusion may be perfectly consistent according to the rules of syllogism, but it may not be true. For example, from the premise 'All men are quadrupeds', one can draw the conclusion. 'Some quadrupeds are men'. This argument is perfectly consistent as it is in accordance with the rules of Conversion. But it is not true. The material truth of a conclusion can be ascertained only when one takes recourse to experience. One can know from experience alone if his reasoning corresponds with facts.

The dialectical criticism of categories often pays more attention to the attainment of self-consistency in reasoning than to truth. The relational categories, e.g., Being and Becoming, Cause and Effect etc. are found to be fraught with self-contradiction and so they are negated. The Mādhyamika negates all the categories of thought, all the views of Reality and establishes the principle of Śūnyatā which alone, according to him, is Truth. The Advaita Vedānta does not go to that extreme. It takes every care to bring its reasoning in conformity with the thought of the Upaniṣads. It negates the relational categories not only in the name of the laws of Logic, e.g. Identity, Contradiction etc., but also in the name of the Upaniṣads, which have been acclaimed by the orthodox philosophical tradition as revealed texts. Thus, it negates Becoming not only because this concept is found to be self-contradictory, but also because its

1   *The Principles of Logic*. Vol. I, p. 149.
2   J S Mill. *A System of Logic*, p. 137.

reality has been negated by the enlightened philosophers of the Upaniṣads. The Upaniṣads follow a two-fold way in their treatment of Becoming. First, they affirm the reality of Matter, Life, Mind etc. which constitute the realm of Becoming and call these principles Brahman (Absolute) and subsequently they negate them. Thus first they affirm Becoming and then they negate it. In this respect, the Advaita Vedānta finds strong support from the Upaniṣads in its negation of Becoming.

Now the question is, what do the Upaniṣads mean when they negate the reality of Matter, Life, Mind etc., of Becoming as such? Does the word negation, *neti neti* of the Upaniṣads, mean 're-jection'; is it a bare denial or it signifies something positive. There is no unanimity among the philosophers of the different schools of Vedānta concerning the meaning of 'negation'. The Advaita Vedānta, like the Mādhyamika, conceives 'negation' in the sense of 'rejection'. Negation, according to the Mādhyamika and the Advaita Vedānta, means a bare denial or exclusion. It does not, according to them, signify any thing positive. Sri Aurobindo does not interpret 'negation' in the sense of a bare denial or exclusion. The word 'negation' used by the philosophers of the Upaniṣads, signifies, according to him, something positive. When 'Becoming' is 'negated' of Brahman, it does not mean that it is treated as unreal or false; it really signifies the transcendence of Brahman (Absolute), its utter freedom from limitations by its own expressions or determinations. It does not deprive Brahman of its power of self-determination, of its real expression in the form or aspect of Becoming. Brahman transcends Becoming; it does not reject it. Thus negation signifies something positive; it signifies the transcendence and absolute freedom of Brahman and not the 'rejection' of the spatio-temporal world or Becoming. Unlike the Mādhyamika and the Advaita Vedānta, Sri Aurobindo conceives 'Negation' as significant. Sri Aurobindo's view of Significant Negation provides a strong foundation to his integral view of Reality or his Integral Advaitism.

(I) *Significant Negation: Bernard Bosanquet*

A most fundamental contribution of Hegel to logic and metaphysics is his view that negativity or contradiction is inherent in the concepts or categories of thought and in the things of the world. It constitutes an essential characteristic of thought and reality. But negativity or contradiction does not create any kind of division or disruption in thought or reality. It does not create any wedge between the different aspects of Reality. Both affirmation and denial, positive and negative are reconciled in the all-embracing unity of thought and reality. Truth, according to Hegel, does not lie in the mere Identity, but in the union of identity with variety.

Negation, according to Hegel, does not mean bare denial or rejection. It must contribute something positive to knowledge. Bosanquet holds that significant negation must be capable of contributing something positive to knowledge. A negative judgment cannot be treated as one of bare exclusion. Negation is intelligible only with reference to a real system which is presupposed by it. Negation, according to Bosanquet, is the conscious expression of difference. In making a negative judgment, one is necessarily conscious of negation or difference. But one is not necessarily conscious in respect of affirmation. Thus a difference is noticed in the subjective attitude of the person in the two cases. But negation itself has a distinct objective reference. It is not of something subjective. Negation is an expression of difference; it is not simply a bare denial or contradiction. 'Negation in its pure form as simple contradiction is the abstraction of difference.' Difference becomes contradiction when it is treated as mere difference or abstraction of difference. Abstraction of difference is conceived as mere difference without identity. Difference apart from identity is conceived as contradiction and negated. Such a denial, according to Bosanquet, is the pure contradictory of the affirmation which it denies. But it is purely a formal negation. It treats contrary terms as contradictories and negates them. As Bosanquet puts it, "The essence of formal negation is to invest the contrary with the character of the contradictory, or to raise mere discrepancy or positive opposition to the level of the absolute or contradictory alternative, which is the abstraction of difference. It is only contradictory negation which allows a conclusion to be formally drawn from the negative; contrary negation does not admit of this. It is only contrary negation which allows any import to be materially attached to the negative; contradictory negation does not admit of this."[1]

---

1. *Logic,* Vol. I, pp. 289-90.

In contradictory negation, a conclusion can be formally drawn from the negative without knowing the things signified by the terms. Such a formal negation or contradiction does not contribute anything positive to knowledge. So it cannot be called significant negation. One can, e.g., formally draw a conclusion from a pair of contradictory terms such as *B* and not-*B*. If a thing is *B*, it cannot be not-*B* and *vice versa*. In the same way, if a thing is not not-*B*, then it must be *B*. *B* and not-*B* cover the whole universe of thought and reality and they leave no room for a third alternative. Thus in formal negation, the laws of Contradiction and Excluded Middle operate in an *a priori* and unconditional way. Such a formal negation cannot be treated as significant. If a negative judgment is taken in the sense of bare exclusion, it cannot be considered as significant, because it would, according to Bosanquet, apply equally well to everything in the world. It does not contribute anything positive to knowledge. It gives only formal truth and does not provide any knowledge of the things of the world or reality. It has its relevance in the field of mathematics and other purely deductive sciences, but not in respect of reality. Thus contradictory negation does not allow any meaning to be materially attached to the negative. So it cannot be treated as significant. Negation, in Bosanquet's view, can have no bearing unless the contraries are limited, so that something follows from the negation. Bare denial amounts to nothing. As Bosanquet puts it, "Thus it appears that bare denial, whether disguised as spurious affirmation, or taken as the mere exclusion of suggested predicates amounts in the strict sense to nothing. The judgments by which it is typified are the exact counterparts of absolute tautology, and like such tautology, are not really judgments at all."[1] They are empty of all contents and do not give knowledge of any situation or fact.

In bare denial or exclusion, identity and difference fall apart and thereby the conditions of intelligible judgment are destroyed. Bosanquet observes, "Pure tautology aims at mere identity, and bare negation at mere difference. It will be found that any meaning which in practice we attach to an apparent tautology or an apparent bare negation is owing to the introduction of difference into the former or of identity into the latter."[2] Difference and Identity

1. *Logic*, Vol. 1, p. 283.
2. *Ibid.*, p. 283.

are not externally related to each other; they are inseparable aspects of everything that exists or can be thought. Thus Bosanquet confirms Hegel's view that identity and variety cannot be treated as different. These two determinations appear to be irreconcilable only when the former is treated as a mere tautology and the latter as a bare denial or negation. But they do not convey, according to Hegel, the complete truth of these determinations. The full truth of these determinations lies in their union. Bosanquet observes, "We must never forget the conclusion which we have reached above, that the unity of judgment does not exclude systematic multiplicity within it."[1]

Difference or variety, according to Hegel, constitutes an essential characteristic of Identity. Identity, apart from variety expresses, as has been stated before, only a one-sided determinateness; it contains only formal truth which is incomplete. Identity can communicate the full truth only when it is conceived in union with variety or difference. Reality is a unity which includes all the diversity within it. Such is the nature of thought as well. The unity of judgment expresses this very nature of thought and Reality. So Bosanquet says that denial, as a form of judgment, must be capable of contributing something positive to knowledge. He says, "All significance then is in this sense *positive* significance, and significant negation must therefore convey something positive."

To Conclude

(i)   Negation does not mean bare denial or exclusion. Such a negation does not contribute anything positive to knowledge. It is merely formal in nature.

(ii) As opposed to formal negation, significant negation must contribute something positive to knowledge.

(iii) Negation is intelligible only with reference to a real system which is presupposed by it. Negation is conscious expression of difference.

(iv) Negation has a distinct objective reference. It is not of some thing subjective.

(v)   Negation as simple contradiction is abstraction of difference;

---

1. *Logic*, Vol. I, p. 284.

it is a mere difference without identity. It is formal negation.
(vi) Formal negation invests the contrary with the character of the
contradictory. Hence no import is materially attached to the
negative.
(vii) In bare denial or exclusion, identity and difference fall apart
and thus the conditions of intelligible judgment are destroyed.
(viii) A negative judgment in the sense of bare exclusion is an
exact counterpart of absolute tautology and hence is not
judgment at all.

(J) *The Mādhyamika Dialectic: Its Nature and Procedure*
Now we proceed to make a critical analysis and evaluation of the
Mādhyamika Dialectic which makes an *a priori* application of the
principles of Formal Logic to determine the nature of concepts and
categories and their relationship. A clear awareness of the limita-
tions and shortcomings of the dialectical procedure of the
Mādhyamika brings into clear light the necessity and importance
of higher reason or the Logic of the Infinite to comprehend the
nature of Reality and its process.

   Dialectic is a criticism of Reason. It comes into operation when
reason becomes conscious of the conflict in which it is involved.
This conflict is the result of the different and opposed views that
are advanced by reason concerning the nature of Reality and its
process. Dialectic tries to remove the conflict inherent in reason
by revealing the contradictions inherent in both the opposites taken
singly or in combination. Once the different and opposite views
are shown to be self-contradictory and false, they are negated and
rejected.

   The Mādhyamika does not try to propound any view of his own
regarding Reality. He keeps himself absolutely free from all the
views. He is fully conscious of the fact that no view of Reality can
be free from contradiction. By a critical analysis and examination
of the concepts and categories of thought and of all the views, he
shows the self-contradiction inherent in them and consequently
rejects them. His rejection of all the views means his denial of the
competence of Reason to comprehend Reality. It constitutes the
main function of the Mādhyamika dialectic. Its function is purely
negative, analytic. As Dr. Murti puts it, "The Mādhyamika dialectic
tries to remove the conflict in reason by rejecting both the oppo-
sites taken singly or in combination. The Mādhyamika is convinced

that the conjunctive[1] or disjunctive[2] synthesis of the opposites is but another view; it labours under the same difficulties. Rejection of all views is the rejection of the competence of Reason to comprehend Reality. The real is transcendent to thought. Rejection of views is not based on any positive grounds or the acceptance of another view; it is solely based on the inner contradiction implicit in each view. The function of the Mādhyamika dialectic, on the logical level, is purely negative, analytic."[3] Negation in the Mādhyamika is purely formal. It is empty of all content. It is clearly witnessed in his dialectical criticism of the categories.

Four alternative views are possible, according to the Mādhyamika, on any subject. They are, namely, Being (*asti*), Non-Being (*nāsti*), both Being and Non-Being (*ubhaya*) and neither Being nor Non-Being (*anubhaya*). He formulates these four types of views in his examination of each category, causality etc., and by showing the self-contradiction inherent in each view (*dṛṣṭi*), he rejects all of them. Thus by rejecting all the views, he propounds the concept of Śūnyatā. Śūnyatā is, according to the Mādhyamika, the rejection of all the views; it is in itself not a view. It is a bare denial of all the views and is not itself positive. The Mādhyamika lays great emphasis on this fact in his analysis and examination of the categories of thought.

To illustrate the nature and procedure of the Mādhyamika dialectic, we may consider the problem of causation. I will quote here at length the Mādhyamika criticism of causation that I have discussed elsewhere.[4]

"The relation between cause and effect has been viewed in four ways. One view advocates identity between cause and effect.[5] The other considers them as different.[6] The third view combines the above two views and considers the two as both identical with and different from each other.[7] The fourth view rejects all these three

---

1. *The Hegelian Synthesis.*
2. *The Jaina Synthesis.*
3. T.R.V. Murti, *The Central Philosophy of Buddhism*, p. 128.
4. R.S. Misra, *Studies in Philosophy and Religion*, pp. 76-78.
5. *The Sāṁkhya.*
6. *The Buddhist and the Nyāya.*
7. *The Jaina.*

alternatives and takes things as produced by chance.[1] The Mādhyamika dialectic examines each view critically and shows its self-contradictory nature. It criticises the Sāṁkhya view which conceives identity between cause and effect. The Sāṁkhya believes in self-becoming. Cause is said to transform itself into effect. It evolves effect out of itself. Thus there is no essential difference between cause and effect, as the latter is not something different from the former. The Mādhyamika points out that there is no meaning in self-production. Candrakīrti, the great commentator on the *Mādhyamika Kārikās* of Nāgārjuna argues that things cannot be produced out of themselves; firstly, because of the futility of the process of self-duplication and secondly, because there can be no end to this process.[2] There can be no necessity of the duplication of what is already present. The Sāṁkhya might reply that the same thing is not produced out of itself. In the effect, the cause produces itself in a transformed condition, in a different form. Between cause and effect, there is a difference in state or form, though there is absolutely no difference in substance. Now the Mādhyamika asks, are the cause and effect identical in respect of this emergent form? They are not. A judgment true of the effect, e.g. table, is not true of the cause, e.g. wood. Thus there is found to be a difference between cause and effect in some sense. Causation implies difference in this view. This goes against identity. So the Sāṁkhya view is involved in this self-contradiction. It advocates identity between cause and effect and yet it cannot do so without admitting difference. In order to maintain identity, it will have to reject 'difference', which will mean giving up causation itself. The notions of identity and causation cannot go together. They are contradictory, discrepant.

The other view which regards cause and effect as different is also shown to be self-contradictory. Candrakīrti contends that if the cause and effect were different, then also there can be no production. Things cannot be produced from other objects totally different from themselves. Because in that case, there will be the contingency of anything being produced out of anything else.[3] If

---

1. *The Materialists and Sceptics.*
2. *na svataḥ utpadyante bhāvāḥ tadutpādavaiyarthyāt, atiprasangadoṣācca.* *Mādhyamika Kārikāvṛtti* 1.3.
3. *na parataḥ utpadyante bhāvāḥ, sarvataḥ sarva-sambha-prasaṅgāt. Ibid.*

98 THE INTEGRAL ADVAITISM OF SRI AUROBINDO

difference between cause and effect is insisted upon, then there can be no relation between them. Where there is absolutely no relation, there can be no causation. If there is difference, there can be no relation. And if there is no relation, there can be no causation. So, if the difference between cause and effect is admitted, causation has to be abandoned altogether. This view is thus found to be not consistent with itself. It is shown to be self-contradictory according to its own accepted canons.

In similar fashion, Candrakīrti brings into light the self-contradiction inherent in the remaining two views also. The third view which plums together *identity* and *difference* is shown to be infected with the shortcomings found in the above two views. Moreover, 'identity' and 'difference' cannot conjoin together to produce objects.[1] According to Candrakīrti, things cannot be produced even without cause. Because in that case, cause-effect relationship will cease to exist altogether. Moreover, there will also arise the contingency of the appearance of the impossibles, such as fragrance in the sky-lotus.[2]

Thus the Mādhyamika subjects all the above-mentioned four views in respect of causation to critical examination and finds them riddled with self-contradiction. This leads him to establish the truth of non-origination (*ajātivāda*). Nāgārjuna says that no object is produced anywhere, at any time. The object is produced neither from itself, nor from the other, nor from the combination of both, nor without cause. Origination is impossible altogether."[3]

The Mādhyamika dialectic makes it crystal clear that causation cannot be explained on grounds of logic or reason. Dr. Murti observes, "The conclusion to which the Mādhyamika is led, as the result of his examination, is that causation cannot rationally be explained. All theories of causation are conceptual devices and makeshifts. Practice does not entail the acceptance of any theory."[4] "The essence of the contradiction is that if the cause and effect were conceived as identical or continuous there is no distinction between the two, we have a colourless static mass; nothing new emerges, and there is no production. If however, they are conceived as distinct and discontinuous, then they become external

---

1. *Mādhyamika Kārikāvṛtti.*
2. *Ibid.*
3. *Mādhyamika Kārikās* 1.3.
4. *Op. cit.*, p. 176.

to each other and the cause is on a par with the non-cause, and the effect has emerged from nowhere as it were; it is uncaused."[1] Bradley also points out, "The dilemma, I think, can now be made plain (a) Causation must be continuous, (b) Causation cannot be continuous."

The Mādhyamika criticism of causation has given us a clear idea of the nature and implications of his dialectic. Now we proceed to make a critical appraisal of his dialectical criticism of the categories, specially, in the light of the concept of Significant Negation. It will help us in having a correct estimate of the merits and shortcomings of the Mādhyamika dialectic, as its understanding and interpretation of Negation is radically different from that of Significant Negation.

(K) A Critical Appraisal of the Mādhyamika Dialectic

(I) The Mādhyamika Criticism of the Concept of Identity

From the above discussion, it is clear that the Mādhyamika proves the self-contradictory nature of all the views, namely, Identity, Difference, both and neither, that have been propounded by the philosophical systems to establish the relationship between cause and effect. His dialectical criticism of causation applies equally well to other relational categories also. Here I propose to make a critical appraisal of his criticism of the concept of Identity.

The Mādhyamika succeeds in showing that the concept of Identity is self-contradictory, because identity necessarily implies difference. The Sāmkhya view that establishes identity between cause and effect is thus found to be self-contradictory. But a critical examination of the Mādhyamika criticism of the theory of Identity makes it crystal clear that he conceives Identity as a tautology, as Formal Logic does. The Formal Logic conceives identity as something that remains perfectly identical with itself, e.g., $A = A$. It retains its essential nature at all times and places. It is necessarily true. If a category of thought or a thing does not remain perfectly identical with itself and implies difference in it, it cannot be treated as self-consistent and cannot be held as true. If it implies difference or variety, it is necessarily self-contradictory and false. Thus the Mādhyamika criticism of the Sāmkhya view of identity between

---

1. Op. cit., p. 177.

cause and effect is perfectly in conformity with the principle of Identity of Formal Logic which, according to Wittgenstein, is a tautology like the principle of Excluded Middle. Being a tautology, the concept of Identity is empty of all content and does not assert anything about any situation or fact. The Mādhyamika finds that the Sāṁkhya view of identity necessarily refers to variety and does describe a certain state of affairs, namely, the production of effects from a cause. This phenomenon cannot be explained in terms of Identity as it happens to be completely empty. It is not supposed to describe any state of affairs. Thus the Sāṁkhya view of identity is necessarily self-contradictory from the point of view of the Mādhyamika.

Thus we find that the Mādhyamika makes an abstract and an absolutely *a priori* application of the principle of Identity of Formal Logic in his dialectical criticism of the Sāṁkhya theory of causation. He makes the same *a priori* approach in his criticism of the other categories also. The categories constitute the structure of experience or reality. The Mādhyamika makes a criticism of the categories apart from and in isolation from experience. This is evident from his arguments that he gives against the production of things out of something else. He argues, as has been stated above, that things cannot be produced out of themselves because there is no necessity of duplication of what is already present. Now this is an absolutely abstract and *a priori* argument. The production of effects out of their causes is a fact of experience. It is on the basis of this established fact that the philosophers have developed different views concerning cause-effect relationship. But the Mādhyamika questions the necessity of the process of production or creation itself. He expects Nature to act in accordance with the laws of Formal logic. And as Nature is not found to act in conformity with these laws, he unhesitatingly passes a sentence of unreality or falsity against it. To say that the Sāṁkhya theory or other views of causation do not provide a thoroughly satisfactory explanation of the world-process on rational grounds is one thing; but to say that all theories of causation "are conceptual devices and makeshifts" is a different thing altogether. The Sāṁkhya, Nyāya, Buddhism etc., have made sustained and honest attempts to make a critical analysis of world-experience and have developed various theories of causation to explain the emergence or creation of things. They do suffer from shortcomings, as none of them has found universal acceptance. But these theories have a direct relation to experience. They present different pictures of reality. So they cannot be characterised as mere constructions of mind which have no basis in experience or reality. They can in no case be treated as mere conceptual devices and makeshifts. The reason of opposition between different theories seems to lie in their different standpoints. As Radhakrishnan observes "The Sāṅkhya and the Vedānta insist that, if the effect is totally distinct from the cause, there cannot be any determining principle to relate the two. The Naiyāyika says that, if the effect is not distinct, we cannot distinguish the two as cause and effect. Both views are justified, though from different standpoints."[1] But the Mādhyamika does not consider any theory of causation as having any logical or rational justification. No theory of causation, according to him, is consistent with itself. So none can be held as true. The Mādhyamika does not take into account the fact of experience. He considers the metaphysical statements as merely analytic in nature, as tautologies. The propositions of logic, according to Wittgenstein, are tautologies and so they are necessarily true. Their self-consistency can be determined a priori without any reference to experience. But the metaphysical propositions cannot, as such, be treated as tautologies. Unlike the propositions of logic, they are not absolutely independent of experience. So their truth cannot be determined a priori. The metaphysical propositions which seem to be independent of experience are purely speculative in character. So they can, in a certain sense, be treated as conceptual devices and makeshifts. The proposition e.g. the cause and effect are identical or one, cannot be considered as merely analytic or a tautology. So any a priori application of the principle of Identity of Formal Logic to determine its truth cannot be justified on rational grounds.

The a priori character of the Mādhyamika dialectic is also evident from the fact that he completely ignores the arguments advanced by Sāṁkhya in support of Satkārya-vāda. The Sāṁkhya gives the following arguments: (i) The non-existent cannot be brought into existence, e.g., sky-flower. (ii) One has to take recourse to a material cause in order to produce an effect. (iii) Anything cannot come out of anything. (iv) Causal efficiency is possessed by that which

---

1. *Indian Philosophy*, Vol. II, p. 98.

has necessary potency. (v) The effect is possessed of the nature of cause.[1] All these arguments advanced by Sāṁkhya make a direct reference to experience. So any *a priori* criticism of the Sāṁkhya theory of causation which takes no notice of experience cannot be considered as logically justified. Regarding the *a priori* criticisms of the Mādhyamika, Dr. Dasgupta rightly observes, "Nāgārjuna's criticisms, are however, largely of an *a priori* nature, and do not treat the concepts in a concrete manner and are not based on the testimony of our psychological experience. The oppositions shown are, therefore, very often of an abstract nature and occasionally degenerate into verbalism. But as a rule they are based on the fundamental relative nature of our experience."[2]

Hegel has given his own interpretation of the principles of Identity and Contradiction, which is radically different from that of Formal Logic. It provides a deep insight into the nature of thought and reality. He agrees with Wittgenstein that the principle of Identity in its positive expression $A = A$ is nothing more than empty tautology. It is without content. He also agrees with Nāgārjuna and other Mādhyamika philosophers that the concept of Identity necessarily implies the concept of difference. But, unlike the Mādhyamikas, he does not conceive the relation between Identity and difference or between cause and effect as self-contradictory and false. The principle of Identity of Formal Logic contains only formal truth which, according to Hegel, is abstract and incomplete. The complete truth lies in the unity of Identity with variety, as the latter constitutes the essential nature of Identity. Identity apart from variety or difference cannot be considered as representing the complete truth either of the concepts of thought or things of the world. The Mādhyamika philosophers, Nāgārjuna, Candrakīrti and others show no awareness of the true nature and implications of the concepts of Identity and difference and their relationship and characterise this relationship as false or unreal.

The Mādhyamika takes great pains to show that the concepts or categories are relational in nature. No category can be explained by itself; it has no intrinsic nature of its own. Each category can be understood only in relation to others. As Dr. Dasgupta puts it, "Nāgārjuna's methods differ considerably from those of Śrīharsh in

1. *Sāṁkhya Kārikā*, 9.
2. *A History of Indian Philosophy*, Vol. II, pp. 170-71.

this that the concepts which he criticised were shown by him to have been intrinsically based and constructed on notions which had no essential nature of their own, but were understood in relation to others. No concept revealed any intrinsic nature of its own, and one could understand a concept only through another, and that again through the former or through another and so on. The entire world-appearance would thus be based on relative conceptions and be false."[1]

Radhakrishnan observes, "Nāgārjuna shows that the whole world of experience is an appearance, a mere network of unintelligible relations. Matter and soul, space and time, cause and substance, motion and rest are all alike the baseless fabric of the vision which leave not a rack behind. Reality must at least be consistent. But the categories through which we construct our reality or experience are unintelligible and self-contradictory. Intelligibility is the minimum expected of reality, but the relations of experience do not possess even that. Things which are not consistent may be actual, but they are not real."[2]

Now we proceed to make a critical evaluation of the Mādhyamika criticism of relational categories.

(II) *The Mādhyamika Criticism of Relational Categories*
The main contention of the Mādhyamikas is that the categories of thought or the objects that have no intrinsic nature of their own and derive their being and nature by mutual dependence are nothing in themselves; they cannot be characterised as real. Their relationship cannot be established either in terms of Identity or difference. Dr. Murti observes, "Relation has to perform two mutually opposed functions: as *connecting* the two terms, in making them relevant to each other, it has to *identify* them; but as connecting the two, it has to differentiate them. Otherwise expressed, relation cannot obtain between entities that are identical with or different from each other". "These insuperable difficulties impel us to the con-clusion that cause and effect, substance and attribute, whole and parts, subject and object etc., are mutually dependent, relative; hence they are not things in themselves."[3] The dialectical criticism

1. *Op. cit.*, p. 170.
2. *Ibid.*, Vol. I, pp. 647-48.
3. *Ibid.*, p. 138.

of the Mādhyamika of the relational categories is based on this thesis.

We have made above a critical appraisal of the Mādhyamika criticism of the concept of Identity. It throws adequate light on his criticism of the relational categories as well. The dialectical criticism of the Mādhyamika is based on his presupposition that a thing can be conceived as real, if it has self-consistency. This presupposition is based on the laws of Formal Logic, namely, Identity, Contradiction etc. The Mādhyamika shows in a thoroughgoing way that no category fulfils the criterion of self-consistency, all are relational in nature. He also proves that the relations between categories are, unintelligible; they are, logically, found to be self-contradictory and false.

The contention of the Mādhyamika that the categories are relational in nature is perfectly true. But his conclusion that relations are unintelligible, self-contradictory and false cannot be held as valid. The reason is that he arrives at this conclusion by an *a priori* and unconditional application of the principles of Identity and Contradiction to the relational categories. He proceeds on the assumption that whatever is found to be inherent with contradiction is necessarily false. As a tautology is always true, contradiction is necessarily false. So a statement that is found to be self-contradictory, is to be negated or rejected.

Here a question arises: How one is to know whether a proposition is self-contradictory or not? If it involves contradiction, how one is to determine whether the contradiction is merely apparent or real? A proposition of logic, e.g., *A* cannot be both *B* and not-*B*, can be easily understood, but it is purely abstract and analytic. In the same way, one can accept the truth of the statement, e.g., the table cannot be both red and not red at the same place and the same time. The truth of both these statements, one analytic and the other descriptive, is evident, because there is no violation of the law of Contradiction in them. The truth or falsity of analytic propositions can be determined *a priori* by the application of the laws of logic. The truth-value of descriptive propositions can also be determined by the application of the principles of logic in the light of experience. The metaphysical propositions are neither purely abstract and analytic, like the propositions of logic, nor they are descriptive in the empirical sense. The concepts and categories of thought, as has been already pointed out, constitute the structure of experience. They are presupposed in every experience; they do not lie within the range of experience and cannot be comprehended by it. The concepts and categories are *a priori* in the sense that they are presupposed in every experience. But they cannot be conceived as absolutely independent of experience, as they constitute its structure. So the propositions of metaphysics cannot be considered as purely abstract and analytic. The concepts and categories and the propositions which express their relationship cannot be conceived as merely abstract and analytic in nature. This being their nature, any *a priori* and unconditional application of the laws of logic, Identity, Contradiction etc., to determine the truth of relational concepts or categories has no rational justification.

The Mādhyamika commits a serious error in his application of the law of Contradiction in an *a priori* and unconditional way to determine the nature of the concepts of Identity and Difference and of the propositions which express their relationship. The propositions of Formal Logic called Contradictions, as has been pointed out before, are conceived as necessarily false, false under all circumstances and conditions. The Mādhyamika dialectic operates on the basis of this very assumption and as it finds the relation of Identity and Difference self-contradictory, it calls it false or unreal, and unceremoniously negates it and rejects it. All the relational categories, cause and effect, substance and attribute, subject and object etc., are thus called unreal and negated. The Mādhyamika here does not show any consciousness of the fact that, unlike the propositions of logic, the propositions of metaphysics do not belong to any of the two extremes, namely, tautologies and contradictions. This classification holds good only in the case of the propositions which are purely abstract and analytic in character. Such propositions are completely empty; they do not describe any fact or situation. They do not present any picture of reality. One can know *a priori* that the one proposition is true and the other is false. But one cannot determine *a priori* the truth or falsity of metaphysical propositions, as they refer to reality and present different pictures of it. Whether the two terms or concepts in a metaphysical proposition, are contradictory or not, can be determined only when they are judged in relation to the Absolute or Reality which constitutes their referent. It is quite possible that the two alternatives of a proposition which appear to be contradictory may not really be so; their apparent contradiction may be resolved in the all-embracing unity of the Absolute.

Thus it is clear that the Mādhyamika commits a grave error, firstly, in applying the law of Contradiction *a priori* to ascertain the truth of metaphysical propositions; secondly, in judging the truth of relational categories without any reference to Reality or the Absolute; and thirdly, in determining the nature of the concepts or categories and their relationship on the basis of the criterion of self-consistency. The principle of consistency can determine only the formal truth of propositions and not their material truth. So it cannot determine *a priori* the truth or falsity of metaphysical propositions, which provide knowledge of Reality. It cannot also determine the nature of metaphysical concepts and categories which, as has been pointed above, are not merely abstract and analytic in nature. Only purely abstract and analytic concepts, categories and propositions can enjoy the privilege of self-consistency and not others which are related to reality, empirical or transcendental. The Mādhyamika ignores these truths altogether. Thus his dialectical criticism of categories suffers from serious shortcomings, as mentioned above.

It is true that the principles of Identity, Contradiction etc. cannot be ignored in any valid reasoning. The conformity to these principles, as has been discussed before, is a precondition for all valid arguments, whether they deal with analytic propositions or other kinds of propositions. In this respect, these principles of logic condition existence. They also condition the propositions which are concrete and express the nature of objects or reality. If a proposition that describes some situation or a certain state of affairs is true, its opposite cannot be true. In this respect, the law of Contradiction conditions even the descriptive propositions and other propositions which are not purely abstract and analytic in nature. It conditions the metaphysical propositions as well. It is true of other principles of logic also. Their chief misuse lies, as has been discussed above, in their *a priori* and unconditional application to propositions which are directly or indirectly related to experience or reality. The Mādhyamika dialectic presents a glaring instance of this misuse of the fundamental principles of logic, specially, Identity and Contradiction.

Hegel's forceful criticism of the laws of Identity and Contradiction as interpreted in Formal logic applies equally well to

Mādhyamika also. The law of Identity, according to Hegel, expresses only a one-sided determinateness which has no truth; it contains only formal truth, which is abstract and incomplete. Truth, according to him, as has been pointed out before, "is complete only in the union of Identity with Variety, and therefore consists only in this unity". The Mādhyamika dialectic is purely analytic in character. It also makes identity into a one-sided determinateness. So, Hegel's criticism of this view of Identity applies with equal force to Mādhyamika also.

Hegel's interpretation of Contradiction also is radically different from that of Formal logic, as has been discussed above. Abstract self-identity has no life. A living unity in Hegel's view contains Contradiction within itself and also overcomes it. Hegel gives Contradiction a higher rank than Identity; he takes Contradiction as the profounder and more fully essential than Identity. He considers Contradiction as the "Negative in its essential determination, the principle of all self movement, which consists of nothing but an exhibition of Contradiction." Hegel lays great emphasis on the fact that Contradictions are reconciled in a unity. He does not consider contradictions or antinomies as irreconcilable in nature. Thought is dynamic and is possessed of the power to manifest itself in its opposite, to become other than what it is and to overcome the contradiction between itself and its 'other' or 'opposite'. Every thought has three moments—thesis, antithesis and synthesis; thus the opposites of thought are synthesised in a unity which constitutes their truth. Hegel conceives Contradictions as inherent in reality; but they are reconciled in it. Reality has the power to become other than what it is and also to overcome the opposition, as has been pointed out above. Thought presents this very picture of reality. The Sāṁkhya theory of Identity between cause and effect expresses this very nature of reality. The contradiction between cause and effect or Identity and difference is reconciled in the unity of reality. The Mādhyamika dialectic, being purely abstract and analytic in character, does not possess the capacity to reconcile the apparent opposition between Identity and Difference and so, it has no other way but to characterise their relationship as false or unreal. It passes the same judgment in respect of other relational categories also.

The Mādhyamika dialectic is based on the presupposition that whatever is contradictory is false or unreal. This presupposition can be sustained only if thought is accepted as purely abstract and analytic in character. It constitutes, in fact, only one aspect of thought and not of thought as a whole. Thought is not only abstract and analytic, but also concrete and dynamic. The abstract and analytic thought operates in an *a priori* and unconditional way, as has been repeatedly pointed out, and with full justification, in the fields of Logic, Mathematics and purely deductive sciences. But its extension and *a priori* and unconditional application in the field of experience or in respect of reality has no rational or logical justification, as has been shown above. So the contention of the Mādhyamika that whatever is contradictory is false and unreal cannot be accepted as true. There is no necessary connection between Contradiction and falsity or unreality. One does not necessarily follow from the other, as the Contradiction between opposites may only be apparent and not real. So the Mādhyamika view of Contradiction itself cannot be held as true. The relations between categories cannot be treated as unreal or false on the basis of this questionable interpretation of Contradiction. Caird has shown that "thought is not only distinction, it is at the same time relation. If it marks off one thing from another, it at the same time connects one thing with another". To quote him again, "If therefore, the law of contradiction be taken as asserting the self-identity of things or thoughts in a sense that excludes their community—in other words, if it be not taken as limited by another law which asserts the relativity of things or thoughts distinguished—it involves a false abstraction. A half-truth is necessarily distorted into a falsehood when taken as a whole truth."

The Mādhyamika simply asserts the self-identity of things or thoughts and excludes their community. He ignores altogether another law which asserts the relativity of things or thoughts distinguished. Thus his interpretation of the laws of identity and Contradiction and of thought itself involves a false abstraction. It is one-sided and contains only a half-truth. He commits a serious error in taking it as a whole truth. The Mādhyamika interpretation of the law of Contradiction suffers from this grave error or shortcoming. It cannot be considered as true. So his judgment that the theory of identity of cause and effect is self-contradictory and false and all the relational categories are false or unreal, involves a false abstraction and cannot be considered as true. From this it follows that the Mādhyamika has no rational justification in negating and rejecting the relational categories by calling them false or unreal. It is true that cause and effect, substance and attribute, whole and parts, subject and object etc., are mutually dependent, relative; they are not things-in-themselves. But from this, it does not necessarily follow that they are false or unreal. Mutual dependence and relativity of things cannot be considered as the criteria of falsity, as the Mādhyamika contends. The different philosophical theories developed about the relationship of cause and effect, substance and attribute etc. may be proved to be self-contradictory and false. But from this it does not follow, that their relationship itself can be treated as false or unreal.

Now a question arises: how is it that none of the philosophical theories is able to explain the relation between cause and effect etc. in a thoroughly adequate and satisfactory way. John Blyth has thrown a good light on this fundamental issue, as we have discussed earlier. He says that modern developments in logic have made it clear that there is no necessary connection between a formal system of logic and the entities to which we try to apply a system.[1] He also makes a very significant observation, "it is no longer plausible to assume that the so-called laws of any one system of logic are identical with the laws of all relational thought and the laws of things." It means that if certain relations between objects in experience do not conform to the order of some logical system, it cannot be said that those relations are unintelligible or false. A system of logic may be developed which may explain relations between objects in experience in an intelligible and rational way.

(L) *Is Negation in the Mādhyamika Dialectic Significant?*
From what we have discussed above, it is clear that Negation in the Mādhyamika dialectic cannot be considered as Significant. In order to be treated as Significant, Negation must contribute something positive to knowledge. But Negation in the Mādhyamika system means a bare denial or exclusion. It is simply a rejection of views which are found to be riddled with self-contradiction. Dr. Murti observes, "Negation has to be understood only in the context of the correction of an error or the cancellation of an illusion. It is admittedly more subjective than affirmation."[2] He

---

1. *Op. cit.*, p. 166.
2. *Op. cit.*, p. 155.

further observes, "Affirmation and negation do not stand on the same footing, and the demand to have something positive in negation is not to understand it correctly. Negative judgment is the *negation of judgment*, and not one more judgment. It is on a higher level of self-consciousness. In affirming we need not be conscious of the affirmation; in negating we are necessarily conscious of the negating function. The two, affirmation and negation, cannot be taken as co-ordinate and equal. They function in different ways."[1]

It is true that in negating one is necessarily conscious of the negating function. But this fact does not make a negative judgment the *negation of judgment*. Bosanquet himself says that negation is the conscious expression of difference. Though negation is more subjective than affirmation, yet it has a clear objective reference. It is not of something purely subjective. A judgment that is negated refers to some fact of experience or provides a view of reality. So it cannot be treated as something purely subjective. It means that the negated cannot be considered as "purely subjective, an appearance". Bosanquet holds that negation is an expression of difference; it is not simply a bare denial or contradiction. He conceives negation in its pure form as simple contradiction, as the abstraction of difference. Difference becomes contradiction when it is treated as abstraction of difference or as mere difference without identity. The Mādhyamika dialectic treats difference as abstraction of difference and so it finds the relationship of Identity and difference, self-contradictory and false. It treats contrary terms as contradictories and negates them. It is a purely formal negation. It does not contribute anything positive to knowledge. Negation, according to Bosanquet, can have no bearing unless the contraries are limited, so that something follows from the negation. Bare denial means nothing. Bosanquet observes, "Thus it appears that bare denial, whether disguised as spurious affirmation, or taken as the mere exclusion of suggested predicates amounts in the strict sense to nothing. The judgments by which it is typified are the exact counterparts of absolute tautology, and like such tautology, are not really judgments at all."[2] The negative judgment of the Mādhyamika

---

1. *Op. cit.*, p. 155.
2. *Logic*, Vol. I, p. 283.

belongs to this category. It is an exact counterpart of absolute tautology and hence is no judgment at all. The Mādhyamikas themselves admit that the negative judgment is the negation of judgment and not one more judgment. Negation in the Mādhyamika dialectic, as has been pointed, above, is a bare denial or exclusion. Here identity and difference fall apart and thereby the conditions of intelligible judgment are destroyed. The Mādhyamika himself is responsible for destroying the conditions which make judgment intelligible. Identity and difference appear to be irreconcilable only when the former is conceived as a mere tautology and the latter as a bare denial or contradiction. The Mādhyamika dialectic moves between the two poles of Tautology and Contradiction. It constitutes its chief shortcoming, as has been shown above. Its criticism of the relational categories suffers from this grave error. On the basis of the *a priori* application of the laws of Identity and Contradiction, the Mādhyamika dialectic negates and rejects the different theories of reality. Thus its function is merely negative. It does not provide any knowledge of reality. So it is clear that negation in the Mādhyamika dialectic is simply formal. It cannot be treated as significant.

Sri Aurobindo does not interpret negation in the sense of rejection of all differences and determinations. Negation signifies transcendence and not denial of determinations. The indeterminability of the Absolute does not deprive it of its power of self-determination. Both are, according to Sri Aurobindo, complementary to each other. They cannot be considered as contradictories. Difference becomes contradiction when it is viewed as mere difference or abstraction of difference.

Sri Aurobindo shows full awareness of the nature and implications of negation and so he does not conceive it in the sense of denial or rejection of attributes and determinations. Negation, according to him, is significant as it provides the knowledge of the Absolute in all its integrality and depth. Sri Aurobindo has given a most authentic and profound interpretation of the Upaniṣadic view of the Absolute on the basis of his concept of higher reason or the Logic of the Infinite. A clear awareness of the limitations of the principles of Formal Logic and the shortcomings of dialectical reasoning enables one to have an adequate understanding and appreciation of the necessity of the higher reason or the Logic of the Infinite. The integral knowledge of the Absolute, on the logical level, is possible only on the basis of the higher reason or the Logic of the Infinite. This higher logic provides a strong rational foundation to Sri Aurobindo's Integral Advaitism.

Now, to understand the real implications and significance of Sri Aurobindo's Integral Advaitism, let us proceed, first, to consider his view of the supreme Reality or the Absolute.

PART II

THE ABSOLUTE

CHAPTER III

THE ABSOLUTE AS EXISTENCE

Our discussion of the general principles of Sri Aurobindo's Integral Advaitism and of the Logic of the Infinite gives us an insight into his conception of the Absolute or Brahman. The Absolute is, as we have pointed out in the preceding chapters, all-inclusive. It includes all the aspects of existence in its all-embracing unity and at the same time it transcends them all. Now we proceed to discuss the nature of the Absolute in detail and will show how it reconciles, according to Sri Aurobindo, all the apparently contradictory aspects of existence in its all-embracing unity.

The Absolute or Brahman manifests itself to our consciousness as an eternal and infinite Self-existence, Self-awareness, and Self-delight of being. So the highest and the best positive affirmation that the human consciousness can make of the Absolute is that it is Sacchidānanda. "The Unknowable knowing itself as Sachchidananda is the one supreme affirmation of Vedanta: it contains all the others or on it they depend. This is the one veritable experience that remains when all appearances have been accounted for negatively by the elimination of their shapes and coverings or positively by the reduction of their names and forms to the constant truth that they contain. For fulfilment of life or for transcendence of life, and whether purity, calm and freedom in the spirit be our aim or puissance, joy and perfection, Sachchidananda is the unknown, omnipresent, indispensable term for which the human consciousness, whether in knowledge and sentiment or in sensation and action, is eternally seeking."[1] In the conception of

1. *L.D.*, Vol. I, p. 56.

Saccidānanda, we find three terms, namely, *Sat* or existence, *Cit* or consciousness and *Ānanda* or bliss. But it does not mean that Saccidānanda is constituted of these three separate principles. The Absolute or Saccidānanda is an indivisible reality. What is called existence is also consciousness and what is consciousness is also bliss. But as these terms have got a special significance attached to them and throw a flood of light on the nature of Saccidānanda or the Absolute, we proceed to study the Absolute in these three aspects, as *Sat* or existence, *Cit* or consciousness, and *Ānanda* or bliss. According to Sri Aurobindo, Saccidānanda is not merely Existence, Consciousness and Bliss but it is also Power or Force. It is not merely *Cit* or Consciousness but it is also Consciousness-Force or *Cit-Śakti*. So we proceed to study Saccidānanda in its aspects of Existence, Consciousness-Force and Bliss. First of all we take up the aspect of *Sat* or Existence.

(A) *Existence—Its Nature and Significance*
Āruṇi, the great philosopher of the Upaniṣads, says that there is one Reality. It is one without a second. It is called by him *sat*.[1] "The world of multiplicity which is the object of man's experience is, according to him, rooted in *Sat* and has evolved out of it. So *Sat* is the substratum of the world. It is also its ultimate cause. Before the evolution of the world, there was, according to Āruṇi, *Sat* alone. It does not mean that *Sat* is not present after the evolution of the world. *Sat* is still there but it appears through innumerable names and forms and is made subject to all sorts of limitations and determinations. Instead of being viewed as the supremely Real and one without a second, it is now apprehended in an individualised condition. Our sense-experience does not perceive the supreme Reality or *Sat* in its pure state. It apprehends it, on the other hand, in the form of particular objects assuming different names and forms. So *Sat* presents itself to our sense-experience and intellect in a modified condition, that is, under the limitations of space, time and cause and under infinite determinations of names and forms, *nāma* and *rūpa*. Our sense-experience is not aware of any fundamental Reality or *Sat* underlying the

---

1. सदेव सोम्येदमग्रआसीदेकमेवाद्वितीयम् । (*Chān.* VI.2)

universe and constituting its essence."[1] As Sri Aurobindo observes "The senses and sense-mind know nothing whatever about any pure or absolute existence. All that our sense-experience tells us of, is form and movement. Forms exist but with an existence that is not pure, rather always mixed, combined, relative. When we go within ourselves, we may get rid of precise forms, but we cannot get rid of movement, of change. Motion of matter in space, motion of change in Time seem to be the condition of existence."[2]

Now a question arises, if *Sat* or Reality cannot be known in its pure state through our sense-experience, what is the ground of positing it at all? Are we not logically justified in denying its reality altogether? The answer is that our reason cannot logically deny the reality of pure Existence or *Sat.* The negation of the supreme Reality or *Sat* is not logically possible, as will be discussed subsequently. This is the unanimous view of the philosophers of the Vedānta. "Sad Brahman, Existence pure, indefinable, infinite, absolute," observes Sri Aurobindo, "is the last concept at which Vedantic analysis arrives in its view of the universe, the fundamental Reality which Vedantic experience discovers behind all the movement and formation which constitute the apparent reality".[3] This supreme truth is realised by man when he transcends his finitude and attains the unconditioned level of spiritual experience. Our sense-experience and thought are conditioned by space, and time, form and movement; hence our consciousness is not aware of the unconditioned Reality, *Sat* lying behind the phenomena and is prone to de .y its reality altogether. It regards movement alone as real and the spaceless, timeless pure existence as nothing but a fiction of mind. "Those who see only this world-energy can declare indeed that there is no such thing; our idea of an eternal stability, an immutable pure existence is a fiction of our intellectual conceptions starting from a false idea of the stable: for there is nothing that is stable; all is movement and our conception of the stable is only an artifice of our mental consciousness by which we secure a standpoint for dealing practically with the movement. It is easy to show that this is true in the movement itself. There is

---

1. R.S. Misra, *Studies in Philosophy and Religion,* p. 39.
2. *L.D.,* Vol. I, p. 85.
3. *Ibid.,* p. 85.

nothing there that is stable. All that appears to be stationary is only a block of movement, a formulation of energy at work which so affects our consciousness that it seems to be still, somewhat as the earth seems to us to be still, somewhat as a train in which we are travelling seems to be still in the midst of a rushing landscape."[1]

(i) Becoming or Process as Ultimately Real: Views of Modern Science, Hume, Bergson and the Buddhists

Some of the great systems of philosophy like that of Bergson, Heraclitus and the Buddhists have affirmed Becoming as the absolute reality and denied the reality of a pure immutable existence or *Sat* altogether. The modern science also has developed this view on the basis of experience and critical investigation of the phenomena of nature or the world-process. According to the modern scientific view, the occurrence of motion need not be accounted for. It assumes that the objects of the world are by their very nature in process. "According to Newton's first law of motion, every moving object continues to move in the same direction and with the same velocity unless it is prevented by external forces. It means that so far as motion is concerned, it needs no explanation. It is only change in the direction or velocity of motion that has to be explained. The notion of first cause is not admitted in the scientific view. According to it, there may be an infinite series of causes and effects with no first cause at all. If God is regarded as the cause of other things, then one may ask for the cause of God's existence as well. The modern mechanical science rejects the notion of ultimate causality altogether. It assumes the unending series of cause-effect relationships. The sequence of cause-effect relationship makes it obvious that one always remains within the sphere of particulars. The events have definite spatio-temporal locations. Hence the earliest cause in any such series of cause-effect relationships cannot be said to be ultimate and self-explanatory. It must be an effect of some equally particular event or set of events in the spatio-temporal process."[2]

"Hume also rejects the notion of a first cause of the world.

1. *L.D.*, Vol. I, p. 94.
2. R.S. Misra, *op. cit.*, p. 55.

According to him, one can trace a particular event to a particular cause on empirical grounds. But one cannot posit God or unconditioned Reality as the cause of the world as a whole on the basis of experience. If we take a chain of twenty events, the first will be the cause of the second, the second of the third and so on. The first will be the effect of the last event in some preceding series. Now in this case, each event in the series has been explained. We do not feel constrained to raise the question about the first cause of the series of events."[1] As Hume observes, "In such a chain or succession of objects, each part is caused by that which preceded it, and causes that which succeeds it—But the whole, you say, wants a cause. I answer, that the uniting of these parts into a whole, like the uniting of several distinct countries into one kingdom, or several distinct members into one body, is performed merely by an arbitrary act of the mind, and has no influence on the nature of things. Did I show you the particular causes of each individual in a collection of twenty particles of matter; I shall think it very unreasonable, should you afterwards ask me, what was the cause of the whole twenty. That is sufficiently explained in explaining the cause of the parts."[2] Thus Hume does not conceive any necessity of positing a changeless Reality as the cause of the world-process.

Bergson also conceives Reality as change or Becoming. The universe is a stream of continual change or becoming. There is nothing that can be called permanent and unchanging behind the subjective and objective orders of existence. Things which appear to be motionless and possessed of qualities are subject to incessant change. On scientific analysis, the so-called static objects resolve themselves into a stream of elementary movements. One may characterise them as vibrations, as ether waves, as electrons and so on. But behind this stream of elementary movements, one does not find any entity that is found to endure through different moments and in which the changes and movements take place. Change alone is real. There is no 'thing' or 'entity' which changes. The individual self is also, according to Bergson, merely a name given to a ceaseless flux of ideas. Our consciousness is changing

1. R.S. Misra, op. cit., p. 55.
2. Dialogues Concerning Natural Religion, Part IX.

every moment. To say that there is something that undergoes change will mean that it is itself other than change. But such a thing is never discerned. The universe is thus one continuous flow, a process, a becoming. Change is the reality of the spatio-temporal world. It is equally the reality of man.

Buddhism also has formulated a philosophy of change. According to the Buddhist view, there is nothing permanent either in the material world or in the vital and mental orders of existence. From the concept of change, the Buddhists have developed the doctrine of momentariness. All things are momentary in nature. The whole world is resolved into ceaseless flux of *dharmas*. What is called self is nothing but a stream of mental *dharmas*. The emergence and disappearance of things are governed by a causal law, called *Pratītyasamutpāda* or the Law of Dependent Origination. This law operates in an automatic way. There is no conscious agency working behind it and governing the temporal process or becoming. According to this law, when a particular thing or event comes into existence, it is followed by another thing or event. On the cause appearing, the effect follows. Every event is conditioned by its preceding event in the series and gives rise to its succeeding event. Thus there is a continuity of the series and not of any unchanging entity. Reality is of the nature of incessant flux or change. It is a stream of becoming.

(ii) *Criticism of the Theories of Becoming*
We do not here propose to give a detailed criticism of the different theories that conceive change or becoming as ultimately real. We shall simply point out some basic difficulties that are inherent in this view and that prove its inadequacy to explain, in a logically satisfactory way, the nature of reality.

"The first objection that can be raised against the theory of change is that, in the absence of conscious Reality or Being guiding and controlling the Process or Becoming, the aggregation of objects is not possible. The emergence of objects out of the events constituting the series or process cannot be accounted for; because the factors or events are themselves non-sentient[1] and also because

1. समुदायिनामचेतनत्वात् । (*S.B.* II.2.18)

no conscious Being or Reality is admitted by the different theories of Becoming as the knower and the controller of the process that could bring about conglomerations.[1] The factors constituting the series cannot themselves account for the emergence of the subjective and the objective orders of existence. One event in the series may give rise to another event. But the preceding event cannot account for the appearance or emergence of objects possessed of different qualities and functions. The emergence of aggregates out of the flux of events cannot be explained. An earlier event, as Śaṅkara observes, may become the cause of just the origination of a later event of the series.[2] It cannot act as cause of the emergence of conglomerations.[3] It may be said that conglomerations or objects themselves constitute the series and one object gives rise to another object. Then the question is, what is the order or rule of succession? A preceding object of the series may give rise to another object of a similar nature or of dissimilar nature.[4] If an earlier object of the series gives rise to another object of the similar nature, then the process of growth and development cannot be explained. The emergence of objects possessed of new qualities or function cannot be explained on this theory. And there will also arise the contingency of unnecessary duplication of things in an unending manner. If, on the other hand, an object of the preceding moment produces an object or effect of a dissimilar nature, then there will arise the contingency of anything being produced out of anything else. And this theory will be subjected to all the criticisms that are made against the *asatkāryavāda*."[5]

The arguments given above make it clear that the emergence of objects cannot be explained on the theory of an unending succession of contingent things constituting a series or process. Contingent things are relative and dependent; they are not self-sufficient. They serve as pointer to a Reality which is beyond space and time and is possessed of supreme consciousness. It alone can provide a rational explanation of the world-process. Unless a first cause exists, "no productive efficiency is actually at work by which

1. अन्यस्य च कस्य चिच्चेतनस्य भोक्तुः प्रशासितुर्वा स्थिरस्य संहन्तुरनभ्युपगमात्. . . . । (S.B. II.2.19)
2. उत्पत्तिमात्रनिमित्तत्वात् । (S.B. II.2.19)
3. न तु संघातोत्पत्तेः किञ्चित्तुनिमित्तं सम्भवति । (S.B. II.2.19)
4. Ibid.
5. Studies in Philosophy and Religion, pp. 58-59.

the effect immediately dependent on it can come into being; no subsequent effects can thus arise; thus, in this event, nothing can exist at all. The supposition of an infinite regress might permit prediction of later events in terms of earlier ones, but it would provide no real explanation of the actual production of any event nor of its having the nature that it does, for nowhere in such a regress do we come upon a cause which we can be sure is really engaged in making its effect arise. All in that case is hypothetical; each effect would exist if its own cause, about which we do not yet know, should have really existed and been able to produce it".[1]

So we may conclude that Becoming or Process is not self-explanatory. The nature of the physical world, of the living beings, cannot be adequately explained on the theory of Becoming as the absolute reality.

(iii) Self or 'I' Inexplicable in Terms of Becoming

"When we take up the problem of self and examine its implications, the inadequacy of the different theories of Becoming becomes more glaring and evident. The phenomenon of remembrance necessitates the acceptance of a self or subject who endures through different moments of experience. The subject who experiences a thing or an event and who remembers it must be one and the same. The statement that 'I saw Mr. X the other day and I am seeing him now' is not possible without the continuance of the self throughout that period. Only a self that continues through different moments of time can make an evaluation of its past experiences. If the self itself were constituted of discrete mental states involved in ceaseless flux or change, the facts of remembrance and evaluation of past experiences would not be possible. So one has to posit the identity of self through the different moments of time."[2]

"The existence of self cannot be explained in terms of any other category of experience. It cannot be resolved into a stream of ideas. So far as the existence of self or 'I' is concerned, it is self-evident. I can significantly ask what I am. It makes no sense to

---

1. E.A. Burtt, *Types of Religious Philosophy*, p. 105.
2. *Studies in Philosophy and Religion*, pp. 60-61.

ask *whether* I am, because the very question presupposes my own existence."

"Being or existence is experienced in its true form in the case of self alone. This experience of self is primary or basic. One may not know *what* the self is. But one does know that it *is*. The experience of self is free from all determinations, all relations. The notion that I *exist* presupposes all the notions about the *nature* of my existence. This awareness of my own existence does not depend on any relations in which I stand. It is also not dependent on any of the attributes that may be predicated of 'I'. Thus, the concept of 'I' transcends all determinations, all relations. It cannot be explained in terms of cause-effect relationship. The notion of the stream of ideas presupposes the existence of 'I'. So this 'I' cannot be explained in terms of the stream of ideas. It cannot be reduced to anything other than itself. It cannot be adequately explained by any theory which regards, 'motion', 'process' or becoming as the ultimate Reality."[1]

The theories of Reality as Becoming or Process breakdown altogether in the case of self or 'I'. "Even if the physical objects were reduced to modes, sense-data, relations etc., the self or 'I' remains in its pure form. An object is not apprehended apart from its qualities and relations to other objects and to self. An object out of all relations to other objects and to self is apparently reduced to nothing. Its very existential character is to be explained in terms of its relations and determinations. But this necessity does not arise in the case of self. The existence of self gives meaning to all our experience. But it does not, as has been stated above, owe its existence to anything other than itself. Thus, unlike the objects, the self is not reduced to nothing, when viewed apart from its relations and determinations."[2] In the state of pure existence, the self may not be characterised as 'this' or 'that' but its very existence is something fundamental. Thus the existence of self, *ātman* is something undeniable and self-evident. This undeniable fact strengthens immeasurably the Vedāntic position which conceives Being or *Sat* as constituting the substratum of 'becoming', of spatio-temporal world.

---

1. *Studies in Philosophy and Religion*, pp. 61-62.
2. *Ibid.*, p. 62.

The Vedānta does not regard Becoming as the absolute Reality. It regards Becoming as not absolute in itself, but as a movement of Being, *Sat.* Sri Aurobindo holds this Vedāntic view. He says, "The very conception of movement carries with it the potentiality of repose and betrays itself as an activity of some existence; the very idea of energy in action carries with it the idea of energy abstaining from action; and an absolute energy not in action is simply and purely absolute existence."[1]

(iv) *Negation of Being: An Impossibility*
Thus the Pure Existence cannot be regarded as a product of imagination or as subordinate to Becoming or movement. It is the Absolute underlying the phenomena and constituting its essence. According to the Vedānta and Sri Aurobindo, thought is constrained to posit the reality of pure existence or the Absolute in order to understand the rationale of the world-process. As Sri Aurobindo remarks, "Neither reason nor experience nor intuition nor imagination bears witness to us of the possibility of a final terminus. All end and beginning presuppose something beyond the end or beginning. An absolute end, an absolute beginning is not only a contradiction in terms, but a contradiction of the essence of things, a violence, a fiction. Infinity imposes itself upon the appearances of the finite by its ineffugable self-existence".[2]

So it is clear that our reason cannot logically deny the reality of pure existence or the Absolute. The system of Śaṅkara which denies the reality of everything else from the metaphysical standpoint posits the fundamental reality of the pure Existence. "We may think away anything, but we cannot think away Being or Existence. Existence is therefore Truth. And in the effort of doing away with Existence, we are conscious of our tacitly assuming it. We can dismiss qualities or attributes of Being, or concrete forms of it, but we cannot put away Existence. The very thought of denial presupposes it. Existence or Being is the ultimate Reality. In fact, the existence of concrete things and appearances implies the notion of existence. Brahman is Existence."[3] Śaṅkara says that one can

1. *L.D.,* Vol. I, pp. 95-96.
2. *Ibid.,* pp. 94-95.
3. M.N. Sirkar, *The System of Vedāntic Thought and Culture,* p. 3.

call a thing unreal only on the ground of something real.[1] Brahman
is called in the scripture the Truth of truths or the Being of all
beings.[2] Another scripture says, one who calls Brahman non-existent
himself becomes non-existent.[3] Brahman as Existence is the
underlying Reality of both the cosmos and the individuals. It is the
Self of the individuals. To deny the reality of pure Existence is to
deny the reality of one's Self which is impossible. The Ātman or
Self, says Śaṅkara, is the essential nature of him who denies it.[4]
Śaṅkara observes that every one is aware of his own Self, no one
thinks that he is not.[5] "The note of scepticism," observes Dr.
Radhakrishnan, "finds its limit in regard to the self, of which we
are immediately conscious".[6] Descartes established the reality of
Self by his famous statement *Cogito Ergo Sum*, meaning 'I think
therefore I am'. But unlike the author of *Cogito ergo sum*, Śaṅkara
does not hold that the existence of Self is guaranteed by the process
of thinking. The existence of Self does not depend on thinking.
As Dr. Radhakrishnan puts it, "If the 'I am' depends on an 'I think',
the 'I think' must also depend on another ergo, and so on, and
it will land us in infinite regress."[7] Hence the knowledge of Self
is prior to all thinking. The existence of Self is, according to Śaṅkara,
not subject to any proof.[8] It is the ground of all proofs, so it is
not itself subject to any proof.[9] Sri Aurobindo agrees with Śaṅkara
in the view that self or Existence is the substratum of all existences,
the cosmic as well as the individual.

(v) *Non-Being: Not a Negation of Being*
It may be said that the scriptures also propound the theory of a
Non-Being or *Asat* which goes against the theory which regards
Being or Existence as the ultimate nature of Reality. The Upaniṣad

1. किंचिद्धि परमार्थमालम्ब्यापरमार्थ: प्रतिषिध्यते । (*S.B.* 3.2.22)
2. सत्यस्य सत्यम् । (*Brh.* 2.1.20.111.6)
3. असन्नेव स भवति, असद् ब्रह्मेति वेद चेत् । (*Tait.* 2.6.1)
4. य एव हि निराकर्ता तदेव तस्य स्वरूपम् । (*S.B.* 2.3.7)
5. सर्वो ह्यात्मास्तित्वं प्रत्येति, न नाहमस्मीति । (*S.B.* 1.1.1)
6. *Indian Philosophy*, Vol. II, p. 476.
7. *An Idealist View of Life*, p. 140.
8. न ह्यात्मा आत्मन: प्रमाणमपेक्ष्य सिध्यति । (*S.B.* 2.3.7)
9. आत्मा तु प्रमाणादिव्यवहाराश्रयत्वात् प्रागेव ।
   प्रमाणादिव्यवहारात् सिध्यति । (*S.B.* 2.3.7)

says, 'Formerly there was only Non-Being or *Asat*. And out of that Non-Being, Being appeared.'[1] But Sri Aurobindo remarks that Non-Being or *Asat* does not really mean a non-existent, a zero or negation of being. "Non-Being is only a word. When we examine the facts it represents, we can no longer be sure that absolute non-existence has any better chance than the infinite Self of being more than an ideative formation of the mind. We really mean by this Nothing something beyond the last term to which we can reduce our purest conception and our most abstract or subtle experience of actual being as we know or conceive it while in the universe. This Nothing then is merely something beyond positive conception. We erect a fiction of nothingness in order to overpass, by the method of total exclusion, all that we can know and consciously are. Actually when we examine closely the Nihil of certain philosophies, we begin to perceive that it is a zero which is All or an indefinable Infinite which appears to the mind a blank, because mind grasps only finite constructions, but is in fact the only true Existence"[2]. The Upaniṣad calls the Absolute, Non-Being or *Asat* only to show that it is beyond all our mental categories. Our highest and purest mental conceptions of Being cannot give us a correct idea of what the pure Existence of the Absolute is. Thus Non-Being or *Asat* is not opposed to Being or *Sat*. Non-Being is simply Being transcending all mental categories.

The word Non-Being or *Asat* has given rise to a great deal of misunderstanding in our philosophical literature. The Mādhyamika conception of *Śūnya* has been generally misunderstood by the thinkers of the other Indian schools. The *Śūnya* of the Mādhyamikas has been taken to mean *Nihil* or Void. But some of the great modern scholars give a different interpretation to the word *Śūnya*. According to these scholars, the Absolute of Nāgārjuna is not a *nihil* or Void but is something which transcends all finite categories. Sri Aurobindo agrees with this view. So the apparent contradiction between the terms Being and Non-Being disappears if we take Non-Being to mean not the negation of being but a Being transcending all finite or mental categories. The word Non-Being or *Asat* gave rise to some misunderstanding even in the

---

1. असद्वा इदमग्र आसीत् । ततो वै सदजायत । (*Tait.* 2.7)
2. *L.D.*, Vol. I, pp. 35-36.

Upaniṣads. One Upaniṣad says, as has been stated above, that formerly there was Non-Being or *Asat* and out of it Being was born. Another Upaniṣad says, how can Being be born out of Non-Being? Being can only come out of Being and not out of Non-Being.[1] "But if we take Non-Being in the sense, not of an inexistent Nihil but of an *X* which exceeds our idea or experience of existence,—a sense, applicable to the Absolute Brahman of the Adwaita as well as the Void or Zero of the Buddhists, the impossibility disappears, for That may very well be the source of being, whether by a conceptual or formative Maya or a manifestation or creation out of itself."[2]

Thus we cannot by any reasoning deny the reality of Being. "The concept of absolute negation is impossible, for so deep and intimate is our conception of Being that any such thought in itself cannot possibly arise.....Negation can only refer to some portion of Being, but becomes entirely meaningless when attributed to Being in its integrity and universality. Absolute non-Being is not thinkable."[3] "Even the illusory structure," says Dr. Radhakrishnan, "cannot be sustained in the atmosphere of a Void. All negation depends on a hidden affirmation. Absolute negation is impossible. Total scepticism is a figment, since such scepticism implies the validity of the sceptic's judgment".[4] One may call the Absolute *Asat* or *Śūnya* but these words do not signify, as has been stated above, a complete negation of being but its complete transcendence of all mental categories. Existence or Being, as has been shown above, is the foundational reality. It is the foundation or the substratum of all Becoming, of the individual and cosmic existence. But the Absolute is not the kind of being or existence which we experience in the world. Its existence is not like that of the objects existing within space and time. Hence it may be called even *Asat* or *Śūnya* from this particular standpoint.

(B) *Existence or Being as Unknowable*
Sri Aurobindo calls the Absolute or pure Existence unknowable. But it only means that the Absolute cannot be known by our

---

1. कथमसतः सज्ञायेतेति । सत्त्वेव सोम्येदमग्र आसीदेकमेवाद्वितीयम् । (*Chān.* 6.2.2)
2. *L.D.*, Vol. I, p. 36 (Footnotes).
3. M.N. Sirkar, *op. cit.*, p. 4.
4. *Indian Philosophy*, Vol. I, p. 662.

sense-experience and thought. Our sense-experience is aware of the objects of the world and works under the limitations of Space and Time. Our reason is constrained, as has been shown above, to posit the existence of the Absolute as the substratum and the foundation of individual and cosmic existence. But our reason cannot directly and immediately realise the Absolute. This does not mean that the Absolute is altogether unknowable. The Absolute can be known and realised by our spiritual and supramental consciousness. So, whereas the Absolute is unknowable to our sense-experience and reason, it is not unknowable to the higher states of consciousness, the spiritual and the supramental consciousness, which can be attained by man in the course of evolution. "It is indefinable and inconceivable," remarks Sri Aurobindo, "by finite and defining Mind; it is ineffable by a mind created speech; it is describable neither by our negations, *neti neti*—for we cannot limit it by saying it is not this, it is not that, nor by our affirmations, for we cannot fix it by saying it is this, it is that, *iti iti*. And yet, though in this way unknowable to us, it is not altogether and in every way unknowable; it is self-evident to itself and, although inexpressible, yet self-evident to a knowledge by identity of which the spiritual being in us must be capable; for that spiritual being is in its essence and its original and intimate reality not other than this Supreme Existence".[1] As the term Non-Being does not, according to Sri Aurobindo, mean the negation of Being, so the term Unknowable does not mean that the Absolute is altogether unknown and unknowable by human knowledge as such, as the agnostics would have us believe.

(i) *Sri Aurobindo's and Kant's View of the Unknowable Compared*

In this respect Sri Aurobindo's view of the Unknowable differs entirely from that of Kant, Spencer and other agnostics. Whereas Kant and Spencer hold that as the Absolute cannot be realised by sense and intellect or reason, so it must always remain unknown and unknowable, Sri Aurobindo maintains that though the Absolute cannot be realised by sense and reason, it can be realised by other processes of knowledge, namely, Intuition and supramental

1. *L.D.*, Vol. II, Part I, pp. 33-34.

consciousness. Sri Aurobindo agrees with Kant and Spencer insofar as they show the incapacity of intellect to grasp the Absolute. Kant makes a critical analysis of the conditions of human knowledge and comes to the conclusion that human beings on account of their congenital incapacity are unable to know the Absolute. All human knowledge, according to him, is conditioned by space, time and other categories. We see things or objects not as they are in themselves but as they appear to us through space, time and other categories. So the human knowledge remains confined to the phenomena and does not know the noumena or things in themselves. Our reason cannot make any judgment about things in themselves. It cannot even say whether things in themselves exist of not. Reason cannot make any positive assertion about God, soul and immortality. Whenever reason tries to pass beyond phenomena and make any judgment with regard to these problems, it is involved in antinomies and contradictions. The categories of the understanding can be applied, according to Kant, only in the region of space and time and not beyond it. Thus Kant confines human knowledge to the region of phenomena or appearance and anything transcending the phenomenal would ever remain for it unknown and unknowable.

Here Sri Aurobindo differs entirely from Kant. According to him Kant is right insofar as he shows the incapacity of the intellect to know the Absolute or things in themselves, but he is perfectly wrong in denying the capacity of knowledge as such to know the Absolute. Apart from intellect, there are other and higher sources of knowledge available to man through which he can realise the Absolute. Man has, according to him, the power to transcend the level of sense and intellect and attain a higher level of consciousness called intuition and supramental consciousness. Kant thinks that by his denial of the capacity of reason to know the Absolute, God, soul etc. he has saved the realm of religion from the encroachments of materialism, scepticism etc. For, if the existence of God cannot be proved by reason, it also cannot be disproved by it. If our knowledge is only phenomenal, reason can have no more right to deny the reality of God than it has to affirm it. As Kant puts it, "I cannot share the opinion so frequently expressed by excellent and thoughtful men who, being fully conscious of the weakness of the proofs hitherto advanced, indulge in a hope that the future would supply us with evident demonstrations of the two cardinal propositions of pure reason, namely, that there is a God, and that there is a future life. I am certain, on the contrary, that this will never be the case....But there is the same apodictic certainty that no man will ever arise to assert the *contrary* with the smallest plausibility, much less dogmatically. For, as he could prove it by means of pure reason only, he would have to prove that a Supreme Being, and that a thinking subject within us as pure intelligence, is *impossible.* But whence will he take the knowledge that would justify him in thus judging synthetically on things far beyond all possible experience? We may, therefore, rest so completely assured that no one will ever really prove the opposite, that there is no need to invent any scholastic arguments."[1]

Thus, Kant finally cries halt to all metaphysical speculations. One can, according to him, give cogent and equally strong arguments for and against such problems as God, world, soul and immortality. As far as pure logic is concerned, these contradictory arguments appear to be equally sound. But the very fact that they contradict each other shows that we have entered a realm where we have no means of knowing anything, where truth cannot be attained by means of logic. As Kant observes, "Both parties beat the air and fight with their own shadows, because they go beyond the limits of nature, where there is nothing they could lay hold of with their dogmatical grasp. They may fight to their heart's content, the shadows which they are cleaving grow together again in one moment, like the heroes in Valhalla, in order to disport themselves once more in these bloodless contests."[2] The categories of the understanding by means of which one comes to have the knowledge of the world are empirically real but transcendentally ideal. They yield valuable and fruitful results only so long as they deal with sense perception or sense-experience. But they become the fruitful source of deception and illusion the moment they try to assert anything about what Kant calls the 'Ideas of Pure Reason,' namely God, the universe and the soul. All our hair-splitting discussion about such questions arises, according to Kant "simply from our filling the gap, due to our ignorance, with paralogisms of reason, and by changing thoughts into things and

---

1. *Critique of Pure Reason,* Max Müller's Translation, p. 595.
2. *Ibid.,* p. 607.

hypostasising them. On this an imaginary science is built up, both by those who assert and by those who deny, some pretending to know about objects of which no human being has any conception, while others make their own representations to be objects, all turning round in a constant circle of ambiguities and contradictions. Nothing but a sober, strict, and just criticism can free us of this dogmatical illusion, which, through theories and systems, deceives so many by an imaginary happiness. It alone can limit our speculative pretensions to the sphere of possible experience, and this not by a shallow scoffing at repeated failures, or by pious sighs over the limits of our reason, but by a demarcation made according to well-established principles, writing the *nihil ulterius* with perfect assurance on those Herculean columns which Nature herself has erected in order that the voyage of reason should be continued so far only as the continuous shores of experience extend—shores which we can never forsake without being driven up on a boundless ocean, which, after deceiving us again and again, makes us in the end cease all our laborious and tedious endeavours as perfectly hopeless".[1]

So it is clear that our abstract logical reason does not enable us to attain any insight into the world of supersensible realities. But it does not mean that the greatest ideas and conceptions that humanity has cherished so long about God, soul, freedom and immortality have no importance and utility for human life. These ideas are imperatively necessary for man's moral and spiritual life. Kant has not denied the existence of the thing-in-itself, of the soul, and of God, but only the possibility of proving the reality of these ideas by means of reason. "True, he combats spiritualistic dogmatism, but the same blow that brings it down overthrows materialism; and though he attacks theism, he likewise demolishes the dogmatic pretensions of the atheists. What he combats to the utmost and pitilessly destroys is the dogmatism of theoretical reason, under whatever form it may present itself, whether as theism or atheism, spiritualism or materialism; is its assumption of authority in the system of our faculties; is the prejudice which attributes metaphysical capacity to the understanding, isolated from the will and

---

1. *Critique of Pure Reason*, (Max Müller's Translation) pp. 319-20.

depending on its own resources. By way of retaliation and here he reveals the depth of his philosophic faith—he concedes a certain metaphysical capacity to practical reason, i.e., to will."[1]

So the Absolute cannot be known by reason, but it can be realised through another avenue of approach, namely, moral will. The Absolute cannot be an object of knowledge but it can be an object of moral will and faith. It is necessary to postulate God, freedom etc. in order to satisfy the demands of the moral law. The moral law demands the actuality of freedom. The moral law or what Kant calls the categorical imperative, claims to be absolute and universal. It asks us to act unconditionally without regard to any considerations save the moral 'ought'. And man can act in accordance with the dictates of the categorical imperative only when he is free, when he can do what he ought to do. So freedom is the necessary prerequisite of the validity of the moral life. But, as man as a part of the phenomenal world is governed by the causal laws, by determinism and necessity in all his acts, so there must be another and higher realm, the noumenal realm where man enjoys the freedom which the moral life demands. Thus man as a natural and intellectual being belongs to the world of sense and suffers from bondage and as a moral being is a member of the intelligible world and enjoys full freedom. "The explanation of the possibility of categorical imperatives, then, is, that the idea of freedom makes me a member of the intelligible world. Were I a member of no other world, all my actions would as a matter of fact always conform to the autonomy of the will. But as I perceive myself to be a member of the world of sense, I can say only, that my actions *ought* to conform to the autonomy of the will."[2] So the guarantee of the world of freedom or the intelligible world is given not by knowledge but by the realisation of the claims of the moral law. The abstract reason is thus subordinated by Kant to moral will or faith. In Kant's view there is no contradiction in man's being simultaneously a member of the two worlds—the world of sense and the intelligible world. "Morality requires us only to be able to think freedom without self-contradiction, not to understand it; it is enough that our conception of the act as free puts no obstacle

---

1. Weber, Alfred, *History of Philosophy*, Frank Thilly's Translation, pp. 463-64.
2. Selections from Kant, *The Metaphysic of Morality*, Watson's Translation, p. 225.

in the way of the conception of it as mechanically necessary, for the act stands in quite a different relation to freedom from that in which it stands to the mechanism of nature. From the critical point of view, therefore, the doctrine of morality and the doctrine of nature may each be true in its own sphere; which could never have been shown had not criticism previously established our unavoidable ignorance of things in themselves, and limited all that we *know* to mere phenomena. I have, therefore, found it necessary to deny *knowledge* of *God, freedom,* and *immortality,* in order to find a place for *faith.*[1] So what is denied by reason is accepted by faith. Thus we find a chasm, an unbridgeable gulf, between knowledge and faith in Kantian philosophy.

In Sri Aurobindo's system, we do not find any antagonism between what are called the phenomenal and the noumenal world, the world of necessity and the world of freedom. This is because, unlike Kant, he does not confine all human knowledge to phenomena. The intelligible world, God, soul, freedom and immortality are, according to him, not only articles of faith and belief, but they can be realised essentially and integrally through supramental consciousness. Thus Sri Aurobindo's conception of the unknowable differs fundamentally from that of Kant. Whereas for Kant, the Absolute remains forever unknown and unknowable, to Sri Aurobindo, it remains unknowable only to sense and reason and not to the higher sources of knowledge. Like Kant, Sri Aurobindo also shows the futility and bankruptcy of our formal and abstract reason or the finite reason so far as the knowledge of the higher realities is concerned. He declares like Kant in unmistakable terms that our unaided abstract and finite reason lands us into inevitable antinomies and contradictions. But unlike Kant, his criticism and analysis of the abstract and finite reason do not land him into agonsticism. Human knowledge in his view is not confined to sense-experience and reason. Man has the capacity to transcend the limitations of his consciousness and attain a higher consciousness, the spiritual and the supramental consciousness, which enable him to realise the Absolute in its essential or differenceless aspect and in its integral aspect.

1. Selections from Kant, *Critique of Pure Reason,* Preface, (Watson's Translation), p. 6.

(ii) *Sri Aurobindo's and Hamilton's View of the Unknowable Compared*

In this respect Sri Aurobindo differs from all other philosophers, like Hamilton, Mansel, Spencer etc. who, following in the footsteps of Kant, confine all knowledge to phenomena. The great contribution of Kant, as Hamilton conceives it, is his demonstration of our ignorance, complete and incurable, of ultimate reality. Since to know is to relate things to mind, that is, to bring it under the conditions of space, time and mental categories, it follows that the unrelated thing, thing-in-itself can never be known. What we know is the object mediated or conditioned by the subject, not the object as it is in itself. According to Kant, when we try to know ourselves we are involved in the same fatal circle of appearance and subjectivity. We know even ourselves as we appear to ourselves and not as we are in ourselves. According to Hamilton this agnosticism of Kant is identical with the Lockian doctrine of the inscrutability of substance, material and spiritual. In both cases alike, we know only the qualities, the appearance and not the substance or the thing-in-itself. "Mind and matter, as known or knowable, are only two different series of phenomena or qualities; mind and matter, as unknown and unknowable, are the two substances in which these two different series of phenomena or qualities are supposed to inhere. The existence of an unknown substance is only an inference we are compelled to make from the existence of known phenomena; and the distinction of two substances is only inferred from the seeming incompatibility of the two series of phenomena to coinhere in one."[1] In Hamilton's view, the source of our ignorance is not in fact the limitation of our faculties so much as the nature of knowledge itself. "Were the number of our faculties coextensive with the modes of being— had we for each of these thousand modes a separate organ competent to make it known to us—still would our whole knowledge be, as it is at present, only of the relative. Of existence absolutely and in itself, we should then be as ignorant as we are now."[2] Thus Hamilton lands us in despair with regard to the knowledge of the

---

1. *Lectures on Metaphysics*, i, 138.
2   *Ibid.*, i, 153.

Absolute or the Unconditioned. But he also concludes, with Kant, that though the knowledge of the Absolute or God is unattainable, yet belief or faith is both possible and necessary. In his view common sense and Intuition, aided by supernatural Revelation may assure us of those truths which lie beyond the sphere of knowledge.

(iii) Sri Aurobindo's and Henry Mansel's View of the Unknowable Compared

Henry Mansel also, following in the footsteps of Hamilton, contends that man's knowledge by its very nature is limited to the finite; so all the arguments put forward for asserting or denying the reality of the Infinite are futile and invalid. The true theology, according to him, is merely 'regulative' and practical, not 'speculative' or scientific. Man can apprehend God and his relation to Him through religious intuition or belief as distinguished from knowledge. Our feeling of dependence, our conviction of moral obligation suggest to us the power and goodness of God. Thus, according to Mansel, we form "regulative ideas of the Deity, which are sufficient to guide our practice, but not to satisfy our intellect; which tell us, not what God is in Himself, but how He wills that we should think of Him".[1] So instead of trying to have an intellectual apprehension of the supersensible realities, we must, according to him, rest satisfied with "the convictions forced upon us by our religious and moral instincts".[2] These convictions cannot be justified by reason and are superior to it. The idea of the Absolute, Hamilton argues, is not only inconceivable but self-contradictory. "In my language Absolute is not opposed to incomplete, but to relative, and means knowledge of an object as it is in itself, apart from its relation to human faculties."[3] Hence "a conception of the Deity, in His absolute existence, appears tc involve a self-contradiction; for conception itself is a limitation, and a conception of the absolute Deity is a limitation of the illimitable".[4]

1. *Limits of Religious Thought*, Bampton Lectures, 1858, p. 84.
2. *Metaphysics*, p. 375.
3. *Limits of Religious Knowledge* (Preface to 4th ed.), p. XXX, note.
4. *Metaphysics*, p. 298.

(iv) *Sri Aurobindo's and Herbert Spencer's View of the Unknowable Compared*

Herbert Spencer subscribes to the doctrine of relativity of knowledge as propounded by Hamilton and Mansel. It is possible, he thinks, to show that man by the very nature of his mind, is necessarily shut out from a knowledge of ultimate reality. We are as incompetent to think or know the Absolute as a deaf man to understand sounds. One can think of a thing only by relating it to another thing, by comparison. But Absolute reality, by definition, is not relative but absolute, and consequently it is beyond our grasp. On the other hand it is implied in all our relative knowledge, since the relative cannot be called relative if there were not something absolute to which it is contrasted. There is, according to Herbert Spencer, a dark region behind the phenomenal world, which he calls the Unknowable or the Absolute.

But it may be objected, if we are limited to phenomena how can we say that there is a dark region behind the phenomenal world? It is because our knowledge is not restricted or confined to the finite, that we come to know of the noumenal sphere. Herbert Spencer should have admitted that only by the knowledge of the Infinite, we know the finite. But then it would have been giving up his agnosticism altogether. The proper conclusion of Herbert Spencer will be or must be that there is no Absolute or the search for the Absolute is meaningless. If the idea of the Absolute is implied in all our relative knowledge, then there is no sense in calling the Absolute unknowable. If on the other hand, knowledge can never reach the Absolute, as Spencer would have us believe, then he has no logical justification even to assert the existence of the Absolute. In this respect Kant's position is better, as he contends that the reality of the Absolute can neither be affirmed nor denied on purely rational grounds.

In the doctrine of the unknowableness of the ultimate reality, Spencer finds a way to reconcile Religion and Science. As he puts it, "If Religion and Science are to be reconciled, the basis of reconciliation must be this deepest, widest, and most certain of all facts—that the Power which the universe manifests to us is utterly inscrutable."[1] The scientific thinker, according to him, "learns at

---

1. *First Principles* (1862), p. 46.

once the greatness and the littleness of the human intellect—its power in dealing with all that comes within the range of experience, its impotence in dealing with all that transcends experience. He realises with a special vividness the utter incomprehensibleness of the simplest fact, considered in itself. He, more than any other truly knows that in its ultimate essence nothing can be known".[1] Thus all our religious and scientific ideas are ultimately found to be merely symbolic representations of Reality and not possessed of the true knowledge of it. "Ultimate religious ideas and ultimate scientific ideas alike turn out to be merely symbols of the actual, not cognitions of it."[2] So we have no idea or thought of ultimate reality or the Absolute. We have only a vague, a dim and indefinite consciousness of the unknowable Reality which lies behind the phenomena of our experience "an indefinite consciousness of the unformed and unlimited", a compelling sense of the mysterious nature of the universe which we inhabit. This indefinite and vague consciousness is the basis of our religious emotion. But it is in a way self-contradictory for Spencer to pronounce that the higher we ascend in the scale of reality or knowledge, the dimmer and dimmer our knowledge becomes.

(C) *Sri Aurobindo's Conception of the Unknowable Compared with that of Vedānta, Bradley and Bergson*

Thus we find that Sri Aurobindo's conception of the unknowable differs fundamentally from that of Kant, Spencer and other agnostics. Whereas the Absolute in Kant and Spencer remains altogether unknowable to human consciousness as such, in Sri Aurobindo's Integral Advaitism, the Absolute is unknowable to the finite mind or reason and not to the higher levels of consciousness. In this respect Sri Aurobindo agrees with the views of the Upaniṣadic sages and with Śaṅkara, Rāmānuja and other Vedāntins. The Vedānta considers sense-experience and intellect as different sources of knowledge. But they can, according to it, give us only the knowledge of the empirical world and not of reality as such. The Real according to the Upaniṣads is that "from which all speech with the

---

1. *First Principles* (1862), pp. 66-67.
2. *Ibid.*, p. 68.

mind turns away unable to reach it".[1] Another Upaniṣad declares,
"The eye does not go there, nor speech nor mind. We do not
know, do not understand how any one can teach it."[2] The knowl-
edge or realisation of Reality cannot be attained by reason.[3] The
ultimate reality cannot be presented in an objective manner which
the senses and the intellect can grasp. "How should one know Him
by whom one knows all this? How should one know the Knower?"[4]
The same Upaniṣad observes, "You cannot see that which is the
witness of vision; you cannot hear that which is the witness of
hearing; you cannot think that which is the thinker of thought; you
cannot know that which is the knower of knowledge."[5]

Thus the Upaniṣads lay great stress on the fact that Reality cannot
be attained by means of intellect or thought. "The Upaniṣads,"
observes Dr. Radhakrishnan, "assert sometimes that thought gives
us imperfect, partial pictures of reality, and at other times that it
is organically incapable of reaching reality. It deals with relations
and cannot grasp the relationless absolute".[6] "Intellect in the sense
of understanding" further observes Dr. Radhakrishnan, "working
with the limited categories of time, space and cause, is inadequate.
Reason also fails, though it takes us beyond understanding. It does
not help us to attain reality, which is not merely an idea, but a
spirit".[7]

The Vedānta from the time of Veda and Upaniṣads up to the
present-day has held fast to intuition. The great propounders of
classical systems of Vedānta like Śaṅkara, Rāmānuja and others
have recognised intuition as the highest source of knowing reality.
The western philosophers like Bradley and Bergson, also regard

1. यतो वाचो निवर्तन्ते अप्राप्य मनसा सह । (*Tait.* 11.4)
2. न तत्र चक्षुर्गच्छति न वागगच्छति नो मनः ।
   न विद्मो न विजानीमो यथैतदनुशिष्यात् ॥ (*Kena,* 1.3)
3. नैषा तर्केण मतिरापनेया । (*Kaṭha.* 1.2.9)
4. येनेदं सर्वं विजानाति तं केन विजानीयात् ।
   विज्ञातारमरे केन विजानीयादिति । (*Bṛh.* 2.4.14)
5. न दृष्टेर्द्रष्टारं पश्येः, न श्रुतेः श्रोतारं शृणुया, न
   मतेर्मन्तारं मन्वीथा, न विज्ञातेर्विज्ञातारं विजानीयाः । (*Bṛh.* 3.4.2)
6. *Indian Philosophy,* Vol. I, p. 175.
7. *Ibid.,* p. 176.

intuition as the highest source of knowing or realising reality. The intellect in Bradley's view is aware only of appearance. The intellect is discursive and separates the 'what' from the 'that', or the content from existence or reality. Hence it is aware only of the appearance of the Absolute and cannot know the Absolute as such. Thus the Absolute, according to Bradley, is unknowable so far as intellect or reason is concerned. The Absolute, Bradley argues, can be realised by intuition or post-reflectional consciousness. The intellect or reason, he declares, must commit suicide if the human consciousness is to know reality. Bergson also holds the view that intellect cuts reality into fragments and thus fails to grasp its essential nature. It is intuition alone which can touch the heart of reality. Of course, the term intuition does not have the same meaning and significance in Śaṅkara, Rāmānuja, Bradley, Bergson and Sri Aurobindo. There is a wide divergence in their views of intuition. But all these philosophers agree in the view that intuition is not mental consciousness or reason. It is a higher consciousness which is attained by man by transcending the limitations of sense and intellect and which is capable of giving us a direct realisation of the ultimate Reality. Thus though the Absolute remains unknowable to sense and intellect, it is known or realised by intuition.

Our intuition can give us the realisation of pure Becoming as well as pure Being. As Sri Aurobindo puts it, "So long as the intuition fixes itself only upon that which we become, we see ourselves as a continual progression of movement and change in consciousness in the eternal succession of Time. We are the river, the flame of the Buddhist illustration. But there is a supreme experience and supreme intuition by which we go back behind our surface self and find that this becoming, change, succession are only a mode of our being and that there is that in us which is not involved at all in the becoming."[1]

It is this great truth that is not apprehended by Kant, Spencer and other agnostics. It is due to the fact, as has been pointed out above, that they regard senses and intellect or reason as the only means of knowledge. They try to know the Absolute in the same way as they know the objects. All the objects must conform to the categories of space, time etc. in order to be known as objects.

---

1. *L.D.*, Vol. I, p. 99.

And as the Absolute transcends all the categories, it is regarded by them as unknown and unknowable. Thus their recognition of senses and intellect as the only sources of knowledge lands them inevitably into agnosticism. Kant who in his *Critique of Pure Reason* wages a relentless war against all sorts of dogmatism, himself falls a prey to another and more perilous dogmatism, namely, agnosticism by confining knowledge to the phenomena. Sri Aurobindo charges all agnosticism with being dominated by a dogmatic mentality. According to him, "all agnosticism is subject to this objection that it may be nothing but our refusal to know, a too ready embracing of an apparent and present restriction or constriction of consciousness, a sense of impotence which may be permitted to the immediate limitations of mind but not to the Jivatman who is one with the Supreme".[1]

The 'Critique of Pure Reason' revealed the secrets of the structure and function of mind as it at present is. It did not try to discover what the mind and consciousness of man can be. Kant, Spencer and others look upon consciousness as static. Man is, according to them, destined to remain confined within the limits of space, time and other categories, so far as the aspect of knowledge is concerned. Thus they take a static view of reason. Reason is beset with all sorts of contradictions and antinomies. It fails to overcome contradictions and antinomies on account of its static nature, as has been clearly shown by the Post-Kantian Idealists, specially Hegel. Sri Aurobindo like Hegel considers consciousness as dynamic. Man as a mental being suffers from all sorts of limitations. But he is, in Sri Aurobindo's view, not bound to remain confined to this limitation forever. Man is man only insofar as he has the prerogative to exceed himself, to overcome his present limitations. Man can attain the highest knowledge of the Absolute or Brahman by exceeding his present limitations. As Sri Aurobindo observes, "The Unknown is not the unknowable;[2] it need not remain the unknown for us, unless we choose ignorance or persist in our first limitations. For to all things that are not unknowable, all things in the universe, there correspond in that universe faculties which can take cognisance of them, and in man, the microcosm, these faculties are always existent and at a certain stage

---

1. *L.D.*, Vol. II, Part I, pp. 332-33.
2. अन्यदेव तद्विदितादथो अविदितादधि । (*Kena.* 1.3)

capable of development. We may choose not to develop them; where they are partially developed, we may discourage and impose on them a kind of atrophy. But, fundamentally, all possible knowledge is knowledge within the power of humanity. And since in man there is the inalienable impulse of Nature towards self-realisation, no struggle of the intellect to limit the action of our capacities within a determined area can forever prevail."[1]

To know the supreme Reality or the Absolute in its essential and integral aspect, we have, in Sri Aurobindo's view, to discover all possible avenues of knowledge that can be attained by man by exceeding his present limitations and not rest content with his present mental consciousness. If Reality does not reveal its essential and integral nature to human mind, it is not the fault of Reality but of our limited and finite mind. So instead of calling Reality or any aspect of it unreal, or a mere postulate of moral will or faith or utterly unknowable, we have to get rid of the limitations of mind and approach the Absolute or supreme Reality through a higher consciousness. It is only then that we can fathom the depth of Reality and realise it in all its essential and integral aspects. This integral realisation of Reality will be possible to man only when he attains supramental consciousness in the course of evolution, as has been stated in the Introduction. The integral knowledge, according to Sri Aurobindo, is present there in man in a latent form. It is not something which has to be created and acquired by mind; "it must rather be discovered or uncovered, it is a Truth that is self-revealed to a spiritual endeavour; for it is there veiled in our deeper and greater self; it is the very stuff of our own spiritual consciousness, and it is by awaking to it even in our surface self that we have to possess it".[2] So the integral Reality has to be approached through integral knowledge and not through partial, limited and fragmentary knowledge like that of sense and mind. It is only when we approach reality through the integral knowledge that we can be saved on the one hand from materialism, agnosticism and scepticism and on the other, from mentalism, and abstract absolutism; from 'The Materialist Denial' and 'The Refusal of the Ascetic'.

So far we have dealt with Sri Aurobindo's conception of Existence

---

1. *L.D.*, Vol. I, p. 16.
2. *L.D.*, Vol. II, Part II, pp. 415-16.

as Unknowable. Now we proceed to discuss the indeterminability of the Absolute or pure Existence.

(D) *Existence as Indeterminability*

As the Absolute or pure Existence is timeless and spaceless, so it is necessarily indeterminate. Brahman, says Śaṅkara, cannot be confined within the bounds of space and time.[1] Brahman as pure Existence is necessarily indeterminate. It is simply Being and is not anything in particular. No attribute or quality can be predicated of this pure Existence. As Sri Aurobindo observes "If this indefinable, infinite, timeless, spaceless Existence is, it is necessarily a pure absolute. It cannot be summed up in any quantity or quantities, it cannot be composed of any quality or combination of qualities. It is not an aggregate of forms or a formal substratum of forms. If all forms, quantities, qualities were to disappear, this would remain. Existence without quantity, without quality, without form is not only conceivable, but it is the one thing we can conceive behind these phenomena."[2] The Upaniṣad calls Brahman partless, without activity, calm, faultless and free from all taints.[3] The sage Yājñavalkya describes Brahman as "neither gross nor subtle, neither short nor long".[4] By denying these contradictory qualities of Brahman, it is meant that Brahman is not a thing or object of the world. These empirical qualities hold good only in the case of the objects of the world and not what is beyond it. To deny these contradictory attributes of Brahman does not mean that it is nothing, because, the *śruti* says, Brahman is pervading all things like ether.[5] Brahman is called the underlying reality of all things or the reality immanent in all things.[6] All these things are Brahman.[7] It means that all the things of the world are in essence Brahman. There is nothing which lies outside Brahman. All this world is

---

1. न देशकालादिविशेषयोग: परमात्मनि कल्पयितुं शक्यते । (*S.B.* 4.3.14)
2. *L.D.*, Vol. I, p. 96.
3. निष्कलं निष्क्रियं शान्तं निरवद्यं निरञ्जनम् । (*Śvet.* 6.19)
4. अस्थूलमनण्वमह्रस्वमदीर्घम् । (*Bṛh.* 3.8.8)
5. आकाशवत्सर्वगतश्च नित्य: । (*Bṛh.* 3.4.1)
6. य आत्मा सर्वान्तर: । (*Bṛh.* 3.4.1)
7. आत्मैवेदं सर्वम् । (*Chān.* 7.25.2)

indeed nothing but the Supreme Brahman.[1] But Brahman as Existence or Brahman in itself cannot be characterised in any way. Brahman has neither genus nor differentia, hence it is incapable of being characterised in any way. It is called unmanifest, unthinkable and without modification.[2] Brahman as Existence transcends all differences. There are no differences in Brahman.[3] Thus Existence is without any quality, quantity, form etc. But Existence is called indeterminable and differenceless, not in the sense that it is altogether devoid of them and hence incapable of manifesting differences and determinations out of itself, but that it exceeds them all. "Necessarily, when we say it is without them, we mean that it exceeds them, that it is something into which they pass in such a way as to cease to be what we call form, quality, quantity and out of which they emerge as form, quality and quantity in the movement."[4] Ordinarily the indeterminate Brahman is supposed to be opposed to all kinds of differences and determinations. But this opposition like that of Being and Non-being can be resolved by having a clear understanding of what the term indeterminate or indeterminable really means.

To say that the Absolute is indeterminable does not mean that it is incapable of manifesting a real cosmos or real determinations out of its being. It is indeterminable in the sense that it cannot be limited by any determination or any possible sum of determinations. It is not incapable of self-determination. The Absolute is thus indeterminable, yet it is at the same time the source of all true self-determinations. Though the Absolute is not limitable or definable by anyone determination or any sum of determinations, yet "it is not bound down to an indeterminable vacancy of pure existence".[5] The indeterminability of the Absolute is, according to Sri Aurobindo, natural and necessary. Without being indeterminable, it would not have been able to create infinite self-determinations out of its being. It is able to evolve or manifest infinite self-determinations out of itself, to be infinitely all things because it is not anything in particular. It is capable of evolving manifold powers out of itself simply because

1. ब्रह्मैवेदं विश्वमिदं वरिष्ठम् । (Mund. 2.2.11)
2. अव्यक्तोऽयमचिन्त्योऽयमविकार्योऽयमुच्यते । (B.G. 2.25)
3. नेह नानास्ति किञ्चन । (Brh. 4.4.19).
4. L.D. Vol. I, pp. 96-97.
5. L.D. Vol. II, Part I, p. 27.

it cannot be identified with any one particular power or sum of powers. It is able to uphold the inexhaustible variety of forms in its being simply because it cannot be characterised by any particular form or sum of forms. Thus the Absolute can be the source, the origin and the substratum of all things, all powers, forms, properties etc. because it is beyond all these; because it cannot be characterised or defined by any one of these determinations or even by all the determinations taken together. Thus the ideterminability of the Absolute "is the natural, the necessary condition both of its infinity of being and its infinity of power of being; it can be infinitely all things because it is nothing in particular and exceeds any definable totality".[1] In spiritual experience, both these aspects of the Absolute are realised. Its indeterminable aspect is characterised by the "fundamental negating positives" of our spiritual experience, such as, "the immobile, immutable Self, the Nirguna Brahman, the Eternal without qualities, the pure featureless one Existence, the Impersonal, the silence void of activities, the Non-Being, the Ineffable and the Unknowable".[2] Similarly, because the Absolute is also the essence and source of all determinations, all creations, hence, it is also characterised by the "fundamental affirming positives" such as, "the Self that becomes all things, the Saguna Brahman, the Eternal with infinite qualities, the One who is the Many, the infinite Person who is the source and foundation of all persons and personalities, the Lord of creation, the Word, the Master of all works and action; it is that which being known all is known; these affirmatives correspond to those negatives".[3]

These two aspects of the supreme Reality or the Absolute, the indeterminate or *nirguna* and the determinate or *saguna* seem to the normal and finite reason to be contradictory and incompatible with each other. Thus, to Śaṅkara, the indeterminate or *nirguna* Brahman is the absolute Reality and the determinate or *saguna* Brahman has merely a relative existence. It is not real in the ultimate or metaphysical sense. If the Absolute is indeterminate or *nirguna*, it cannot be determinate or *saguna* as it involves self-contradiction. So the Absolute, according to Śaṅkara, is devoid of all determinations. On the other hand, according to Rāmānuja and

1. *L.D.*, Vol. II, Part I, p. 27.
2. *Ibid.*, p. 27.
3. *Ibid.*, p. 27.

Hegel, the Absolute is determinate. It is inclusive of all determinations. All the determinations and differences are integrated and assimilated in the concrete whole or the Absolute. To call the Absolute indeterminate is, according to them, to indulge in a mere abstraction. But, according to Sri Aurobindo, both the indeterminate and the determinate, the *nirguṇa* and *saguṇa,* the impersonal and personal are the fundamental aspects or poises of the Absolute. In this respect, we may compare Sri Aurobindo's view of the Absolute with that of Spinoza.

(E) *Sri Aurobindo's and Spinoza's View of the Absolute Compared*
Spinoza calls the Absolute, Substance. He regards the Absolute or Substance as both transcending all attributes and as the centre of all attributes. It means that the Absolute or Substance is both indeterminate and determinate. Now it is difficult for reason to reconcile both these opposed views of the Absolute. It seems to be self-contradictory to assert that the Absolute is both indeterminate as well as determinate. In Spinoza's philosophy we do not find any solution regarding this difficult problem. He does not give any logical explanation how the transcendental substance becomes the centre of infinite attributes or modes. *Natura Naturans* and *Natura Naturata* form the two aspects of the same Substance or Absolute, but Spinoza does not explain how these two aspects of the Substance can be reconciled. This problem has given rise to two opposite views regarding Spinoza's system.

One view holds that the finite world, the world of particulars or *natura naturata* is not a real manifestation of Substance or the Absolute but is a product or subjective creation of our finite and ignorant mind. Substance, according to this view, does not transform itself into attributes and modes. On the other hand, it is our distorted and finite understanding that conceives attributes and modes in an indeterminate and differenceless substance. Spinoza's definition of attributes lends support to this view. Spinoza defines attribute as that which the intellect perceives as constituting the essence of the substance. If this definition is literally interpreted, it would mean that the attribute does not really exist in the Substance, is not a part and parcel of it but is superimposed by the human intellect on the Substance. Thus it will be regarded as having only a subjective existence, as existing only in the individual or finite mind and not in reality. Attributes and modes according to this interpretation will be taken as nothing but the substance viewed through the distorted imagination of the percipient. It will mean that the attributes and modes will not be regarded as having any ontological status but only an epistemic status. The finite world, the *Natura Naturata,* the world of becoming will be reduced to the status of unreality.

According to another view, the attributes and modes are the real modifications or products of Substance. Spinoza regards Substance as consisting of infinite attributes. According to this view it is wholly unnecessary to interpret Spinoza's definition of attributes in a subjectivist sense, simply in order to reconcile the seemingly contradictory theses of Spinoza. "In fact, the contradiction is purely imaginary and arises from a misconception. The celebrated statement *determinatio negatio est* does not signify determination is negation, but *limitation* is negation. By calling God *ens absolute indeterminatum,* Spinoza does not mean to say that God is an absolutely indeterminate being, or non-being, or negative being, but, on the contrary, that he has absolutely *unlimited* attributes, or absolutely *infinite* perfections—that he is a positive, concrete, most real being, the being who unites in himself all possible attributes and possesses them without limitation."[1] "Spinoza evidently intended to forestall the objections of the non-attributists[2] by ascribing to God *infinita attributa,* which seems to mean both *infinite attributes* and an *infinity of attributes.*"[3] According to this view, to say that the Absolute is indeterminate will not mean that it is devoid of all attributes but that it is possessed of infinite attributes. Spinoza holds that the Absolute is possessed of infinite attributes of which the human mind or intellect can perceive only two, namely, extension and thought. Thus the absolute is necessarily in a way indeterminable to the human intellect.

Now if this view is admitted and the Absolute is taken to be possessed of infinite attributes, then it cannot logically be called indeterminate. Whether the Absolute is possessed of a limited number of attributes or of infinite attributes it will be called de-

1. Weber, Alfred, *op. cit.,* p. 331.
2. "Who maintain that to give attributes to God means to limit him."
3. Weber, Alfred, *op. cit.,* p. 331.

terminate and not indeterminate. There is no sense in calling such an Absolute indeterminate. The finite or particular things are possessed of a limited number of attributes. God or Absolute may be taken to be possessed of infinite attributes. But the infinite number of attributes cannot make the Absolute indeterminate. So like the Absolute of Rāmānuja and Hegel, the Absolute of Spinoza should be called determinate or *saguṇa* and not indeterminate or *nirguṇa* and determinate or *saguṇa* simultaneously. Secondly, to say that *determination negatio est* does not mean, that determination is negation but that *limitation* is negation does not solve the contradiction. To determine the Absolute means putting a limitation upon it. And to limit the Absolute means to negate its absoluteness, because a limited Absolute is a contradiction in terms. Hence *determinatio negatio est* can only mean that determination is negation. Spinoza does not seem to be conscious of this contradiction in his philosophy because he does not give any explanation to reconcile these opposed elements in his system.

Sri Aurobindo tries to solve the opposition between the indeterminate and the determinate aspects of the Absolute. According to him, the indeterminate and determinate aspects of the Absolute appear as contradictory only to our finite mind or reason. But to the higher reason or supramental cognition, they do not appear as contradictory and incompatible with each other. As Sri Aurobindo puts it, "For it is not possible in a supramental cognition to split asunder the two sides of the One Existence—even to speak of them as sides is excessive, for they are in each other, their co-existence or one-existence is eternal and their powers sustaining each other found the self-manifestation of the Infinite."[1] Sri Aurobindo of course does not deny the possibility of having an exclusive spiritual experience of any one of the aspects of the Absolute. Such experiences will of course be valid but their validity will be confined to the particular fields. As he observes, "But neither is the separate cognition of them entirely an illusion or a complete error of the Ignorance; this too has its validity for spiritual experience."[2] Any such exclusive experience of one aspect of Reality cannot deny the possibility of having other equally valid and cogent spiritual experiences. It is quite possible, Sri Aurobindo argues, to

---

1. *L.D.*, Vol. II, Part I, pp. 27-28.
2. *Ibid.*, p. 28.

have an integral experience of the Absolute in our supramental cognition. The indeterminate and the determinate aspects of the Absolute seem to be incompatible to each other both to our normal reason as well as to our spiritual experience simply because we are still in the stage of mind. We judge Reality by the standard of mind and hence fall helplessly into the mud and mire of inevitable antinomies, contradictions, divisions and separations. It is only when we ascend to the higher stages of consciousness and ulti- mately to the Supermind that we can have an integral, comprehen- sive and harmonious experience of both the aspects of the Abso- lute, of *saguṇa* as well as *nirguṇa* simultaneously. Then we are no longer bewildered by the antinomies or contradictions. The One and the Many, the Infinite and the Finite—all seem to be the complementary aspects of the same Reality. The negative aspect of the Absolute, as has already been shown above, carries in it the freedom of the Absolute from the limitations of its own determi- nations. But not only does it guarantee the freedom of the Abso- lute but it also enables the individual souls to get rid of all kinds of bondage and limitations, disengage themselves from the phe- nomenal creations of nature and also have mastery and supremacy over all the laws, processes and workings of Prakṛti or lower nature. It is the infinite freedom of the Absolute that enables the individu- als to keep themselves free from all cosmic workings and effects and enjoy the calm and undisturbed silence of their immutable existence. It is the same freedom that enables them to indulge in all sorts of phenomenal or worldly activities without infringing in any way the eternal calm, the undisturbed silence and the inef- fable bliss of their immutable and transcendent existence. As Sri Aurobindo puts it, "Those that seem to us negative carry in them the freedom of the Infinite from limitation by its own determina- tions; their realisation disengages the spirit within, liberates us and enables us to participate in this supremacy: thus, when once we pass into or through the experience of immutable self, we are no longer bound and limited in the inner status of our being by the determinations and creations of Nature. On the other, the dynamic side, this original freedom enables the consciousness to create a world of determinations without being bound by it: it enables it also to withdraw from what it has created and recreate in a higher truth formula. It is on this freedom that is based the spirit's power of infinite variation of the truth possibilities of existence and also its capacity to create without tying itself to its workings, any and every form of Necessity or system of order: the individual being too by experience of these negating absolutes can participate in that dynamic liberty, can pass from one order of self-formulation to a higher order."[1]

Sri Aurobindo does admit that it is not possible to solve the riddle of existence on the basis of the finite reason. One cannot make any reconciliation between One and Many, Being and Becoming, Indeterminate and Determinate on the basis of the finite or abstract reason. Our finite reason is confronted with all sorts of contradictions which it finds itself unable to solve. So Sri Aurobindo puts forward the conception of the supramental consciousness which does not suffer from the limitations of finite mind and, which enjoys an all-embracing and integral experience of all the aspects of existence or reality. Sri Aurobindo's conception of the higher reason or the supramental consciousness does not only provide an answer to the difficulties in Spinoza's conception of the Absolute but also helps us to solve the contradictions inherent in the systems of Rāmānuja, Hegel, Bradley, Śaṅkara and others, as we shall show in subsequent chapters.

We have discussed before how Sri Aurobindo tries to solve the riddle of the law of contradiction by the higher reason or what he calls the logic of the Infinite and how he arrives at his Integral Advaitism which reconciles and synthesises all the so-called contradictory aspects of existence and does not deny the reality of any of them.

We have so far studied the Absolute in its aspect of Existence. Now we proceed to study the Absolute or Brahman in its aspect of Cit-Śakti or Consciousness-force.

---

1. *L.D.*, Vol. II, Part I, p. 28.

CHAPTER IV

THE ABSOLUTE AS
CONSCIOUSNESS-FORCE

The Absolute, according to Sri Aurobindo, is not only pure Being or Existence, but is also Consciousness-Force. As reason is constrained to posit pure Being or Existence underlying the phenomena, so it is constrained to posit a force as constituting the phenomena. The world is the product or creation of force. As Sri Aurobindo says, "However the phenomenon of consciousness may be explained, whether Nature be an inert impulse or a conscious principle, it is certainly Force; the principle of things is a formative movement of energies, all forms are born of meeting and mutual adaptation between unshaped forces, all sensation and action is a response of something in a form of Force to the contacts of other forms of Force. This is the world as we experience it and from this experience we must always start."[1] "Physical analysis of Matter by modern Science," he further observes, "has come to the same general conclusion, even if a few last doubts linger. Intuition and experience confirm this concord of Science and Philosophy. Pure reason finds in it the satisfaction of its own essential conceptions. For even in the view of the world as essentially an act of consciousness, an act is implied and in the act movement of Force, play of Energy. This also, when we examine from within our own experience, proves to be the fundamental nature of the world. All our activities are the play of the triple force of the old philosophies,

---

1. *L.D.*, Vol. I, p. 103.

knowledge-force, desire-force, action-force, and all these prove to be really three streams of one original and identical Power, Adya Shakti. Even our states of rest are only equable state or equilibrium of the play of her movement".[1] Thus our reason is constrained to posit the reality of an ultimate creative force in order to explain our experience.

But the Absolute is not only movement or force. It is, as we have shown above, also pure Existence. We are aware of the Absolute as movement or Becoming but the Absolute is not subject to movement or Becoming. It is an Existence which remains immutable and unaffected by any movement. Now the problem is, how can we posit these contradictory aspects in the Absolute? If the Absolute is pure Existence, how can it be movement or force at the same time?

(A) *Existence and Force: Their Relation*

As we have shown before Sri Aurobindo does not find any opposition between Being and Becoming or Existence and Force. It is only our finite and abstract reason which finds all sorts of contradictions and oppositions between them and not our higher reason or the logic of the Infinite. Force, according to Sri Aurobindo, is inherent in Existence. As he puts it, "Shiva and Kali, Brahman and Shakti are one and not two who are separable. Force inherent in existence may be at rest or it may be in motion, but when it is at rest, it exists nonetheless and is not abolished, diminished or in any way essentially altered."[2] Thus the opposition between Existence and Force is very much removed, if we admit this dual status of Force, of rest as well as movement. To say that the Force is inherent in Existence or Being does not mean, as we have shown above, that the Absolute ceases to be a pure immutable Being. Thus there can be no contradiction in asserting that Force is inherent in Existence. "This reply is so entirely rational and in accordance with the nature of things that we need not hesitate to accept it. For it is impossible, as it is contradictory to reason, to suppose that Force is a thing alien to the one and infinite existence and entered into it from outside or was non-existent and arose in

---

1. *L.D.*, pp. 103-04.
2. *Ibid.*, Vol. I, p. 104.

it at some point in Time."[1] The very presence of Force does not make the Absolute or Brahman subject to movement.[2] "In a conscious existence which is absolute, independent of its formations, not determined by its works, we must suppose an inherent freedom to manifest or not to manifest the potentiality of movement. A Brahman compelled by Prakriti is not Brahman, but an inert Infinite with an active content in it more powerful than the continent, a conscious holder of Force of whom his Force is master. If we say that it is compelled by itself as Force, by its own nature, we do not get rid of the contradiction, the evasion of our first postulate. We have got back to an Existence which is really nothing but Force, Force at rest or in movement, absolute Force perhaps, but not Absolute Being."[3] The Absolute in Sri Aurobindo's view is possessed of Force but is not subject to it. It manifests itself as Force both in its static and dynamic aspects and at the same time it transcends both these aspects.

(B) Force as Conscious in Nature

Now it is clear that the Absolute is Existence as well as Force and it is by means of Force that It manifests itself as the world and the individual souls. Now the problem is, what is the nature of Force? Is it conscious or unconscious? Sri Aurobindo's answer is that Force is conscious. It is not unconscious or jaḍa as the materialists would have us believe. The phenomenon of consciousness according to Sri Aurobindo cannot be explained if the ultimate creative force is regarded as unconscious. The contention of the materialists that consciousness is the product of matter is challenged by Sri Aurobindo. He refutes the contention of the materialist that the brain secretes thought as the liver secretes bile. As he says, "Materialism indeed insists that, whatever the extension of consciousness, it is a material phenomenon inseparable from our physical organs and not their utiliser but their result. This orthodox contention, however, is no longer able to hold the field against the tide of increasing knowledge. Its explanations are becoming more and more inadequate and strained. It is becoming always

1. L.D., Vol. I, pp. 104-05.
2. Ibid., pp. 106-07.
3. Ibid., pp. 106-07.

clearer that not only does the capacity of our total consciousness far exceed that of our organs, the senses, the nerves, the brain but even for our ordinary thought and consciousness these organs are only their habitual instruments and not their generators. Consciousness uses the brain which its upward strivings have produced, brain has not produced nor does it use the consciousness."[1] "Our physical organism no more causes or explains thought and consciousness than the construction of an engine causes or explains the motive-power of steam or electricity."[2]

Sri Aurobindo argues that consciousness is present in a latent manner in plant and matter also. Consciousness is not only present in living organisms but it is, according to him, present in plant and matter also though in a latent manner. In plant, the consciousness is intuitively present. "The seeking and shrinkings of the plant, its pleasure and pain, its sleep and its wakefulness and all that strange life whose truth an Indian scientist has brought to light by rigidly scientific methods, are all movements of consciousness, but, as far as we can see, not of mentality. There is then a sub-mental, a vital consciousness which has precisely the initial reactions as the mental, but is different in the constitution of its self-experience, even as that which is superconscient is in the constitution of its self-experience different from the mental being."[3] What is true of plant is also in a sense true of matter. The range of consciousness does not cease with plant but extends to the material world also.[4]

Sri Aurobindo is one with the Vedānta and Hegel that consciousness is present even in the material world though in a latent manner. And he is confronted with the same difficulty to explain in a rational manner the presence of consciousness in matter. The difficulty is aggravated by the fact that matter seems to be a complete negation of consciousness. But Sri Aurobindo is not prepared to admit any sudden gulf in Nature. "Thought," he says "has a right to suppose a unity where that unity is confessed by all other classes of phenomena and in one class only, not denied, but merely more concealed than in others. And if we suppose the unity to be unbroken,

1. *L.D.*, Vol. I, p. 108.
2. *Ibid.*, p. 108.
3. *Ibid.*, p. 110.
4. *Ibid.*, pp. 110-11.

we then arrive at the existence of consciousness in all forms of the Force which is at work in the world".[1] The emergence of consciousness out of the forms of matter can be explained only if it is regarded as potentially and in a latent manner present in matter. "Nothing can evolve out of Matter which is not therein already contained." Thus reason is constrained to posit consciousness as the principle underlying the operations of the creative Energy. The creative force is conscious in its nature though it may not manifest consciousness in its outward working. The Divine by his energy manifests the world in accordance with his own law, the divine law, as we have indicated above. There is the supreme consciousness underlying the whole world-show and guiding its destiny. "Consciousness is the great underlying fact, the universal witness for whom the world is a field, the senses instruments. To that witness the worlds and their objects appeal for their reality and for the one world and the many, for the physical equally with the supraphysical we have no other evidence that they exist."[2] Thus instead of assuming consciousness as the product of the material energy, we have to regard it as the supreme fundamental principle underlying the world and directing its operations. Without admitting the primacy of this supreme conscious principle, we cannot affirm even the existence of the world or of ourselves. The Upaniṣad also asserts: By His shining everything shines, by His light, everything is illumined.[3] But this consciousness is not our individual egoistic consciousness born in the course of evolution. As Sri Aurobindo observes, "For the witness, if he exists, is not the individual embodied mind born in the world, but that cosmic consciousness embracing the universe and appearing as an immanent Intelligence in all its works to which either world subsists eternally and really as its own active existence or else from which it is born and into which it disappears by an act of knowledge or by an act of conscious power. Not organised Mind, but that which, calm and eternal, broods equally in the living earth and the living human body and to which mind and senses are dispensable in-

---

1. *L.D.*, Vol. I, p. 111.
2. *Ibid.*, p. 24.
3. तमेवभान्तमनुभाति सर्वं।
   तस्य भासा सर्वमिदं विभाति ॥ (*Muṇḍ.* 2.2.10)

struments, is the witness of cosmic existence and its Lord."[1]

The presence of consciousness in the ultimate creative force is also proved by the fact that there is seen an element of purpose or design in its workings. Not only the human beings who are normally possessed of mental consciousness know how to adjust themselves to their environment, but the animals, including the lowest insects are also able to make a perfect adjustment, though in a very limited and stereotyped manner, to their surroundings. Thus Sri Aurobindo observes, "We see, for instance, in the animal, operations of a perfect purposefulness and an exact, indeed a scientifically minute knowledge which are quite beyond the capacities of the animal mentality and which man himself can only acquire by long culture and education and even then uses with a much less sure rapidity. We are entitled to see in this general fact the proof of a conscious Force at work in the animal and the insect which is more intelligent, more purposeful, more aware of its intention, its ends, its means, its conditions than the highest mentality yet manifested in any individual form on earth. And in the operations of inanimate Nature we find the same pervading characteristic of a supreme hidden intelligence, "hidden in the modes of its own workings".

Thus Sri Aurobindo strikes at the very roots of materialism. Whereas materialism holds that consciousness is the product of material energy, Sri Aurobindo contends that matter itself is the product of Conscious Force. The Upaniṣads hold that *cit* as energy creates the world. The world is said to have been manifested by the Absolute or Brahman by his force of will.[2] Another Upaniṣad observes, "In the beginning there was only the Self. There was nothing else besides it. He thought, "May I create the world." He created these worlds."[3] The *Brahma-Sūtra* says that the first cause of the world is an intelligent principle.[4] Sri Aurobindo also holds that the Absolute as *Cit-Śakti* creates or manifests the world.

But the conception of a conscious Force at the root of the

---

1. *L.D.*, Vol. I, p. 26.
2. तदैक्षत बहुस्यां प्रजायेयेति । (*Chān.* 6.2.3)
3. आत्मा व इदमेक एवाग्र आसीत् । नान्यत् किञ्चनमिषत् ।
   स ईक्षत लोकान्नु सृजा इति । स इमाँल्लोकानसृजत् । (*Ait.* 1.1.1)
4. ईक्षतेर्नाशब्दम् । (*Br. Sū.* 1.1.5)

world-process may be challenged on the ground that there is a large element in Nature's operations to which we give the name of waste. The occurrence of earthquake, drought, volcanic eruptions etc. cannot be said to be the work of a conscious and intelligent Force. "But obviously," says Sri Aurobindo, "this is an objection based on the limitations of our human intellect which seeks to impose its own particular rationality, good enough for limited human ends, on the general operation of the world-Force. We see only part of Nature's purpose and all that does not subserve that part we call waste. Yet even our own human action is full of an apparent waste, so appearing from the individual point of view, which yet, we may be sure, subserves well enough the large and universal purpose of things. That part of her intention which we can detect, Nature gets done surely enough in spite of, perhaps really by virtue of her apparent waste. We may well trust to her in the rest which we do not yet detect".[1] We have, according to Sri Aurobindo, no right to look at the cosmic process from our mental standard. What we call waste may not necessarily be so from the standpoint of Nature's ulterior purpose. Thus we cannot deny the presence of consciousness in Nature's workings simply on the ground that there is a large element of waste in it. "Man's consciousness," observes Sri Aurobindo "can be nothing else than a form of Nature's consciousness. It is there in other involved froms below Mind, it emerges in Mind, it shall ascend into yet superior forms beyond Mind. For the Force that builds the worlds is a conscious Force, the Existence which manifests itself in them is conscious Being and a perfect emergence of its potentialities in form is the sole object which we can rationally conceive for its manifestation of this world of forms".[2]

(C) Characteristics of Conscious Force

It is due to its conscious Force or Māyā that Brahman manifests itself as the universe and the individual souls. The secret of this manifestation is found in the three essential characterstics of Māyā or Conscious Force, namely, of infinite self-variation, of self-limitation and of self-absorption.

The Conscious Force or Māyā of Brahman is not restricted to

---

1. *L.D.*, Vol. I, pp. 112-13.
2. *Ibid.*, p. 113.

one particular state of consciousness or "to one state or law of its action; it can be many things simultaneously, have many coordinated movements which to the finite reason may seem contradictory; it is one but innumerably manifold, infinitely plastic, inexhaustibly adaptable".[1] "Māyā is the supreme and universal consciousness and force of the Eternal and Infinite and, being by its very nature unbound and illimitable, it can put forth many states of consciousness at a time, many dispositions of its Force, without ceasing to be the same consciousness-force for ever."[2] The individual consciousness can see itself as a limited and phenomenal being. It can also put off its apparent limitations and see itself as a universal and a transcendent being. The underlying consciousness being one and the same, there is no essential difficulty in passing from one status to another. The one being can thus experience or realise itself triply from any of these three statuses.

The second characteristic of the Infinite consciousness or conscious Force is, as has been stated above, its power of self-limitation. It is the subordinate movement of the Infinite consciousness determining itself within the bounds of Space and Time. This power of self-limitation expresses itself in the form of individual self-limitation and cosmic self-limitation. But though Brahman by its capacity of self-limitation expresses itself in the form of individual beings or souls, yet the individual souls are not unaware of their essential and integral nature. The spiritual individual is aware of himself, of his essential and integral nature. "Spiritual individuality means," observes Sri Aurobindo, "that each individual self or spirit is a centre of self-vision and all-vision; the circumstance—the boundless circumference, as we may say—of this vision may be the same for all, but the centre may be different—not located as in a spatial point in a spatial circle, but a psychological centre related with others through a coexistence of the diversely conscious Many in the universal being".[3] The world will be the same for all the spiritual individuals but each individual will see it from his own standpoint, his own self-nature and self-being. Though all the spiritual individuals are, in essence, the same, yet they have their individual differentiations. This self-limitation is not

1. *L.D.*, Vol. II, Part I, p. 57.
2. *Ibid.*, p. 57.
3. *Ibid.*, p. 58.

fundamental but only "an individual specialisation of a common universality or totality; the spiritual individual would act from his own centre of the one truth and according to his self-nature, but on a common basis and not with any blindness to other-self and other-nature. It would be consciousness limiting its action with full knowledge, and not a movement of ignorance".[1]

Apart from the individual self-limitation, there is also the cosmic limitation of the Infinite consciousness. It is this power of limitation that is responsible for the existence and working of the universe. The Infinite consciousness supports the universe with only a certain part of itself and holds back all that is not needed for the cosmic movement. In the same way the self-determination of Mind, Life and Matter takes place according to the same principle. This power of self-limitation of Infinite and illimitable consciousness appears contradictory to our normal reason. But the Logic of the Infinite shows that this is also one of its powers. Because the Infinite consciousness is beyond all limitations, hence it can determine itself freely in innumerable ways. These self-determinations of the Infinite consciousness do not effect any division in it. They exist in the Infinite consciousness and are pervaded by it on all sides. So, on the basis of the higher reason or the Logic of the Infinite, we can understand the possibility of the individual and cosmic limitation of the Infinite consciousness. But the power of self-limitation does not as yet give us any account of the ignorance and the binding and blinding limitation of our phenomenal consciousness, our individual ego.

This is made clear in the third characteristic of the Infinite consciousness—its power of self-absorption. This self-absorption takes place in two ways: that of superconscience and of Inconscience. In the state of Superconscience, the Infinite consciousness takes a plunge into itself, into a state of pure self-awareness. This is a state of pure self-awareness of the Being. In this state, there is no knowledge of the individual or universal existence. The Infinite consciousness takes a plunge again into a state of utter darkness, called the Inconscient. The being of the Infinite is there, though it seems there more like an infinite non-

1. *L.D.*, Vol. II, Part I, pp. 58-59.

being. The Being is there in the Inconscient in the state of perfect self-oblivion. Its consciousness and force are also there intrinsically in that apparent non-being. It is out of the Inconscient that an ordered world is created. The truth of the Infinite consciousness lies hidden in the apparently automatic and blind working of the energy or force of the Inconscient. The states of the Superconscient and the Inconscient are that of the total self-absorption of the Infinite consciousness. There is also a partial self-absorption of the Infinite consciousness confined to a particular status such as of Mind, Life and Matter. This throws light incidentally on the opposition made by our minds between the indeterminate or *nirguṇa* and the determinate or *saguṇa* Brahman. These different aspects are possible due to the power of self-absorption of the Infinite consciousness. When the Infinite Consciousness confines itself to one particular status it becomes apparently oblivious of its other states. The whole of the Infinite Consciousness remains there behind the special status, but that particular state of Consciousness is not aware of It. The Consciousness confined to the *nirguṇa* aspect is not aware of the *saguṇa* and *vice versa*. "Yet it is now evident," observes Sri Aurobindo, "that to the Infinite Consciousness both the static and the dynamic are possible; these are two of its statuses and both can be present simultaneously in the universal awareness, the one witnessing the other and supporting it or not looking at it and yet automatically supporting it; or the silence and status may be there penetrating the activity or throwing it up like an ocean immobile below throwing up a mobility of waves on its surface".[1] Thus it is clear that Brahman by its conscious power or Consciousness-Force can manifest itself in different ways without falling from its transcendental status.

(D) *Fundamental Aspects of Existence and Consciousness-Force*

The fundamental principle of Existence manifests itself in relation to the universe in three aspects: self or Ātman, spirit or Puruṣa and God or Īśvara. In the same way the Consciousness-Force of Brahman manifests itself as Māyā, Prakṛti and Śakti corresponding to

1. *L.D.*, Vol. II, Part I, p. 61.

the three aspects of Existence—Ātman, Puruṣa and Īśvara respectively. As Consciousness-Force is inherent in the Self-existence of the Absolute and exists in an inalienable and inseparable union with Him, in the same way, the three aspects of Consciousness-Force, namely, Māyā, Prakṛti and Śakti exist fundamentally in an inseparable union with the three corresponding aspects of Self-Existence. Now we proceed to study these fundamental aspects, namely, Ātman-Māyā, Puruṣa-Prakṛti and Īśvara-Śakti and see how they bridge the gulf between the transcendent Brahman and the relative universe.

(i) Ātman-Māyā

Let us first of all take up the aspect of Ātman-Māyā. Brahman expresses itself in the universe as the Self of all existence, Ātman, the cosmic Self. But it also expresses itself as the Supreme Self transcendent of its own cosmicity and at the same time as individual universal in each being. Māyā or Consciousness-Force expresses itself as the self-power, Ātma-Śakti of the Ātman. We become aware of this aspect of Brahman first in a "status in silence, an immobile immutable being, self-existent, pervading the whole universe, omnipresent in all, but not dynamic or active, aloof from the ever mobile energy of Maya".[1] In the same way we can become aware of it as the Puruṣa, the conscious Being, separate from Prakṛti, standing aloof from the creation of the threefold guṇas. But this is only one aspect, the aspect of status or silence of Brahman. This is an essential realisation but not total realisation according to Sri Aurobindo. Brahman can also be realised in its power, in its creative and dynamic aspect. The power that creates the world is the power of the Self and not something apart from it. "As we cannot separate Fire and the power of Fire," remarks Sri Aurobindo "so we cannot separate the Divine Reality and its Consciousness-Force, Cit-Shakti".[2] The Self or Ātman is nevertheless a fundamental aspect of Brahman with a distinct emphasis on its impersonal aspect. It is to be noted that by the word Ātman we do not mean only the universal or the cosmic Self. Ātman is a comprehensive term and includes all the aspects of existence—

---

1. *L.D.*, Vol. II, Part I, p. 63.
2. *Ibid.*, p. 63.

the individual, the universal and the transcendent. It is due to this comprehensive nature of the Ātman that the individual self can realise its unity with the cosmic self and also with the transcendent Self beyond the cosmos. By the realisation of Self one can attain "individual liberation, a static-universality, a Nature—transcendence".[1] Though the Self can be experienced in its dynamic and creative aspect also, yet freedom and impersonality are essentially and, always the nature of the Self. By the realisation of the Self, the individual becomes free from the subjection of Prakṛti, from the shackles of its threefold *guṇas*. It is in this sense that Sri Aurobindo observes that "To realise the Self is to realise the eternal freedom of the Spirit."[2]

But the realisation of the transcendent Self is often accompanied by a great danger. It leads the individual to think that the self alone is real and the universe is unreal or false. The individual according to Sri Aurobindo, "finds soon that this separation in his consciousness has an immense liberative power, for by it he is no longer bound to the Ignorance, the Inconscience; it no longer appears to him the very nature of himself and things but an illusion which can be overcome or at least a temporary wrong self-experience, Maya. It is tempting to regard it as only a contradiction of the Divine, an incomprehensible mystery-play, masque or travesty of the Infinite—and so it irresistibly seems to his experience at times, on one side the luminous verity of Brahman, on the other a dark illusion of Maya".[3] But this is not the final realisation of the Ātman and its power. On a deeper and a higher realisation, Māyā appears not as contradictory of Brahman or as unreal but as a power of Brahman. As Sri Aurobindo puts it, "But something in him will not allow him to cut existence thus permanently in two and, looking more closely, he discovers that in this half-light or darkness too is the Eternal—it is the Brahman who is here with this face of Maya."[4] "This is the beginning of a growing spiritual experience," he further observes, "which reveals to him more and

1. *L.D.*, Vol. II, Part I, p. 64.
2. *Ibid.*, p. 64.
3. *The Synthesis of Yoga*, Part I, pp. 136-37.
4. *Ibid.*, p. 137.

more that what seemed to him dark incomprehensible Maya was all the time no other than the Consciousness—Puissance of the Eternal timeless and illimitable beyond the universe but spread out there under a mask of bright and dark opposites for the miracle of the slow manifestation of the Divine in Mind and Life and Matter".[1] The individual now realises his unity with the Divine both in its aspect of Existence and Consciousness-Force. Now whereas formerly Existence and Māyā seemed to be quite contradictory of each other, now they appear to be one with each other and as different faces of the same Reality. As Sri Aurobindo says, "The once conflicting but now biune duality of Brahman-Maya stands revealed to him as the first great dynamic aspect of the Self of all selves, the Master of existence, the Lord of the world-sacrifice and of his sacrifice."[2]

(ii) *Puruṣa-Prakṛti*

On another line of approach, one experiences the Absolute or Brahman in its aspect of Puruṣa-Prakṛti. "The Conscious Being, Purusha," says Sri Aurobindo, "is the Self as originator, witness, support and lord and enjoyer of the forms and works of Nature".[3] The aspect of Self or Ātman has been seen to be essentially transcendental and impersonal in character. The Puruṣa aspect is characteristically universal-individual and though it is separate from Nature, yet it is intimately connected with her. Nature acts not for her own sake but for the Puruṣa. The Puruṣa though essentially impersonal and universal in character, yet puts on a more personal aspect as the Sāṁkhyas hold. Then we have the plurality of souls to enjoy one common universal Nature. It is Nature that acts and not the Puruṣa. The Puruṣa or Conscious Being imparts its consciousness to Nature and is itself the witness of the workings or actions of Nature. Nature cannot indulge in its cosmic workings without the sanction of the Puruṣa. The Puruṣa is free to give or withdraw its sanction from the movements of Nature. But this freedom of withdrawing its sanction and holding itself back from

---

1. *The Synthesis of Yoga*, Part I, p. 137.
2. *Ibid.*, p. 138.
3. *L.D.*, Vol. II, Part I, p. 64.

being involved in the workings of Nature cannot be attained unless the Puruṣa has realised his real being, his separation from the products of Nature. In the state of ignorance, the Puruṣa is simply passive and gives automatic sanction to all the movements of Nature. In that state he becomes so much identified with his body-mind organism that he does not realise his distinct and separate identity and so is led away by the powerful forces of nature like a straw by the mighty movements of winds. It is the state of utter subjection of Puruṣa to the forces of Nature. As Sri Aurobindo states, "If the Purusha in us is passive and allows Nature to act, accepting all she imposes on him, giving a constant automatic sanction, then the soul in mind, life, body, the mental, vital, physical being in us, becomes subject to our nature, ruled by its formation, driven by its activities; that is the normal state of our ignorance."[1] But if the Puruṣa becomes aware of itself, realises its distinct identity from the creations of Nature, it keeps itself back from the movements of Nature. Then the soul is able to realise its freedom from the subjection of Nature. As long as the soul remains identified with the physical, vital, mental organism, it cannot realise its freedom. Then it considers itself the doer of all actions and the cause of all movements. But on the realisation of freedom it sees itself inactive and considers Nature to be the cause of all movements and individual and cosmic workings. In this state the soul has the freedom of accepting the workings of Nature and giving its sanction or keeping itself aloof from them. Now if it gives its sanction, it does it voluntarily and in full knowledge. Its sanction is no longer automatic and passive. At this stage the soul gets the power and freedom to effect a direct transformation in its relationship with Nature. It can indulge in the cosmic play voluntarily and in full consciousness of its real being. Whereas formerly it was involved in the movement of Nature involuntarily, passively and unconsciously, now it does it in full consciousness and knowledge and while involved in its workings, it considers itself as separate from Nature and its creations. Or it may stand back from the works of nature and merge itself into the silence of the Self. The soul is also free to effect a drastic change in the formations of its present

---

1. *L.D.*, Vol. II, Part I, p. 65.

nature. It can rise to a higher level of existence and can recreate the individual existence. That is, it can make the present physical and mental formations of our being fit to receive the higher powers of the soul and work in accordance with its higher nature. At this stage, the Puruṣa is no longer under the subjection of Nature. It becomes now lord or master of its nature, Īśvara.

Sri Aurobindo's conception of Puruṣa-Prakṛti is more comprehensive and integral than that of the Sāṁkhya philosophy. The Sāṁkhya holds Puruṣa and Prakṛti to be eternally separate entities but in relation to each other. Prakṛti or Nature is an executive power. Apart from the Puruṣa or the conscious principle, Prakṛti or Nature is inert, mechanical, inconscient. Puruṣa is conscious but inactive. Nature is active but devoid of all consciousness. Whatever consciousness is found in the constituents of Nature is the reflection of the consciousness of Puruṣa. Mind and intelligence become conscious by the consciousness of Puruṣa. Moreover the Sāṁkhya believes in the plurality of souls. According to Sri Aurobindo, all these positions of the Sāṁkhya are perfectly valid in experience but he considers them only as pragmatic truths and not the fundamental truth of soul or of Nature. Prakṛti or Nature, according to him, though apparently inconscient, conceals a secret consciousness as becomes evident when the principles of life and mind evolve during the course of evolution. In the same way the conscious being or Puruṣa is many in its individual souls but in its real nature it is one and the same in all. Giving his own view of Puruṣa and Prakṛti, Sri Aurobindo observes, "Prakriti presents itself as an inconscient Energy in the material world, but, as the scale of consciousness rises, she reveals herself more and more as a conscious-force and we perceive that even her inconscience concealed a secret consciousness; so too conscious being is many in its individual souls, but in its self we can perceive it as one in all and one in its own essential existence".[1] Moreover, according to Sri Aurobindo, though the experience of soul and nature as dual is true, the experience of their unity is also true and more fundamental in nature. Nature is able to impose its forms and workings on Being simply because it is the force of Being. The Being can

---

1. *L.D.*, Vol. II, Part I, p. 67.

control Nature, can become its lord or master simply because it is its own nature. Even in the state of ignorance and passivity, Nature cannot continue its process without the consent and sanction of the Being or Puruṣa. So this close relationship between Being and Nature shows that the two are not fundamentally separate and alien to each other. "The duality," says Sri Aurobindo, "is a position taken up, a double status accepted for the operations of the self-manifestation of the being; but there is no eternal and fundamental separateness and dualism of Being and its Consciousness-Force, of the Soul and Nature".[1]

Hence the duality between Soul and Nature is only apparent and not real. "An apparent duality is created in order that there may be a free action of Nature working itself out with the support of the Spirit and again a free and masterful action of the Spirit controlling and working out Nature."[2] The duality is also necessary that the Spirit may be free to withdraw itself from the formations of Nature, dissolve them and create a new or higher formation. The Puruṣa aspect and the Prakṛti aspect always go together. The Spirit and the Consciousness-Force assume the various grades corresponding to each other. In the supreme status, the Spirit is the supreme Being, Puruṣottama and the Consciousness-Force is his supreme Nature or as the Gītā calls it, Parā-Prakṛti. In each status of the gradations of Nature, the Spirit makes a corresponding manifestation. In the status of Mind, the Spirit manifests as the mental being, in Life-Nature, it becomes the vital being. In the grade of Matter, it becomes physical being. In Supermind, the Spirit becomes the being of knowledge and in the supreme transcendent status, it manifests itself as the Being of Bliss and pure Existence. In man, the Spirit is present as the Psychic Entity, the inner Self behind all the formulations of our phenomenal nature and supporting them. Thus it is clear that the Puruṣa and Prakṛti, though apparently different from each other in certain modes of manifestation, are one in essence. They are the fundamental aspects of the same Reality or Brahman. "Wherever there is Prakriti," says Sri Aurobindo, "there is Purusha; wherever there is Purusha, there is Prakriti".[3]

1. *L.D.*, Vol. II, Part I, p. 67.
2. *Ibid.*, pp. 67-68.
3. *The Synthesis of Yoga*, Part I, p. 139.

Thus Sri Aurobindo makes a decisive improvement on the position of the Sāṁkhya with regard to its conception of Puruṣa and Prakṛti. There is, as has been stated above, an underlying unity behind the apparent duality of Puruṣa and Prakṛti. In the same way there is the fundamental oneness of Puruṣa behind the apparent diversity of many souls according to Sri Aurobindo. In the supramental status the Puruṣa and Prakṛti do not appear as opposed to and independent of each other but as the inseparable aspects of the same Reality. As Sri Aurobindo puts it, "At a certain spiritual and supramental level the Duality becomes still more perfectly Two-in-one, the Master Soul with the Conscious Force within it, and its potentiality disowns all barriers and breaks through every limit. Thus this once separate, now biune duality of Purusha-Prakriti is revealed to him in all its truth as the second great instrumental and effective aspect of the soul of all souls, the Master of existence, the Lord of the Sacrifice".[1]

(iii) *Īśvara-Śakti*

Now we come to the third aspect in which the Absolute or Brahman manifests itself in the universe. It is the dual aspect of Īśvara-Śakti. As Sri Aurobindo puts it, "On yet another line of approach the seeker meets another corresponding but in aspect distinct Duality in which the biune character is more immediately apparent—the dynamic Duality of Ishwara-shakti."[2] Īśvara is the Lord and creator of the universe. The Being is in its fundamental nature master of its nature. In the first aspect of the Reality we have seen that the Māyā or power of the Ātman created the universe out of the stuff of and by the support of Ātman. The Ātman was necessary as the substratum of the universe. Apart from Ātman, Māyā could neither create the universe out of nothing, nor could it support it in the void. Though the Ātman represents the state of silence and immobility, yet its support and sanction is necessary for the creation and movement of the universe. In the same way, in the second aspect, the aspect of Puruṣa-Prakṛti, we have seen that though the Puruṣa is inactive, yet its consent whether involuntary and auto-

---

1. *The Synthesis of Yoga*, Part I, p. 140.
2. *Ibid.*, p. 140.

matic or voluntary is necessary to support the workings of Nature. But in these two aspects of Reality, the Being though fundamentally and essentially is the master of its nature, yet outwardly it does not appear to be so. But in the third aspect of the Reality, the Divine Being or Īśvara is not fundamentally but also overtly seen as the omnipotent ruler of its nature. He is seen as the omnipotent, omniscient and omnipresent Being, the creator of the individual and cosmic existences, the great dynamo of all the individual, cosmic and supra-cosmic powers and energies, the supreme Puruṣa present in the heart of all existences, the lord and ruler of all works, the Enjoyer of all delight, the father and friend of all creatures, the great depository of eternal peace, happiness and bliss. This aspect of Reality is in a certain sense, the most comprehensive of all the aspects, for all the aspects are here united in single formation. Īśvara is supra-cosmic as well as intracosmic. He is the divine Inhabitant of all the individual beings, the underlying reality of the universe and also the transcendent Being. Thus, Īśvara is, according to Sri Aurobindo, not the God of popular religions, the personal God who is limited by his qualities and is individual and separate from all others. Īśvara is neither the *saguṇa* Brahman possessed of all qualities nor *nirguṇa* Brahman devoid of all qualities. "Neither is this the Saguna Brahman active and possessed of qualities, for that is only one side of the being of the Ishwara; the Nirguna immobile and without qualities is another aspect of His existence. Ishwara is Brahman the Reality, Self, Spirit, revealed as possessor, enjoyer of his own self-existence, creator of the universe and one with it, Pantheos, and yet superior to it, the Eternal, the Infinite, the Ineffable, the Divine Transcendence."[1]

All these three aspects taken together give a complete view of the relation between the Self-Existence and Consciousness-Force. They also make it clear that there is no contradiction or incompatability between the individual, the cosmic and the transcendent Existence. In the aspects of Ātman-Māyā and Puruṣa-Prakṛti, there is an apparent duality. Being and Force in both these aspects appear to be separate from each other. There is an apparent duality between the static Ātman and dynamic Māyā, between the inactive but conscient Puruṣa and the active but inconscient

1. *L.D.*, Vol. II, Part I, pp. 69-70.

Prakṛti. But when we come to the aspect of Īśvara-Śakti, we find that the Force or Śakti is itself the power of the Being, the Self-Existent, the Īśvara. Īśvara is the lord of Śakti and of all things. "Being and its Consciousness-Force, Spirit and Nature cannot be fundamentally dual: what Nature does is really done by the Spirit."[1] So there is no fundamental duality between Existence and Consciousness-Force. They are inseparable and inalienable from each other. If they appear as distinct from each other in certain aspects of Reality, it is only to serve some pragmatic purpose. There the duality is merely apparent and not real. There is a truth in the perception of duality. The perception of duality is valid but to say that the duality is the ultimate truth is far from truth. The fundamental and ultimate truth is the realisation of their unity and not their separateness and duality. The Consciousness-Force as Māyā is "conceptively creative of all things" as Prakṛti, it is "made dynamically executive, working out all things under the witnessing eye of the Conscious Being, the Self or Spirit", as Śakti, it is both "conceptively creative and dynamically executive of all the divine workings". "One Being, One Reality as Self bases, supports, informs, as Purusha or conscious Being experiences, as Ishwara wills, governs and possesses its world of manifestation created and kept in motion and action by its own Consciousness-Force or Self-Power, Maya, Prakriti, Shakti."[2]

These three aspects of Existence and Consciousness-Force constitute the whole realm of duality. Existence and Consciousness-Force in their transcendent or ultimate status are one and the same. There are no distinctions and differences in the ultimate state of the Absolute. Śiva and Śakti are ultimately one and do not appear as dual in the transcendent status. But in the manifestation, the ultimate Reality or Saccidānanda appears in the dual aspects of Īśvara-Śakti, Ātman-Māyā and Puruṣa-Prakṛti. These are the fundamental dual aspects of the ultimate Reality or Brahman. In our gross universe, Existence and Consciousness-Force of Brahman appear as *Jīva* and *Jagat* or world. We can solve the riddle of the universe and establish its relation with Brahman only if we take account of all these dual aspects. Otherwise, we cannot relate the world to the transcendent and differenceless Absolute. Ordinarily

1. *L.D.*, Vol. II, Part I, p. 74.
2. *Ibid.*, p. 76.

Jīva, the individual soul and *Jagat* or the world appear as quite opposed to and independent of each other. But as we rise in the higher planes of consciousness, we find that the *Jīva* and *Jagat* are not really opposed to and independent of each other but are the dual aspect of the same Reality. To the consciousness of Īśvara, the world has no independent existence. It is a part and parcel of Him. Śakti is not opposed to Īśvara. The world is seen to be the manifestation of His Śakti or power. Īśvara is the supreme Subject to which the whole world is object. But here the world-object is not seen by the Subject as something different from or opposed to it but as a part of it. The distinction between Īśvara, Jīva and the world is there but Jīva and *Jagat* or world do not appear as apart from, and independent of Īśvara. Not only that; they are seen to be part and parcel of Īśvara, as constituted of the stuff of His power of Śakti. The unity of Īśvara is there intact, but it is expressing itself in the multiplicity. Beyond this is the differenceless unity of the transcendent Absolute where Existence or Consciousness-Force, Śiva and Śakti remain in an inseparable and indistinguishable manner. No play of duality, no movement of the world can affect this ineffable and unutterable unity of the Absolute or Brahman. This state of the Absolute, the highest and the ultimate state is beyond all differences. All differences fall short of the Absolute. But it does not mean that the differences and duality are unreal. Duality is nothing but the manifestation of the Absolute, hence is real. But the Absolute in its highest status cannot be characterised by any of the categories which are applicable in the realm of duality. Thus Sri Aurobindo arrives at an Integral Advaitism without denying the reality of the world and the individual souls. We have seen that he has been able to arrive at his Integral Advaitism by his conception of the ultimate creative force as conscious in nature.

(E) Conception of Śakti in Śāktaism and Sri Aurobindo's System Compared

Sri Aurobindo's conception of Conscious Force resembles that of Śāktaism. In fact, his conception of Conscious Force or Cit-Śakti is taken from Tantra. We find the direct influence of both the Vedāntic and the Tāntric systems in his conception of the Absolute. He himself observes in one of his letters, "It is only if you approach the Supreme through his double aspect of Sat and Chit-Shakti, double but inseparable, that the total truth of things can become manifest to the inner experience. This other side was developed by the Shakta Tantrics. The two together, the Vedantic and the Tantric truth unified, can arrive at an integral knowledge."[1] In Śāktaism, the ultimate creative force is considered as Conscious in nature. The Ultimate Reality consists of *Śiva* and *Śakti* in an inseparable and indistinguishable union with each other. Śiva is represented as omnipresent, pure consciousness (prakāśa), impersonal and inactive. It is pure being transcending all relativity. Śiva and Śakti are related to each other as *Prakāśa* and *Vimarśa*. Vimarśa is, according to Bhāskarācārya, the spontaneous vibration of the ultimate reality. "The first touch of relation in the pure Absolute is *Vimarśa*, which gives rise to the world of distinctions. Vimarśa or Śakti is the power latent in the absolute or pure consciousness. It is the Absolute personified; consciousness become a subject, and it passes over into its opposite, the not-self or the object. If Śiva is consciousness (cit), Śakti is the formative energy of consciousness, Cidrūpiṇī."[2] Sir John Woodroffe observes, "Śiva and Śakti are not two independent Realities but one Realty in two aspects, namely static and kinetic....Śakti or Power is that, which, in itself unchangeable, produces out of itself as Material Cause the world of change. Common language speaks of the Power of Śiva, but strictly Power or Śakti is Śiva. When the one Reality or Brahman is regarded as the Changeless Consciousness it is called Śiva; when it is regarded as the power of Consciousness or Consciousness-Power which projects the universe from out of itself, it is called Śakti. It is a fundamental doctrine that there is no Śiva without Śakti, nor Śakti without Śiva....Śakti is only the active power of actionless Consciousness (Śiva)."[3] Thus the whole world is the creation of Śakti which is one with Śiva. Śiva by himself cannot create the world. As we find it clearly stated in the opening verse of *Saundaryalaharī*, "Śiva, when he is united with Śakti is able to create; otherwise he is unable even to move."[4] But the unity or

---

1. *Letters of Sri Aurobindo*, 1947 Ed., pp. 52-53.
2. Radhakrishnan, *Indian Philosophy*, Vol. II, p. 735.
3. *The World as Power, Reality*, pp. 81-82.
4. शिव: शक्त्या युक्तो यदि भवति शक्त: प्रभवितुं ।
   न चेदेवं देवो न खलु कुशल: स्पन्दितुमपि ॥

oneness of Śiva and Śakti, is not disturbed by the process of creation. "In the perfect experience of ānanda, Śiva and Śakti are indistinguishable. The two coalesce in one being. Śiva answers to the indeterminate Brahman in a state of quiescence; Śakti is determinate Brahman endowed with *icchā* (will), *jñāna* (knowledge), and *kriyā* (action) projecting the whole objective universe. Śiva and Śakti are one, since force is inherent in existence. The force may be at rest or in action, but it exists none the less in both the states. The potentiality of the whole object-world exists as the Śakti of Śiva."[1]

The supreme Śakti does not create the world while remaining in its pure transcendent status. It has to put itself in the garb of Prakṛti in order to manifest the world. So our gross universe is created by Prakṛiti which is non-conscious. But this Prakṛti is unconscious only in its outward appearance. It is ultimately conscious in nature. "Prakṛti or māyā is looked upon as of the substance of Devī. Within the womb of Śakti is māyā or prakṛti, the matrix of the universe, potential in *pralaya*, active in creation."[2]

"Within, so to say, the womb of Śakti is Māyā or Prakṛti, the matrix of the universe which during cosmic inaction or Mahāpralaya is potential and latent even as fire is latent within wood. Māyā or Prakṛti is not a non-reality, nor a state of equilibrium of certain things; nor is it a something—nothing, something little (yatkiñcit), an idea (bhāva). It is immutable and permanent as the triple aspect already mentioned. It enfolds to use chemical phraseology, a triad of Guṇas or Reals, which mutating and combining, make up the appearance of the ever-changing world, and which in Mahāpralaya, are withdrawn within the bosom from where they emerged. Māyā or Prakṛti, it must be understood, is ever in association with cit, be it in Mahāpralaya or in evolution; for there is only One without a second, and Prakṛti must be an inseparable part or power of It."[3]

Thus a clear-cut distinction is made between the two aspects of Śakti in Śāktaism, namely, first, Śakti as Māyā or Prakṛti and second as ultimate conscious power and it is shown that what we call Māyā or Prakṛti is nothing but the outward aspect of the supreme conscious Force. Thus Śāktaism escapes from the dualism of ul-

1. Radhakrishnan, *op. cit.*, Vol. II, p. 735.
2. *Ibid.*, p. 736.
3. *Principles of Tantra*, Part II (Edited by Arthur Avalon), p. xvii-xviii (Introduction).

timate Reality and creative Force by conceiving Śakti or Force as
conscious and as One with Śiva. The conception of Śakti in this
system is definitely superior to that of the Vedānta. The *Tantras*
have taken great care to emphasise this conscious nature of the
supreme Śakti and its oneness and inseparability with Śiva or the
transcendent Reality. "The notion seems to prevail that what the
Tāntriks posit by Śakti is dead matter, Prakṛti. Nothing can be
farther from this unwarrantable conclusion. Śakti, as that which is
potential, is much more expressive than Brahman considered as
something neutral. Prakṛti, the matrix of the universe of names and
forms, is the veil through which alone it is possible to approach
the Sat-Cit-Ānanda Brahman by the human consciousness. It is the
destiny of human consciousness, which is relative to merge itself
into the one true Consciousness, which is absolute, and thus to
fulfil the end and aim of life. The *Tantra,* therefore, along with
all other spiritual sciences, worships the Absolute through that in
which it is manifested."¹ It is said further, "Cit or Śakti is self-
manifesting. But immutable, undifferentiated Prakṛti is the only
ground in which it can manifest itself so as to be cognisable to
the self, be it of man or of Devatā. Prakṛti, therefore, is not a 'veil,'
but, on the other hand, is Śakti itself in Evolution."²

Thus we find a close resemblance of Sri Aurobindo's concep-
tion of Śakti or Conscious Force with that of Śāktaism. As he
observes, "In all that is done in the universe, the Divine through
his Shakti is behind all action but he is veiled by his Yoga Maya
and works through the ego of the Jiva in the lower nature."³ "The
One whom we adore as the Mother is the divine Conscious Force
that dominates all existence, one and yet so many-sided that to
follow her movement is impossible even for the quickest mind and
for the freest and most vast intelligence."⁴ In the vein of Tāntric
description, Sri Aurobindo observes further, "The One original tran-
scendent Shakti, the Mother stands above all the worlds and bears
in her eternal consciousness the Supreme Divine. Alone, she
harbours the absolute Power and the ineffable Presence; contain-
ing or calling the Truths that have to be manifested, she brings

1. *Principles of Tantra,* (Introduction) p. xviii-xix.
2. *Ibid.,* p. xix.
3. *The Mother,* (1946 Ed.), p. 11.
4. *Ibid.,* pp. 36-37.

them down from the Mystery in which they were hidden into the light of her infinite consciousness and gives them a form of force in her omnipotent power and her boundless life and a body in the universe."[1] "The supreme is manifest in her forever as the everlasting Sachchidananda, manifested through her in the worlds as the one and dual consciousness of Ishwara-Shakti and the dual principles of Purusha-Prakriti, embodied by her in the worlds and in the Planes and the Gods and their Energies and figures because of her as all that is in the known worlds and in unknown others. All is her play with the Supreme; all is her manifestation of the mysteries of the Eternal, the miracles of the Infinite. All is she, for all are parcel and portion of the divine Conscious Force. Nothing can be here or elsewhere but what she decides and the Supreme sanctions; nothing can take shape except what she moved by the Supreme perceives and forms after casting it into seed in her creating Ananda."[2] It is Mother who forms the connecting link between the individual, the universal and the transcendent aspects of the Absolute. Sri Aurobindo observes, "There are three ways of being of the Mother of which you can become aware when you enter into touch of oneness with the Conscious Force that upholds us and the universe. Transcendent, the original supreme Shakti stands above the worlds and links the creation to the ever unmanifest mystery of the Supreme. Universal, the cosmic Mahashakti, she creates all these beings and contains and enters, supports and conducts all these million processes and forces. Individual, she embodies the power of these two vaster ways of her existence, makes them living and near to us and mediates between the human personality and the diving Nature."[3] Thus we find that the conception of Śakti in Śāktaism and Sri Aurobindo's system is fundamentally the same though there are certain important differences in other respects.

(F) Conception of Śakti in Kashmir Śaivism and Sri Aurobindo's System Compared

We find a distinct leaning towards Advaitism in Kashmir Śaivism. In this system Śiva is regarded as the ultimate reality. He enjoys

---

1. *The Mother*, p. 39.
2. *Ibid.*, pp. 40-41.
3. *Ibid.*, pp. 38-39.

infinite consciousness and unrestricted independence. It is Śiva who manifests himself in the dual forms of subject and object, as the experiencer as well as the experienced. He creates the world by the mere force of his will. "He makes the world appear in himself as if it were distinct from himself, though not so really; even as objects appear in a mirror. God is as unaffected by the objects of his creation as the mirror is by the images reflected in it. By his own wonderful power (Śakti) inherent in him, God appears in the form of souls and constitutes objects for their experiences. The only reality is the unlimited pure self, the one and only substratum of the universe, whose activity (spanda, vibration) is the cause of all distinctions."[1]

Śiva is the changeless reality underlying the universe. Śiva remains changeless in spite of his manifesting the entire universe by his energy or Śakti. His Śakti has an infinity of aspects, the chief of which are cit (intelligence), Ānanda (bliss), Icchā (will), Jñāna (knowledge) and Kriyā (creative power). Thus the force or energy of Śiva is conscious in nature. It manifests the five transcendental categories, namely, Śivatattva, Śaktitattva, Sadāśiva, Īśvaratattva and Sadvidyā. These five transcendental categories constitute the higher or pure creation.

The lower creation consists of the phenomenal world. The phenomenal world is created by the force of Māyā. "The first manifestation of the impure creation is Māyā. It is this Tattva, the manifestation of which, first of all, apparently breaks the unity of the Universal Self. It is the most distinctive power of the Universal Self in its creative aspect. It manifests diversity independently of any external helper or prompter. It is conceived both as the power of obscuration and as the primary cause of all the limited manifestation. In its former aspect, it is often referred to as "Moha" and in the latter as Parāniśa. Its effect also by transference of epithet (upacāra) is spoken of as māyā."[2] The Māyā as the force of obscuration makes the one Universal Self appear as innumerable individual selves who are ignorant of their real nature and enjoy only a limited amount of the powers of knowledge and action. It

1. Radhakrishnan, op. cit., Vol. II, pp. 732-33.
2. K.C. Pandey, Abhinavagupta: An Historical and Philosophical Study, pp. 244-45.

is on account of its throwing the individual selves into this delusion that it is also referred to as "Moha".[1]

Thus the higher creation is manifested by the supreme conscious force or Śakti and the lower creation by Māyā. The recognition of a subordinate power, namely, Māyā is logically necessary in this system. For if Śakti is regarded as the creator of the world then the phenomena of ignorance and limitation cannot be explained. "The supposition of Māyā as a principle of obscuration is both necessary and logical. For, if the Ultimate Reality is possessed of all the five powers, Cit, Ānand, Icchā, Jñāna and Kriyā, and so is perfect in every way and the universe is identical with it, it has to be explained; where does the plurality of selves with all their limitations come from; and what is the cause of the limited creation which forms the object of experience of the limited beings? To account for these facts, or rather, to answer these questions it is that the Māyā is supposed to be the force of obscuration. As such, Māyā Tattva hides the true nature of the Self so that not only all its five powers are obscured but the universe also, which was in relation of identity with it disappears. Thus there arises the occasion for the other aspect of Māyā, viz., as the cause of the limited universe to come into play and produce the limited universe in all its parts almost simultaneously much as emblic myrobalan (āmalakī), being forcefully struck with a staff, lets fall its fruits."[2]

But the principle of Māyā does not affect the unity of the Absolute or Śiva in this system because it is itself the manifestation of the supreme Reality. It is not something independent of Śiva or the supreme Reality. Hence it does not constitute a limit to it. In this respect we find an agreement between Sri Aurobindo's system and Kashmir Śaivism. Sri Aurobindo also looks upon the world as a creation of ignorance. But this ignorance itself is the form of the

1. (a) मोहयत्यनेन शक्तिविशेषेण इति वा मोहो मायाशक्ति: ।
        Īśvara Pratyabhijñā Vimarsini (Kashmir), 1.35.
   (b) माया च नाम देवस्य शक्तिरव्यतिरेकिणी ।
        भेदावभासस्वातन्त्र्यं तथा हि स तया कृत: ॥ (Tantrāloka vi. 116)
2. K.C. Pandey, op. cit., pp. 245-46.
   सा माया क्षोभमापन्ना विश्वं सूते समन्तत: ।
   दण्डाहतेवामलकी फलानि किल यद्यपि ॥ (Tantrāloka vi. 128).

supreme Reality, being nothing else than its power of self-limitation. The world is a creation of ignorance, of lower nature or what the Gītā calls Aparā Prakṛti. But the power of ignorance is not something essentially opposed to the power of knowledge. Prakṛti is according to him not opposed to conscious force or *cit-śakti*, but is its external aspect. The real force of the Absolute is conscious in nature but it assumes the garb of unconsciousness or ignorance in order to manifest itself in the different limited and transitory forms of the world. The Advaitism of Sri Aurobindo's system as well as of Kashmir Śaivism is maintained due to the fact that in both of these systems, the supreme creative force is looked upon as conscious in nature and the unconscious force, Māyā or Prakṛti is regarded as a limited manifestation and an external garb of the supreme conscious force. Thus they are able to affirm the oneness of the Absolute without denying the reality of the world.

We find this distinction in the conception of force indicated in the *Gītā* also.

(G) *Gītā's Classification of Force into Parā and Aparā Prakṛti*

The main purpose of the Gītā's classification of the two Natures, the Spiritual and the phenomenal or as the Gītā puts it, the Parā and the Aparā Prakṛti, is to give an integral knowledge of the whole of Existence or to arrive at a full and complete knowledge of the supreme Being. The Supreme Nature or the Parā Prakṛti is described by the Gītā as the inherent power of the divine Being. It is one with the Divine in its being and essence. The Divine is the Being. The supreme Nature is his Power. This is the creative principle inherent in the supreme Puruṣa. It is as Sri Aurobindo says, "the executive power of the Purusha, his activity of being—not a separate entity but himself in Power." There is no dualism between the supreme Being and the creative force. Both are one and the same. The supreme Nature is only the power aspect of the supreme Being. It is as Sri Aurobindo calls in "The Life Divine" The Consciousness-Force or *Cit-Śakti*. The lower nature or Aparā Prakṛti is the principle of ignorance. It works through the three *guṇas*, namely, *sattva* or the principle of light or wisdom, *rajas* or the principle of activity and *tamas* or the principle of darkness and inertia. It is, as the Sāṁkhya says, the cause of all the phenomenal or cosmic creation. This is described by the *Gītā* as consisting of the eightfold general principles—the five elements or conditions of material being, mind, reason and ego.[1] All these manifold existences, all these phenomenal becomings are under the subjection of these three modes of Nature. But there is behind the working of the lower Nature, the secret and invisible principle of the supreme Nature which is really directing all its operations.[2] The lower Nature in the course of its evolution presents the principles and the workings of the higher Nature in a strictly limited, perverted and distorted manner. But nevertheless, it does not bring forth anything independently of itself. It derives the essence of all phenomena from the supreme Nature. The supreme Nature becomes the multiple individual souls in order to support the phenomenal becoming.

According to Sri Aurobindo, the *Gītā* solves the dualism between the supreme Being and the creative force by conceiving the latter as conscious in nature and as one with it in its transcendent status. Though the phenomenal world according to the *Gītā* is the creation of Aparā Prakṛti, yet the Aparā Prakṛti is in Sri Aurobindo's view not anything opposed to Parā Prakṛti but only its outward and limited aspect. Thus the Aparā Prakṛti can be reconciled and integrated with the Absolute or the supreme Being without affecting its unity. The reason of the dualism of the Sāṁkhya is that it stops at the lower nature or Aparā Prakṛti and has got no idea of the higher nature or Parā Prakṛti. As he observes, "The *Gītā* also, if it stopped there, would have to make the same incurable antinomy between the Self and cosmic Nature which would then be only the Maya of the three gunas and all this cosmic existence would be simply the result of this Maya; it could be nothing else. But there is something else, there is a higher principle, a nature of spirit, *parā-praktir me*. There is a supreme nature of the Divine which is the real source of cosmic existence and its fundamental creative force and effective energy and of which the other lower and ignorant Nature is only a derivation and a dark shadow. In this highest dynamics, Purusha and Prakriti are one. Prakriti there

1. भूमिरापोऽनलो वायुः खं मनो बुद्धिरेव च ।
   अहंकार इतीयं मे भिन्ना प्रकृतिरष्टधा ॥ (*B.G.* 7.4)
2. अपरेयमितस्त्वन्यां प्रकृतिं विद्धि मे पराम् ।
   जीवभूतां महाबाहो ययेदं धार्यते जगत् ॥ (*B.G.* 7.5)

is only the will and the executive power of the Purusha, his activity of being not a separate entity, but himself in Power."[1] Thus the Gītā arrives at an integral monism by conceiving nature as not anything opposed to the Divine but only as a part of Him and one with Him in essence.

Sri Aurobindo's integral Advaitism is, as has been shown above, also based on this fundamental unity between the Absolute and its creative force or cit-śakti. Sri Aurobindo further adds to Gītā's conception of Parā and Aparā Prakṛti his idea of evolution by which the Aparā Prakṛti ultimately evolves into Parā Prakṛti. Thus the creative force and the Absolute are ultimately one with each other. It is this fundamental unity that reconciles all the so-called oppositions between the individual, the cosmic and the transcendent aspects of Existence, as we have shown in the foregoing pages.

---

1. *Essays on the Gītā*, Second Series (1945 Ed.), pp. 6-7.

CHAPTER V

THE ABSOLUTE AS BLISS

(A) *Bliss as the Essence of all Existence*

The third aspect of the Absolute is Bliss. As the Absolute is Existence and Conscious Force, so it is also Bliss.[1] "This primary, ultimate and eternal Existence as seen by the Vedāntins" observes Sri Aurobindo "is not merely bare existence, or a conscious existence whose consciousness is crude force or power; it is a conscious existence the very term of whose being, the very term of whose consciousness is bliss. As in absolute existence there can be no nothingness, no night of inconscience, no deficiency, that is to say, no failure of Force—for if there were any of these things, it would not be absolute—so also there can be no suffering, no negation of delight".[2] "Absoluteness of conscious existence, further says Sri Aurobindo, "is illimitable bliss of conscious existence; the two are only different phrases for the same thing. All illimitableness, all infinity, all absoluteness is pure delight".[3] The Upaniṣad also says, 'That which is infinite is bliss, there is no bliss in the finite.'[4] The finite according to Śaṅkara is not possessed of bliss for the reason that it is full of desires which are the root cause of all sufferings.[5] The infinite, says Śaṅkara, is full of the nature of

1. आनन्दो ब्रह्मेति व्यजानात् । (*Tait.* 3.6)
2. *L.D.*, Vol. I, pp. 114-15.
3. *Ibid.*, p. 115.
4. यो वै भूमा तत्सुखं नाल्पे सुखमस्ति । (*Chān.* 7.23.1)
5. अतस्तस्मिन्नल्पे सुखं नास्ति ।
   अल्पस्याधिकतृष्णाहेतुत्वात् ।
   तृष्णा च दुःखबीजम् । (Śaṅkara's Commentary, *Chān.* 7.23.1)

bliss as it is free from all desires that inevitably lead to all sorts of sufferings.[1] That desires are the real causes of our sufferings and that the more one gets rid of desires, the more one is freed from sufferings is seen in our everyday life. As Sri Aurobindo puts it, "Even our relative humanity has this experience that all dissatisfaction means a limit, an obstacle—satisfaction comes by realisation of something withheld, by the surpassing of the limit, the overcoming of the obstacle."[2] Thus one cannot hope to enjoy the infinite bliss, within the limits of the finite existence. In order to enjoy the infinite bliss, one has to rise high and transcend all one's spatial and temporal limitations.

The bliss of Brahman is not limited to any one particular status. It does not only manifest itself in Being but in Becoming as well. As Sri Aurobindo puts it, "The self-delight of Brahman is not limited, however, by the still and motionless possession of its absolute self-being. Just as its force of consciousness is capable of throwing itself into forms infinitely and with an endless variation, so also its self-delight is capable of movement, of variation, of revelling in that infinite flux and mutability of itself represented by numberless teeming universes. To loose forth and enjoy this infinite movement and variation of its self-delight is the object of its extensive or creative play of Force."[3] Thus Sri Aurobindo holds the Upaniṣadic view that the universe comes out of Brahman. "From Delight all these beings are born, by Delight they exist and grow, to Delight they return."[4] Bliss or Delight constitutes the content or value aspect of the Absolute. It is the content or value aspect of the Absolute that gives concreteness to it. Without content or value, the Absolute will be mere abstract entity. To call the ultimate Reality merely existence or existence-consciousness and ignore its aspect of bliss or value is to give a one-sided view of it. To take away its value aspect means depriving it of all its concreteness. The importance of both these aspects of the Absolute is expressed by

---

1. अतो भूमैव सुखम् ।
   तृष्णादिदुःखबीजत्वासम्भवाद्धूम्नः । (Śaṅkara's Commentary, Chān. 7.23.1)
2. L.D., Vol. I, p. 115.
3. Ibid., p. 115.
4. आनन्दाद्धयेव खल्विमानि भूतानि जायन्ते । आनन्देन जातानि जीवन्ति ।
   आनन्दं प्रयन्त्यभिसंविशन्ति । (Tait. 3.6)

Bradley in the following words, "If we take up anything considered real, no matter what it is, we find in it two aspects. There are always two things we can say about it; and if we cannot say both, we have not got reality. There is a "what" and a "that", an existence and a content and the two are inseparable. That anything should be, and yet should be nothing in particular, or that a quality should not qualify and give a character to anything is obviously impossible. If we try to get the "that" by itself, we do not get it, for either we have it qualified or else we fail utterly. If we try to get the "what" by itself, we find at once that it is not all. It points to something beyond, and cannot exist by itself and as a bare adjective. Neither of these aspects, if you isolate it, can be taken as real, or indeed in that case is itself any longer. They are distinguishable only and not divisible."[1] Hence it is necessary that both these aspects, the aspect of existence and of content or value must be considered in order to have a comprehensive grasp of the Absolute. Not only these two aspects but the aspect of consciousness also holds equal importance in the Vedānta and in Sri Aurobindo's system. Following the view of the ancient sages, Sri Aurobindo gives a comprehensive account of the Absolute. The Absolute, according to him, as we have seen above, is Existence, Consciousness-Force and Bliss. Sri Aurobindo holds that the Absolute cannot be ultimately identified even with our conception of Saccidānanda. But Saccidānanda is the best description that our language can give in a positive manner of the Absolute. All the beings of the universe depend for their existence on the bliss of Brahman. "Who indeed would breathe, who will live, if this Bliss were not in the ether."[2] Brahman is called *rasa* or bliss. Bliss forms the constitutive stuff and the essence of all things.

There is in fact no way of measuring the bliss of Brahman. But a beautiful and suggestive attempt has been made in the *Taittirīyopaniṣad* to give us the calculus of the bliss of Brahman.[3] There it is stated that a young man, noble, resolute, strong and of good learning who is also the lord of earth can be said to be possessed of the highest of human joys. The joy of one hundred

1. *Appearance and Reality* (2nd Ed. revised, pp. 162-63).
2. को ह्येवान्यात् कः प्राण्याद् यदेष आकाश आनन्दो न स्यात् । (*Tait.* 2.7)
3. *Tait.* 2.8.

such human beings will equal the joy of one human genius. The joy of one hundred such human genii will equal the joy of one heavenly genius. The joy of the manes who live in the long-enduring world is hundred times more than that of heavenly genius. In this way the joy of the higher and higher grades of beings is said to be hundred times more than those of the beings immediately preceding them. And last of all comes Brahmā, who is said to be possessed of highest joy among all manifested beings. Now a sage who is full of revelation and is one with Brahman possesses all these grades of joy severally and simultaneously. Thus in this manner we can make an intellectual appreciation of the bliss of Brahman. But we can realise the bliss of Brahman through intuition. Our senses and intellect can give us only a shadow of the absolute bliss. It is only when one gets rid of the limitations of the ego and realises his psychic entity within that he can enjoy the bliss of Brahman. The happiness or joy that is found in the world of duality, in the different grades of manifestation, is nothing but a part of the absolute bliss. As Śaṅkara observes, "the empirical or the finite bliss is also a part of the bliss of Brahman".[1] The beings of the various grades of manifestation, e.g., from the human being up to Brahmā are not able to realise the pure and immeasurable bliss of Brahman on account of their knowledge being superseded by ignorance in different degrees. They are able to realise the bliss of Brahman partially in accordance with their knowledge and capacity. The bliss of Brahman is eternal, imperishable and absolute; while the bliss of beings of different grades of manifestation is finite and unstable. But the partial, fragmentary and unstable finite bliss is destined to be transformed into the absolute bliss during the course of evolution. The human being according to Sri Aurobindo is destined to enjoy the bliss of the Absolute in full measure by undergoing triple transformation—the psychic, the spiritual and the supramental.

The search for happiness may be said to be ingrained in every living creature. All beings try to avoid pain and seek pleasure. As Freud says, "They seek happiness, they want to be happy and to

---

1. एतस्यैवानन्दस्यान्यानि भूतानि मात्रामुपजीवन्ति ।
        (Brh. 4.3.32, Śaṅkara's Commentary)
  लौकिकोऽप्यानदो ब्रह्मानन्दस्यैव मात्रा ।
        (Tait. 2.8, Śaṅkara's Commentary)

remain so."[1] "To find happiness," observes another modern author, "is the desire, the craving of every human creature, whether expressed in words or vaguely felt as a something that is lacking."[2] But the trouble is that one scarcely finds true happiness in life. The pleasure derived from sense enjoyment is not lasting. It is associated in some way or other with pain. All worldly pleasures are in some measure fraught with pain. "Every sweet has its sour" as Emerson observes in his Essay on 'Compensation'. The *Bhagavadgītā* also says, "The enjoyments that are based on sense-contact are verily wombs of pain....." "All pleasures terminate in pain, as all bright flames terminate in the darkness of smoke."[3] It is true that the ascetics have sometimes gone to extremes in denouncing sense-pleasure. But there is a great truth in the statement that pleasure is relative and that it is generally associated with pain. Freud says, "As we see, it is simply the pleasure principle which draws up the programme of life's purposes....yet its programme is in conflict with the whole world, with the macrocosm as much as with the microcosm. The whole constitution of things runs counter to it, one might say that the intention that man should be happy is not included in the scheme of 'creation'."[4] "The goal towards which the pleasure-principle impels us—of becoming happy—is not attainable. There are many paths by which the happiness attainable for man can be reached, but none which is certain to take him to it."[5] "What is called happiness in its narrowest sense comes from the satisfaction—most often instantaneous—of pent-up needs which have reached great intensity and by its very nature can only be a transitory experience. When any condition desired by the pleasure principle is protracted, it results in a feeling of mild comfort; we are so constituted that we can only intensely enjoy contrasts much less intensely states in themselves. Our possibilities of happiness

1. Freud, *Civilization and its Discontents*, pp. 26-27.
2. Hutchinson, *Hypnotism and Self-education*, p. 80.
3. सर्वस्या एव पर्यन्ते सुखाशायाश्च संस्थितम् ।
   मालिन्यं दु:खमप्येवं ज्वालाया इव कज्जलम् ।
   (*The Yoga-Vāsiṣṭha* V. 49. 6-7) Vide Dɪ. B.L. Atreya, *The Philosophy of the Yoga-Vāsiṣṭha*, p. 390.
4. Freud, *Civilisation and its Discontents*, p. 27.
5. *Ibid.*, pp. 41-42.

are thus limited from the very start by our very constitution."[1] This
view of Freud holds good to a very great extent as far as the finite
individual is concerned. The finite creature is certainly bound by
all sorts of limitations. Hence the possibilities of happiness for him
can be said to be limited by his very constitution. But the fact is
that the finite being is not destined to remain always finite. Man
has within him the power and the capacity to transcend all sorts
of limitations and become one with the infinite. He can enjoy real
happiness only when he realises his real self, the Ātman, which
is one with the Infinite or Brahman.

The highest end of man's life is the realisation of Self. But the
tragedy of man's life is that he is not ordinarily aware of his self.
He identifies himself with his psycho-physical organism and with
the objects of the world but remains unaware of his self. The result
is that he is deprived of the real joy of life and becomes subject
to all sorts of sufferings and ultimately meets death. Thus the lower
desires have to be cancelled if one aims to attain immortality. As
Maitreyī says, "What shall I do with that which will not make me
immortal."[2] It is the realisation of Self or Ātman alone that makes
one immortal and enables one to enjoy the supreme and absolute
bliss. The human being according to the sage Yājñavalkya loves
the objects and beings of the world not for their own sake but
for the sake of the Self. "It is not for the sake of the husband that
he is loved but for one's own sake that he is loved."[3] Similarly
Yājñavalkya goes on to say that the love for wife, sons, wealth and
all other things and beings of the world is not in reality for their
own sake but for the sake of one's own self. It means that the
things of the world are not possessed of any intrinsic value in
themselves. Whatever value they are seen to be possessed of is
simply derived from the self. But it should be remembered that
the word 'self' here does not really mean the empirical self or ego
but the transcendental self which is one with Brahman. It is Brahman

1. Freud, *Civilisation and its Discontents*, pp. 27-28.
2. येनाहं नामृता स्यां किमहं तेन कुर्याम् । (*Brh.* 2.4.3)
3. न वा अरे पत्युः कामाय पतिः प्रियो भवति । आत्मनस्तु कामाय पतिः प्रियो भवति ।(*Brh.* 2.4.5)

which is really the abode of bliss[1] and not any finite object or being. The bliss of Brahman underlies all our finite existence and constitutes its essence.

(B) *Purpose of Creation*

Now a question arises, why should Brahman manifest the world at all? What is the purpose of creation? "Why should Brahman, perfect, absolute, infinite, needing nothing, desiring nothing, at all throw out force of consciousness to create in itself these worlds of forms?" Sri Aurobindo answers this fundamental question in one word, "for delight". We have already given answer to the question of the 'How' of the world-process from the standpoint of Sri Aurobindo. We have seen that Brahman manifests the world by its conscious force through the process of self-concentration. Brahman is possessed of the power of self-variation, self-limitation and self-absorption. Hence it finds no insurmountable difficulty in manifesting itself in the forms of the world. Now, we have to consider the question of the 'why' of the world-process.

Sri Aurobindo's answer that Brahman manifests the world for delight may appear outwardly as a sort of a poetic answer to a philosophical problem, but it has a great and deep significance behind it. The fact is that Brahman can have no purpose in creating or manifesting the world. It cannot be guided or governed by any purpose in manifesting the world. Brahman is full of all perfections. And to say that Brahman has some purpose in creating the world will mean that it wants to attain through the process of creation something which it has not. And that is impossible. Hence there can be no purpose of Brahman in creating the world. The world is a mere spontaneous creation of Brahman. It is a Līlā or sport of Brahman. It is created out of Bliss, by Bliss and for Bliss. Līlā indicates a spontaneous sportive activity of Brahman as distinguished from a self-conscious volitional effort. The concept of Līlā signifies freedom as distinguished from necessity. Śaṅkara says that even as a king or his minister whose all wishes have been fulfilled engage themselves in acts for mere pastime without any particular motive, and as the inhaling and exaling of air take place

---

1. रसो वै स: । (*Tait.* 2.7)

without any purpose for it is their very nature, so also Brahman without any purpose engages Itself by its very nature in creating this world of diversity. We cannot attribute any other motive to Īśvara either by reasoning or on the basis of scriptures. And no body can question the nature of a thing as to why it is what it is.[1] Śaṅkara says further that though in the world we may find some subtle reason even in mere sportive or natural acts, yet no motive can be attributed to God as He is full of all perfections as the scriptures say.[2] Lord Kṛṣṇa says, "O Pārtha! in all the three worlds there is nothing that I have to accomplish. I have neither anything which is not attained by me nor anything which is to be attained, and yet I remain in action."[3] Thus the question of 'why' of creation, though it outwardly appears so very fundamental ultimately becomes illegitimate. To ask why Brahman creates the world is to question the very nature of Brahman. As we cannot ask why Brahman is what it is, so we cannot ask why Brahman manifests itself in the forms of the world.

But it may be said that the Upaniṣads mention various purposes which God had in creating the world. For example, it is said that Being only was in the beginning, one only, without a second. It thought, May I be Many, may I grow forth: 'It sent forth-fire.'[4] Thus such purposes as becoming many, growing forth etc. seem to be attributed to Brahman. Another Upaniṣad says, "In the beginning, there was nothing whatsoever. This world was covered over with Death, with Hunger, for hunger is death. He created the mind, thinking, 'Let me have a mind'."[5] It is also said that He desired, 'Let me have a second form (body)'.[6] These and many other passages seem to speak of different purposes which God had in creating the world.

---

1. *S.B.* 2.1.33.
2. यदि नाभ लोके लीलास्वपि किञ्चित् सूक्ष्मं प्रयोजनमुत्प्रेक्ष्यते, तथापि नैवात्र किञ्चित् प्रयोजनमुत्प्रेक्षितुं शक्यते, आप्तकामश्रुतेः । (*S.B.* 2.1.33)
3. न मे पार्थास्ति कर्तव्यं त्रिषु लोकेषु किञ्चन ।
नानवाप्तमवाप्तव्यं वर्तएव च कर्मणि ॥ (*B.G.* 3.22)
4. तदैक्षत बहुस्यां प्रजायेयेति तत्तेजोऽसृजत । (*Chān.* 6.2.3)
5. नैवेह किंचनाग्र आसीन्मृत्युनैवेदमावृतमासीत् । अशनायया, अशनाया हि मृत्यु; तन्मनोऽकुरुत, आत्मन्वी स्यामिति । (*Bṛh.* 1.2.1)
6. सोऽकामयत, द्वितीयो म आत्मा जायेतेति । (*Bṛh.* 1.2.4)

But we should not interpret these words from our own human standpoint. It has already been stated above that God is full of all perfections, so we cannot attribute any motive or desire to God. What these words mean, in fact, is that the Being who creates or manifests the world is conscious and not an unconscious principle. The word 'desire' really signifies the presence of consciousness in the creative principle. We find this very clearly stated in the Brahma-Sūtra where it is said that the first cause cannot be Pradhān or the unconscious Nature because thinking is attributed to it by the scriptures.[1] So the scriptures which seem to attribute various purposes to God really mean to establish the fact of the supreme role of Consciousness in creation. Thus the standpoint of Sri Aurobindo as well as of Śaṅkara and other Vedāntins is not contradicted by the scriptures. Hence it is clear that creation is a pure Līlā, an expression of the spontaneous and sportive activity of God. Sri Aurobindo calls the whole of creation a Līlā, "the play, the child's joy, the poet's joy, the actor's joy, the mechanician's joy of the Soul of things eternally young, perpetually inexhaustible, creating and recreating Himself in Himself for the sheer bliss of that self-creation, of that self-representation—Himself the play, Himself the player, Himself the playground.

(C) The Problem of Evil

Now a question arises, if the world is a Līlā of Brahman, if it is manifested out of the bliss of Brahman, then whence come pain, suffering and evil. The world is manifested out of the bliss of Brahman, hence it must be full of happiness and bliss. But it presents just the opposite picture. Here bliss seems to be conspicuous by its absence and in its place one finds oneself confronted everywhere with the phenomena of pain, suffering and evil. The world instead of appearing as the abode of bliss presents itself as a vale of tears. Now this presents a serious challenge to the monistic or Advaitic position. "The problem of evil is a stumbling block to all monistic conception."[2]

Evil seems to be a direct contradictory of bliss. It seems to be opposed to all that is good, beautiful, blissful and so on. "By good,

---

1. ईक्षतेर्नाशब्दम् । (*Br. Sū.* 1.1.5)
2. Radhakrishnan, *Indian Philosophy*, Vol. I, p. 242.

as we mortals experience it, we mean something that, when it comes or is expected, we actively welcome, try to attain or keep, and regard with content. By evil in general as it is in our experience, we mean whatever we find in any sense repugnant and intolerable.... We mean (by evil) precisely whatever we regard as something to be gotten rid of, shrunken from, put out of sight, of hearing, of memory, eschewed, expelled, assailed, or otherwise directly or indirectly resisted. By good we mean whatever we regard as something to be welcomed, pursued, won, grasped, held, persisted in, preserved. And we show all this in our acts in presence of any grade of good or evil, sensuous, aesthetic, ideal or moral...whether you regard us as animals or as moralists, whether it is a sweet taste, a poem, a virtue or God that we look to as good; or whether it is a burn or a temptation, an outward physical foe or a stealthy, inward, ideal enemy that we regard as evil."[1] In a general way it may be said that the good in all its senses is desirable and the evil is undesirable.[2] Ethically, one may also say in a broad sense that "Good is what ought to be, evil is what ought not to be."[3] These definitions or descriptions of good and evil clearly show that they are diametrically opposed to each other. They are considered as opposed to each other in our practical life. The whole problem of morality rests on the opposition of good and evil. But the problem is, can we regard good and evil as opposed to each other metaphysically also as they are so regarded in our practical and moral life? Can the Absolute as good and blissful be regarded as opposed to evil, pain, suffering etc.?

If we regard evil as opposed to the bliss of the Absolute then we will inevitably land in a hopeless dualism. We will then have to believe in two equally real and independent principles—one of good and the other of evil. But these two principles will in that case be always confronting each other like two hostile forces and one will not be able to reconcile them. One cannot find a solution of the riddle of existence by acquiescing meekly in such a rank dualism. So evil cannot be regarded as ultimately opposed to the bliss of the Absolute, if monism or Advaitism is to be maintained. It cannot at least be regarded as an independent principle. But if

1. Royce, *Studies of Good and Evil*, 18.
2. *Vide* Sidgwick, *Methods of Ethics*, London, 1901, p. 110.
3. Naville, *Problem of Evil*.

it is regarded as dependent on the Absolute then it has to be explained how such a principle which appears quite contradictory of the Absolute does not affect its unity and integrity. It must be shown that the presence of evil does not put a limitation upon the Absolute, does not affect Its absoluteness. Here lies the main difficulty. The monists can neither give evil an independent status nor are they able to make a reconciliation between the Absolute and evil without seriously jeopardising their monistic position. In most of the monistic systems evil seems to maintain jealously its identity and existence like a lonely island in the ocean of the Infinite. Thus it has proved a sumbling block to all monistic systems.

Sri Aurobindo does not take a pessimistic view of life and existence. To the pessimist, the world is full of sorrow and suffering and there is no joy in life. It is true that nobody can deny the fact that there is suffering in life. But the pessimist of the extreme type is so much obsessed by the spectacle of sorrow and suffering that he obstinately refuses to admit any joy in life and considers all optimistic thoughts about life as mere ramblings of a depraved and a deluded mind. As Schopenhauer puts it, "To me optimism, when it is not merely the thoughtless talk of such as harbour nothing but words under their low foreheads, appears not merely as an absurd, but also as a really wicked way of thinking, as a bitter mockery of the unspeakable suffering of humanity."[1] Sri Aurobindo does not agree with this view. According to him, such a pessimistic view suffers from an exaggeration, an error of perspective. If we look at life and existence dispassionately and with a sole view to accurate and unemotional appreciation, we shall according to him find "that the sum of the pleasure of existence far exceeds the sum of the pain of existence—appearances and individual cases to the contrary not withstanding—and that the active or passive, surface or underlying pleasure of existence is the normal state of nature, pain a contrary occurrence temporarily suspending or overlaying that normal state. But for that very reason the lesser sum of pain affects us more intensely and often looms larger than the greater sum of pleasure; precisely because

---

1. Schopenhauer, *The World as Will and Idea*, Eng. tr., i, 420.

the latter is normal, we do not treasure it, hardly even observe it unless it intensifies into some acuter form of itself, into a wave of happiness, a crest of joy or ecstasy".[1]

But even if it is granted that the sum of pleasures preponderates over that of pain, it cannot be gainsaid that the very presence of pain and evil constitutes a problem. If all is Saccidānanda, how can pain and suffering at all exist? This is the real problem which has to be solved from the standpoint of Sri Aurobindo.

One may try to solve the problem of pain and evil by saying that they are meant for a trial and an ordeal. The stoics regarded evil as good as a disciplinary agent. On this point Sencca writes in his de providentia: "Fragile are the plants that grow in a sunny valley." And Epictetus observes: "God sends me hither and thither, shows me to man as poor, without authority, and sick....not because He hates me....but with the view of exercising me and of using me as a witness to others". These may be very fine and noble sentiments but they do not solve the problem of evil. This does not explain the suffering which destroys the very possibility of moral improvement as we see in cases of insanity etc. This raises the question about the goodness of God.

Sri Aurobindo contends that one cannot escape from the problem of pain and evil by saying that pain is a trial and an ordeal for it will lead to the denial of the goodness of God. "For one who invents torture as a means of test or ordeal, stands convicted either of deliberate cruelty or of moral insensibility and, if a moral being at all, is inferior to the highest instinct of his own creatures."[2]

But to escape moral difficulty one may try to explain the problem of pain and evil by taking recourse to the law of Karma. One may say that pain and evil are the inevitable results and natural punishments of one's evil deeds done in the past. But the question is, "Who created or why or whence was created that moral evil which entails the punishment of pain and sufferings? And seeing that moral evil is in reality a form of mental disease or ignorance, who or what created this law or inevitable connection which punishes a mental disease or act of ignorance by a recoil so terrible, by tortures often so extreme and monstrous?"[3] Man indulges

---

1. *L.D.*, Vol. I, pp. 116-17.
2. *Ibid.*, p. 118.
3. *Ibid.*, p. 118.

in evil deeds on account of ignorance. But ignorance is not the creation of man. Man is on the other hand the product of ignorance. So the moral evil that a man commits on account of ignorance must not be met with such a dire punishment. A good and benevolent God cannot be expected to inflict such dire pain and sufferings on man for the evil acts that he does under the sway of ignorance. Thus the law of Karma does not explain the problem of evil. "The inexorable law of Karma is irreconcilable with a supreme moral and personal Deity, and therefore the clear logic of Buddha denied the existence of any free and all governing personal God; all personality he declared to be a creation of ignorance and subject to Karma."[1]

The solution of the problem of pain and evil will depend mainly on the relationship between God and the world. If one assumes the existence of an extra-cosmic personal God who has created pain, evil and suffering for his creatures but Himself stands above them then the problem of pain and evil will remain unexplained. If God inflicts pain and suffering on his creatures but himself remains unaffected by them then he is not a benevolent and all loving God. And if he allows the world to be driven and ruled by an inexorable law and keeps himself aloof without giving any aid to the suffering creatures then he cannot be called omnipotent, all-good and all-loving. Thus it is clear that on the theory of an extra-cosmic God either his benevolence or goodness or omnipotance is questioned. On no theory of an extra-cosmic moral God, can evil and suffering be explained—the creation of evil and suffering—except by an unsatisfactory subterfuge which avoids the question at issue instead of answering it or a plain or implied Manicheanism which practically annuls the Godhead in attempting to justify its ways or excuse its works.[2] Thus the theory of an extra-cosmic personal God is to be rejected altogether. The Vedānta does not regard Saccidānanda as an extra-cosmic God. Saccidānanda manifests Himself in the forms of the world. He is both transcendent and immanent. He is manifesting Himself in each and every creature. The sufferings which the different creatures have to bear is indirectly borne by Saccidānanda himself. So now the problem

1. L.D., Vol. I, p. 118.
2. Ibid., pp. 118-19.

is, how Saccidānanda who is Existence—Consciousness—Bliss admits into Himself "that which is not bliss, that which seems to be its positive negation". In this way we find that half of the moral difficulty is removed. Now Saccidānanda cannot be charged with cruelty as He Himself indirectly bears the pain and suffering of the embodied being. But though his goodness and benevolence may in this way be maintained, yet his omnipotence and omniscience may certainly be questioned. It may be asked how Saccidānanda being all-powerful and all-knowing came to manifest the phenomena of pain, suffering and evil in his being. If He had to create pain, suffering and evil in spite of Himself then it means that He is not omnipotent and if He created them without knowing their full consequences then it means that He is not omniscient. Thus the principles of pain, suffering and evil seem to throw a serious challenge to the monistic conception.

(D) Sri Aurobindo's Solution of the Problem of Evil

Sri Aurobindo tries to meet this challenge boldly and squarely. The principles of pain, suffering and evil seem to present a formidable challenge to the Absolute because we look at them from a very narrow angle. We look at this problem from our human standpoint, from our individualistic standpoint and fail to look at it from a universal standpoint. The problem of pain and evil may appear quite different to us if we look at it from a universal standpoint. As Royce puts it; we see things in the temporal series; the problem may be quite other sub-specie eternitatis.[1] The result of our having a narrow view is that we want to impose our own ethical conceptions on the whole of existence. We think that ethical principles are true of reality as a whole. Rashdall says, "It is of the essence of the moral consciousness, as it actually exists, to claim universal validity; if it possesses no such validity, it is not merely particular moral judgments that are false and delusive, but the whole idea that there is such a thing as an end which absolutely ought to be promoted, and that we have a power (more or less adequate) of determining what that something is."[2] "The word 'good' means the same in him (God) and in us, else it means nothing to us."[3]

---

1. Royce, *The World and the Individual*.
2. Rashdall, *Theory of Good and Evil*, ii, 270.
3. W.N. Clarke, *Outline of Christian Theology*, Edin. 1898, p. 69.

This view will mean that morality is the ultimate characteristic of reality. But Sri Aurobindo calls such a view narrow and partial. He contends that we do not live in an ethical world. "The attempt of human thought to force an ethical meaning into the whole of Nature," he observes, "is one of those acts of wilful and obstinate self-confusion, one of those pathetic attempts of the human being to read himself, his limited habitual human self into all things and judge them from the standpoint he has personally evolved, which most effectively prevent him from arriving at real knowledge and complete sight."[1] This view is also held by other idealists of the present day, such as Bradley, Bosanquet etc. Like Sri Aurobindo they also hold that morality is a peculiar feature of human life and does not constitute the ultimate characteristic of reality. Reality is supra-ethical and transcends the limitations of moral laws. Bradley calls morality an appearance, for it represents a conflict and an opposition between the ideal that is to be attained and the real that falls short of it. The opposition between good and evil is not finally resolved in the moral plane. But they are resolved and reconciled in the ultimate reality. "Error and evil are facts and most assuredly there are degrees of each; and whether anything is better or worse, does without any doubt make a difference to the Absolute. And certainly the better any thing is, the less totally in the end is its being overruled. But nothing, however good, can in the end be real precisely as it appears. Evil and good in short, are not ultimate; they are relative factors which cannot retain their special characters in the whole."[2] Thus reality is ultimately beyond good and evil.

Ethics according to Sri Aurobindo not only does not form the essential characteristic of reality but it is not the essential feature of the whole of nature also. It is the essential characteristic, as has been said above, of human life. Material nature is not ethical. The mechanical law which governs it takes no cognisance of good and evil, mercy and justice etc. As Mill says, "In sober truth, nearly all the things which men are hanged or imprisoned for doing to one another, are nature's everyday performances....Nature impales men,...and has hundreds of other hideous deaths in reserve, such

1. *L.D.*, Vol. I. p. 118.
2. *Appearance and Reality*, p. 430.

as the cruelty of a...Domitan never surpassed. All this Nature does with the most supercilious disregard both of mercy and of justice."[1] Animal or vital Nature also is non-ethical. We do not blame the tiger and other ferocious animals for killing their prey as we do not blame the storm, fire etc., for bringing disaster on living beings. In animal life we find the presence of evil in the form of pain. We may broadly consider evil as of two kinds—physical evil or pain and moral evil or sin. Animals have only the consciousness of pain and not of sin. They do not suffer from moral evil.[2] Thus animal life cannot be called ethical. It is human being who suffers from both—physical evil and moral evil. He is ethical in the sense that he is conscious of good and evil. But it must not be inferred that these values are unreal and are merely the constructions of mind. They have got an objective validity. "The moral law has a real existence, there is such a thing as an absolute Morality, there is something absolutely true or false in ethical judgments, whether we or any number of human beings at any given time actually think so or not. Such a belief is distinctly implied in what we mean by morality. The idea of such an unconditional, objectively valid, Moral Law or ideal undoubtedly exists as a psychological fact."[3] True ethics begins with our consciousness of moral values, of moral law. It manifests itself in the human life. It is human being who suffers from evil and who tries to get rid of it. Evil does not exist in the Absolute or Saccidānanda. The all-knowing and blissful Saccidānanda cannot have evil inherent in it. Evil cannot also exist in the individual soul, for the soul as we have stated above, is the seat of immortality and bliss. Evil manifests itself in the cosmos and there also in the human life. It is mind that is the seat of evil. Thus it is clear that evil is not the essential characteristic of the whole of cosmos. It emerges only at a certain stage of evolution, that is in the plane of mind. So Sri Aurobindo calls ethics a stage in evolution. The factor which is common to all the stages is the urge of Saccidānanda towards self-expression. "This urge is at first non-ethical, then infra-ethical in the animal, then in the intelligent animal even anti-ethical for it permits us to approve hurt done to others

1. J.S. Mill, *Essay on Nature.*
2. *L.D.*, Vol. II, Part I, p. 382.
3. Rashdall, *op. cit.*, ii, 211.

which we disapprove when done to ourselves. In this respect man even now is only half-ethical. And just as all below us is infra-ethical, so there may be that above us whither we shall eventually arrive, which is supra-ethical, has no need of ethics."[1] Ethics serves a very useful purpose in human life. It enables man to free himself slowly and gradually from the clutches of ignorance and prepare himself for receiving the light of the Divine. "The ethical impulse and attitude, so important to humanity, is a means by which it struggles out of the lower harmony and universality based upon inconscience and broken up by Life into individual discords towards a higher harmony and universality based upon conscient oneness with all existences. Arriving at that goal, this means will no longer be necessary or even possible, since the qualities and oppositions on which it depends will naturally dissolve and disappear in the final reconciliation."[2]

Thus it is clear that the ethical standpoint applies only to a temporary phase of existence and it cannot be applied to the whole of existence. As Sri Aurobindo points out, "If then, the ethical standpoint applies only to a temporary though all-important passage from one universality to another, we cannot apply it to the total solution of the problem of the universe. To do otherwise is to run into the peril of falsifying all the facts of the universe, all the meaning of the evolution behind and beyond us in order to suit a temporary outlook and a half-evolved view of the utility of things. The world has three layers, infra-ethical, ethical and supra-ethical. We have to find that which is common to all; for only so can we resolve the problem."[3] And the common factor as we have stated above is the urge of Saccidānanda towards self-expression. It is Saccidānanda who manifests himself in these different grades, namely, infra-ethical, ethical and supra-ethical. Matter, Life and Mind are nothing but the self-expressions of Saccidānanda. In the same way pain, pleasure, evil etc. are also the results of the self-expression of Saccidānanda in the world of ignorance. All these principles can be ultimately reduced to Saccidānanda. Hence pain, evil etc. cannot be called contradictories

1. *L.D.*, Vol. I, pp. 121-22.
2. *Ibid.*, p. 122.
3. *Ibid.*, p. 122.

of the bliss of Saccidānanda and so they cannot challenge the monistic position.

The bliss of the Absolute is different from pleasure or joy as we experience it in daily life. While pleasure, joy etc. are particular, ephemeral and dependent in nature like their opposites pain, evil etc., the bliss of the Absolute is universal, permanent and self-existent. It manifests pain, pleasure etc. out of itself in the stage of mind. Sri Aurobindo calls pleasure and pain the positive and negative currents of Delight or Bliss. Thus it is clear that pain and evil are not opposed to the Absolute but are the modes of the manifestation of the Absolute. They could be called contradictories of the Absolute only if they were independent of the Absolute or if they had an independent origin. Pain, evil, pleasure etc. are the results of the imperfect manifestation of the Absolute. The contradictions of the world and of human life are due to the fact that the Absolute has not yet manifested itself fully in the world. The world is still ruled by the principles of inconscience and ignorance. Pain, evil etc. are the products of inconscience and ignorance. But they are not the permanent characteristics of the world. They will be eliminated in the higher stages of evolution. "To accept evil as a given fact, and not to seek to overcome it, is possible only in so far as one is oneself evil."[1] The world is not destined to be ruled by ignorance and inconscience forever. The principles of inconscience and ignorance are destined to be transformed according to Sri Aurobindo into that of consciousness and knowledge and the world of necessity is destined to be transformed into the world of freedom in the course of evolution, as we shall show in detail in a subsequent chapter.

Thus it is the principle of evolution which offers a practical solution of the problem of evil. The evolutionary standpoint enables us to reconcile evil with the Absolute without affecting in any way the Advaitic position. Evil does not form a permanent characteristic of the world. It emerges at a certain stage in the course of evolution and is destined to be transformed into good or bliss when the evolution reaches a higher or the supramental stage. Then there will no more remain the problem of evil. Thus the presence of evil at the present stage of evolution cannot challenge the monistic position. Not only that; Sri Aurobindo's

---

1. C.E.M. Joad, *God and Evil*, p. 236.

Integral Advaitism is not affected in any way by the phenomena of Ignorance, world etc. as we shall show in subsequent chapters. This is due to the fact that he finds a practical solution also of these problems in the principle of evolution. Śaṅkara and the Śaṅkarites are forced to call evil unreal in order to maintain their Advaitism. But according to Sri Aurobindo it is only an escape from the problem and not its real solution. Sri Aurobindo recognises the reality of evil yet he shows us the way how evil is to be transformed ultimately into good in the higher stages of evolution. Sri Aurobindo does not call evil the product of individual's ignorance. He does not think that evil will be eliminated from earth by the cancellation of individual's ignorance. Ignorance and Inconscience have to be banished from earth-consciousness itself if evil is to be eliminated finally from the world. The liberation of a few individual souls from the bondage and tyranny of evil and ignorance will not liberate the whole world. Sri Aurobindo stands for cosmic liberation and not for individual liberation alone. The liberation of the cosmos from inconscience, ignorance, evil etc. will be possible only when the supramental principle will make a descent into the earth-consciousness and effect a radical transformation in its nature, as we will show in a subsequent chapter. According to Sri Aurobindo there can be no final solution of the problem of evil "until we have turned our inconscience into the greater consciousness, made the truth of self and spirit our life-basis and transformed our ignorance into a higher knowledge. All other expedients will only be make-shifts or blind issues; a complete and radical transformation of our nature is the only true solution".[1]

Sri Aurobindo does not regard pain, evil and error as having any absoluteness in them like Truth and Good. They have no absoluteness in them, howsoever immeasurable they may appear to be. "If pain becomes immeasurable, it ends itself or ends that in which it manifests or collapses into insensibility or in rare circumstances, it may turn into ecstasy of Ānanda. If evil becomes sole and immeasurable, it would destroy the world or destroy that which bore and supported it; it would bring things and itself back by disintegration into non-existence."[2] Pain and Evil are the results of

1. L.D., Vol. II, Part I, p. 406
2. Ibid., pp. 379-80

ignorance and so they will be transformed into knowledge by the descent of the supramental principle. But Truth and Good will not be eliminated from the world by the descent of the Supermind. On the other hand they will attain full perfection and absoluteness in that state. At present Truth and Good seem to be relative like error and evil. But they are essentially possessed of absoluteness. Sri Aurobindo contends that "the relation of truth to falsehood, of good to evil is not a mutual dependence, but is in the nature of a contradiction as of light and shadow; a shadow depends on light for its existence, but light does not depend for its existence on the shadow. The relation between the Absolute and these contraries of some of its fundamental aspects is not that they are opposite fundamental aspects of the Absolute; falsehood and evil have no fundamentality, no power of infinity or eternal being, no self-existence even by latency in the Self-Existent, no authenticity of an original inherence".[1]

Thus it is clear that the presence of pain and evil in no way contradicts the universal principle of Bliss which lies at the root of all existence and constitutes its essence. The principle of Bliss which is present in a latent manner in the earth-consciousness at the present stage will manifest itself fully, according to Sri Aurobindo, after the supramental transformation has taken place. Then the world of pain and evil will be transformed into the world of bliss. The Vedāntins, as has already been stated, call the world the Līlā of the Divine. "World-existence," observes Sri Aurobindo, "is the ecstatic dance of Shiva which multiplies the body of the God numberlessly to the view; it leaves that white existence pre-cisely where and what it was, ever is and ever will be; its sole absolute object is the joy of the dancing".[2] It is only when the principle of bliss will fully manifest itself in the world that it will be truly entitled to be called the Līlā of the Divine or Saccidānanda.

Now we proceed to discuss the nature of the Absolute in its creative aspect called the Supermind.

1. *L.D.*, Vol. II, Part I, p. 373.
2. *Ibid.*, Vol. I, p. 100.

CHAPTER VI

THE ABSOLUTE AS SUPERMIND

The merit of Sri Aurobindo's conception of the Absolute lies, as we have seen in the preceding chapters, in its integral and all-comprehensive character. It finds no real opposition or incompatibility between the so-called irreconcilable and incompatible aspects of existence, e.g., Being and Becoming, One and Many etc. The antinomies and contradictions exist, in fact, not in Reality itself but in our limited and half-blind finite reason. While the logic of the finite fails to realise this basic truth and lays the charge of contradictions and antinomies at the door of Reality itself, the Logic of the Infinite, on the contrary, perceives unity, harmony and reconciliation and holds mind responsible for its partial, fragmentary and distorted view of Reality. The finite world, according to Sri Aurobindo, does not stand in opposition to the Absolute or the Infinite, but is its manifestation. But the problem is, how can the spaceless, timeless and immutable Absolute manifest itself as the finite circumscribed by the limitations of space and time? We have here to account for the evolution of the world in space and time out of the spaceless and timeless self-concentration of the Absolute. The apparently diametrically opposite nature of the Absolute and the world does not warrant a smooth transition from the former to the latter. Sri Aurobindo holds that the difficulty in the evolution of the world out of the Absolute can be solved if we admit an intermediate principle between the transcendent and relationless Absolute and the finite world, namely, the Supermind. The Absolute, according to Sri Aurobindo, manifests the world through the Supermind.

THE INTEGRAL ADVAITISM OF SRI AUROBINDO

(A) *The Supermind as Creator*

It has been stated in a previous chapter that the Absolute manifests the world through its Conscious Force. The Supermind is nothing else but the Conscious Force working according to some fixed truth, some definite principle or law. The Conscious Force of the Absolute "does not work directly or with a sovereign irresponsibility like a magician building up worlds and universes by the mere fiat of its word. We perceive a process, we are aware of a law".[1] The Infinite Conscious Force has to put itself under the limitations of its own law or ·..ih in order to manifest the universe. As Sri Aurobindo puts it, "Infinite consciousness in its infinite action can produce only infinite results; to settle upon a fixed Truth or order of truths and build a world in conformity with that which is fixed, demands a selective faculty of knowledge commissioned to shape finite appearance out of the infinite Reality".[2] This selective faculty of knowledge is called by Sri Aurbindo Supermind. The Vedic seers called this power Māyā, the divine power. "Maya meant for them the power of infinite consciousness to comprehend, contain in itself and measure out, that is to say, to form—for form is delimitation—Name and Shape out of the vast illimitable Truth of infinite existence".[3]

We cannot regard the world as the creation of mind. "Mind," observes Sri Aurobindo, "is not sufficient to explain existence in the universe. Infinite consciousness must first translate itself into infinite faculty of knowledge or, as we call it from our point of view, omniscience".[4] Mind is not, in fact, an instrument of knowledge. It deals not with the Reality itself but with appearances. It is merely an instrument meant to serve some pragmatic purpose. It cannot claim to be the creator of the finite world as the subjective idealists would have us believe. Thus Sri Aurobindo differs from the other idealists who recognise Mind alone as the creator of the world or regard it as the only mediator between the Absolute and the world. Even an infinite Mind which would be free from our limitations cannot be regarded as the creator of the universe. Such a mind according to Sri Aurobindo would be quite different from

---

1. *L.D.*, Vol. I, p. 144.
2. *Ibid.*, p. 145.
3. *Ibid.*, p. 145.
4. *Ibid.*, p. 148.

the definition of mind as we know it. It would be the supramental Truth. "An infinite Mind constituted in the terms of mentality as we know it could only create an infinite chaos, a vast clash of chance, accident, vicissitude wandering towards an indeterminate end after which it would be always tentatively groping and aspiring. An infinite, omniscient, omnipotent Mind would not be mind at all, but supramental knowledge".[1] Thus Sri Aurobindo rejects the views which recognise mind, whether individual or universal Mind as the creator of the world. The world, according to him is, as has been stated above, manifested by a supramental principle out of the being of Saccidānanda or the Absolute.

The problem of creation has always proved a hard nut to crack for the monistic philosophy of both the East and the West. To keep the one ultimate and fundamental reality intact and at the same time to give satisfactory explanation of the world of diversity has always seemed to be undoubtedly a baffling problem. To remain perfectly true to the monistic principle and at the same time to do justice to the phenomenal world is a hard duty of monistic philosophy. A general tendency in the monists both in our country and in the west has been to maintain their monism at the cost of the phenomenal world. The phenomenal world has either been denied any reality altogether or has been given a very subordinate and inferior status. Thus the monistic philosophers have, in general, failed to arrive at an Integral monism which affirms the oneness of the Absolute and at the same time gives the world the highest status by regarding it as nothing else but the Absolute itself in a particular poise. If they have tried to present the Reality in its untarnished form, they have denied the reality of the world and if they have maintained the reality of the world, they have compromised the oneness of the Reality or the Absolute. The superiority of Sri Aurobindo's conception of the Absolute over that of the other monistic philosophers lies in its integral and all-comprehensive character. He maintains the perfect oneness of the Absolute without denying the reality of the world. He establishes the indeterminability of the Absolute without denying the reality of its determinate aspect. He is able to establish his Integral Advaitism on the basis of the Supermind or the Supramental consciousness. The failure of the other monistic philosophers in establishing an

---

1. *L.D.*, Vol. I, p. 149.

Integral Advaitism is mainly due to the fact that they are not aware of this integral and all-comprehensive consciousness, namely the Supermind. We can see this fact clearly and realise the importance of Sri Aurobindo's conception of the supermind by comparing Sri Aurobindo's view of the Absolute with some great monistic systems of our country as well as of the west. We have already compared Sri Aurobindo's view of the Absolute with that of Spinoza, Hegel, Kant etc., in the preceding chapters. Now we proceed to compare Sri Aurobindo's view of the Absolute with that of Rāmānuja, Śaṅkara and Bradley.

(i) Rāmānuja's and Sri Aurobindo's View of the Absolute Compared

Rāmānuja regards the Absolute as determinate and personal. It is a supreme and perfect personality which includes and embraces the finite world and souls in its being. Thus the Absolute or God has internal difference (svagatabheda). Cit and acit, souls and matter are the predicates of God.[1] Brahman or God is the supreme reality of which the world is the body. Brahman is self-dependent but the souls and the world depend on Brahman for their being and existence.[2] "Souls, and matter are comprehended within the unity of the Lord's essence and are related to the Supreme as attributes to a substance, as parts to whole or as body to the soul which animates it."[3] Unlike Śaṅkara, Rāmānuja regards being (sat), consciousness (cit) and bliss (ānanda) as the qualities of the Absolute or Brahman which give it a character and a personality.

The pluralistic universe is as real as God. But though it is as real as God, yet it depends on the latter, as has been stated above, for its existence. God is both immanent and transcendent. "God is not to be regarded as simply the immanent ground, for then God will have to be conceived as wholly differentiated into the "many" or the "many" will have to be conceived as wholly absorbed into the undifferentiated oneness of God. To Rāmānuja, God is both the transcendent and the immanent ground of the world. God is

1. चिदचिद्विशिष्ट ईश्वर: ।
2. सर्वं परमपुरुषेण सर्वात्मना स्वार्थे नियाम्यं धार्यं तच्छेषतैकस्वरूपमिति सर्वं चेतनाचेतनं तस्य शरीरम् ।
(Śrī Bhāṣya 11.1.9).
3. Radhakrishnan, Indian Philosophy, Vol. II, p. 684.

a person, and not a mere totality of other persons, and so he cannot be confused with the thinking individuals and the objects of their thought."[1] Rāmānuja argues that one cannot attain the knowledge of a differenceless Absolute. All knowledge rests on the relationship of subject and predicate, of substance and attributes. Unlike Śaṅkara, Rāmānuja holds that an identity expresses itself in and through the differences. Whereas a judgment expresses the identity of subject and predicate, it also at the same time signifies a difference between them. If we negate all differences we cannot affirm even the identity. We can know a thing or a subject only through its attributes. If we negate all the attributes and differences we reduce it to an abstraction. Thus the Absolute in Rāmānuja's view cannot be devoid of attributes and differences, which are integrated and harmonised in its being. The indeterminateness of the Absolute, according to him, simply means that it is devoid of finite and imperfect attributes and not of all attributes whatsoever. Brahman is possessed of infinite attributes which cannot be conceived by the finite mind. The Upaniṣads which deny plurality mean according to Rāmānuja simply this that the plurality cannot have any existence apart from and independent of Brahman. They do not negate plurality as such. The plurality exists in the being of Brahman and as an integral part of It. Thus the Absolute of Rāmānuja can be expressed as identity-in-difference.

But certain difficulties may be raised against Rāmānuja's view of the Absolute. The world, according to Rāmānuja, constitutes the body of God. Souls and matter are said to be the attributes of God. But the problem is that as the attributes undergo the process of change, it becomes difficult to conceive how God remains unchanged. If God remains unchanged in spite of the changing condition of his attributes, then the attributes cannot be said to be an integral part of God. To say otherwise is to get involved in contradiction. And if God changes along with his changing attributes, then he cannot be called a supremely perfect Being. "Brahman has absolutely non-conditioned existence, which is not the case with non-intelligent matter, which is the abode of change

1. Radhakrishnan, op. cit., pp. 685-86.

and the souls implicated in matter. But it is difficult to conceive how Brahman could be supposed to be unchangeable in view of the changing conditions of his attributes, souls and matter."[1] The phenomenon of change is difficult to explain in a changeless Absolute. As Dr. Radhakrishnan observes, "If the Absolute is supposed to be a transcendent changeless existence, it is a problem how such an Absolute, which has no history, includes the time process and the evolution of the world. Unless Rāmānuja is willing to explain away the immutable perfection of the Absolute, and substitute for it a perpetually changing process, a sort of progressing perfection, he cannot give us any satisfactory explanation of the relation of the souls of the Absolute to its body."[2] Thus it may be said that the relation between the finite and the Infinite cannot be logically explained in Rāmānuja's system. "Śaṅkara's difficulty, that from Brahman, which is absolute perfection, the world of imperfection cannot be said to take its rise, at any rate that it is impossible for the finite mind to account for the rise of the finite from out of the infinite, does not trouble Rāmānuja, since he is willing to accept on the authority of the Śruti that the finite springs from the infinite."[3]

The objections which are raised against Rāmānuja's system may be raised against Sri Aurobindo's system also. It may be said that Sri Aurobindo commits a self-contradiction in saying that the Absolute is changeless and at the same time manifests itself as the world. But such objections hold true and appear to be unanswerable only so long as we accept the judgment of the abstract and formal reason. But to a higher and synthetic reason, as we have elaborately shown in a preceding chapter, these objections do not appear as formidable and unanswerable in any way. Our finite reason is hypnotised by the magic of words and concepts and hence fails to find the truth lying behind them. To the finite or abstract reason the Absolute cannot be both changeless and changing; but to the higher reason, there is no contradiction in assuming Being and Becoming as the complementary aspects of the Absolute. To the higher reason the word changeless does not mean that the Absolute is incapable of manifesting itself or undergoing any

1. Radhakrishnan, op. cit., p. 699.
2. Ibid., p. 716.
3. Ibid., p. 699.

change at all. It only means that the Absolute is not bound or limited by the phenomena of change. The whole essence of the Absolute is not exhausted in change or Becoming. The Absolute does manifest itself as Becoming or changing world but at the same time it maintains its integrity as immutable pure Existence. To quote again Sri Aurobindo's statement, "The immutability of the Identical does not consist in a monotone of changeless sameness incapable of variation; it consists in an unchangeableness of being which is capable of endless formation of being, but which no differentiation can destroy or impair or minimise."[1] If we regard the Absolute as changeless, meaning thereby that it is incapable of undergoing any change at all, then we put a kind of limitation on the Absolute. In our anxiety to keep the Absolute free from the filthy touch of the world, we impose a kind of impotence on the Absolute. The Absolute becomes limited to one particular status and the world of change or becoming appears as something foreign to it. If we are to maintain the perfect absoluteness of the Absolute, we are to regard it as both transcendent and immanent, Being and Becoming simultaneously. It is true that all these concepts or categories fall short of the Absolute. We cannot in reality describe the Absolute by any of these categories. But the best positive description of the Absolute that can be given from our intellectual standpoint is that the Absolute is both transcendent and immanent. The changelessness and the transcendence of the Absolute simply means that it exceeds the limitations of change or becoming.

By undergoing change, the Absolute does not become subject to any limitation. It undergoes change or becoming by its own free will and through its own powers. Hence there is no question of subjection or limitation in the case of the Absolute. All the limitation in the case of the Absolute is self-imposed. Hence it cannot be called a limitation in the real sense. The Absolute is free from all limitations. But it is also equally free to put itself under limitation. To say that the Absolute is a supremely perfect Being and so any change in the Absolute will be incompatible with its perfection is not true. It has already been said that creation is a sport

---

1. *L.D.*, Vol. II, Part I, pp. 55-56.

or Līlā of Brahman. The Absolute could fall from its perfection if it had been compelled by any other agency to manifest the world. The Absolute will no more remain an Absolute if it has to work under a necessity foreign to its own nature. "Reality as a whole is free from external compulsion; its motion can be explained as a spontaneous movement from within."[1] The perfection of the Absolute does not deprive it of its Power to indulge in a sportive act of creation. So if we proceed to examine or investigate the nature of reality from the standpoint of our formal and abstract reason, we are sure to be confronted by the insoluble contradictions. But we can solve these riddles if we take recourse to the higher reason which is not deluded by the magic of words but fathoms the depth of reality. So the objections which were raised against Rāmānuja's system can be satisfactorily answered if we proceed on the basis of the higher logic. Sri Aurobindo has not tried to seek any easy escape from these baffling problems. According to him, it is necessary to examine first of all our own tools before applying them to Reality. The secrets of reality can be revealed to us only if we rise above the limitations of our formal logic and take recourse to the higher logic or the logic of the Infinite.

Now we proceed to examine the system of Śaṅkara and see how far our higher reason or the logic of the Infinite enable us to answer the difficulties raised in it with regard to the relationship between the finite and the Infinite.

(ii) Śaṅkara's and Sri Aurobindo's View of the Absolute Compared

The Absolute or Brahman according to Śaṅkara is a timeless and spaceless reality. It is indeterminate. No attribute or quality can be applied to it. Brahman cannot be characterised as a whole of which the finite souls and the objects of the world can be called parts. The categories of part and whole are empirical categories and hence they cannot be applied to the transcendent Absolute. In the same way Brahman cannot be called a substance which has for its attributes the finite souls and the world. It cannot be characterised even as cause. The relation of cause and effect can be

---

1. Paulsen, *Introduction to Philosophy*, p. 233.

true in the case of things within time. It cannot hold good in the case of a timeless and spaceless reality. The "Self is not a category at all, and, consequently it cannot be said to be even a system or a relational whole or, again, a unity in-difference. On the contrary, it is the ultimate, non-relational consciousness, which is necessarily distinctionless, unobjectifiable, and immediate. Whatever is relational and mediated cannot be the Self, though relativity and mediatedness belong to the very nature of the objects".[1] Brahman is neither bound by temporal nor spatial relations. Thus it is a differenceless and relationless reality. There are no differences in Brahman, says the Upaniṣad.[2] To the knower of Brahman everything becomes the Self, so he ceases to see differences altogether.[3]

Brahman, according to Śaṅkara, cannot be called a person. Personality is always constituted of the two elements of self and not-self. The self in order to be conscious of itself must confront the not-self. The self can realise its personality only through the not-self. If we take away the not-self, the self as a person also disappears. The concept of personality thus signifies dependence on something else. "If we use the term personality in a different sense," observes Dr. Radhakrishnan, "in which it does not demand any dependence on another then it is an illegitimate use".[4] So Brahman is impersonal and differenceless and not personal in nature.

The Upaniṣads or the Śrutis, according to Śaṅkara, give us a two-fold view or reality. On the one hand, they give us the knowledge of reality as it is and on the other hand they describe it as it appears to our consciousness with its attributes or qualifications. The creatorship of Brahman is the qualification per accidens or *taṭastha lakṣaṇa* of it. In its essential nature Brahman is said to be the principle of Existence, Consciousness and Bliss. This is its essential nature or *svarūpa lakṣaṇa*. Brahman as creator is related to the world. As creator, it is called Īśvara or lord of the universe. It is the determinate or *saguṇa* Brahman. But Īśvara or *saguṇa*

---

1. Prof. A.C. Mukerji, *The Nature of Self,* pp. 338-39.
2. नेह नानास्ति किञ्चन । (*Bṛh.* 4.4.19)
3. यत्र त्वस्य सर्वमात्मैवाभूत्तत्केन कं पश्येत् । (*Bṛh.* 4.5.14)
4. *Indian Philosophy,* Vol. II, p. 536.

Brahman cannot be characterised as the highest or ultimate reality. Īśvara or *saguṇa* Brahman is an identity-in-difference. It is a universal consciousness which has internal distinctions within it. It is mediated by the consciousness of the finite souls and the world. It is a complex of the Infinite and the finite and not the Infinite in its perfect purity. The consciousness of Īśvara is limited by the distinction of subject and object, of the finite souls and the world within it. "The immanent and all-inclusive consciousness, though it represents the centre of all centres of experience and is fully aware of the entire experience and presentation still suffers within itself a limitation of the division of subject and object. And so long as it has the consciousness of presentation, it has a sense of an outness, which is a barrier to its absoluteness. And an outness, which is an expression of self to self, though often claimed to be not strictly an outness cannot be reconciled in the Absolute, for an expression has a differentiating implication inasmuch as it is an effort to be away from the centre. Śaṅkara has, therefore, conceived the Absolute to be denying all relational consciousness, it is the centre which has no circumstance, it is the focus which shines in itself, but does not throw out its splendour. It is expression. It is real, for it is continuity. It persists. And Śaṅkara claims that we finally get to such an existence, which denies and transcends all relational import."[1]

In this respect Śaṅkara's view is similar to that of the Buddhist Absolutists, the Vijñānavādins and the Mādhyamikas who also conceive the Absolute as transcending all relational categories. Aśvaghoṣa regards the Absolute or Bhūta-tathatā as exceeding all categorical limitations. "Thus we understand that Suchness (Bhūta-tathatā) is neither that which is existence nor that which is non-existence, nor that which is at once existence and non-existence; that it is neither that which is unity, nor that which is plurality, nor that which is not at once unity or plurality".[2] "It is Śūnya (non-being) because it transcends all forms of separation and individuation; it is Aśūnya, because all possible things in the world emanate from it".[3] "This Bhūta-tathatā is neither that which is existent nor that which is non-existent, nor that which is at once existent

1. M.N. Sircar, *Comparative Studies in Vedāntism*, p. 132.
2. Suzuki, *Awakening of Faith*, p. 59.
3. *Ibid.*, p. 58, note.

and non-existent, nor that which is not at once existent and non-existent. It is neither that which is plurality, nor that which is at once unity and plurality, nor that which is not at once unity and plurality. It is negative in the sense that it is beyond all that is conditional, and it is positive in the sense that it holds all within it. It cannot be comprehended by any kind of particularisation or distinction. It is only by transcending the range of our intellectual category and the comprehension of the limited range of finite phenomena that we can get a glimpse of it. It cannot be comprehended by the particularising consciousness of all beings, and we thus may call it negation (Śūnyatā), in this sense."[1] Nāgārjuna also conceives the Absolute or Tathāgata as above all relational experience. He says, "It should not be said that Tathāgata is Śūnya or Aśūnya or both or neither. The name given to Him is conventional. In the state of calmness (Nirvāṇa) the four kinds of ideas, permanent, impermanent, both or neither, cannot exist".[2] The term Śūnya in Nāgārjuna's view does not mean nothingness. Nāgārjuna admits the existence of a supreme or higher reality though he considers it to be not an object of experience. "The Absolute is neither existent nor non-existent nor both existent and non-existent, nor different from both non-existence and existence".[3] "To the Mādhyamikas reason and language apply only to the finite world. To transfer the finite categories to the infinite would be like attempting to measure the heat of the sun by the ordinary thermometer".[4] The Absolute in the Mādhyamika system according to Candrakīrti repels all predicates including those of being and non-being and he complains that people ignorantly identify such an Absolute with the doctrine of non-being.[5] Thus it is clear from these statements that both Śankara as well as the Buddhist absolutists regard the Absolute as transcending all relational categories. Madhva is to a certain extent right in his view that the Śūnya of the Buddhists and Brahman of the Vedāntins are one and the same.[6]

1. Dr. Dasgupta, *Indian Idealism*, pp. 80-81.
2. *Mādhyamika Kārikās*, XXII. 11.12.
3. अस्ति नास्ति उभय अनुभय इति चतुष्कोटि विनिर्मुक्तं शून्यत्वम् ।
4. Radhakrishnan, *op. cit.*, Vol. I, p. 663.
5. *Mūla-Mādhymika-kārikās*, ed. by Poussin, p. 499.
6. यच्छून्यवादिन: शून्यं तदेव ब्रह्म मायिन: । (*Tattvoddyota*, p. 245)

So Brahman cannot be regarded as both indeterminate and determinate, *nirguṇa* and *saguṇa* simultaneously. Śaṅkara does not agree with Bhāskara in his view that Brahman as cause is one while as effect it is many.[1] "A reality that has two sides or can be experienced in two ways is not the highest reality. The sides are dissolved the moment we touch the fountain of being. We catch aspects of the Absolute when we look at it from the outside. In itself, the Absolute is without sides, without forms, and without any element of duality or *guṇas.*"[2] The same thing, observes Śaṅkara, cannot be said to be with and without attributes as it involves self-contradiction.[3] The finite world is ultimately regarded as unreal due to *avidyā*. Brahman creates or manifests the world by Māyā or *avidyā*. It is *avidyā* which makes us see the world, the individual souls and Īśvara in place of Brahman. When the knowledge of Brahman is attained and *avidyā* or ignorance is cancelled, then the whole world-show disappears from one's view. The world is empirically real and transcendentally ideal or unreal. It has only an epistemic status and no ontological status in Śaṅkara's system.

Śaṅkara's conception of the Absolute can be considered an improvement on Hegel's and Rāmānuja's conception of the Absolute insofar as the former views it as an unconditioned, differenceless and unmediated principle while the latter regard it as a mediated principle and as a whole including and integrating all the differences in it. The Absolute of Hegel and Rāmānuja cannot be really called perfectly unconditioned and independent. The Absolute and the world in Hegel's system, as we have shown in a preceding chapter, are mutually dependent. The Absolute cannot exist as Absolute without the world. The Absolute of Rāmānuja is also conditioned by the finite souls and the world. Unlike Śaṅkara, Rāmānuja does not make any distinction between God or Īśvara and the Absolute. But the conception of God or Īśvara has meaning and significance only in relation to the world and finite souls. If we take away the world and the individual souls, the *Creatorship and Godship* of God disappear altogether. Though Rāmānuja regards God as both immanent and transcen-

1. कार्यरूपेण नानात्वमभेद: कारणात्मना । (*Bhāskara-bhāṣya* 1.1.4)
2. Radhakrishnan, *op. cit.*, Vol. II, p. 541.
3. नह्येकं वस्तु स्वत एव रूपादिविशेषोपेतं तद्विपरीतं चेत्यवधारयितुं शक्यं विरोधात् । (*S.B.* 3.2.11)

dent, yet it is not a complete and perfect transcendence. The Absolute of Hegel and Rāmānuja is universal in nature which integrates and synthesises all the particulars within it. But it cannot strictly be called a perfectly transcendent Absolute. So Śaṅkara's conception of the Absolute marks a definite advance over that of Rāmānuja and Hegel insofar as he represents the Absolute in its perfectly transcendent and essential nature.

But Śaṅkara's conception of the Absolute suffers from a great drawback also. The defect or drawback is that he does not give any place to the world in his conception of reality. The world and the individual souls are said, as has been stated above, to be ultimately unreal. In order to present the Absolute in its perfect purity, integrity and transcendence, Śaṅkara reduces the world to unreality from the ontological standpoint. The experience of the world is due to ignorance. "Philosophy in Śaṅkara is a denial of immanent life and an assertion of transcendent consciousness. Though Śaṅkara would accept a continuity of the immanent life, still he would not conceive and grant a history in the Absolute. And he has sacrificed the history to the fixity of an unchangeable and unchanged Absolute. Philosophy is essentially a transcendence in which the immanent life and consciousness has no meaning, no existence. Śaṅkara has not reconciled the claims of relative experience and transcendent consciousness. Such reconciliation has been thought an impossibility and to the integral Absolute has been sacrificed the truth and revelations of relative consciousness. This plurality of relative consciousness is due to nescience. It has no *raison d'etre* in the Absolute."[1]

Śaṅkara considers a synthesis between the indeterminate and the determinate, the impersonal and personal Absolute as impossible. But the question is that the Absolute may transcend the finite, but the experience of the finite requires some explanation. How the world of space and time came to manifest itself in the transcendent Absolute? Śaṅkara simply says that the world is due to Māyā; but how Māyā came to operate in the Absolute is not explained by him. Even if the world is unreal or illusory in nature it has to be explained. "If....we attempt to write off the appearance

---

1. M.N. Sircar, *Comparative Studies in Vedāntism*, pp. 133-34.

of difference as mere illusion due to partial vision, the difficulty remains. For the task of making a real unity generate an apparent diversity is not less than that of accounting for its generation of a real diversity. Unity in fact can no more account for error than for diversity."[1] The finite souls and *avidyā* are said to be beginningless though liable to end on the attainment of knowledge. "But how side by side with Absolute consciousness this polarity of opposites exists; how, if not in the Absolute consciousness but in it as locus, the finite centres of consciousness are formed are problems that pass human comprehension and the philosophy of Absolute monism has sought to solve the problem by categorically denying it."[2] "How do we manage to deceive ourselves into seeking a transformation and plurality, where in reality the Brahman alone is? On this question our authors give no information."[3] Śaṅkara has not been able to explain adequately the nature of *avidyā* and its relation to Brahman. A similar difficulty exists in the Mahāyāna Buddhism. "As to the question how and why this negative principle of ignorance came to assert itself in the body of Suchness, we are at a loss where to find an authoritative and definite answer to it."[4]

Śaṅkara considers it impossible to explain how the One became Many. The manifold would have a status in experience but it has no status in reality. This is a puzzle. Śaṅkara "leaves the problem of the one and the many as almost insoluble and inexplicable. Human reason is not equal to the task. The reality of the many may not be felt in liberation, still the appearance requires an explanation. And this seems to be a puzzle. The impress of the transcendent consciousness the empiric mind cannot receive and hold and the faculty of intelligence is inherently incapable of transcending the relativity of subject and object. Śaṅkara seems to feel that philosophy cannot sufficiently comprehend how the one becomes the many. This appears to be the implication of the māyā doctrine".[5]

1. C.E.M. Joad, *Introduction to Modern Philosophy*.
2. M.N. Sircar, *op. cit.*, p. 135.
3. Deussen, *The System of Vedānta*, p. 392.
4. Suzuki, *Outline of Mahāyāna Buddhism*, p. 116.
5. M.N. Sircar, *op. cit.*, p. 136.

Now let us see how far we can solve the difficulty of Śaṅkara from the standpoint of Sri Aurobindo. The main objection which Śaṅkara raises against the conception of change in Brahman is that Brahman cannot be both changeless and changing simultaneously.[1] Brahman cannot be said to be possessed of the two states of rest and motion because it is immutable (Kūṭastha).[2] This conclusion is arrived at by an *a priori* application of the abstract and formal law of contradiction to the statements which reveal the nature of Brahman. But it is not logically justified, as we have shown before. We have already shown that this objection appears to be formidable and unanswerable only to the finite reason which takes only a superficial view of different concepts and does not penetrate into their real meaning. The word changeless, according to Sri Aurobindo, as we have stated above, does not mean that it is incapable of undergoing any change at all but that it remains unaffected by the world of change or becoming. Its whole reality is not exhausted in the Becoming. The pure Existence, as we have shown in preceding chapter, remains absolutely unaffected by the whole phenomena of Becoming. Thus, the changelessness of Brahman only means that it exceeds all change and not that it is incapable of indulging in a voluntary and sportive creative activity. To say that Brahman is differenceless or indeterminate does not mean that it is devoid of all determinations and that it is incapable of manifesting determinations out of its being, but it means that it exceeds all determinations. If we say that Brahman is only changeless and is incapable of manifesting self-determinations out of its being, we put a limitation upon the infinity and absoluteness of Brahman.

Vācaspati's Dialectical Criticism of the Concept of Change and its Answer

The Vedāntins of Śaṅkara school have taken great pains to show that the concept of change in the Absolute is self-contradictory. They have tried to show that if the concept of change in the Absolute is admitted, then the Absolute can no longer remain unaffected and its absoluteness will be compromised. Vācaspati

---

1. नह्येकस्य ब्रह्मण: परिणामधर्मत्वं तद्रहितत्वं च शक्यं प्रतिपत्तुम् । (S.B. 2.1.14)
2. न हि कूटस्थस्य ब्रह्मण: स्थितिगतिवदनेकधर्माश्रयत्वं सम्भवति । (S.B. 2.1.14)

shows the impossibility of conceiving change in the Absolute in the following manner. If transformation implies a complete change in the being of cause, knowledge would be impossible, for it makes every state of existence different from the previous state. If by transformation is meant a change not of the whole but of the parts of its being, then the question arises, whether these parts are different from or identical with the whole cause. If we affirm the first alternative, then we have to admit a synthesis between the two which is logically impossible. If the second alternative is accepted then we will have to admit that the complete being of cause is changed which means that the effect is entirely a different thing.[1] He further argues, "what is the nature of the entire cause that is transformed into diversified forms? Is it partless or is it endowed with parts? If it be partless, it goes to prove that complete change is produced in the primordial cause in every form of transformation and the effect must be eternal. If we accept the second alternative, the primordial cause becomes no longer eternal but perishable".[2] Thus it is clear that whether we regard the Absolute as changing in part or in whole, its absoluteness is affected and it is reduced to the level of the finite. So we cannot logically conceive, according to this view, any change in the Absolute without indulging in self-contradiction. If we regard the Absolute as partless and admit change in it, then it means that the whole of the Absolute is changed, which means that it has ceased to be absolute, and if we admit that a part of the Absolute changes, then it means that the Absolute consists of parts and is thus perishable like other finite entities. Thus the Absolute is reduced to the level of a finite and perishable entity if the concept of change or transformation is introduced in it.

Now this difficulty arises on account of our taking an abstract view of the concept of change. We seem to proceed on the assumption that we can conceive only two kinds of change in a thing; that is, if a thing changes, it can change either wholly or partially. But this view of change either in part or in whole is largely based on our experience of the material world. If a change

1. Vide Bhāmatī, p. 117, Bhāmatī-Kalpataru Nirṇaya Sāgar Edn.
2. A.B. Shastri, Studies in Post-Śaṅkara Dialectics, p. 174. Vide Bhāmatī, Kalpataru 1.1.4.

takes place in a material thing, then either the whole of the thing is changed or it is changed in part only. If, for example, milk changes into curd, then it ceases to be milk. It means that the whole of milk is changed or transformed into curd and thus it no more keeps its identity as milk. In the same way a thing may change in part only, e.g., a part of gold may be transformed into a jewel. Thus in the world of matter we see things changing either in whole or in parts. Now if these are the only two ways in which we can understand the concept of change, then certainly the difficulties raised by Vācaspati cannot be solved and his criticism against the concept of change in the Absolute cannot be answered.

But if we take the trouble to look at the world of experience we find that the phenomenon of change is not confined to these two alternatives only. In the vital world, the phenomenon of change does not necessarily take place in either of these two ways, namely, in part or in whole. In the vital world, we find wholes coming out of wholes. The mother gives birth to a son. The son is a whole coming out of another whole, the mother. In the world of life, all creation takes place in the form of wholes. One whole is generated by another whole. This is generally the process of creation in the world of life. Now the child is born of mother. In this relationship of mother and child we cannot apply our logic of whole and part. Here mother maintains her identity in spite of giving birth to a child. So we cannot say that the whole of mother is changed. We also cannot say that a part of mother has been transformed into the child. The individuality of the mother is not seen to be broken into parts or fragments by bringing forth an issue. Hence it cannot logically be said that some part of mother is changed and the other part remains unchanged. So the relationship of mother and child is clearly a case of a whole coming out of another whole. The categories of part and whole cannot be applied to it. Now if this is true of the world of life, it is not difficult for us to conceive that it may be much more true in the case of the Absolute or Brahman. We can fairly say that in manifesting the world, Brahman does not change either in part or in whole. Brahman maintains its unity in spite of manifesting itself into different centres of our world-experience. "That incoercible unity in all divisions and diversities," to quote again Sri Aurobindo's words, "is the mathematics of the Infinite, indicated in a verse of the Upaniṣads—'This is the complete and That is the complete; subtract the complete from the complete, the complete is the remainder' ".[1] So the change in Brahman does not take place in accordance with the mathematics of our finite and abstract reason but in accordance with the 'mathematics of the Infinite'. So it is clear that Brahman undergoes change in a different manner altogether from what we see in the material world. The attempt on the part of the finite reason to apply the logic of whole and part etc. in case of the Absolute to prove the impossibility of admitting change in it is thus vain and futile. The real tragedy with the dialectical reasoning lies in the fact that we try to judge reality in abstraction. Our reason abstracts itself from the world of experience and reality and then tries to pass judgments on them. Such attempts on the part of reason are thus bound to end in failure. We can hope to attain a greater insight into reality only if we switch on the light of experience in the dark chambers of our abstract reason. The more our reason gets rid of its abstraction, the more it will be fit to understand the world of experience and reality. In order to understand the truth of reality, our finite logic has to transform itself ultimately into the logic of the Infinite.

So, if we look at the concept of change from the standpoint of higher reason or the logic of the Infinite we find that it does not affect the oneness and immutability of the Absolute in any manner. The concept of change is, according to the higher reason, quite consistent with the immutability and the transcendence of the Absolute. The greatness of Śaṅkara lies in the fact that he lays great stress on the perfect transcendence of the Absolute. Sri Aurobindo agrees with Śaṅkara insofar as he argues that the Absolute transcends all our categories. But the main defect in Śaṅkara lies in the fact that he tries to judge the relationship between the Absolute and the world from the standpoint of our abstract reason. Because he cannot explain the relationship between the Absolute and the world from the standpoint of our abstract reason, so he calls the latter unreal or false. The phenomenon of change is attributed by the Śaṅkarites to ignorance. Brahman, it is said, does not really manifest the world out of itself, but it appears as the world due

---

1. *L.D.*, Vol. II, Part I, p. 53.

पूर्णमदः पूर्णमिदं पूर्णात्पूर्णमुदच्यते ।
पूर्णस्य पूर्णमादाय पूर्णमेवावशिष्यते ॥

to ignorance. Thus the doctrine of *pariṇāma* or real change in Brahman is rejected and that of *vivarta* which denies real change is upheld by the Śaṅkarites. "*Vivartavāda* is, therefore, the denial of causation and the assertion of identity. It presupposes *pariṇāma* or effectual transformation, for the identity is intelligible as the denial of the manifold. This denial requires a position, and as such we posit a world through a law of causation and then deny it to indicate the illusoriness of position and the reality of the identity. To establish unqualified monism on a secure basis, Vedāntism simultaneously asserts and denies the manifold existence in the identity of Being. If the world of appearance altogether be denied an existence in identity—there would arise a gulf between the transcendent being and immanent experience, and a metaphysical dualism would be the result. To counteract this possibility of thought, the manifold world is posited and then denied. Logically, affirmation goes before denial "is" before "is not."[1]

It is said that logically affirmation precedes negation. One can affirm a thing unconsciously but one cannot deny it unconsciously. One can affirm a snake in place of rope unconsciously but one cannot deny it unconsciously. Negation or denial is thus always said to be conscious. Sarvajñātmamuni, a great teacher of the Śaṅkara school, says that *vivarta* presupposes *pariṇāma*. When our reason reaches *pariṇāmavāda*, it logically makes a transition to *Vivartavāda*.[2]

Now this contention of the Śaṅkarites cannot be granted as it is based on our abstract reason. The doctrine of *pariṇāma* appears to be quite logical if viewed from the standpoint of higher reason, as we have fully shown above. *Vivartavāda* is simply a refusal to explain causation. "We may still go further and say that *vivartavāda* is a frank confession of a failure to exactly determine causation."[3] Dr. Dasgupta rightly remarks, "The difficulty that many of the *sūtras* of Bādarāyana give us a *pariṇāma* view of causation was realised by Sarvajñātma Muni, who tried to explain it away by suggesting that the *pariṇāma* theory was discussed approvingly in the *sūtras*

1. M.N. Sircar, *op. cit.*, p. 105.
2. विवर्तवादस्य हि पूर्वभूमिर्वेदान्तवादे परिणामवाद: ।
   व्यवस्थितेऽस्मिन् परिणामवादे स्वयं समायाति विवर्तवाद: ।
   Vide Śaṁksepaśārirakam, p. 40, Chān. 11.61 (Benares Edn.).
3. M.N. Sircar, *op. cit.*, p. 106.

only because this theory was nearest to the *vivarta*, and by initiating people to the *pariṇāma* theory it would be easier to lead them to the *vivarta* theory, as hinted in *sūtra* 11.1.14."[1]

Śaṅkarites fight shy of affirming the truth of causation due to the fear that it will compromise the transcendence of the Absolute. To say that the Absolute is beyond all categories and is a transcendent reality and at the same time to admit that it is the cause of the world, is according to them, self-contradictory. "Causality holds good as long as we are confined to the empirical world, but when we transcend the phenomenal world and judge the effect from the metaphysical standpoint, it is non-existent or false. Experience must presuppose the chain of causation, but beyond experience, it has no validity."[2]

It is true that Brahman cannot be described as simply creator from the ultimate standpoint. Sri Aurobindo is one with Śaṅkara in holding the view that ultimately Brahman transcends cause-effect relationship. But to say that Brahman transcends cause-effect relationship is one thing and to say that the creatorship of Brahman is unreal is a different thing altogether. Brahman, according to Sri Aurobindo, ultimately transcends all relationships including the cause-effect relationship. But it does not mean that he is not also the creator or the cause of the world. We can understand the truth of this statement to some extent if we look at the facts of our everyday experience. We may take, for example, the relationship of father and son. Father is the cause of the son. But the whole individuality of father is not based on his relationship with the son. Father is not only a father of his son, but he is a man also. So a man as father is necessarily related to his son. His existence as father solely depends on his relationship with his son. But his existence as man does not depend on that of his son. So man as man transcends the relationship of father and son. He is no doubt a father but he is also something more. He is primarily a man, an individual, who is above the relationship of father and son. Hence his existence as man and his existence as father do not seem to be incompatible with each other. He is simultaneously man as well as a father. If we take away the son, he will cease to exist as a father but he will not cease to exist as a man. So we cannot

---

1. S.N. Dasgupta, *A History of Indian Philosophy*, Vol. II, p. 45.
2. A.B. Shastri, *op. cit.*, p. 174.

describe a man by the category of either father or of man. He is both father as well as man. Man has a complex personality. So it cannot be described by any single category. If it is said that a Man is a father, it will not express the whole truth of his personality. Again, if it is said that man is man, it will also not express the whole truth of his complex personality. We do not mean to say that man is a transcendent being altogether. Here we only mean to indicate that even a human being also transcends in some measure all sorts of relationships.

Now if this is true in the case of man, it will undoubtedly be true to a far greater extent in the case of the Absolute which transcends all limitations. The Absolute as creator is necessarily related to the world. But the Absolute as Absolute transcends its aspect of creatorship and is above the cause-effect relationship. And as it is not incompatible for a man to be both a man and a father, in the same way it is not incompatible for the Absolute to be both the Absolute and the creator of the world. The Absolute is integral in nature. So it cannot be confined within the limits of any single category or any sum of categories. Sri Aurobindo lays great stress on the fact that the creatorship of the Absolute is in no way incompatible with its absoluteness. To say that the Absolute is above all relations does not necessarily mean that all relations that are predicated of the Absolute are false or unreal. If it is said that man as man transcends the relationship of father and son it does not mean that his relationship with his son as father is false or unreal. The transcendence of the Absolute only means that the whole truth of the Absolute cannot be expressed by relational categories. The relational categories, according to Sri Aurobindo, are imperfect but not false or unreal, as the Śaṅkarites would have us believe. All the categories are the self-determinations of the Absolute. They express the nature of the Absolute though in an imperfect and more or less distorted manner. But on that very ground they cannot be said to be unreal and contradictory of the Absolute. To know the Absolute in an integral manner, we have not only to look at the transcendent aspect of the Absolute but also its immanent or its relational aspect.

Though Śaṅkarites look upon the Absolute as transcending all categories, yet their abstract logic puts a kind of limitation upon its absoluteness by confining it within the limits of categories. By saying that the Absolute cannot change, the Śaṅkarites confine it within the category of Being. Similarly by saying that the Absolute is not self-conscious, they confine it within the category of pure consciousness. If we regard the Absolute as changeless meaning thereby that it is incapable of manifesting the world, it means clearly that the Absolute not only transcends the world but is also opposed to it. The Absolute as Being not only transcends becoming but is also opposed to it. Though the Śaṅkarites deny the fact of the opposition of the Absolute and the world from the ontological or ultimate standpoint, yet their logic inevitably leads one to this conclusion. If the Absolute is incapable of change, then it is certainly opposed to the world and not only transcends it. The Śaṅkarites might say that we experience the world only so long as we are in ignorance. The moment we have the realisation of the transcendent Absolute, the experience of the world vanishes from our view. But whether we experience the world or not in the state of ultimate realisation, it is there. The very fact of experience is to be explained. The world is on a lower plane than the Absolute. So if the consciousness reaches the plane of the Absolute and is identified with it, it may cease to experience the world. But it does not mean that the lower plane, namely, the world is cancelled altogether. The experience of the world may be cancelled for the individual who realises the Absolute but the world itself is not cancelled. Now if the experience of the world cannot be explained by the Absolute and requires some other entity like ignorance or māyā to explain it, then it clearly means that the Absolute not only transcends the world but is also opposed to it. And this opposition cannot fail to put a limitation upon the Absolute.

In the same way if we regard the Absolute as pure consciousness and not self-conscious, we confine the Absolute, as has been stated above, to the category of pure consciousness. The Śaṅkarites hold that the Absolute derives the power of self-consciousness through its association with māyā or ignorance. In this respect the view of Śaṅkarites resembles that of Kant. As Kant holds that the pure subject or pure consciousness becomes self-conscious through its association with sensibility, in the same way the Śaṅkarites hold that the pure conscious Absolute becomes self-conscious through its association with ignorance or Māyā. The concept of self-consciousness shows a dependence on something else. Hence it cannot characterise the Absolute in its ultimate status. Now if the view that the Absolute assumes the nature of self-consciousness through its association with ignorance be admitted then it will mean that there is something foreign to the nature of the Absolute and is thus opposed to it. To say that the Absolute ultimately transcends ignorance does not mean that ignorance as such does not exist. We cannot dispense with the empirical reality altogether simply by saying that it has no place in the Absolute. It will simply mean that we confine the Absolute to a particular status, namely, the status of pure consciousness. The Absolute as pure consciousness and the Absolute as self-conscious are not necessarily incompatible with each other. The Absolute can be regarded as both transcendent and immanent, as pure consciousness and self-conscious from the standpoint of higher reason. To say that the Absolute ultimately transcends self-consciousness does not necessarily mean that it is not possessed of self-consciousness also. The Absolute cannot be characterised as simply pure consciousness or simply self-conscious. It is both as well as it is beyond both. But the abstract reason of the Śaṅkarites does not enable them to conceive the Absolute in its integral aspect. They are confronted on all sides by antinomies and contradictions and the only way left for them to escape from this contradiction is to deny the reality of Change or Becoming.

We can solve all the contradictions if we admit an integral consciousness which is able to realise the reality in all its aspects. In the system of Śaṅkara, intuition is said to give us the knowledge of the transcendent Absolute and reason and sense experience give us the knowledge of the world. There is no such consciousness which can have the knowledge of the Absolute as well as of the world. Īśvara who is supposed to be possessed of integral consciousness is called unreal from the ontological standpoint. But in Sri Aurobindo's system we have the Supermind possessed of integral consciousness. It is the creative aspect of the Absolute or Brahman. It is the Absolute itself playing the role of the creator. It is this consciousness which bridges the gulf between the Infinite and the finite. The logic of the Infinite is the logic of this supramental consciousness. Without this supramental principle we cannot hope to solve the riddle of existence.

The truth of this statement is further confirmed if we compare Sri Aurobindo's conception of the Absolute with that of Bradley.

(iii) *Sri Aurobindo's and Bradley's View of the Absolute
       Compared*

The Absolute, according to Bradley, is a single, all-inclusive, and
perfectly harmonious reality. The human intellect does not grasp
the essential nature of the Absolute but only its appearances. But
Bradley, unlike Śaṅkara, does not call these appearances unreal.
The appearances are real and they are synthesised, harmonised
and integrated in the all-embracing unity of the Absolute. But these
appearances do not exist in the Absolute in the same manner as
they appear to the human consciousness. They are transformed
and transmuted in the Absolute consciousness. As Bradley ob-
serves, "The Absolute, we may say in general has no assets beyond
appearances; and again with appearances alone to its credit, the
Absolute would be bankrupt. All of these are worthless alike apart
from transmutation. But on the other hand once more, since the
amount of change is different in each case, appearances differ
widely in their degrees of truth and reality. There are predicates
which, in comparison with others, are false and unreal."[1] All ap-
pearances are not transformed and transmuted alike. Some appear-
ances require greater transformation and transmutation than the
others in order to be harmonised, synthesised and integrated in
the Absolute. The more an appearance requires to be transformed
and transmuted the less reality it is said to possess in Bradley's
system. "The more an appearance, in being corrected, is trans-
formed and destroyed, the less reality can such an appearance
contain; or, to put it otherwise, the less genuinely does it represent
the Real."[2] All the contradictions of our finite experiences are
resolved, according to Bradley, in the all-embracing unity of the
Absolute. "Spirit is a unity of the manifold in which the externality
of the manifold has utterly ceased. The universal here is immanent
in the parts, and its system does not lie somewhere outside and
in the relations between them. It is above the relational form and
has absorbed it in a higher unity, a whole in which there is no
division between elements and laws."[3]
    Bradley regards the Absolute as above its internal distinctions

1. *Appearance and Reality* (1893), p. 489.
2. *Ibid.*, p. 376.
3. *Ibid.*, p. 498.

and at the same time conceives it as inclusive of all distinctions. "The Absolute stands above its internal distinctions. It does not eject them, it includes them. The Absolute is the concrete identity of all extremes." This is a puzzle to the finite reason. If the Absolute is admitted to be above all internal differences, then it cannot logically be considered to be inclusive of differences or distinctions. Sri Aurobindo maintains the perfect transcendence of the Absolute as well as its immanence on the basis of the higher logic. But Bradley is not in a position to do so. He does not explain how the Absolute synthesises all the differences within it and how it ultimately resolves their contradictions. Bradley himself says, "We do not know why and how the Absolute divides itself into centres or the way in which, so divided, it still remains one. The relation of the many experiences to the single experience and so to one another is, in the end, beyond us."[1]

Thus Bradley fails to explain the relationship between the One and the Many, though he asserts that the Absolute is a harmonious system and has all the differences integrated in its unity. Now it is clear that from the metaphysical standpoint the system of Bradley cannot be said to be an improvement upon those of Rāmānuja and Hegel. Bradley's Absolute can also be characterised as an identity-in-difference. It is true that Bradley calls his Absolute a non-relational whole which cannot be characterised even as Spirit. But as we cannot conceive the Absolute apart from all differences or appearances, so it is difficult for us to conceive how such an Absolute can be called non-relational in a strict sense. Appearances, according to Bradley, are a necessary part of the Absolute. The Absolute does not become non-relational only by saying that the appearances get transformed and transmuted in the Absolute. So we can say without being unfair to Bradley that his Absolute is an identity-in-difference. Intuition, according to Bradley, gives us a harmonious view of reality. All the distinctions and differences are said to be harmonised in the all-embracing unity of the Absolute. The Absolute cannot be considered in itself apart from the differences. It is known in and through the differences. So the Absolute of Bradley also can be represented by the principle of identity-in-difference, as we have also indicated in a previous

---

1. *Appearance and Reality*, p. 527.

chapter. Unlike Śaṅkara, Bradley does not hold that in intuition all the differences and distinctions are dissolved altogether. They are, according to him, integrated and harmonised, as has been stated above, in the all-embracing unity of the Absolute. In this respect we do not find any great difference between Hegel's Reason and Bradley's Intuition. Hegel also holds that the self-conscious Reason reconciles all differences within its all-embracing unity. We have already stated in a preceding chapter that Hegel's Reason has a great deal of intuitive element in it. William James makes a profound and striking observation about Hegel, when he asks, "What reader of Hegel can doubt that sense of a perfected being with all the otherness soaked up into itself, which dominates his whole philosophy must have come from the prominence in his consciousness of mystic moods."[1] Our view that Hegel's Reason has a great deal of intuitive element in it is supported by Hegel's own statement. Comparing religion with philosophy, Hegel observes, "It is not the concern of philosophy to produce religion in any individual. Its existence is, on the contrary, presupposed as forming what is fundamental in every one. So far as man's essential nature is concerned, nothing new is to be introduced into him. To try to do this would be as absurd as to give a dog printed writings to chew, under the idea that in this way you could put mind into it. He who has not extended his spiritual interests beyond the hurry and bustle of this finite world, nor succeeded in lifting himself above this life through aspiration, through the anticipation, through the feeling of the Eternal, and who has not yet gazed upon the pure ether of the soul, does not possess in himself that element which it is our object here to comprehend."[2]

So it is clear that Hegel's reason is not an abstract entity which separates the 'what' from 'that'. It is an all-inclusive whole which integrates and harmonises all the differences within it. Bradley would have been saved from the trouble of hurling many scathing but unjustified criticisms against Hegel's View of Reason, had he grasped the intuitive element present in it. Bradley has also not been able to present any satisfactory view of the Absolute, as we have shown above. His Absolute cannot be regarded as perfect

---

1. *Varieties of Religious Experience* (1906), p. 389.
2. *Philosophy of Religion*, E.T. (1895), i, p. 4.

and unconditioned inasmuch as it is also conditioned by the internal distinctions like the Absolute of Rāmānuja and Hegel. It is the Absolute of Śaṅkara which can really be regarded as perfectly transcendent and unconditioned. But the main defect in Śaṅkara's view is that he has denied the reality of the world.

Thus it is clear that neither Spinoza nor Hegel nor Rāmānuja nor Bradley nor Śaṅkara has been able to present a satisfactory view of reality. None of them can solve the contradictions between the One and the many or between the Infinite and the finite. Spinoza simply asserts the Absolute as both indeterminate and determinate but does not show how they can be reconciled with each other. Hegel and Rāmānuja solve the contradiction by denying the indeterminate and relationless Absolute altogether. Bradley simply asserts that the contradictions of the finite experiences are resolved in the unity, harmony and integrity of the Absolute but does not explain how this miracle happens at all. Śaṅkara solves the contradiction between the indeterminate and the determinate, between the Absolute and the world by simply denying the ultimate reality of the latter altogether.

Sri Aurobindo regards all these views as partial and one-sided. The reason of the failure of these philosophers to solve the problem of the One and the Many, of the indeterminability and determinability is, according to Sri Aurobindo, this, that they make a mental approach to solve these problems. Though Śaṅkara, Bradley, Rāmānuja and Spinoza proclaim that reality cannot be realised and grasped by mind, yet they try to understand Reality and its process from the standpoint of mind. They apply their finite and mental logic to understand the supralogical Reality and its process, hence their failure becomes inevitable. These philosophers have only two courses open to them. If they go by their logic, they have to deny, like Śaṅkara, Hegel and Rāmānuja, some aspect of Reality or if they affirm the truth of all the aspects of Reality, they have to do it like Spinoza at the cost of their logic. The self-consistency of thought demands the denial or abrogation of some fundamental aspect of experience and the self-consistency of experience demands the sacrifice of the fundamental laws of thought. It is between these two extremes that the monistic thought generally moves.

Sri Aurobindo tries to steer clear of these two extremes by making not a mental but, as has been stated above, a supramental approach to reality. It is only the supramental consciousness that can have an integral view of reality and not the mental consciousness or mind-dominated intuition. What appears as contradictory to our mental consciousness appears, according to him, simply complementary to the supramental consciousness. It is only our supramental consciousness that can give us an all-integral view of the Absolute as both transcendent and immanent. Sri Aurobindo has a most comprehensive and integral view of the Absolute. "Sri Aurobindo's Absolute is a most remarkable conception. Philosophically one could say, it is an Absolute in an absolutely absolute way. It is governed by its own logic of the Absolute, the logic of the finite and the relative being inadequate for it. The former conceptions of the Absolute in the history of philosophy have often suffered in one way or another from some taint of the relative. Here the Absolute is a real Absolute, which is personal as well as impersonal, complete and perfect as well as dynamic and evolutionary and an infinite lot more."[1] Our mind cannot have an all-embracing view of the Absolute. It cannot also make a reconciliation between the Absolute and the relative. Only the supermind is possessed of this integral vision.

Sri Aurobindo's conception of supermind enables him to deal effectively with the problem of creation and to find a proper reconciliation between the Absolute and the finite world. The Supermind is to him a link between the Absolute and the finite world. Unlike mind it is fully aware of the indivisible, unitary and self-concentrated consciousness of Saccidānanda in which there are no separating distinctions. It also contains the essential truth of the world and creates the world of multiplicity out of the indivisible, unitary and self-concentrated being of Saccidānanda. So, above the Supermind we have the pure being of Saccidānanda and below it, the analytic consciousness of mind which knows only by division and separation and has only an indirect and secondary apprehension of unity and infinity. The Supermind succeeds where mind fails. "That which is an apparent discord to the mind because it considers each thing separately in itself," says Sri Aurobindo "is

---

1. Dr. Indra Sen, *Problem of Life and Sri Aurobindo*, Sri Aurobindo Mandir Annual (1943), pp. 48-49.

an element of the general ever-present and ever-developing harmony to the Supermind because it views all things in a multiple unity".[1]

It is this infinite and fundamental truth-consciousness that can solve effectively the problem of creation. It contains the secrets of creation within itself. Thus it is by following the logic of the infinite based on this supramental truth-consciousness that one can hope to unveil the secrets of Reality and to find the truth of man, world and God. It is because of its intermediate position that Sri Aurobindo calls the supermind the child of Saccidānanda and parent of the Mind. Between Saccidānanda and Mind, observes Sri Aurobindo, "is this comprehensive and creative consciousness by its power of pervading and comprehending knowledge the child of that self-awareness by identity which is the poise of the Brahman and by its power of projecting, confronting, apprehending knowledge parent of that awareness by distinction which is the process of Mind.[2] Mind cannot have an all-embracing vision of the whole. It can only deal with parts. It has the idea of the whole as "an assemblage of parts or a totality of properties and accidents". Hence its view of things and of reality is fragmentary, partial and one-sided. To have a greater, a profounder and a real knowledge, "Mind has to make room for another consciousness which will fulfil Mind by transcending it or reverse and so rectify its operations after leaping beyond it; the summit of mental knowledge is only a vaulting-board from which that leap can be taken".[3] "Mind," further says Sri Aurobindo, "is a passage, not a culmination". Hence it is clear that we cannot solve the problem of One and the Many or any other problems by the help of mind. It will only land us into paradoxes and inconsistencies. To have a comprehensive and real view of reality, we have to take recourse to a higher consciousness and a higher logic. This higher or supramental consciousness will not find any real contradiction existing between Saccidānanda and the world and will present a harmonious and a comprehensive view of all the aspects of existence, the individual, the universal and the transcendent.

1. *L.D.*, Vol. I, p. 170.
2. *Ibid.*, p. 157.
3. *Ibid.*, p. 160.

We have to realise that the unitarian and indivisible conscious-
ness of Saccidānanda cannot be a thing without contents. If it is
an original self-concentration it must be that which contains all
things in another manner than in this temporal and spatial mani-
festation. It is our narrow, partial and false understanding of the
nature of unitarian consciousness of Saccidānanda that makes us
conceive the existence of the world incompatible with it. It should
be noted that this state of pure unitarian indivisible consciousness
is but a poise of the being of Saccidānanda or of the utterly in-
effable and inconceivable Existence. We can be aware of
Saccidānanda in its pure unitarian consciousness, in its timeless
and spaceless concentration. We can also be aware of Saccidānanda
in an another poise, in a dynamic, all-comprehending equal self-
extension, also known as Supermind. Then we have a third poise
of Saccidānanda, the world of diversity that seems to mind as
offering a direct challenge to the pure poise of unity. Thus we see
that the world is neither illusory nor unreal. It is the manifestation
of Saccidānanda. Prior to the state of manifestation it exists in a
potential form in the pure indivisible being of Saccidānanda. It is
brought into existence by the dynamic and all powerful Supermind
out of the original self-concentration of Saccidānanda and held by
it in the state of perfect harmony and reconciliation. It is the
Supermind which holds a proper balance between the One and
the Many. Referring to this supramental poise of Saccidānanda, Sri
Aurobindo observes, it is "its firm self-extension in the Truth-
consciousness which contains and upholds the diffusion and
prevents it from being a real disintegration, maintains unity in
utmost diversity and stability in utmost mutability, insists on har-
mony in the appearance of an all-pervading strife and collision,
keeps eternal cosmos where Mind would arrive only at a chaos
eternally attempting to form itself. This is the Supermind, the Truth-
consciousness, the Real-Idea which knows itself and all that be-
comes".[1] Thus it is clear that for the all-embracing, all-comprehend-
ing and all-constituting consciousness of the Supermind, there can
exist no paradoxes, inconsistencies or contradictions. These are all
the creations of mind and have no place in the supramental truth-
consciousness.

The Supermind does not create the world in an arbitrary man-

----

1. *L.D.*, Vol. I, p. 161.

ner. The manifestation of the world takes place according to some principle, some causal relationship. This causal principle is the Divine Law. The supreme Being takes recourse to its own law in order to create the world. The Divine Law is the underlying principle of the whole of cosmic existence. All the animate and inanimate existences are carried on in their evolutionary journey by the truth of the Divine Law. The essence of the Divine Law is, in the opinion of Sri Aurobindo, "an inevitable self-development of the truth of the thing that is, an Idea, in the very essence of what is developed; it is a previously fixed determination of relative movements out of the stuff of infinite possibility".[1]

This Law is not an abstract principle. The creation or the manifestation of the world must be a play of conscious force. Hence the principle which manifests all things and secretly guides their movements must be a knowledge-will or Conscious Force. This principle of knowledge-will or Conscious Force must not be confused with mental consciousness. Mind is only a product or creation of this Law. It does not possess or govern it and is not aware of its essential nature. Mind moves only in the domain of phenomena, whereas this Law lies at the root of phenomenal existence. It is immanent in the cosmic existence as well as transcendent of it. This Law or the principle of knowledge-will is in possession of the unity of things and out of it manifests the world of multiplicity. But mind is not in possession of this essential and infinite unity and is also only imperfectly aware of a part of multiplicity.

(B) *Supermind as Truth-Consciousness or Real-Idea*

This Divine Law or the principle of Conscious Force or knowledge-will is the truth of the Supermind which is also known as Truth-consciousness, as Real-Idea. Whatever is in the being of the Supermind, observes Sri Aurobindo, "takes form as self-knowledge, as Truth-Consciousness as Real-Idea, and that self-knowledge being also self-force, fulfils or realises itself inevitably in Time and Space".[2]

The word 'Supermind' is rather ambiguous. It may be taken as the highest and purest form of mental consciousness which is far

---

1. *L.D.*, Vol. I, p. 181.
2. *Ibid.*, p. 182.

above the ordinary plane of normal mind. Thus there will be only a difference of degree between these two planes of consciousness and not of kind. The mind itself will become super-eminent and lifted above ordinary mentality and so there will not result any radical change in the consciousness. Or the Supermind may be understood in the sense of all that is beyond mind. Then it will assume a too extensive comprehensiveness which would include in it Saccidānanda and even the ineffable and the unknowable. But the Supermind is neither the mind raised to the highest degree of consciousness nor it includes the Absolute in itself. It is radically different from mind. Though it manifests Mind yet it is quite different from it in nature. Similarly above the Supermind, we have Saccidānanda and the supreme Unknowable. There are intervening grades between Mind and the Supermind such as the Higher Mind, the illumined Mind, Intuition and Overmind. But all these grades lie in the lower hemisphere and in the world of ignorance. The Supermind belongs to the higher hemisphere and shines in perfect knowledge and supreme light. So the term Supermind has a definite meaning and must not be confused with mental consciousness on the one hand and with Saccidānanda on the other.

In order to give a precise meaning to the term Supermind, Sri Aurobindo calls it the "Truth-Consciousness".[1] Sri Aurobindo has borrowed this significant term from the *Ṛg-Veda* and uses it "to delimit the connotation of the more elastic phrase, Supermind" The Truth-Consciousness is present everywhere in the universe as an ordering self-knowledge and manifests the cosmos in the light of its own law. Saccidānanda, as we know, contains infinite potentiality in itself. The infinite potentiality by itself might give rise to the play of unaccountable powers, may lead to a play of "uncontrolled unbounded chance". Thus, in place of a harmonious and well-ordered cosmos, we would have a perfect chaos. Hence some law, some guiding or ordering principle of self-knowledge is required to bring about the manifestation of cosmos out of the infinite potentiality of the Absolute and regulate its movement. "If there were only infinite potentiality," says Sri Aurobindo, "without any law of guiding truth and harmonious self-vision, without any

---

1. *ṛta-cit.*

predetermining Idea in the very seed of things cast out for evolution, the world could be nothing but a teeming, amorphous, confused uncertainty".[1] But the cosmos does not present the picture of a chaos or uncertainty. We see everywhere a certain order in the manifestation and development of things. It is all due to the presence of the Truth-Consciousness within it. It possesses in its own being the vision or self-knowledge of the truth or law that governs each potentiality. It has the full knowledge of all the other potentialities and the harmonious relationship that exists between them. Thus it has the full-awareness of each thing both in its potentiality and in actuality. It has the self-awareness of the past, present and future of a thing. It has the full and perfect knowledge of the what and the how of things. It knows eternally how to create, what to create and when to create this world of manifestation. "The world", says Sri Aurobindo, "expresses a foreseen Truth, obeys a pre-determining will, realises an original formative self-vision, it is the growing image of a divine creation".[2] Thus the Truth-consciousness regulates and orders the manifestation, working and development of the cosmos and keeps the law in the world. The creation does not manifest any thing new. It manifests what was originally contained in the potential form, in the seed state. Each thing is what it is by virtue of this Truth-Consciousness inherent within it. At each moment it is guided by this principle and becomes in the end what it was in potential form prior to the state of manifestation. "Each thing in Nature," contends Sri Aurobindo, "whether animate or inanimate, mentally self-conscious or not self-conscious, is governed in its being and in its operations by an indwelling vision and power, to us subsconscient or inconscient because we are not conscious of it, but not inconscient to itself, rather profoundly and universally conscient".[3] It is for this reason that even those things which have no intelligence seem to do the work of intelligence. The plant and the animal obey subconsciously and the man half-consciously the real-idea of the divine Supermind within it. Our phenomenal existence seems to be governed by our mental consciousness. But mind, in fact, is not aware of the truth of being in which "self-knowledge is inseparable from

---

1. *L.D.*, Vol. I, p. 160.
2. *Ibid.*, p. 151.
3. *Ibid.*, p. 171.

self-existence". It is a principle or product of ignorance. It has to obey though only half-consciously the law of the Truth-Consciousness or the Real-Idea within it. But mind is not destined to remain in this shackled condition forever. It has its eternal perfection in the Real-Idea. Not only mind but the other two terms of the lower hemisphere also, namely Life and Body enjoy the eternal perfection in the Supreme Truth-Consciousness or the Real-Idea. Our phenomenal existence is on its way to become what it originally is in the Real-Idea. "The type of all perfection towards which we grow," says Sri Aurobindo, "the terms of our highest evolution must already be held in the divine Real-Idea; they must be there formed and conscious for us to grow towards and into them: for that pre-existence in the divine knowledge is what our human mentality names and seeks as the Ideal".[1] What we consider as Ideal is not something non-existent. It is the eternal Reality which we have not yet realised in our temporal existence. By calling the Supermind the Real-Idea, Sri Aurobindo means that it is not mental thought or imagination. It is the Reality illumining itself by its own light. The idea of mind does not express the real formations of being. But the Real-Idea expresses the real truth of being. The meaning of the Real-Idea becomes clear from the following words of Sri Aurobindo: it is "a power of Conscious Force expressive of real-being, and partaking of its nature, and neither a child of the void nor a weaver of fictions. It is conscious Reality throwing itself into mutable forms of its own imperishable and immutable substance".

Thus we see the supreme importance of the fundamental and dynamic principle of knowledge and will, whether we call it the Supermind, the Truth-Consciousness or the Real-Idea, to reconcile in a harmonious vision the apparently opposite and contradictory aspects of the supreme Reality. "The conception of the Supermind," as Dr. Maitra significantly observes, "is the pivot round which the whole of Sri Aurobindo's philosophy moves".[2]

Yet it must not be regarded that this principle is entirely alien to us. It is indeed far above the plane of human consciousness and is radically different from it. But the plane of supramental consciousness is not essentially impenetrable to the surging waves of

---

1. *L.D.*, Vol. I, p. 204.
2. *Introduction to The Philosophy of Sri Aurobindo*, p. 29.

human consciousness which has broken through all the barriers of ignorance, limitation and division. The supramental principle is the highest plane of our own essential dynamic being and consciousness. Hence it is not inaccessible to the human consciousness. The individual is capable of not only inferring it or having distant glimpses of this supreme Truth but also of realising it and having an integral experience of it. But it requires the greatest and superhuman effort on the part of human consciousness to make an ascent to the supramental plane. In the unforgettable moments of greatest superhuman experience the individual may rise up to the plane of the supramental existence and descend again. But according to Sri Aurobindo, the permanent ascent to the highest plane of the supramental existence is the supreme ideal for our evolving human consciousness which aspires not for the complete annihilation of our dynamic existence, but for its supreme perfection.

The principle of the Supermind is not any original and novel conception of Sri Aurobindo. He himself says that the gospel of the divine and immortal Supermind is contained in the cryptic verses of the Veda. The Vedic seers conceived this Supermind "as a vastness beyond the ordinary firmaments of our consciousness in which truth of being is luminously one with all that expresses it and assures inevitably the truth of vision, formulation, arrangement, word, act and movement and therefore truth also of result of movement, result of action and expression, infallible ordinance or law".[1] This was the principle of luminous truth and harmony of being. The Gods are but the powers of the Supermind and are its creation. In their knowledge they are possessed of this "truth-consciousness" and in their action of the "seer-will". The principle of harmony pervades everywhere in the supermind. "Light is here one with force, the vibration of knowledge with the rhythm of the will and both are one, perfectly and without seeking, groping and effort, with the assured result."[2] Thus the Vedic seers had an unmistakable vision of the nature of the Supermind. They did not regard the world as unreal or simply as a creation of Māyā. The world was to them the real creation of the supreme Divine. They

---

1. *L.D.*, Vol. I, pp. 155-56.
2. *Ibid.*, p. 156.

saw everywhere in the world the divine qualities of beauty, harmony and joy. They had the vision of the Supermind as the upholder of the Divine Law, of Dharma, of moral order. The Supermind is thus characterised by Sri Aurobindo as "the beginning and end of all creation and arrangement, the Alpha and the Omega, the starting-point of all-differentiation, the instrument of all-unification, originative, executive and consummative of all realised or realisable harmonies".[1] The Supermind is, in fact, not the whole of the Absolute reality. It is, as has been already observed, the dynamic and creative aspect of Saccidānanda. As Sri Aurobindo observes, "we have to regard therefore this all-containing, all-originating, all-consummating Supermind as the nature of the Divine Being, not indeed in its absolute self-existence, but in its action as the Lord and Creator of its own worlds. This is the truth of that which we call God".[2] "It has the knowledge of the One, but is able to draw out of the One its hidden multitudes; it manifests the Many, but does not lose itself in their differentiations. And shall we not say that its very existence points back to something beyond our supreme perception of the ineffable Unity,—Something ineffable and mentally inconceivable not because of its unity and indivisibility, but because of its freedom from even these formulations of our mind,— Something beyond both unity and multiplicity? That would be the utter Absolute and real which yet justifies to us both our knowledge of God and our knowledge of the world."[3]

Now we proceed to discuss the triple status of the Supermind called by Sri Aurobindo, the comprehending consciousness, the apprehending consciousness and the projecting consciousness.

(C) The Triple Status of Supermind

In the foregoing pages we have dealt to some extent with the first and primary poise of the Supermind. We have seen that it is not the pure unitarian consciousness of Saccidānanda. It is not the timeless, spaceless self-concentrated unity of Saccidānanda which annihilates all distinctions and does not justify the existence of the temporal and spatial order or cosmos. The Supermind is the dynamic, creative and self-extended aspect of Saccidānanda. We have

---

1. *L.D.*, Vol. I, p. 158.
2. *Ibid.*, p. 166.
3. *Ibid.*, p. 158.

already seen that there is no essential opposition between the static and dynamic aspects of Saccidānanda. The one does not annihilate the existence of the other but is, on the other hand, complementary to it. So this dynamic and creative Supermind is an equally real aspect of Saccidānanda. It is "an equal self-extension of Sachchidananda, all-comprehending, all-possessing, all-constituting". But this all, according to Sri Aurobindo, is not to be taken in a plural sense. This all is one, not many. In this primary and fundamental status of the Supermind, there is no individualisation. In this poise, there is an equal self-extension of consciousness. There is, as yet, no concentration of consciousness that may support an individual development. The multiplicity is there but all the multiple forms are the forms of the Divine Being and are not in any degree separate existences. The multiplicity does not present itself as multiplicity to this primary Supermind. The Supermind, in this status, will know the whole world of multiplicity as itself. The real significance and meaning of this all-comprehending and all-inclusive oneness will become clear from the following significant imagery of Sri Aurobindo. "Somewhat as the thoughts and images that occur in our mind are not separate existence to us, but forms taken by our consciousness, so are all names and forms to this primary Supermind."[1] The creation or the world of multiplicity is the pure divine ideation and free formation of the Infinite. But this cosmic play of the Infinite consciousness is not unreal or false. It is real play of the Divine consciousness. Thus this status of the Supermind represents the truth of all comprehensive, all-inclusive and all-embracing unity. The one here has become all without losing its oneness. When the reflection of this supreme status of all-comprehensive and self-extended unity falls on our stilled and purified self, we lose all the sense of individuality. The consciousness of individuality and separate existence is merged altogether in all-embracing and all-unifying vision of unity.

In this poise, there is no difference between the Conscious Force and Being. The Conscious Force is the power of Being and is inseparably one with the Being. There is also no difference between subject and object. The divine soul will have no sense of otherness. All the manifold creation seems to it to be itself and not anything other than itself. There is also here no difference between consciousness and force or knowledge and will. "The

---

1. *L.D.*, Vol. I, p. 184.

divine soul in this poise," says Sri Aurobindo, "would make no difference between Conscious-Soul and Force-Soul, for all force would be action of consciousness, nor between Matter and Spirit since all would be simply form of Spirit".[1] The consciousness in this poise is called by Sri Aurobindo the comprehending consciousness. Our Vedic seers, according to him, were aware of a distinction in the operations of the Supermind "between knowledge by a comprehending and pervading consciousness which is very near to subjective knowledge by identity and knowledge by a projecting, confronting, apprehending consciousness which is the beginning of objective cognition". As the all-comprehensive, all-pervading, all-inhabiting cosmic vision of this primary poise of the divine Supermind comprehends all things in being and static self-awareness, subjective, timeless and spaceless, so it comprehends all things in dynamic knowledge and self-extension and governs their objective self-manifestation in temporal and spatial order.

The Supermind is, in this poise, not distributed or divided. It is everywhere the single and equal Brahman, *Samam Brahman*. There is no independent centre of existence in this status. It pervades the whole creation as one. It is one in multiplicity. This extended unity of the Supermind in Time and Space is closely related to the timeless and spaceless absolute unity. "That high concentration of unity in the unextended Brahman," says Sri Aurobindo, "must necessarily translate itself in the extension by this equal pervasive concentration, this indivisible comprehension of all things, this universal undistributed immanence, this unity which no play of multiplicity can abrogate or diminish".[2] The characteristic of equal concentration is peculiar to the comprehending consciousness of the Supermind. There is an equal concentration of this consciousness in the smallest things as well as in the greatest things. This all-comprehensive poise of the Supermind is best expressed by the characteristic formula, *All this is, indeed, Brahman.*[3] It is the unity that holds the whole world of diversity in its close embrace. The diversity is real because it is ultimately nothing but Brahman. Not only the reality underlying all these existences is Brahman but all

---

1. *L.D.*, Vol. I, p. 184.
2. *Ibid.*, p. 175.
3. सर्वं खल्विदं ब्रह्म । (*Chān.* 3.14.1)

these existences themselves are nothing but the forms of Brahman. It is Brahman expressing itself in the multitude of forms. The supramental consciousness will affirm all these existences as itself. In the whole world of multiplicity it will find itself and itself alone. There is no other to it in this primary status.

The second poise of the Supermind is called the apprehending consciousness or *Prajñā*. In this poise we have, for the first time, the fundamental division between the Divine consciousness and its Force or between Puruṣa and Prakṛti. The Divine Consciousness stands back from the movement which it contains and realises it by the apprehending consciousness. It is the support of the movement of Prakṛti, inhabits itself in all the works of nature but keeps itself at the same time, aloof from it. Though itself indivisible it seems to distribute itself in the forms of nature.[1] Thus, here, we come across the fundamental distinction between subject and object or Puruṣa and Prakṛti or self and not-self. But the Puruṣa and Prakṛti or subject and object do not appear as totally different and contradictory entities. The subject and object are fundamentally one as we find in the first status. There we do not find any distinction between consciousness and force. So there is merely a practical differentiation between consciousness and force or subject and object and not an essential difference between them. The same indivisible divine consciousness places itself as subject to view itself as object. The divine consciousness as subject views itself as object and not as anything other than itself. The object is nothing but the manifestation of subject. The relationship between the subject and the object or Divine Consciousness and Force is beautifully compared to that of a poet and his creation. That apprehending consciousness, the *prajñā* places, "the working of the indivisible All, active and formative, as a process and object of creative knowledge before the consciousness of the same All, originative and cognisant as the possessor and witness of its own working,—somewhat as a poet views the creations of his own consciousness placed before him in it as if they were things other than the creator and his creative force, yet all the time they are really no more than the play of self-formation of his own being in itself and are indivisible there from their creator".[2]

---

1. अविभक्तं च भूतेषु विभक्तमिव च स्थितम् । (*B.G.* 13.17)
2. *L.D.*, Vol. I, p. 206.

So the Divine consciousness would view all the objects as essentially the forms of itself. It would realise itself as the stable Conscious-Self in each name and form. But in this poise there is a concentration of the divine Consciousness within the framework of space and time. The comprehending consciousness expressed itself as an equal concentration. But here we have an unequal concentration. So the Divine Consciousness in this poise would also realise itself as a concentration of Conscious-Self which supports the individual forms and keeps their separate individuality. Thus we have the distinction between the individual Divine or *Jīvātman* and the universal Divine. The concentration that supports the soul-form would be the individual Divine. The universal Divine would realise all the soul-forms as itself. But there will be a difference in its relationship. It will be related to each soul-form separately and in each soul-form it would establish a separate relation with all the other soul-forms. The individual Divine or *Jīvātman* would realise itself as a soul-form and soul-movement of the universal Divine. By the comprehending consciousness it would be able to realise its unity with the One and with all the other soul-forms and by the apprehending consciousness it would realise itself as different form the One and from other soul-forms. Thus it is capable of enjoying its individual movement as well as its oneness with One and with all other soul-forms. Thus, in this poise we find the relationship of Identity-in-difference between One and the many. The same 'One' manifests as the many and the 'many' are essentially conscious of their fundamental oneness. There is no essential difference between the one and the many, but only a practical differentiation. In this status, we have the consciousness of the unity qualified by the difference. The unity is yet the predominant principle. The 'many' enjoy free difference in unity. So unity is the predominant feature of this poise and difference is merely secondary. In the first poise there was only the consciousness of unity. The 'many' did not appear as many but as 'One'. But here the relationship is that of unity in multiplicity. A practical distinction has been created, according to Sri Aurobindo, "between the knower, knowledge and the known; between the Lord, His force and the children and works of the Force, between the Enjoyer, the Enjoyment and the Enjoyed, between the Self, Maya and the becomings of the Self." But in this poise, the Divine Consciousness, as we have observed above, is fully aware that it is itself that has expressed itself in different ways and forms. So all the difference is secondary and is based on the fundamental principle of unity.

In the third poise of the Supermind, the conscious Soul no longer remains concentrated in knowledge observing and governing the movements of its Force or Prakṛti, but projects itself into the movement and identifies itself with each form of itself. In each form the Divine Soul or Puruṣa dwells with his Nature and from this artificial centre of consciousness he establishes his relationship with other forms of himself and with the One. Now the vision of the Puruṣa is directed according to the will and knowledge appropriate to each soul-form. "The Purusha in each form," says Sri Aurobindo, "actively identifies himself with each; he delimits himself in that and sets off his other forms against it in his consciousness as containing his otherselves which are identical with him in being but different in relation, different in the various extent, various range of movement and various views of the one substance, force, consciousness, delight which each is actually deploying at any given moment of Time or in any given field of Space".[1] In this poise we have distinct emphasis on the aspect of multiplicity. The Puruṣa identifies himself with each soul-form and views other soul-forms as different from itself. Though it is true that there is no essential difference yet there is the consciousness of duality predominant in this status. The realisation of unity would be, according to Sri Aurobindo, "a supreme accompaniment and constant culmiation of all experience". In the second poise we have seen, unity was the dominant principle. It was characterised as the unity qualified by a subordinate dualism. The 'Many' in that poise were well aware of their fundamental unity. But in this tertiary poise the consciousness of multiplicity comes in the forefront. For all practical purposes the Puruṣa or Jīvātman identifies himself with each soul-form and considers himself as different from the other soul-forms and from the One or the universal Divine. But the individual Divine or Jīvātman is still conscious of itself as the manifestation of the One. It is conscious of its power of conscious self-manifestation or self-creation, "of its multiple self-concentration conceived

<hr>

1. *L.D.*, Vol. I, p. 208.

so as to govern and enjoy manifoldly its manifold existence in the extension of Time and Space; this true spiritual individual would not arrogate to itself an independent or separate existence".[1]

But even in the third poise of the Supermind there is no lapse into ignorance. "For the individual Divine would still be conscious of itself as the result of the One and of its power of conscious self-creation that is to say, of its multiple self-concentration conceived so as to govern and enjoy manifoldly its manifold existence in the extension of Time and Space; this true spiritual individual would not arrogate to itself an independent or separate existence. It would only affirm the truth of the differentiating movement along with the truth of the stable unity regarding them as the upper and lower poles of the same truth, the foundation and culmination of the same divine play; and it would insist on the joy of the differentiation as necessary to the fullness of the joy of the unity."[2] Hence we cannot stamp any of these three poises with the stigma of falsehood and illusion. In the supramental plane, diversity is not governed by ignorance. The diversity is dependent on unity but it does not suffer from ignorance. Unity is logically prior to diversity. Hence diversity cannot be called unreal or the product of ignorance. "We can only assert the priority of the oneness to the multiplicity, a priority not in time but in relation of consciousness, and no statement of supreme spiritual experience, no Vedantic philosophy denies this priority or the eternal dependence of the Many on the One. It is because in Time the Many seem not to be eternal but to manifest out of the One and return into it as their essence that their reality is denied; but it might equally be reasoned that the eternal persistence or if you will, the eternal recurrence of the manifestation in Time is a proof that the Divine multiplicity is an eternal fact of the Supreme beyond Time no less than the Divine unity; otherwise it could not have this characteristic of inevitable eternal recurrence in Time."[3]

Now it is clear that in the supramental plane, the soul is aware of the unity maintaining the diversity and constituting its essence. But in the empirical world, in the spatio-temporal world, the soul is not aware of the fundamental principle of unity. The individual

1. *L.D.*, Vol. I, pp. 186-87.
2. *Ibid.*, pp. 186-87.
3. *Ibid.*, pp. 187-88.

sees diversity all round him but he is not aware of the unity. Our mind is naturally aware of the diversity but has no knowledge of the unity lying behind it. Now the problem is, what is the cause of this limitation? What is the cause of our forgetfulness of our real self and existence? This is due to a new factor, the principle of ignorance. As Sri Aurobindo puts it, "A new factor, a new action of conscious force is therefore needed to create the operation of a helplessly limited as opposed to a freely limiting mind—that is to say, of mind subject to its own play and deceived by it as opposed to mind master of its own play and viewing it in its truth, the creature mind as opposed to the divine. That new factor is *Avidya*, the self-ignoring faculty which separates the action of mind from the action of the supermind that originated and still governs it from behind the veil."[1] So it is clear that in order to understand the nature of the empirical world and of our individual existence, it is necessary first of all to probe into the secrets of *Avidyā* or ignorance. We now proceed to discuss the nature and significance of ignorance and see how the supreme Spirit takes a plunge into ignorance in order to manifest the cosmos.

---

1. *L.D.*, Vol. I, p. 209.

PART III

CREATION OR DESCENT

CHAPTER VII

CONCEPTION OF IGNORANCE

(A) *Plunge of the Spirit into Ignorance: The Origin of Ignorance*

We have indicated in the preceding chapter that the Absolute or the supreme Spirit takes a plunge into ignorance in order to create or manifest the world. Now the problem is, how the supreme consciousness that is beyond all limitations puts itself in the form of ignorance? "How could this manifold ignorance or this narrowly self-limiting and separative knowledge arise and come into action or maintain itself in action in an absolute Being who must be absolute consciousness and therefore cannot be subject to ignorance? How is even an apparent division effectively operated and kept in continuance in the indivisible."[1]

The Absolute is not only pure consciousness but is also possessed of force called conscious force or *cit-śakti*, as we have explained in detail in a preceding chapter. The conscious force of the Absolute is possessed of the power of self-variation, self-limitation and self-absorption. The Absolute through its conscious force puts itself under limitation in order to manifest the world. The conscious force energises itself or, to adopt the Vedic terminology, performs *tapas* in order to manifest the world. "Tapas" observes Sri Aurobindo, "means literally heat, afterwards any kind of energism, *askesis*, austerity of conscious force acting upon itself or its object. The world was created by Tapas in the form, says

---

the ancient image of an egg, which being broken, again by Tapas, heat of incubation of conscious force, the Puruṣa emerged, soul in Nature, like a bird from the egg."[1] "By energism of Consciousness or Tapas, Brahman is massed; from that Matter is born and from Matter, Life and Mind and the worlds."[2] Similarly another Upaniṣad describes the process of creation thus: "He desired, "May I be Many,'' He concentrated in Tapas, by Tapas he created the world; creating he entered into it; entering he became the existent and the beyond-existence, he became the expressed and the unexpressed, he became knowledge and ignorance, he became the truth and the falsehood: he became the truth, even all this whatever that is, "That truth" they call him.[3] "Energism of consciousness is Brahman."[4] These statements of the Upaniṣads clearly indicate the nature and process of creation. It is Brahman that has created or manifested the world by the process of self-concentration or self-modification of its conscious force. This conscious force of Brahma manifests itself in apparently contradictory aspects as truth and untruth, knowledge and ignorance and so on. The conscious force of Brahman has to assume the form of ignorance in order to manifest the world. Thus Ignorance is the result of the self-concentration or self-modification of conscious force. "Ignorance must be part of the movement of the One—a development of its consciousness knowingly adopted, to which it is not forcibly subjected but which it uses for its cosmic purpose."[5] The modification or limitation of the supreme consciousness is voluntary and self-willed and not arbitrary and forced. So now we have to trace the origin of ignorance in the dynamic aspect of the supreme Reality or Conscious Force. As Sri Aurobindo puts it, "since the ignorance is a phenomenon of the dynamic action of Force of Consciousness, not an essential fact but a creation, a consequence of that action, it is this Force aspect of Consciousness that it will be fruitful to consider".[6]

---

1. *L.D.*, Vol. II, Part I, p. 336 (Footnotes).
2. तपसा चीयते ब्रह्म ततोऽन्नमभिजायते । (*Muṇḍ* 1.1.8)
   अन्नात् प्राणो मन: सत्यं लोका: कर्मसु चामृतम् । (*L.D.*, Vol. II, Part I, p. 330)
3. *Tait.* 2.6.1.
4. तपो ब्रह्मेति ।
5. *L.D.*, Vol. II, Part I, pp. 333-34.
6. *Ibid.*, p. 335.

From our study of the nature of the Absolute it is clear that ignorance does not exist in it. The pure indivisible consciousness of the Absolute has no place for ignorance. The Absolute or Saccidānanda is self-luminous, hence it has nothing to do with ignorance. Ignorance does not exist in the creative aspect of the Absolute, namely, the Supermind also. The triple poise of the Supermind, as we have seen in the preceding chapter, has no place for ignorance. Though there is diversity, yet it is as we have stated in the preceding chapter, not governed by ignorance. The higher existence, the triple plane of Saccidānanda and the Supermind are not contaminated by ignorance. Supermind manifests the triple plane of Existence, Consciousness and bliss out of the indivisible and differenceless unity of Saccidānanda. But though there is the manifestation of the triple plane out of the indivisible unity of Saccidānanda, yet there is no ignorance. Thus it is clear that ignorance does not exist in Saccidānanda. It does not exist, as has been stated above and in the preceding chapter, in the Supermind also.

So it is clear that ignorance is not original and primal in nature. It appears at a later stage of the movement of consciousness-force when it is apparently absorbed in some partial movement and concentration of itself. All the other planes of consciousness are put behind the concentrated form. Hence such a concentrated form becomes ignorant of the other planes of existence. This form of consciousness appears in the stage of mind. Mind is separated on account of self-concentration or self-absorption of conscious force from its spiritual and supramental basis and hence is ignorant of reality. "The origin of the Ignorance must then be sought for in some self-absorbed concentration of Tapas, of Conscious Force in action on a separate movement of the Force; to us this takes the appearance of mind identifying itself also in the movement separately with each of the forms resulting from it."[1] Thus when the Spirit makes a descent from Supermind to mind, there emerges the principle of ignorance. "It is on the plane of mind that the putting back of the real self-consciousness becomes possible."[2] The total separation of mind from its original source, the Supermind,

---

1. *L.D.*, Vol. II, Part I, p. 347.
2. *Ibid.*, p. 363.

becomes possible on account of a veil falling between them. It exists in the Overmind. Thus the beginning of ignorance is found in the overmind. As Sri Aurobindo puts it: "Such a veil exists, says the Upanishad,[1] constituted by the action of mind itself; it is in Overmind a golden lid which hides the face of the supramental Truth but reflects its image; in Mind it becomes a more opaque and smoky-luminous coverture."[2] On account of this veil, the mental consciousness is confined to the diversity, and moves away from the consciousness of unity. There are different levels of consciousness existing between Supermind and Mind, the chief of which as stated by Sri Aurobindo are the Higher Mind, the Illumined Mind Intuition and Overmind. We will discuss the nature and function of these grades of existence and consciousness in our chapters on Evolution. But here the point to be noted is that the conscious force of the Absolute goes on diminishing as it descends more and more in the lower grades and ultimately it assumes the form of ignorance when it reaches Mind. But the exclusive concentration of conscious force does not stop here, that is, at the stage of mind. It makes a further descent into the vital plane and thus undergoes a further diminution in consciousness. The identification and absorption of consciousness-force with a partial and exclusive movement goes still further until mind becomes oblivious even of the knowledge of diversity and is ultimately reduced to inconscience when the Spirit finally makes a descent into Matter. "This is the last stage of the descent of consciousness, an abysmal sleep, a fathomless trance of consciousness which is the profound basis of the action of material Nature."[3] The principle of ignorance lies midway between the supreme consciousness and the total inconscience. But ignorance and inconscience are the exclusive and separative movements of the same Consciousness Force which assumes these apparently opposite and contradictory forms in order to proceed with the work of creation.[4] Thus it is clear that the world of mind, life and matter is created or manifested by the Absolute or the Supermind through ignorance. And this ignorance

1. हिरण्मयेन पात्रेण सत्यस्यापिहितं मुखम् ।
   तत् त्वं पूषन्नपावृणु सत्यधर्माय दृष्टये ॥ (Īśa. 15).
2. *L.D.*, Vol. II, Part I, p. 363.
3. *Ibid.*, p.64.
4. *Ibid.*, p. 359.

is nothing but the self-concentrated or self-limited form of the supreme conscious force or *Cit-śakti* of the Absolute. So our study of the process of the lapse of Spirit into Ignorance and the origin of Ignorance gives us a real insight into its nature also. So now we proceed to discuss the nature of ignorance.

(B) *Nature of Ignorance*

The Integral Advaitism of Sri Aurobindo does not look upon Ignorance as something opposed to knowledge. Ignorance is, according to Sri Aurobindo, nothing else but a self-limitation or self-concentration of consciousness or knowledge. The supreme Consciousness which manifests itself at one stage as knowledge, appears at the other stage as ignorance. Hence knowledge and ignorance are not essentially opposed to each other. They are the different but the complementary aspects of the same reality.

(i) *Vedic View of Knowledge and Ignorance*

Sri Aurobindo contends that this view of the nature of knowledge and ignorance was originally held in Veda. The distinction between knowledge and ignorance begins with the hymns of the *Ṛg-Veda*. Knowledge there means the perception of the truth, the right, *satyam ṛtam*; ignorance means the unconsciousness of the truth and the right. The knowledge and ignorance are called in the *Ṛg-Veda* '*Citti*' and '*Acitti*' respectively. "Ignorance," observes Sri Aurobindo, "is the absence of the divine eye of perception which gives us the sight of the supramental Truth; it is the non-perceiving principle in our consciousness as opposed to the truth perceiving consciousness and knowledge".[1] It does not mean that ignorance according to the Vedic sages was a pure and entire absence of knowledge. It is limited or false knowledge and not the real and true knowledge of things. On account of its limitation, it creates a false and distorted view of things. Hence it is also called in *Ṛg-Veda* undivine Māyā or Adevī Māyā as opposed to the Divine knowledge or Devī Māyā. The undivine Māyā creates false mental forms and appearances, but it is still "a formative power of knowledge, the true magic of the supreme Mage, the Divine Magician" and is not something totally opposed to the Divine knowledge.

---

1. *L.D.*, Vol. II, Part I, pp. 236-37.

The Divine Māyā is the knowledge of the truth of things, of their unity which "the gods possess and on which they found their own eternal action and creation and their building of their powers in human beings". It means that ignorance is in its nature a dividing mental knowledge which does not grasp the unity and essential nature of things but gives us only a particular, fragmentary and partial view of them. Knowledge, on the other hand, is that which gives us the unitary and the universal view of things and has an integral and all-comprehensive view of the whole of existence. But ignorance is not considered here as opposed to knowledge. It is still knowledge but a limited and fragmentary knowledge which instead of revealing the essential truth of things gives us a false and distorted view of them.

(ii) *The Upaniṣadic View of Knowledge and Ignorance*
In the Upaniṣads the original Vedic terms regarding knowledge and ignorance have been replaced by the terms *Vidyā* and *Avidyā*. Thus we find a change in our conception of knowledge and ignorance. *Vidyā* or knowledge in its highest spiritual sense came to mean the knowledge of the One and *avidyā* or ignorance came to mean purely and trenchantly the knowledge of the many as divorced from the knowledge of the One. Thus we find a change in the conception of knowledge and ignorance in the Upaniṣads from that of the Veda. "The complex associations," says Sri Aurobindo, "the rich contents, the luminous penumbra of varied and corollary ideas and significant figures which belonged to the conception of the Vedic words, were largely lost in a language more precise and metaphysical, less psychological and flexible".[1] But even then there is no real opposition between the two terms, knowledge and ignorance, as is found in the later Vedānta. In the Upaniṣads, *Avidyā* is not considered as an original illusion of a consciousness that can be equated with dream or hallucination. The Upaniṣads according to Sri Aurobindo, do not lay sole emphasis on knowledge only but they make it necessary for us to have an integral view of the domains of knowledge as well as ignorance. If the Upaniṣads declare that the man who passes his life in ignorance wanders about stumbling like a blind man led by the

---

1. *L.D.*, Vol. II, Part I, p. 238.

blind and goes from death to death, they also declare that he who
takes recourse to knowledge only, enters as if into a blinder dark-
ness than he who follows after the ignorance[1] and that the man
who knows Brahman as both the One and the Many, as both the
Becoming and the Non-Becoming, crosses by the ignorance, by
the experience of the multiplicity, beyond death and by knowl-
edge takes possession of Immortality.[2] So the Upaniṣads do not
make any inseparable division between knowledge and ignorance.
The status of becoming which is the sphere of ignorance is simply
the manifestation of the Being. "The status of becoming," says Sri
Aurobindo, "is inferior to the status of Being, but still it is the
Being that becomes all that is in the universe".[3] So the Upaniṣads
make a clear distinction between the fields of knowledge and
ignorance but they do not make a rigid division and opposition
between them. Knowledge and ignorance are not according to
them entirely separated from each other. Ignorance, according to
the Upaniṣads, is not entirely opposed to knowledge but is a lower
and inferior kind of knowledge. Hence there exists no real oppo-
sition or antinomy between them.

(iii) Conception of Ignorance in the Advaita Vedānta
But when we come to the Advaita Vedānta, we find a total sepa-
ration between the principles of knowledge and ignorance. Knowl-
edge and ignorance are regarded here as entirely opposed to each
other like light and darkness. Ignorance or Avidyā is called unreal
or false in nature. By calling it unreal, the Advaitins do not mean
that it is non-existent. Avidyā exists, but it is not real. Avidyā is
real from the empirical standpoint but is unreal from the transcen-
dental standpoint. Hence it is strictly called neither real nor unreal
but indescribable or anirvacanīya. The Advaitins have to posit this
entity in order to explain the world-process. But they are not able
to determine its real nature. It is considered to be an inconsistent
category, a self-contradictory principle. Had it been consistent, it.

1. अन्धं तम: प्रविशन्ति येऽविद्यामुपासते ।
   ततो भूय इव ते तमो य उ विद्यायां रता: ॥ (Īśa. IX)
2. विद्यां चाविद्यां च यस्तद्वेदोभयं सह ।
   अविद्यया मृत्युं तीर्त्वा विद्ययाऽमृतमश्नुते ॥ (Īśa. II)
3. L.D., Vol. II, Part I, p. 239.

would not have been called *avidyā* at all. It is based on Brahman, yet it is a baseless illusion opposed to all reason and cannot stand the test of logic even as darkness cannot stand the sun.[1] *Avidyā* cannot be surpassed by anything in shamelessness. It despises all reason and logic and yet,it exists like Brahman itself.[2] According to Vimuktātman, *Avidyā* is indescribable only in the sense that it cannot be described either as real or as unreal, and not in the sense that nothing can be said about it.[3] It is positive in nature (*bhāvarūpam*). It is also called a material energy by Padmapāda.[4] It is said to be possessed of two characteristics, one of concealing the real nature of Brahman (*āvaraṇa*) and the other consists in presenting the false and unreal objects in its place (*vikṣepa*). *Avidyā* lasts so long as the individual does not get enlightenment. The moment one enjoys the bliss of Brahman, for him *avidyā* is cancelled altogether. *Avidyā* or *Ajñāna*, according to Citsukha, is beginningless and positive and is cancelled by knowledge.[5] The world is nothing but the presentation of *avidyā* or ignorance. There is only Brahman and no world in reality but due to the dynamic activity of *avidyā* or the principle of ignorance we see the world in place of Brahman. Brahman according to the Advaitins does not really manifest the world. It only appears as the world due to the force of *avidyā*. So whatever we perceive in the state of *avidyā* is false or illusory. *Avidyā* does not provide us with real knowledge of any kind. It is not the knowledge of the many that are real. It is the knowledge of unreal or illusory many. Hence it is itself unreal or false. The dawn of knowledge will mean the complete cancellation of ignorance along with its products. So knowledge and ignorance cannot exist simultaneously. With the dawn of knowledge ignorance disappears altogether. Hence the

---

1. सेयं भ्रान्तिर्निरालन्बा सर्वन्यायविरोधिनी ।
   सहते न विचारं सा तमो यद्वद् दिवाकरम् ॥ (*Naiṣkarmyasiddhi*, pp. 111, 66)
2. अहो! धाष्र्यमविद्याया न कश्चिदतिवर्तते ।
   प्रमाणं वस्त्वनादृत्य परमात्मेव तिष्ठति ॥ (*Ibid.*, 111, 111)
3. तेन सदसत्वाभ्याम् अनिर्वचनीया, न पुनरवाच्येति । (*Iṣṭa-Siddhi*, p. 35)
4. जडात्मिका अविद्याशक्ति: ।
5. अनादि भावरूपं यद् विज्ञानेन विलीयते ।
   तदज्ञानमिति प्राज्ञा लक्षणं संप्रचक्षते ॥
   अनादित्वे सति भावरूपं विज्ञाननिरस्यमज्ञानम् । (*Tattva-Pradīpikā*, p. 57)

two principles, that is, knowledge and ignorance cannot be re-
conciled with each other. A total separation occurs here between
them. Thus we find a clear transition and change in the meaning
of these two terms from the time of Veda to the period of the
classical Vedānta. In the Vedic view the knowledge of the One is
knowledge but the knowledge of the Many is also a knowledge
though a limited or inferior kind of knowledge. But in the
Upaniṣads, the knowledge of the Many is called ignorance and the
knowledge of the One or the supreme Reality alone is called
knowledge. Thus a separation between knowledge and ignorance
had taken place but still the Absolute separation and opposition
had not yet occurred there. Ignorance is considered there as dif-
ferent in nature from knowledge but it does not stand in oppo-
sition to knowledge. The knowledge of the One does not mean
the abrogation of the knowledge of the Many. But when we come
to the later Vedānta, the Advaita Vedānta, we find a complete
separation and opposition between the two terms of knowledge
and ignorance. The knowledge of Brahman or the One does,
according to the Advaita Vedānta, mean the cancellation or the
abrogation of the knowledge of the world or the many. Hence
they are considered as totally opposed to each other. Thus the
separation between knowledge and ignorance which was started
in the Upaniṣads finds its logical culmination in the Advaita Vedānta.
The Advaita school does not find any way to reconcile these two
contradictory and opposite principles. Hence it has to cancel in-
evitably one principle, namely, ignorance and its product, the world,
in order to establish its monism.

(iv) Criticism of the Advaita View of Ignorance

Now we proceed to make a critical examination of this doctrine
of Māyā in the light of the philosophy of Sri Aurobindo. We have
to see what are its merits and defects, what is its real significance
and value and whether it is inevitable and necessary to explain the
process of creation or manifestation of the world.

The first question that Sri Aurobindo raises with regard to Māyā
is, who is the percipient of Māyā? There must be someone who
perceives the illusion or Māyā. The illusion can exist only for some
subject. Now the Advaitins of Śaṅkara school differ among them-
selves regarding the problem of the seat or substratum of igno-
rance. It is true that from the transcendent standpoint, the Śaṅkarites

do not believe in any other entity except Brahman. But so long as the empirical show of existence lasts, they have to give some explanation regarding the seat or support of ignorance. There are two views in the Advaita Vedānta regarding the seat or support of ignorance—one of Vācaspati and his school and the other of the Vivaraṇa school. According to Vācaspati, *Jīva* or the individual soul is the support of ignorance or nescience. And according to the Vivaraṇa school represented by Sarvajñātma Muni, Prakāśātman, Ānandabodhācārya and others, ignorance has for its substratum Brahman. Now both these views seem to be full of difficulties. Sri Aurobindo makes a critical examination of both these views and shows the self-contradictions inherent in them. None of these views can, according to them, explain satisfactorily the nature of Māyā and its relation with Brahman and the individual souls.

Brahman as the Percipient of Māyā or Ignorance: Its Criticism
Now let us first take the view of the Vivaraṇa school which regards Brahman as the seat of or the percipient of Māyā, Sri Aurobindo examines all possible alternatives that can be put forward to show the relationship between Brahman and Māyā and shows that they are all full of self-contradiction. If Brahman were the percipient of Māyā, then the illusion cannot persist for a moment. The true consciousness of Brahman is the cosciousness of self, an aware-ness of its own pure existence. The pure consciousness of Brah-man can have no awareness of an illusion or the illusory world-show. If Brahman perceives the world with its pure consciousness, then the world must be real and must be nothing but Brahman, because Brahman alone is real. But the world and the things of the world according to the Advaitins are merely the apparent forms of Brahman and not Brahman itself. Brahman is the reality under-lying these forms while these forms are regarded as the creation of Māyā. So now the position is this. Brahman cannot be the percipient of Māyā or its creation, the world, because it is illusory, unreal and false. But at the same time it cannot be said that because Brahman cannot be the percipient of Māyā or the world-show, so it does not exist; because the experience of the world is a fact. Brahman cannot be the percipient of the world, still the world exists. This is the dilemma that we are required to solve.

The existence of the world is a fact. If the world is regarded as unreal or illusory, yet it requires some consciousness to create it or perceive it. Now Māyā being regarded as the creator of the world must be supposed to be possessed of this conscious power of creating illusion. As there is no consciousness but that of Brahman, Māyā must be supposed to be a power of Brahman. But it has already been shown that the pure consciousness of Brahman cannot perceive illusion or illusory world. Then it may be supposed that there is a double status of Brahman-Consciousness— one conscious of the pure existence of Brahman, the supreme Reality, and the other conscious of the cosmos or the illusory world. The unreal world has nothing to do with the pure existence of Brahman. It is not made of the substance of Brahman and is but a creation of Māyā, But if this view were regarded as true then it directly contradicts the statement of the Upaniṣads that "the world is made out of the supreme Existence, is a becoming, an outcome or product of the eternal Being". Brahman will no longer be regarded as the material cause of the universe. But the recognition of this dual consciousness of Brahman, though it goes against the statement of śrutis, has to be admitted in this view in order to solve the mystery of Māyā. "This dual consciousness," says Sri Aurobindo, "offers itself as the sole plausible explanation of the riddle of a real eternal percipient, an unreal Percept, and a Perception that is a half real creator of unreal Percepts".[1]

If we reject the notion of this dual consciousness and regard Māyā as the sole conscious power of Brahman, we may, says Sri Aurobindo, regard Māyā as "Brahman's power of cosmic Imagination inherent in his eternal being creating out of nothing names, forms and happenings that are not in any way real." But Brahman cannot stand in need of a power of imagination to create the world show. The power of imagination is required by the limited and partial beings with an ignorant consciousness. They have to supplement their ignorance by imaginations and conjectures. Brahman who is blissful and perfect in itself has no need to create an unreal Time and Space with all the organic and inorganic objects by its power of imagination. This solution according to Sri Aurobindo is logically untenable.

Regarding Māyā as the sole conscious power of Brahman, we may conceive Māyā as a "subjective action of Brahman-Consciousness emerging out of its silence and superconscient immobility and

1. L.D., Vol. II, Part I, p. 181.

passing through experiences that are real because they are part of
the consciousness of Brahman but unreal because they are not
part of Its being".¹ But Brahman has no distinction of subject and
object. To say that Māyā is a subjective action of Brahman con-
sciousness is nothing but to impose the limitation of human mind
on Brahman. Again, the distinction between the consciousness
and being of Brahman is not valid. Hence the objects of the world
cannot be merely a creation of subjective action of Brahman-con-
sciousness and utterly devoid of its being. Brahman will be aware
by his true consciousness of the illusions imposed on him and
would know them as illusions. Only some being in the phenom-
enal world will be deluded by the creation of Māyā. This duality
is experienced by the individual soul when it frees itself from the
works of nature and has the awareness within of the pure exist-
ence of Brahman or self and knows the phenomenal world as
unreal but on the surface has to act as if it were real. But this
solution, according to Sri Aurobindo, negates the sole and indi-
visible pure existence and pure awareness of Brahman. It creates
a dualism within its featureless unity. All these solutions which
have been offered to solve the mystery of Māyā must be regarded
as u˙ tenable "unless we modify our first view of the Reality and
concede to it a power of manifold status of consciousness or a
power of manifold status of existence".²

Even if it were admitted that Brahman has a dual consciousness,
still it cannot be a dual power of knowledge-ignorance. Brahman
can have no ignorance and cannot be subject to Māyā. To say that
Brahman has ignorance is to impose the limitations of our own
consciousness on Brahman. "An Ignorance", says Sri Aurobindo,
"which occurs or intervenes in the course of manifestation as a
result of a subordinate action of consciousness and as part of
divine cosmic plan and its evolutionary meaning, is one thing and
is logically conceivable; a meaningless ignorance or illusion eternal
in the original consciousness of the Reality is another thing and
not easily conceivable; it appears as a violent mental construction
which has no likelihood of validity in the truth of the Absolute."³

1. *L.D.*, Vol. II, Part I, p. 181.
2. *Ibid.*, p. 183.
3. *Ibid.*, p. 183.

The dual consciousness can thus have no ignorance. It is fully conscious of the pure existence of Brahman and at the same time is aware of the illusory world and knows it as unreal and illusory. But it is difficult to understand why a will or power of Brahman should create only illusions and not realities of the Real. It seems incredible, observes Sri Aurobindo, "that the sole power of the Reality should be to manifest something contrary to itself or to create non-existent things in an illusory universe".[1]

One other solution may be put forward which does not concede to Māyā and her works even an empirical existence. According to it the question how the illusion was generated, how the universe is related to Brahman is illegitimate. The universe does not exist at all, Māyā is non-existent, Brahman is the sole truth and nothing exists besides Brahman. This view is known in Advaita Vedānta as *Ajātivāda* or doctrine of non-origination of the world and is associated with the name of Gauḍapāda. Gauḍapāda shows the self-contradictions inherent in the theory of causation and arrives at the doctrine of *ajāti*. He says, "Neither the unreal nor the real can have the unreal as their cause; nor can the real have the real as its cause......and how could the real be the cause of the unreal."[2] "Nothing is produced either by itself or by another, nor is anything in fact produced, whether it be being, or non-being, or either."[3] Thus the difficulties of causation led Gauḍapāda to deny the manifestation of the world altogether. But the problem is, if a real universe does not exist, a cosmic illusion exists and we have to explain how this illusion came into being, what is its relation or non-relation to the Reality. To deny the existence of the universe altogether is nothing but fleeing away from the face of a real and difficult problem. The dilemma of an immutable Reality and an illusory dynamism, the two absolutely contradictory of each other still remains and we are obliged to find some way to solve it.

---

1. *L.D.*, Vol. II, Part I, p. 184.
2. नास्त्यसद्धेतुकमसत्सदसद्धेतुकं तथा ।
   सच्च सद्धेतुकं नास्ति सद्धेतुकमसत्कृतः ॥ (*Kārikā*, iv, 40)
3. स्वतो वा परतो वापि न किंचिद्वस्तु जायते ।
   सदसत्सदसद्वापि न किंचिद्वस्तु जायते ॥ (*Ibid.*, iv, 22)

Individual as the Percipient of Māyā or Ignorance: Its Criticism
So long Brahman was regarded as the percipient of Māyā. But this
theory is self-contradictory and has not been able to explain
adequately either the true nature of Māyā or its relation to Brah-
man. Now we proceed to consider the theory of Vācaspati which
regards the *Jīva* or the individual soul as the seat of or percipient
of *māyā* or *avidyā*. If the *Jīva* or the finite self be regarded as the
seat of *avidyā*, the question is, how can the finite self being itself
a creation of *avidyā* be the seat of *avidyā*? Finitude is a mode of
avidyā. It is *avidyā* that makes the infinite appear as the finite. The
Advaita Vedānta ascribes all finitude to *avidyā* or nescience. So the
finite self or *Jīva* being the product of *avidyā* cannot be the seat
or support of it. In the same way Īśvara-consciousness is also
subject to the limitation of *avidyā*. Hence it also cannot on the
same ground be called the seat of *avidyā*. Thus Vācaspati cannot
escape the charge of begging the question by conceiving *avidyā*
as located in the *Jīva*-consciousness.

Finally, it may be said that the individual and the universe are
unreal; but Māyā, as it confronts and imposes itself on Brahman,
acquires a certain reality. It is owing to this acquired reality of Māyā
that the universe and the individual also appear as real. But the
question is, for whom is the experience of the universe valid and
for whom does it cease by liberation or extinction or withdrawal?
It must be valid for the individual and it must cease to exist on
the liberation of the individual. It means that the individual is a
real entity. But in the illusionist hypothesis the individual is merely
illusory. Now an unreal or illusory being cannot put on reality and
suffer from a real bondage and get a real liberation. If the experience
of the universe and bondage and liberation have any meaning or
significance then the individual must have some reality. And this
individual consciousness can be nothing else than the conscious-
ness or being of Brahman who projects itself in Māyā. But if it is
so, then it will, on the one hand, falsify the illusionist theory of the
pure unreality of the individual self and, on the other hand, it will
have to be explained, how the consciousness or being of Brahman
happened to become subject to Māyā. So the problem of the
individual subject, his experience of the universe, his bondage and
liberation cannot be explained on the illusionist hypothesis. As Sri
Aurobindo observes, "In the Monistic view the individual soul is
one with the Supreme, its sense of separateness an ignorance,

escape from the sense of separateness and identity with the Supreme its salvation. But who then profits by this escape? Not the supreme Self, for it is supposed to be always and inalienably free, still, silent, pure. Not the world, for that remains constantly in the bondage and is not freed by the escape of any individual soul from the universal illusion. It is the individual soul itself which effects its supreme good by escaping from the sorrow and the division into the peace and the bliss. There would seem then to be some kind of reality of the individual soul as distinct from the world and from the Supreme even in the event of freedom and illumination. But for the illusionist the individual soul is an illusion and non-existent except in the inexplicable mystery of Māyā. Therefore we arrive at the escape of an illusory non-existent soul from an illusory non-existent bondage in an illusory non-existent world as the supreme good which that non-existent soul has to pursue."[1]

From the above discussion it is clear that we cannot explain the nature of Māyā or Avidyā and its relation to Brahman whether we regard Māyā as located in Brahman or in the individual soul. All these difficulties arise due to the fact that the Śaṅkarites do not regard the creative force as real. Sri Aurobindo escapes the difficulties of the Śaṅkarites by conceiving the creative force as real in nature and as one with Brahman. As we have seen above, Sri Aurobindo regards Ignorance which manifests the world of Mind, Life and Matter as real in nature and as a modification or self-limitation of the supreme conscious force of the Absolute or Brahman. Ignorance, according to him, has its seat neither in Brahman nor in the individual soul. It is located in Mind. Ignorance is not an original principle which may affect the unity of Brahman. By conceiving Ignorance as a modification of the supreme conscious force of Brahman, Sri Aurobindo maintains the oneness of the Absolute and at the same time is able to explain the world process.

Now we proceed to discuss critically some analogies which are generally put forward by the Śaṅkarites in support of their theory of the unreality of the world. First of all we will take up the analogy of dream and will show that dream experience does not support the doctrine of the unreality of the world.

---

1. *L.D.*, Vol. I, pp. 49-50.

(v) *Doctrine of the Unreality of the World not Supported by Dream*

Dream is regarded as unreal because its experiences have no validity for our waking consciousness. Dream lies midway between our waking consciousness and deep sleep. Dream-experience ceases to exist and has no validity either for our waking consciousness or deep sleep. Hence it is felt to be unreal. But this is no ground, argues Sri Aurobindo, for our calling dream unreal. There may be different states of consciousness each valid in itself. One may pass from one state of consciousness to another and become forgetful of the previous state or even if one remembers its contents, they may be considered illusory. But it does not mean that the present state of consciousness is real and that of another or previous state unreal. "If earth circumstances begin to seem unreal to a soul passing into a different world or another plane of consciousness, that would not prove their unreality; similarly, the fact that world-existence seems unreal to us when we pass into the spiritual silence or into some Nirvana, does not of itself prove that the cosmos was all the time an illusion. The world is real to the consciousness dwelling in it, an unconditioned existence is real to the consciousness absorbed in Nirvana; that is all that is established."[1] So it cannot be said that as the unreality of dream world is proved by our waking consciousness, so the unreality of the waking world is proved when one enters the transcendent consciousness. The experience of the world may cease to exist for the individual who realises the transcendent but it will not prove the unreality of the spatio-temporal world itself.

Moreover, dream experience and waking experience are quite different in character. Our waking experience is coherent in nature while this coherence is generally absent in dream. Our waking experience is conditioned by the categories of space, time and cause. But dream experience cannot be brought under categorical determinations. Hence the analogy of dream cannot be applied to our waking consciousness. As Sri Aurobindo puts it, "But the second reason for refusing credit to our sleep experience is that a dream is something evanescent without antecedents and without a se-

1. *L.D.*, Vol. II, Part I, p. 153.

quel; ordinarily, too, it is without any sufficient coherence or any significance intelligible to our waking being If our dreams wore like our waking life an aspect of coherence, each night taking up and carrying farther a past continuous and connected sleep experience as each day takes up again our waking world-experience, then dreams would assume to our mind quite another character. There is therefore no analogy between a dream and waking life; these are experiences quite different in their character, validity, order."[1] It is said that our life also lacks inner coherence and significance. But it appears so due to the limitation in our understanding. Our limited mental consciousness is not able to grasp the full truth and significance of life. But when one enters within and begins to see life from within, its incoherence disappears and its real significance is fully revealed. "There is no surface incoherence in life, it rather appears to our minds as a chain of firm sequences, and, if that is a mental delusion, as is sometimes alleged, if the sequence is created by our minds and does not actually exist in life that does not remove the difference of the two states of consciousness." The disparity between the waking and the dream life is further proved by the fact that whereas the former is to a considerable extent controlled by the ego, the latter is devoid of it. The evanescence of our waking life cannot be put on a par with dream. The evanescence of a dream is radical and one dream has no connection with another; but the evanescence of the waking life is of details—there is no evidence of evanescence in the connected totality of world-experience.[2] "Our bodies perish but souls proceed from birth to birth through the ages; stars and planets may disappear after a lapse of aeons or of many light-cycles, but universe, cosmic existence may well be a permanent as it is certainly a continuous activity; there is nothing to prove that the Infinite Energy which creates it has an end or a beginning either of itself or of its action."[3] Thus there is too great disparateness between dream-life and waking life to make the analogy applicable. Even if dream life is unreal, it does not prove in any way the unreality of our waking life.

1. *L.D.*, Vol. II, Part I, p. 153.
2. *Ibid.*, p. 154.
3. *Ibid.*, p. 154.

But it cannot be said dogmatically that dreams are totally unreal and without any significance. Psycho-analysis has thrown a flood of light on the nature and significance of our dream life. Freud has shown how closely our dream experiences are connected with our waking life. If we are able to understand fully the nature of dreams, they may cease to appear as perfectly incoherent and devoid of all significance. So whether dream-experience is regarded as real or unreal, it will in no way support the theory of the unreality of the world.

Now we proceed to examine critically the nature of illusions and hallucinations and will show that according to Sri Aurobindo illusions and hallucinations also do not support the theory of the unreality of the world.

(vi) *Theory of the Unreality of the World not Supported by Illusions and Hallucinations*

The Śaṅkarites try to prove the unreality of the world by their theory of superimposition. According to them, in illusion, we have two things, one real and the other unreal. And illusion is the result of the superimposition of an unreal entity on a real thing. We may take, for example, the analogy of rope-snake. In illusion we mistake rope for snake. The snake according to them is an unreal entity. Its unreality is proved by the fact that when rope is recognised as rope, the snake disappears altogether. By calling it unreal, the Advaitins do not mean that it is perfectly non-existent like the sky-flower, hare's horn, a barren woman's son etc. As long as the illusion lasts, it is perceived as real but its unreality becomes evident when the illusion is cancelled. Hence it is strictly neither real nor unreal or non-existent. So the Advaitins call it indescribable (*anirvacanīya*) and their theory of illusion is called *anirvacanīya-khyāti*. On the strength of this analogy, the Śaṅkarites try to prove the unreality of the world. As snake is superimposed on the rope, so the world is also according to them superimposed on Brahman. And as the existence of snake is cancelled on the perception of rope, so the existence of the world is cancelled on the realisation of Brahman. Snake has existence only in knowledge or in the consciousness of the percipient. It has no independent existence. It has only an epistemic status and no ontological status. In the same way the world also enjoys only an epistemic status and no ontological status. It does not mean that the world is the creation of an individual mind like snake. The Advaitins generally make a distinction between empirical reality and illusion. The former is called *vyāvahārika satya* and the latter *prātibhāsika satya*. The Vijñānavādins also make a distinction between the empirical experience and the illusory experience. What the Advaitins call *vyāvahārika satya* is called by the Vijñānavādins *paratantra satya*; and the *prātibhāsika satya* or illusory experience is called by the Vijñānavādins *parikalpita satya*. The spatio-temporal world which is called *vyāvahārika* or *paratantra* is true for all our practical purposes. But the *prātibhāsika* or *parikalpita* experience is purely imaginary. It serves no practical purpose. The empirical world is independent of the individual consciousness but the illusory object does not enjoy an independent existence. The reality of the empirical or phenomenal world is cancelled only on the realisation of the transcendent reality but the reality of illusory object is cancelled in our empirical or mental consciousness itself. Thus there is a vast difference between the empirical world and the world of illusion. But the empirical world is also said to have only an epistemic status for the reason that its experience is cancelled on the realisation of the transcendent.

Sri Aurobindo holds that the analogies based on the illusory experiences do not prove the unreality of the world. The false image which is imposed on an object is not of something quite non-existent. It is an image of something real and existent but not present at the place in which its image is erroneously imposed by our mind. It is not entirely a new creation. "A mirage is the image of a city, an oasis, running water or of other absent things, and if these things did not exist, the false image of them, whether raised up by the mind or reflected in the desert air, would not be there to delude the mind with a false sense of reality. A snake exists and its existence and form are known to the victim of the momentary hallucination: if it had not been so, the delusion would not have been created; for it is a form resemblance of the seen reality to another reality previously known elsewhere that is the origin of error."[1] So these analogies do not prove the unreality of the world. The analogy would have been applicable if the world we experience had been the copy or image of a true world which

---

1. *L.D.*, Vol. II, Part I, p. 165.

existed elsewhere. As Sri Aurobindo puts it, "The analogy therefore is unhelpful; it would be valid only if our image of the universe were a falsity reflecting a true universe which is not here but elsewhere or else if it were a false imaged manifestation of the Reality replacing in the mind or covering with its distorted resemblance a true manifestation. But here the world is a non-existent form of things, an illusory construction imposed on the bare Reality, on the sole Existent which is forever empty of things and formless: there would be a true analogy only if our vision constructed in the void air of the desert a figure of things that exist nowhere, or else if it imposed on a bare ground both rope and snake and other figures that equally existed nowhere."[1]

Sri Aurobindo holds that in illusion we wrongly combine an object given in perception with a memory image on account of some similarity in their form which also represents a real object existing elsewhere and experienced in the past. "All mental or sense hallucinations are really misrepresentations or misplacements or impossible combinations or false developments of things that are in themselves existent or possible or in some way within or allied to the province of the real. All mental errors and illusions are the result of an ignorance which miscombines its data or proceeds falsely upon a previous or present or possible content of knowledge."[2] Thus it comes to this that the things which are related or combined together in illusion are not false though their relation or combination is false. According to the Śaṅkarites, in illusion one of the terms of the relation is also false. But Sri Aurobindo argues that the terms which are related are not false but their relation is false.[3] A memory image which represents a real object seen in the past is projected on an external object. So error consists in our projecting a memory image on an external object due to ignorance. Had there been, for example, no snake, there would not be the projection of snake on rope. So the contention of the Śaṅkarites that snake itself is false is not true. Only the projection of snake on rope is false and not the snake itself.

Śaṅkara and the Śaṅkarites maintain that the object presented in illusion is not merely a memory image. On the contrary, it is

---

1. *L.D.*, Vol. II, Part I, p. 165.
2. *Ibid.*, pp. 165-66.
3. Compare the Nyāya-Vaiśeṣika and the Bhāṭṭa views of error.

a new creation altogether. Though the illusory object is a creation of mind without any objective validity of its own, yet it is quite distinct form memory insofar as it has an outward or objective reference outside the mind while memory is purely mental in its character having no objective reference. "The presentation of silver on the locus in oyster-silver superimposition is not a mere objectification of a memory-image. It is, on the contrary, an entirely new creation due to the operation of *avidyā* which has a twofold capacity—screening and creation. If the silver were an objectification of a past memory-image the form of judgment should have been 'this is that silver' instead of the form 'this is silver', and in this very illustration, this twofold capacity is equally patent. *Avidyā* here screens the real nature of the 'this' or locus which is oyster by shutting out from view its special features and creates a new silver which the percipient cognises. The silver we see in erroneous perception, says Vācaspati, is not that of the market but is an entirely new creation on the mother-of-pearl—a novel appearance in a definite point of time and space and this spatial and temporal mark is sufficient to indicate its existence ás different from a similar object perceived in a different place at a different time."[1]

We do not regard the objection put forward by the Advaitins against regarding silver as an objectification of a memory-image as sound. The argument that if silver had been an objectification of a memory-image then the form of judgment should have been 'this is that silver' instead of the form 'this is silver' is not valid. The reason is that this objectification of a memory-image is not a conscious process. The memory-image is imposed on an external object unconsciously. Had it been a conscious process then only the form of judgment could have been 'this is that silver'. Illusion is due to our unconscious identification of a memory-image with an external object. Thus it cannot be said that the object presented in an illusion is a new creation or a novel appearance generated by *avidyā*. Mind cannot create things out of void. Its highest flights of imagination also have some basis in experience. It cannot create snake or silver as has been stated above if it had no such experience in the past. A man who has never seen a snake cannot mistake a rope for snake.[2] Thus the illusory object cannot be called

1. A.B. Shastri, *Studies in Post-Śaṅkara Dialectics*, pp. 240-41.
2. *L.D.*, Vol. II, Part I, p. 167.

a novel appearance or a new creation as the Śankarites would have us believe. The illusory object is in reality a memory-image of an object existing elsewhere. Sri Aurobindo also holds, like Śankara and the Śankarites, that illusion or error is the result of our ignorance. But whereas Śankara and the Śankarites hold that ignorance creates a new entity altogether different from memory, Sri Aurobindo holds that ignorance only projects memory image on an external object. According to Sri Aurobindo, the analogies of rope-snake, oyster-silver etc. could have been applied in determining the relationship of Brahman and the world only if the world had been regarded as real. As Sri Aurobindo puts it, "The analogy of mental hallucination would only be applicable if we admit a Brahman without names, forms or relations and a world of names, forms and relations as equal realities imposed one upon the other, the rope in the place of the snake, or the snake in the place of the rope—an attribution, it might be, of the activities of the Saguna to the quiescence of the Nirguna. But if both are real, both must be either separate aspects of the Reality or co-ordinate aspects, positive and negative poles of the one Existence. Any error or confusion of Mind between them would not be a creative cosmic Illusion, but only a wrong perception of realities, a wrong relation created by the Ignorance."[1]

Thus it is clear that the analogies of our illusory experiences do not support the theory of the unreality of the world. "What we see in the universe is that a diversity of the identical is everywhere the fundamental operation of cosmic Nature; but here it presents itself, not as an illusion, but as a various real formation out of one original substance. A Reality of oneness manifesting itself in a reality of numberless forms and powers of its being is what we confront everywhere. There is no doubt in its process a mystery, even a magic, but there is nothing to show that it is a magic of the unreal and not a working of a Consciousness and Force of being of the omnipotent Real, a self-creation operated by an eternal self-knowledge."[2]

(vii) *The Changing Character of the Universe does not Prove its Unreality*

Śankara and the Śankarites call the universe unreal also because

1. *L.D.*, Vol. II, Part I, p. 166.
2. *Ibid.*, p. 167.

of the fact that it is temporary and perishable and not eternal and imperishable. In support of his theory of the unreality of the universe Śankara quotes the famous illustration given in the Upaniṣad of clay and the pots. There it is said that the different modifications of clay are merely a name born of speech and have no substantial reality. The clay alone is real.[1] The modifications of the clay perish and go back to the earth leaving behind them nothing but clay. Hence this analogy, according to Śankara, goes to prove that the supreme Brahman is alone real and the world being the manifestation of Brahman is unreal. But this analogy, according to Sri Aurobindo, can tell more convincingly the other way. The pot is real on account of being made out of the substance of clay which is real. Even if it disappears its previous existence cannot be denied or thought to have been unreal or illusory. So the relation between the clay and the pot or between Brahman and the world is not that of an original Reality and a phenomenal unreality but is that of dependence. It has to be admitted that the pot as such cannot exist apart from clay. In the same way it may be said that the world as such being the manifestations of Brahman cannot exist apart from Brahman. So the significance of the analogy of clay and pot is to show the dependence of the world on Brahman and to prove their essential oneness and not to signify the unreality of the world. Śankara lays great stress on the word 'alone' where it is said, the clay alone is real. But the word 'alone' does not mean that pot is unreal but that it has no other existence apart from clay. Moreover, the pot form according to Sri Aurobindo is an eternal possibility of clay and it can manifest at any time if the clay exists. So we may suppose that "the power of manifestation is inherent in Brahman and continues to act either continuously in Time-eternity or in an eternal recurrence". The universe has a different order of Reality from the transcendent Brahman, but for that very reason it has no need to be called transcendentally unreal or unreal to that transcendence. But Śankara's main difficulty in regarding the universe as real is that he regards the Real as immutable, eternal and differenceless. But this definition of the Real is, according to Sri Aurobindo, a purely intellectual conception, an ideative distinction, a mental construction and has no binding for a substantial and integral experience. The contradiction which seems

---

1. वाचारम्भणं विकारो नामधेयं मृत्तिकेत्येव सत्यम् । (*Chān.* 6.1.4)

270   THE INTEGRAL ADVAITISM OF SRI AUROBINDO

to exist between the eternal supracosmic Reality and the temporary world is merely verbal. The world-existence is in fact not contradictory to the supracosmic Existence but is dependent on it. "It cannot be the final truth," observes Sri Aurobindo, "that the Supreme Consciousness has no regard upon the universe or that it regards it as a fiction which its self in Time upholds as real. The cosmic can only exist by dependence on the supracosmic; Brahman in Time must have some significance for Brahman in timeless eternity; otherwise there could be no self and spirit in things and therefore no basis for temporal existence".[1]

Sri Aurobindo contends that in Śaṅkara's philosophy we find a contradiction between reason and intuition. Intuition is intensely aware of the transcendent, immutable Absolute and has no awareness of the world. Reason is intensely aware of the world but has no realisation of the Absolute. This conflict compels Śaṅkara to take recourse to the doctrine of Māyā. The main purpose of this theory or its main function is to reconcile the two perfectly contradictory experiences of reason and intuition. But Sri Aurobindo contends that though "it opens a way out from their contradiction", yet "it is not a solution, it does not resolve the contradiction". The solution of this contradiction lies only in a higher consciousness, the supramental consciousness. To a higher consciousness, they do not appear as involving any such contradiction. Sri Aurobindo is definite and emphatic in his view that whatever unreality we find in existence lies really in our ignorant and limited mind and we have to get rid of it. Then we will have no reason to call the world unreal. "It is an ignorance of self and the world," observes Sri Aurobindo, "that has to be overcome and not an illusion, a figment of individuality and world-existence".[2] He is of the opinion that to bridge the gulf between the cosmos and the transcendent Reality we have to pass beyond the intellect. It is abstract intellectual reason that raises and perpetuates contradictions everywhere in the Reality. In Brahman-consciousness the divergences and contradictions cannot exist. The divisions of the intellectual reason are all connected by a real thread of unity in a higher or supramental consciousness. The mystery of the world is supra-rational and hence it cannot be fathomed by our dividing and limited intellect. But

1. *L.D.*, Vol. II, Part I, p. 196.
2. *Ibid.*, p. 205.

the universe cannot surely remain a mystery to a higher or divine consciousness. As he says, "It cannot be that to that self-creative supreme consciousness the world is an incomprehensible mystery or that it is to it an illusion that is yet not altogether an illusion, a reality that is yet unreal."[1] It is only by rising into the higher and dynamic planes of consciousness that man can fathom and ultimately solve the mystery of the universe and find a real reconciliation between the two apparently contradictory but in fact complementary aspects of Reality, namely, the static and the dynamic.

If the world does not reveal to us in its forms the Reality, it is not because it is unreal but because "it is a progressive self-expression, a manifestation, an evolving self-development of that in Time which our consciousness cannot yet see in its total or its essential significance".[2] All finite forms are nothing but the Infinite in essence. Matter to our finite reason seems merely a hard immobile entity. But to a scientific mind it appears as a force or energy in its essence. But if one goes still further and looks at matter from the spiritual standpoint, then matter seems nothing else but Brahman in essence. So a spiritual consciousness which is capable of having a simultaneous experience of both the sides of Existence will see matter not in its isolation as matter but as Brahman. It will not deny the truth of matter but to it matter as such will merely appear as a mode of the self-expression of Brahman. Matter to that divine consciousness will not appear as contradictory of spirit but itself the Spirit, as a mode of self-formation and self-expression of the Spirit. There are no contradictions in Reality, no feeling of contradiction in the divine consciousness. The only field where contradictions reign supreme and have their full sway is our finite and limited mind which is governed in its operations by the laws of Formal logic which are purely abstract and analytic in character and cannot determine *a priori* the relationship between the Absolute and the world.

It is sometimes said that the universe cannot be a manifestation, because the Absolute has no need of manifestation as it is manifest to itself eternally. But it can equally be said that "the Reality has no need to create a Mayic universe."[3] "The Absolute can have no

1. *L.D.*, Vol. II, Part I, p. 206.
2. *Ibid.*, pp. 206-07.
3. *Ibid.*, p. 207.

need of anything; but still there can be—not coercive of its freedom, not binding on it, but an expression of its self-force, the result of its Will to become—an imperative of a supreme self-effectuating force, a necessity of self-creation born of the power of the Absolute to see itself in Time".[1] The force of the Absolute which manifests the universe is not bound to remain always in a potential form and at rest. It is free to keep itself at rest and to express itself in the infinite forms of the universe in Time. "If the Absolute," remarks Sri Aurobindo, "is self evident to itself in eternal Timelessness it can also be self-manifest to itself in eternal motion of Time". So the universe is nothing but a real self-manifestation of the Absolute. To call it unreal or illusory is according to Sri Aurobindo "a superfluous conception, otiose and unnecessarily embarassing".

What we can call unreal or unreal reality is our ego or our sense of separativeness. As long as we are in ignorance or are ego-bound individuals, we consider ourselves and other things as self-existent. We do not realise our essential identity with the universe or with the transcendent Existence. But when we transcend the ego and realise our essential self, this narrow sense of separativeness disappears. The individual still remains but he does not consider himself as self-existent and apart from everyone else but exists as "being and power and manifestation of the Infinite". He still maintains his individuality but the sense of separativeness and isolation is no longer there. So unlike Śaṅkara, Sri Aurobindo does not consider the ego as the only constitutive factor of individuality. They are one in considering the ego or sense of separativeness unreal, but whereas Śaṅkara holds that the individuality ends with the disappearance of ego, Sri Aurobindo does not think so. On the contrary, according to him, the true individual only emerges when the ego consciousness completely disappears. He now becomes a spiritual Puruṣa a portion of the Divine.

(viii) *Theory of Māyā Unable to Solve the Riddle of Existence*
The theory of Māyā according to Sri Aurobindo instead of solving the problem of existence renders it for ever insoluble. It regards all our experiences in the universe as unreal. "In the thesis of the pure unreality of Maya" observes Sri Aurobindo "all knowledge as

---

1. *L.D.*, Vol. II, Part I, p. 207.

well as all ignorance, the knowledge that frees us no less than the ignorance that binds us, world-acceptance and world-refusal, are two sides of an illusion; for there is nothing to accept or refuse, no body to accept or refuse it. All the time it was only the immutable superconscient Reality that at all existed; the bondage and release were only appearances, not a reality".[1] But if it is so, the process of negation cannot stop here. If all the experiences of the individual consciousness turn out to be illusory then there is no guarantee that its spiritual experiences are not illusions; and if so its experience of the immutable, differenceless Reality may also turn out to be perfectly illusory. If all the objects of the universe are illusory including the universe itself then there is no guarantee that the experience of the pure, silent, static and immutable self is also not illusory, "since that too comes to us in a mind moulded of delusion and formed in a body created by an illusion".[2] The intellect which can deny the reality of all things can as well deny the reality of the transcendent experience. "The Buddhist,'' says Sri Aurobindo, "took this last step and refused reality to the Self on the ground that it was as much as the rest a construction of the mind; they cut not only God but the eternal Self and impersonal Brahman out of the picture."[3]

So according to Sri Aurobindo it is essential that along with the reality of Ātman or Brahman we should also accept the universe as real. For if the beings of whom Brahman is the self are unreal or illusory then the reality of Brahman can also be questioned. The experience "I am that," can, according to Sri Aurobindo have no basis in the theory of Māyā for there is no 'I', only 'that'. In the same way, the experience "I am He" is doubly ignorant, for if there is no universe there cannot be a Lord of the universe. Unlike Śaṅkara, Sri Aurobindo holds that the experience "I am That" can have any significance only when there is a real eternal spiritual Puruṣa apart from our changing phenomenal being. The individual self according to Sri Aurobindo maintains its identity even after the realisation of its essential nature. But then though it maintains its individual existence yet it considers itself a portion of the Divine and one with it in its essential nature. The individual spiritual

1. *L.D.*, Vol. II, Part I, p. 209.
2. *Ibid.*, p. 210.
3. *Ibid.*, p. 210.

Puruṣa has full awareness of its identity with the universal and the transcendent aspects of Reality.

"The theory of Illusion," observes Sri Aurobindo, "cuts the knot of the world problem, it does not disentangle it; it is an escape, not a solution; a flight of the spirit is not a sufficient victory for the being embodied in this world of the becoming; it effects a separation from Nature, not a liberation and fulfilment of our nature."[1] The proper solution of the riddle of existence can only be that which reconciles all the aspects of existence and recognises the proper significance of each in its own place. But Illusionism or Māyāvāda does not do that, but deprives all knowledge and experience except the realisation of the transcendent Brahman, of reality and significance.

The Advaita view according to Sri Aurobindo suffers from the defect that it annihilates one aspect of reality altogether in order to escape from an apparent contradiction. The original Vedāntic conception according to him does not consider the supreme Reality and the world or knowledge and ignorance as opposed to or contradictory of each other. But the Advaita Vedānta considers the problem of knowledge and ignorance from the standpoint of the dialectical intellect and hence falls inevitably into the mesh of contradictions. Sri Aurobindo takes his stand on the Vedic or Upaniṣadic conception and departs from the "fine excesses of the dialectical intellect". As he observes, "While giving every tribute to the magnificent fearlessness of these extreme conclusions, to the uncompromising logical force and acuity of these speculations, inexpugnable so long as the premises are granted, admitting the truth of two of the main contentions, the sole Reality of Brahman and the fact that our normal conceptions about ourselves and world-existence are stamped with ignorance, are imperfect, are misleading, we are obliged to withdraw from the hold so power-fully laid by this conception of Maya on the intelligence."[2]

(ix) Sri Aurobindo's Solution of the Riddle of Existence
In order to do this one has to fathom the true nature of knowledge and ignorance. In the opinion of Sri Aurobindo, the solution of the problem of knowledge and ignorance cannot be properly

---

1. *L.D.*, Vol. II, Part I, p. 211.
2. *Ibid.*, p. 240.

attained simply by an examination of words and ideas or by a dialectical discussion. It may be attained by a total and comprehensive observation and penetration of the essential facts of consciousness—the surface consciousness as well as the other planes of consciousness that lie below or above the surface consciousness. Sri Aurobindo is of the view that one cannot attain any comprehensive and essential knowledge about oneself or the world or the ultimate Reality by means of dialectical discussions. "For the dialectical intellect," observes Sri Aurobindo, "is not a sufficient judge of essential or spiritual truths; moreover, very often, by its propensity to deal with words and abstract ideas as if they were binding realities, it wears them as chains and does not look freely beyond them to the essential and total facts of our existence".[1] Our dialectical discussions are, according to Sri Aurobindo, not absolutely free from our psychological prejudices. They are largely determined by one's attitude, temperament or turn of mind. Sri Aurobindo aims to get rid of these psychological prejudices whether mental, intellectual or spiritual as much as possible. "Our principle in such an inquiry," says Sri Aurobindo, "must be to see and know; the dialectical intellect is to be used only so far as it helps to clarify our arrangement and justify our expression of the vision and the knowledge, but it cannot be allowed to govern our conceptions and exclude truth that does not fall within the rigid frame of its logic".[2] "Illusion, knowledge and Ignorance," further says Sri Aurobindo, "are terms or results of our consciousness and it is only by looking deeply into our consciousness that we can discover and determine the character and relations of the knowledge and the ignorance or of the illusion if it exists, and the Reality".[3] So Sri Aurobindo aims at making a comprehensive examination of all the planes of consciousness in order to have a comprehensive and integral view of the whole of Reality. All the difficulties of the Advaita Vedānta are, as has been stated above, due to the fact that it makes a separation between the supreme Reality or Brahman and the creative and dynamic force or Māyā. The Advaita Vedānta treats difference between Brahman and Māyā as abstraction of

---

1. *L.D.*, Vol. II, Part I, p. 241.
2. *Ibid.*, p. 242.
3. *Ibid.*, p. 242.

difference, that is, mere difference without identity. So it feels constrained to conceive this difference as contradiction. Its dialectic based on the abstract laws of formal logic does not find any way to reconcile these two principles. Hence it has to establish the truth of the one principle at the cost of the other. But the dynamic and integral method of Sri Aurobindo does not find itself obstructed by the so-called antinomies or contradictions, as we have shown in the preceding chapters. The supreme Reality and the creative force appear as opposed to each other only to the finite or formal logic and not to the logic of the infinite or dynamic logic. It sees no opposition in the "One becoming or being always many and the Many being or becoming the one."

In reality there is no opposition between Brahman and the world. But the finite mind conceives this opposition as existing in reality itself and not in its own limited and imperfect view. So the principles that appear to the finite intellect as opposed to Brahman are in reality merely different powers of Brahman manifested in the course of its involution or self-concentration. So "what we call Ignorance is", observes Sri Aurobindo, "not really anything else than a power of the one divine Knowledge—Will or Maya; it is the capacity of the One Consciousness similarly to regulate, to hold back, measure, relate in a particular way the action of its knowledge. Knowledge and Ignorance will then be, not two irreconcilable principles, one creative of world-existence, the other intolerant and destructive of it, but two co-existent powers both present in the universe itself, diversely operating in the conduct of its processes but one in their essence and able to pass by a natural transmutation into each other. But in their fundamental relation Ignorance would not be an equal co-existent, it would be dependent on knowledge, a limitation or a contrary action of knowledge".[1] Thus we find that the Advaitism of Sri Aurobindo unlike that of the Māyāvāda does not exclude or deny the reality of the world or the creative force or Māyā. His Advaitism is able to reconcile the apparent opposition between them. And he succeeds in doing this by his dynamic conception of Reality. The static conception of Reality does not find favour with Sri Aurobindo. According to him neither the supreme Reality or Brahman nor the world is static

---

1. *L.D.*, Vol. II, Part I, p. 247.

in nature. The creative force is, as we have shown in detail, in a preceding chapter, the power of Brahman that manifests itself in different forms and powers. And it is this supreme creative or dynamic force that bridges the gulf or reconciles the apparent opposition between Brahman and the world.

(C) *Boundaries of Ignorance*

Owing to the exclusive and separative movement of Consciousness-Force, mind suffers from a many-sided ignorance. Mind has the awareness of only a small part of our being and of the objective world. "A superficial observation of our waking consciousness shows us," says Sri Aurobindo, "that of a great part of our individual being and becoming we are quite ignorant; it is to us the inconscient, just as much as the life of the plant, the metal, the earth, the elements".[1] But the superficial or waking consciousness is not the whole of our being. "We are not only what we know of ourselves," says Sri Aurobindo, "but an immense more which we do not know; our momentary personality is only a bubble on the ocean of our existence".[2] When one extends the range of one's experience and dives deeper into his self, one becomes aware of the other vaster and higher grades of consciousness—the subconscient, the subliminal and the superconscient and so on. These different ranges of consciousness constitute the major part of our consciousness and being. Our surface consciousness or being is, as Sri Aurobindo says, merely a bubble on the ocean of our integral existence. Comparing our surface personality with our whole being, Sri Aurobindo characteristically says, "our mind and ego are like the crown and dome of a temple jutting out from the waves while the great body of the building is submerged under the surface of the waters".[3] Thus it is clear that the normal or surface consciousness of man suffers from a many-sided ignorance. The boundaries of ignorance extend far and wide.

According to Sri Aurobindo, man suffers from a sevenfold ignorance namely, the original, the cosmic, the egoistic, the temporal, the psychological, the constitutional and the practical. We are

1. *L.D.*, Vol. II, Part I, p. 318.
2. *Ibid.*, p. 318.
3. *Ibid.*, p. 319.

ignorant of the true nature of the Absolute. The Absolute is the source of all Being and Becoming but we consider some partial aspects of being or some temporal relations of becoming as the whole truth of existence. This is, according to Sri Aurobindo, the first, the original ignorance. The second, the cosmic ignorance, consists in our being ignorant of the true nature of the immobile, immutable, spaceless, timeless and impersonal self and considering the phenomenal or the cosmic becoming in Time and Space as the whole truth of existence. Similarly, the egoistic ignorance consists in our being ignorant of our universal self, the cosmic existence, the cosmic consciousness, our unity with all the beings and considering ourselves as phenomenal creatures, the egoistic beings possessed of a limited mentality, vitality and corporeality. The temporal ignorance is due to our being helplessly identified with this body, with this life and being ignorant and forgetful of our past lives, of our eternal becoming in Time.

Even in this body, we are only aware of our surface consciousness, our phenomenal existence and are utterly ignorant of our large and complex being, of our superconscient, subconscient and subliminal spheres of consciousness and existence. This is the fifth, the psychological ignorance. The sixth, the constitutional ignorance consists in regarding the mind, life or body or any two of these or all the three as the essential truths of our being and "losing sight of that which constitutes them and determines by its occult presence and is meant to determine sovereignly by its emergence their operations". Thus on account of this manifold ignorance, we fail to live in harmony with all the beings and thus lose the true enjoyment of our life. We, moreover, suffer from pain, evil, error, are ignorant in our thought, will, sensations, actions and thus fail to adapt and accommodate ourselves to the environment and grope blindly in a maze of darkness and ignorance. This is the seventh, the practical ignorance.

But man, in Sri Aurobindo's view, is not destined to remain confined within the narrow walls of this many-sided ignorance. This many-sided ignorance is destined to be transformed into many-sided and integral knowledge, as will be shown in the chapter on "Evolution." "A many-sided Ignorance striving to become an all-embracing knowledge is the definition of the consciousness of man the mental being—or, looking at it from another side, we may say equally that it is a limited separative awareness of things striving to become an integral consciousness and an integral knowledge."[1] The integral knowledge will mean the cancellation and the transcending of the boundaries of ignorance. It will mean a comprehensive and perfect knowledge of the Absolute, the Self, the cosmic existence and consciousness, the eternal soul or spirit, the deeper and the higher layers of our existence, namely, the subconscient, the subliminal and the superconscient, the essential truth and the true constitution of our being and lastly the true harmony of ourselves with the whole of existence and working in the world as an instrument of the Divine. As Sri Aurobindo puts it, "it will mean the knowledge of the Absolute as the origin of all things; the knowledge of the Self, the spirit, the Being and of the cosmos as the Self's becoming, the becoming of the Being, a manifestation of the Spirit; the knowledge of the world as one with us in the consciousness of our true self, thus cancelling our division from it by the separative idea and life of ego; the knowledge of our psychic entity and its immortal persistence in Time beyond death and earth-existence; the knowledge of our greater and inner existence behind the surface, the knowledge of our mind, life and body in its true relation to the self within and the superconscient spiritual and supramental being above them; the knowledge, finally, of the true harmony and true use of our thought, will and action and a change of all our nature into a conscious expression of the truth of the Spirit, the self, the Divinity, the integral spiritual Reality".[2]

(D) *Purpose of Ignorance*

An examination of the sevenfold order of Ignorance has made it clear that the emergence of the phenomenon of ignorance was necessary for the manifestation of the world and the individual life. Each side of the manifold ignorance has, according to Sri Aurobindo, got its own justification and serves a necessary purpose in the scheme of creation. In his present existence man lives and acts under the subjection of Nature or Prakṛti. He lives from moment to moment, being carried along the sweeping currents of Time. Had he been living in his timeless being, he would not have thrown himself in the stream of Time. Living in his superconscient

---

1. *L.D.*, Vol. II, Part I, p. 329.
2. *Ibid.*, p. 442.

or subliminal self, man would not have acted in accordance with the dictates and the capacities of surface mentality. His actions, thoughts and movements would have been quite different from what they are when he is guided by his surface consciousness. He would have been able to enjoy only the universal view of things and would not have seen things from the individual standpoint. His individuality or personality would in that case, not come into being. "He has to put on the temporal, the psychological, the egoistic ignorance," observes Sri Aurobindo, "in order to protect himself against the light of the infinite and the largeness of the universal so as to develop behind this defence his temporal individuality in the cosmos."[1] The emergence of Ignorance is not necessary for all kinds of cosmic manifestation. The cosmic manifestation can take place even without ignorance. But that would be quite different manifestation from that in which we live. It would according to Sri Aruobindo, "be confined to the higher worlds of the divine Existence or to a typal non-evolving cosmos where each being lived in the whole light of its own law of nature, and this obverse manifestation, this evolving cycle, would be impossible. What is here the goal would be then the eternal condition; what is here a stage would be the perpetual type of existence".[2] But it may be asked, what would be the harm if this mutable and perishable cosmos and the individual life full of all kinds of pains, sufferings and limitations would not have come into existence? The answer of Sri Aurobindo is that in that case the purpose of Saccidānanda would not be served. The supreme spirit put on the garb of ignorance in order to enjoy the pleasure of self-discovery. "It is to find himself in the apparent opposites of his being and his nature," observes Sri Aurobindo, "that Sachchidananda descends into the material Nescience and puts on its phenomenal ignorance as a superficial mask in which he hides himself from his own conscious energy, leaving it self-forgetful and absorbed in its works and forms".[3] The greater the resistance put by the material and inconscient nature, the greater the joy the spirit attains in the course of its self-discovery. "Not to return as speedily as may be to heavens," says Sri Aurobindo, "where perfect

1. *L.D.*, Vol. II, Part I, pp. 360-61.
2. *Ibid.*, p. 361.
3. *Ibid.*, p. 361.

light and joy are eternal or to the supracosmic bliss is the object of this cosmic cycle, nor merely to repeat a purposeless round in a long unsatisfactory groove of ignorance seeking for knowledge and never finding it perfectly—in that case the ignorance would be either an inexplicable blunder of the All-conscient or a painful and purposeless Necessity equally inexplicable—but to realise the Ananda of the Self in other condition than the supra-cosmic, in cosmic being, and to find its heaven of joy and light even in the oppositions offered by the terms of an embodied material existence, by struggle therefore towards the joy of self-discovery, would seem to be the true object of the birth of the soul in the human body and of the labour of the human race in the series of its cycles".[1] Thus Sri Aurobindo does not regard ignorance as a "blunder and a fall, but a purposeful descent; not a curse, but a divine opportunity".[2]

(E) *Integral Advaitism not Affected by Ignorance*

Thus Sri Aurobindo does not regard ignorance as putting in any way a limitation upon the Absolute. Ignorance being nothing else than the concentrated form of knowledge itself in a particular phase of manifestation, is not opposed to knowledge. Had ignorance derived its origin from any other source than knowledge itself or had it been original and primary in nature, then it could put a limitation upon Brahman or pure Consciousness. The monistic or Advaitic position of Sri Aurobindo would have been affected because there would be a principle over and above that of Brahman to put a limitation upon it. But ignorance in Sri Aurobindo's view is dependent on Brahman and has got its origin in a particular movement of its Conscious Force. Moreover, ignorance will in the course of evolution transform itself into knowledge. Hence there is no question of ignorance constituting a limit to the Absolute or Brahman.

So the contention of Śaṅkara and the Śaṅkarites that if ignorance is regarded as real, then it will affect the Advaitic or monistic position has no truth in it from the standpoint of Sri Aurobindo.

---

1. *L.D.*, Vol. II, Part I, p. 362.
2. *Ibid.*, p. 362.

He agrees with Śaṅkara in his view that ignorance does not put a real limitation upon the Absolute. But whereas Śaṅkara holds that the Absolute or Brahman is not affected for the reason that ignorance is unreal or false, Sri Aurobindo holds that the Absolute remains unaffected by the ignorance because the latter is merely its mode or manifestation and not anything opposed to it. Hence it is not necessary to regard ignorance as unreal or false in order to establish the advaitic or monistic position. The reality of ignorance thus does not put any limitation upon the Absolute or contradict its nature from the standpoint of Sri Aurobindo.

The failure of Śaṅkara and other advaitins of his school to establish integral Advaitism by admitting the reality of the creative principle or ignorance and its product, the world, is due to the fact that they regard ignorance as something opposed to Brahman though not independent of it. Ignorance is regarded in the Advaita Vedānta as material in nature[1] and thus opposed to the pure consciousness of Brahman. So if ignorance is regarded as real, then it will certainly, being opposed to Brahman, constitute a limitation upon it and so the Advaitic position cannot be maintained. It will involve a certain dualism in it. So the only way left for the Advaitins or Māyāvādins is to deny the reality of the ignorance and its product, the world, in order to maintain their Advaitism.

But Sri Aurobindo is saved from this difficulty due to the fact that he does not regard the creative force as material or unconscious in nature. He calls it *cit-śakti* or consciousness-force. It is a conscious power inseparable from Brahman. It assumes the form of unconsciousness and materiality only at a certain stage of manifestation. Thus it does not limit the Absolute in any manner. The objection that if Brahman is immutable and if it is one with the creative force, a change in creative-force will mean a change in the being of Brahman which goes against its immutability arises, as has been shown in our chapters on the Absolute, due to the limitations of mind. The opposition between the Immutable and the Mutable, the One and the Many, the Subject and the Object arises on account of the fact that our mind takes a narrow view of all these terms and conceptions. By an enlargement of these terms they cease to appear, as has been stated above, incompatible

---

1. जडात्मिका अविद्याशक्ति: ।

or contradictory to each other. So, instead of getting rid of the creative principle and its product, the world, to establish Advaitism, we have to get rid of the limitations of mind and arrive at an integral view of things, words and ideas in the view of Sri Aurobindo. It is only then that one can arrive at a real Advaitism, a concrete and integral Advaitism, instead of the abstract Advaitism of the Māyāvādins. According to Sri Aurobindo, contradictions do not really exist in reality but in our limited, ignorant and partial mind or intellect. So instead of sacrificing reality or any part of it at the altar of mind or intellect, we have to sacrifice the limitations of mind at the altar of reality. We have to replace the narrow and limited mental view by the supramental and integral view in order to have an all-embracing view of reality. It is by making an integral approach to reality that one can establish the integral Advaitism.

An objection is sometimes raised, can the power of self-limitation exist in the Absolute Consciousness? If it does, will it not mean a negation of the Absolute itself and thus a denial of Advaitism. Thus a distinguished critic observes: "Can Absolute knowledge contain within itself the principle of its own limitation? Briefly, can ignorance reside in knowledge as a certain action of knowledge itself?.... Is this any kind of monism? Is not monism disrupted from within?"[1]

This objection against Sri Aurobindo's position is based on the famous dictum 'determinatio negatio est,' meaning, determination or limitation is negation. But this dictum is only partially true. It is true in the case of the determination or limitation that is imposed on reality from outside, by something external to it. But it is not true in the case of the voluntary self-determination or self-limitation of reality. As Sri Aurobindo puts it: "All conscious self-limitation is a power for its special purpose, not a weakness; all concentration is a force of conscious being, not a disability."[2] "This power of self-limitation for a particular working," further says Sri Aurobindo, "instead of being incompatible with the absolute conscious force of that Being, is precisely one of the powers we should expect to exist among the manifold energies of the

1. G.R. Malkani, *Proceedings of the Indian Philosophical Congress*, 1950, pp. 116-17.
2. *L.D.*, Vol. II, Part I, pp. 365-66.

Infinite".[1] Hence all determination or limitation does not necessarily mean negation of the Absolute. The Absolute is called indeterminable, as has been stated in our chapters on the Absolute, in the sense that it cannot be limited by any determination or any possible sum of determinations. It does not mean that it is incapable of self-determination. Though the Absolute is not limitable or definable by any determination or any sum of determinations, yet, "it is not bound down to an indeterminable vacancy of pure existence". The indeterminability of the Absolute, according to Sri Aurobindo, "is the natural, the necessary condition of its infinity of being and its infinity of power of being".

Thus it is clear that the presence of ignorance or of the principle of self-limitation in the Absolute does not mean a denial of its absoluteness. It does not take away anything from the perfection of the Absolute. Self-determination cannot be put on a par with external determination. Hence the monism or Advaitism of Sri Aurobindo is neither "disrupted from within" nor from without. The charge of disruption of monism arises due to a complete misunderstanding of Sri Aurobindo's conception of reality and a rigid adherence to the formula: determination is negation. The Advaitism of Sri Aurobindo could be affected or disrupted only if the ignorance were regarded, as has been indicated above, as something opposed to the Absolute knowledge.

Sri Aurobindo is able to reconcile all the apparent contradictions due to the fact that he makes an integral instead of a partial approach to the problem of reality. By making this integral or comprehensive approach to all the fundamental problems of reality, he has shown that we can arrive at a concrete Advaitism which remains intact, unaffected and unassailed by its so-called contradictories, e.g., ignorance, inconscience, finitude, error, evil and so on.

Now we proceed to discuss the nature of the principles of Mind, Life and Matter which constitute the three stages in the descent of the Absolute or Saccidānanda into the spatio-temporal world through the principle of Ignorance.

---

1. *L.D.*, Vol. II, Part I, p. 366.

CHAPTER VIII

STAGES OF DESCENT OR INVOLUTION

(1) *Mind*

Mind is the manifestation or the result of the self-concentration or the self-modification of the Supermind. It is the principle or faculty of knowledge in man. It is mind which enables man to be aware of himself and of the subjective and the objective orders of existence. But the ways of knowing one's own existence and of the subjective and the objective orders of existence differ from each other. There are, according to Sri Aurobindo, four ways in which man becomes aware of his own existence as well as that of the subjective and the objective world. As Sri Aurobindo puts it, "A knowledge by identity, a knowledge by intimate direct contact, a knowledge by separative direct contact, a wholly separative knowledge by indirect contact are the four cognitive methods of Nature."[1]

(A) *The Four Ways of Mental Knowledge*

The human mind is aware of its own existence through a knowledge by identity. The knowledge by identity in its purest form is illustrated in the surface mind only by one's direct self-consciousness or self-awareness of one's existence. The knowledge of one's own self is the surest kind of knowledge possible to human mind. Man has no doubt about his own existence. He may doubt the

---

1. *L.D.*, Vol. II, Part I, p. 280.

existence of other things but he can have no doubt about his own existence. He can consider the whole universe, the whole of objective existence as nothing but a dream or an illusion but cannot consider his own essential existence, his own self or I as illusory. Some element of awareness by identity is also illustrated in the case of one's temporary identification with one's mental states. For example, when one gets angry, one's whole consciousness seems to be a wave of anger. Other passions also, e.g., love, grief, joy etc., occupy the whole of one's consciousness. So the individual for the moment loses in a way his self-consciousness and is aware only of the particular mental or emotional state. In the case of thought also the thinker sometimes loses his own self-consciousness and becomes for the moment a movement of thought or thinking. He does not either reflect or observe himself nor is he able to control his feeling or movements at the time of his identification with his particular emotion or passion. But every passing wave of emotion or thought does not involve the whole of our personality or consciousness. As Sri Aurobindo puts it, "But very ordinarily there is a double movement; a part of ourselves becomes the thought or the passion, another part of us either accompanies it with a certain adherence or follows it closely and knows it by an intimate direct contact which falls short of identification or entire self-oblivion in the movement."[1]

This will be made clear if we analyse our mental experience. In all functioning of mentality, we have according to Sri Aurobindo, four elements, "the object of mental consciousness, the act of mental consciousness, the occasion and the subject".[2] In our subjective experience, "the object is always some state or movement or wave of the conscious being, anger, grief or other emotion, hunger or other vital craving, impulse or inner life reaction or some form of sensation, perception or thought activity".[3] It means that the object of our subjective experience may be any cognitive, affective or conative state of our psychophysical organism. The act is the process of observing or evaluating the inner movements of our conscious being. "The act," says Sri Aurobindo, "is some

1. *L.D.*, Vol. II, Part I, p. 280.
2. *Ibid.*, p. 267.
3. *Ibid.*, p. 267.

kind of mental observation and conceptual valuation of this movement or wave or else a mental sensation of it in which observation and valuation may be involved and even lost—so that in this act the mental person may either separate the act and the object by a distinguishing perception or confuse them together indistinguishably. That is to say, he may either simply become a movement, let us put it, of angry consciousness, not at all standing back from that activity, not reflecting or observing himself, not controlling the feeling or the accompanying action or he may observe what he becomes and reflect on it, with this seeing or perception in his mind "I am angry".[1] In the former case we have the illustration of knowledge by identity in which the subject or mental person, the act of conscious self-experience, and the objective mental state are identified into one wave of conscious force in movement. In the second case, the act or process of self-experience partly detaches itself from the object. "Thus by this act of partial detachment," observes Sri Aurobindo, "we are able not only to experience ourselves dynamically in the becoming, in the process of movement of conscious force itself, but to stand back, perceive and observe ourselves and, if the detachment is sufficient, to control our feeling and action, control to some extent our becoming".[2] Thus one has the intimate and direct awareness of one's own subjective experience. Whereas in the former case, one loses altogether one's self-consciousness and becomes merely a wave of anger, passion etc., in the latter case, one is conscious of one's wrath or of one's passionate state. In the former case, the whole personality of the individual is eclipsed for the moment by a state of passion or emotion. In the latter case the individual has the capacity to control to some extent the disturbed state of his organism. But the latter state is not free from defect.

In this act of self-observation, there is a partial detachment of the act from the object, but not of the mental person or the subject from the mental act or process. The mental person or the subject and the mental act or process are rolled up in each other. The mental person is also not sufficiently detached or separated from the emotional becoming. So in the case of the knowledge by intimate direct contact there is neither the total detachment of the

---

1. *L.D.*, Vol. II, Part I, p. 267.
2. *Ibid.*, p. 268.

subject from the object nor of the subject from the mental act. "I am aware of myself," says Sri Aurobindo, "in an angry becoming of my conscious stuff of being and in a thought perception of this becoming but all thought-perception also is a becoming and not myself, and this I do not yet sufficiently realise; I am identified with my mental activities and involved in them, not free and separate. I do not yet directly become aware of myself apart from my becomings and my perception of them, apart from the forms of active consciousness which I assume in the waves of the sea of conscious force, which is the stuff of my mental and life nature".[1] According to Sri Aurobindo, the whole of our subjective existence is not exhausted in the ever changing mental states. There is something called the self or the subject, which is over and above the changing conscious experience. But we are not aware of the pure subject or self as long as we remain identified with the different states of mind. As Sri Aurobindo puts it, "It is when I entirely detach the mental person from his act of self-experience that I become fully aware first, of the sheer ego, in the end, of the witness self or the thinking mental Person, the something or someone who becomes angry and observes it but is not limited or determined in his being by the anger or the perception. He is, on the contrary, a constant factor aware of unlimited succession of conscious movements and conscious experience of movements and aware of his own being in that succession; but he can be aware of it also behind that succession, supporting it, containing it, always the same in fact of being and force of being beyond the changing forms or arrangements of his conscious force. He is thus the self that is immutably and at the same time the Self that becomes eternally in the succession of Time."[2] In this way, we have the knowledge or awareness of our subjective experience by what Sri Aurobindo calls, a knowledge by separative direct contact. The knowledge of our inner movements is, according to Sri Aurobindo, of a double nature, separation and direct contact: "for even when we detach ourselves, this close contact is maintained; our knowledge is always based on a direct touch, on a cognition by direct awareness carrying in it a certain element of identity. The more

1. *L.D.*, Vol. II, Part I, p. 268.
2. *Ibid.*, pp. 268-69.

separative attitude is ordinarily the method of our reason in ob-
serving and knowing our inner movements; the more intimate is
the method of the dynamic part of mind associating itself with our
sensations, feelings, and desires: but in this association too the
thinking mind can intervene and exercise a separative dissociated
observation and control over both the dynamic self-associating
part of mind and the vital or physical movement".[1] In our subjec-
tive experience, we have the direct contact of consciousness with
the object. Whether the subject or the self detaches itself partially
or entirely from the objective mental state, its awareness of the
object is always based on a direct contact. Our subjective expe-
rience is always characterised by a certain intimacy, immediacy and
directness.

But the knowledge of the external world does not possess the
characteristics of intimacy, immediacy and directness. In the knowl-
edge of the external world, the subject or mental person considers
the world or the object to be different from and independent of
himself. One does not identify oneself with external objects. One
also does not identify oneself with other human beings, with their
thoughts, feelings and desires and other subjective movements
with that directness and immediacy as one does in the case of his
own subjective experience. So neither one can know external objects
by way of identity nor by way of direct contact. Whatever knowl-
edge we have of the external objects or of other human beings
is primarily through the senses. It is the senses, e.g., sight, hearing,
touch etc., which establish a contact between the subject and the
object. The senses seem to initiate some kind of a direct intimacy
with the object of knowledge. But this is according to Sri Aurobindo,
not a real directness, a real intimacy, "for what we get by our sense
is not the inner or intimate touch of the thing itself, but an image
of it or a vibration or nerve message in ourselves through which
we have to learn to know it".[2] But if human knowledge were to
depend on sense-experience alone, then it could know little or
nothing about the object. The senses alone do not give any def-
inite idea of the object of experience. "But there intervenes,"
observes Sri Aurobindo, "a sense-mind intuition which seizes the

---

1. *L.D.*, Vol. II, Part I, p. 283.
2. *Ibid.*, p. 284.

suggestion of the image or vibration and equates it with the object, a vital intuition which seizes the energy or figure of power of the object through another kind of vibration created by the sense contact, and an intuition of the perceptive mind which at once forms a right idea of the object from all this evidence."[1] Whatever is deficient in the interpretation of the image thus constructed is filled up by the intervention of the reason or the total understanding intelligence. The sense-experience provides us only with the raw material. This raw material has to be arranged and synthesised by the sense mind, the vital mind, the perceptive mind and reason in order to have a definite and vivid knowledge of the object. As Sri Aurobindo puts it, "our world-knowledge is therefore a difficult structure made up of the imperfect documentation of the sense-image, an intuitional interpretation of it by the perceptive mind, life-mind, and sense-mind, and a supplementary filling up, correction, addition of supplementary knowledge, coordination, by the reason".[2]

(B) The Inadequacy of Mental Knowledge

But still the knowledge of the external world gained by mind is partial, narrow and imperfect. The human mind takes recourse to its various intellectual faculties, namely, imagination, speculation, reflection, impartial weighing and reasoning, inference etc., in order to arrive at a more complete and satisfactory knowledge of the world. But still it does not fully succeed in its endeavour. As Sri Aurobindo puts it, "After all that the result still remains a half-certain, half dubious accumulation of acquired indirect knowledge, a mass of significant images and ideative representations, abstract thought counters, hypotheses, theories, generalisations, but also with all that a mass of doubts and a never-ending debate and enquiry."[3] But not only is our knowledge of the external world imperfect, but our knowledge of the self and the subjective existence is also narrow and imperfect. We have a very meagre and pitifully insufficient knowledge of our surface existence only, of our apparent phenomenal self and nature and are not aware of

---

1. L.D., Vol. II, Part I, p. 284.
2. Ibid., p. 285.
3. Ibid., p. 285.

our true self and the true meaning of our existence. "We really persuade ourselves," observes Bergson, "that by setting concept beside concept we are reconstructing the whole of the object with its parts, thus obtaining so to speak, its intellectual equivalent. In this way we believe that we can form a faithful representation of duration by setting in line the concepts of unity, multiplicity, continuity, finite or infinite divisibility etc. There precisely is the illusion. There also is the danger. Just insofar as abstract ideas can render service to analysis, that is, to the scientific study of the object in its relation to other objects, so far are they incapable of replacing intuition, that is, the metaphysical investigation of what is essential and unique in the object".[1]

So our surface consciousness or mental knowledge is a state of knowledge but it is a limited, imperfect and inadequate knowledge and hence can be called a kind of ignorance. The human mind is ignorant of the true nature of the world. It cannot have a direct and intimate knowledge of the world but has to depend on the sense experience to establish contact with the world. It does not know the world as it is but as it appears to the senses. Thus our mind knows only the phenomena and not the noumena or the reality underlying the world. Not only that. The mental being does not have a true and integral knowledge of its own self and existence. Though it has a direct knowledge of itself yet its knowledge, as has been stated above, is restricted to the surface. "It is quite evident," observes Sri Aurobindo, "that we know ourselves with only a superficial knowledge—the sources of our consciousness and thought are a mystery; the true nature of our mind, emotions, sensations is a mystery; our cause of being and our end of being, the significance of our life and its activities are a mystery: this could not be if we had a real self-knowledge and a real world-knowledge".[2]

But now the question is, why is our mental knowledge about ourselves, our subjective and objective existence so very imperfect and narrow? The reason of the limitation of human knowledge lies in the fact that the whole consciousness in man ordinarily remains concentrated on the surface. This self-concentration of the Divine

---

1. *An Introduction to Metaphysics* (1913), E.T., pp. 15-17.
2. *L.D.*, Vol. II, Part I, p. 286.

consciousness-force on the surface enables the individual to enjoy its ego-centric individuality and carry on its activities without being aware of the deeper layers of its consciousness and existence. "The ego-sense," observes Sri Aurobindo, "is only a preparatory device and a first basis for the development of real self-knowledge in the mental being. Developing from inconscience to self-conscience, from nescience of self and things to knowledge of self and things, the Mind in forms arrives thus far that it is aware of all its superficially conscious becoming as related to an "I" which it always is. That "I" it partly identifies with the conscious becoming, partly thinks of it as something other than the becoming and superior to it, even perhaps eternal and unchanging".[1] The ego-sense is generally considered the cause of our bondage. It becomes the cause of bondage only when the individual begins to consider his surface embodied existence as all in all and regards his higher self and existence as merely a figment of mind. Otherwise it is the ego-sense that makes us self-conscious and aware of our individuality. The animals are also conscious of the objects. But they cannot be said to be possessed of self-consciousness. They cannot consider themselves apart from and independent of all other objects and living beings. "Possibly, in the lower animal," says Sri Aurobindo "the sense of ego, the sense of individuality would not, if analysed, go much farther than a sensational imprecise or less precise realisation of continuity and identity and separateness from others in the moments of Time. But in man there is in addition a co-ordinating mind of knowledge which, basing itself on the united action of the mind-sense and the memory arrives at the distinct idea—while it retains also the first constant intuitive perception—of an ego which senses, feels, remembers, thinks and which is the same whether it remembers or does not remember".[2] It is the ego which lies behind and at the root of all human experience. It is the principle that makes a synthesis of all experience and makes it a coherent whole. As Sri Aurobindo puts it, "Mind-sense is the basis, memory the thread on which experiences are strung by the self-experiencing mind: but it is the coordinating faculty of mind, which, relating together all the material that memory provides and

1. *L.D.*, Vol. II, Part I, pp. 275-76.
2. *Ibid.*, pp. 273-74.

all its linkings of past, present and future, relates them also to an "I" who is the same in all the moments of Time and in spite of all the changes of experience and personality." The object is an object only in relation to a subject. Without being aware of oneself as the subject, one cannot be aware of the object as object. "This action of knowledge in man, this co-ordinating intelligence, this formulation of self-consciousness and self-experience," observes Sri Aurobindo, "is higher than the memory-ego and sense-ego of the animal and therefore, we may suppose nearer to real self-knowledge".[1] So the ego-sense as it is manifested in man serves a great purpose in human life and experience. It endows man, as has been stated above, with self-consciousness and thus opens the way for him to proceed towards the realisation of his real self and existence.

But the knowledge based on a separative ego-sense suffers from narrowness, limitation and imperfection due to certain definite reasons. As Sri Aurobindo puts it, "First it is a knowledge of our superficial mental activity and its experiences and with regard to all the large rest of our becoming that is behind, it is an Ignorance. Secondly, it is a knowledge only of being and becoming as limited to the individual self and its experiences; all the rest of the world is to it not-self, something, that is to say, which it does not realise as part of its own being but as some outside existence presented to its separate consciousness. This happens because it has no direct conscious knowledge of this larger existence and nature such as the individual has of his own being and becoming. Here too there is a knowledge asserting itself in the midst of a vast ignorance. Thirdly, the true relation between the being and the becoming has not been worked out on the basis of perfect self-knowledge but rather by the Ignorance, by a partial knowledge."[2]

The individual, thus, remains in ignorance as long as he tenaciously keeps himself confined within the limits of his ego-consciousness. But he is not bound to remain forever a prisoner of his ego. The ego does not represent our true individuality. The true individual, the psychic entity lies within. Man can transcend the limitations of his ego and realise his true and essential being within himself. So our ignorance is not something irremediable. As

---

1. *L.D.*, Vol. II, Part I, p. 274.
2. *Ibid.*, p. 276.

Dr. Radhakrishnan observes, "*Avidyā* is not inevitable, though quite natural. If it were inevitable, there is no point in asking us to get rid of it. We cannot strive against the inevitable. We cannot know what cannot be known. It is possible for us to check the course of *avidyā*, and it shows that we are really greater than our habits."[1] Sri Aurobindo holds the view that *avidyā* is not an essential and integral part of human consciousness. It is merely a passing phase of human life. Unlike Kant, Sri Aurobindo does not hold the view that knowledge is confined to phenomena and cannot know the reality underlying it. It is only human consciousness as it is in the present state of existence that is confined to phenomena and is conditioned by the categories of space, time and cause. But mental knowledge does in no way mark the apex of the evolution of human consciousness. There are levels of consciousness higher than that of mind and man can reach those higher levels of consciousness and existence individually as well as collectively in the course of evolution. "Our self-ignorance and our world-ignorance can only grow towards integral self-knowledge and integral world-knowledge in proportion as our limited ego and its half-blind consciousness open to a greater inner existence and consciousness and a true self-being and become aware too of the not-self outside it also as self—on one side a Nature constituent of our own nature, on the other an Existence which is a boundless continuation of our own self-being. Our being has to break the walls of ego-consciousness which it has created, it has to extend itself beyond its body and inhabit the body of the universe. In place of its knowledge by indirect contact, or in addition to it, it must arrive at a knowledge by direct contact and proceed to a knowledge by identity."[2] It means that in order to have an integral, direct and immediate consciousness of oneself and of the external world one has to rise above the plane of mind and become one with the Supermind. Mind being nothing else but the self-concentration and self-manifestation of the Supermind, it can again become one with its original source, the Supermind, by an opposite process of self-expansion during the course of evolution.

At present mind has to depend for a knowledge of itself as well

---

1. *Indian Philosophy*, Vol. II, p. 508.
2. *L.D.*, Vol. II, Part I, p. 288.

as of the world on its various mental and intellectual faculties, specially, on memory. It is memory that links the past with the present. Man can know of his present existence by a direct self-awareness. But it is only by the aid of memory that he can be aware of his past life and link it with his present existence. "Memory, in the dividing consciousness," observes Sri Aurobindo, "is a crutch upon which mind supports itself as it stumbles on driven helplessly, without possibility of stay or pause, in the rushing speed of Time. Memory is a poverty-stricken substitute for an integral direct abiding consciousness of self and a direct integral or global perception of things".[1] In the absence of the integral consciousness, it is memory that effects the integration of man's personality. As Sri Aurobindo puts it, "for while all that it can do for the mind with regard to its direct self-consciousness is to remind it that it existed and was the same in the past as in the present, it becomes in our differentiated or surface self-experience an important power linking together past and present experiences, past and present personality, preventing chaos and dissociation and assuring the continuity of the stream in the surface mind".[2] But the human consciousness stands in need of memory and other mental faculties in order to be aware of its own existence as well as of the external world only so long as it remains confined within the limits of the ego. But at last when it transcends the artificial limitations of the ego-sense, its various mental faculties are shaken off altogether and replaced by an integral and all-embracing supramental consciousness. It is only when the mental consciousness is totally transformed by the supramental consciousness that man can, as has been stated above, enjoy an integral and real knowledge of his own essential existence and can realise his identity with the whole of the cosmos.

Sri Aurobindo takes into account the different grades of consciousness—the subconscious, the submental, the subliminal and the superconscient and shows that unless the light of spirit penetrates into the darkest regions of man's personality and transforms it by its light and power, the latter cannot enjoy perfect freedom, harmony and integration.

---

1. *L.D.*, Vol. II, Part I, p. 258.
2. *Ibid.*, pp. 266-67.

(C) *The Subconscious, the Submental, the Subliminal and
    the Superconscient*

The subconscious region is generally supposed to lie below the
normal and waking consciousness, below the level of mind and
conscious life. It is the inferior and obscure consciousness which
operates in the purely physical and vital parts of our being. Our
mind is not aware of all the workings of our physical and vital
being. The purely physical and vital being has its own law, it has
its own principle of consciousness which is termed subconscient
or more properly submental. Mind has thus no control over this
subconscious region. "That part of us which we can strictly call
subconscient because it is below the level of mind and conscious
life, inferior and obscure, covers the purely physical and vital
elements of our constitution of bodily being, unmentalised, unob-
served by the mind, uncontrolled by it in their action."[1] In itself,
the physical and vital being is not self-conscious. It is not pos-
sessed of mental awareness. This consciousness "operates in the
cells and nerves and all the corporeal stuff and·adjusts their life
process and automatic responses". The subconscient is aware of
our vital and physical desires, cravings, movements and directs our
automatic and involuntary movements and responses. In the
subconscient, says Sri Aurobindo, "there is no organised self-con-
sciousness, but only a sense of action and reaction, movement,
impulse and desire, need, necessary activities imposed by Nature,
hunger, instinct, pain, insensibility and pleasure". Sri Aurobindo
makes a distinction between submental and subconscient. Accord-
ing to him the physical and vital consciousness, the vital or physi-
cal substratum should be strictly called submental rather than
subconscient. For, he says, the vital and physical awareness though
different from mind, "is a nervous and sensational and automati-
cally dynamic mode of consciousness"; it has its own law of re-
actions to contacts and does not depend on mind for the aware-
ness and perception of its action and movements. Hence it is more
properly to be termed as submental because it is also a grade of
consciousness different from mind. Generally no distinction is made
between the subconscious and the submental. The regions lying
below the mental level, namely, the vital and the physical being

---

1. *L.D.*, Vol. II, Part II, p. 537.

are called, as has been stated above, subconscious. But as the physical and the vital being has a consciousness of its own though different from mind, so it should, according to Sri Aurobindo, be more properly called submental rather than subconscious. The subconscious according to him is other than the vital and physical being. It is bereft of even physical and vital consciousness. "The true subconscious," observes Sri Aurobindo, "is other than this vital or physical substratum; it is the Inconscient vibrating on the borders of consciousness, sending up its motions to be changed into conscious stuff, swallowing into its depth impressions of past experience as seeds of unconscious habit and returning them constantly but often chaotically to the surface consciousness, missioning upwards much futile or perilous stuff of which the origin is obscure to us, in dream, in mechanical repetitions of all kinds, in untraceable impulsions and motives, in mental, vital, physical perturbations and upheavals, in dumb, automatic necessities of our obscurest part of nature".[1] The true subconscious thus contains within it a store of past impressions, memories and experiences. It constitutes much of the stuff of our waking consciousness. These impressions of past experience remain dormant in the subconscious and can surge up in sleep or even in an unguarded and absent-minded waking state assuming different forms. They assume the forms of dreams. All the thoughts, impulses, desires etc., rejected by the waking consciousness sink in the depth of subconscious and surge up at any moment in the surface consciousness and with sometimes disastrous consequences, assuming the "forms of mechanical mind action or suggestion, forms of automatic vital reaction or impulse, forms of physical abnormality or nervous perturbance, forms of morbidity, disease, unbalance".

The subconscious cannot be explored by our surface consciousness or mind. A descent of mind into the subconscient would "plunge us into incoherence or into sleep or a dull trance or a comatose torpor". The subconscient region can be explored, examined and controlled by the subliminal and the supraconscient and not by the mental consciousness. As Sri Aurobindo puts it, "A mental scrutiny or insight can give us some indirect and constructive idea of these hidden activities; but it is only by drawing back

---

1. *L.D.*, Vol. II, Part I, pp. 322-23.

into the subliminal or by ascending into the superconscient and from these looking down or extending ourselves into these obscure depths that we can become directly aware and in control of the secrets of our subconscient physical, vital and mental nature."[1] The control of the subconscient is regarded by Sri Aurobindo as of utmost importance for a higher or divine life. "For the subconscient," remarks Sri Aurobindo, "is the Inconscient in the process of becoming conscious; it is a support and even a root of our inferior parts of being and their movements. It sustains and reinforces all in us that clings most and refuses to change, our mechanical recurrences of unintelligent thought, our persistent obstinacies of feeling, sensation, impulse, propensity, our uncontrolled fixities of character. The animal in us, the infernal also— has its lair of retreat in the dense jungle·of the subconscious. To penetrate there, to bring in light and establish a control, is indispensable for the completeness of any higher life, for any integral transformation of nature.[2]

The subliminal self is different from the subconscious. It is possessed of mind, life, senses like the surface being. But they extend to wider domains, have wider powers and are free from our limitations. The subliminal says Sri Aurobindo, "includes the large action of an inner intelligence and inner sense-mind, of an inner vital, even of an inner subtle-physical being which upholds and embraces our waking consciousness".[3] Our waking consciousness and being is merely an exteriorised portion, a fragmentary, distorted, vulgarised and mutilated part of the real and inner being. The subliminal remains constantly working behind our normal or waking self and is to a great extent responsible for our responses, movements and actions. Our whole personality is also in a great measure the outcome of the influences, motives and powers proceeding out of the subliminal self. The subliminal also opens itself to the universal consciousness. It is aware of the presence and working of universal Mind, universal Life, universal subtle Matter-force. Thus the subliminal self exceeds the limitations of our surface or physical mind and physical senses. Man can have a control over his life-energies, mind-energies, can get rid of limitations, distortions

1. *L.D.*, Vol. II, Part II, pp. 538-39.
2. *Ibid.*, p. 539.
3. *Ibid.*, p. 539.

and divisions of surface mind only when the veil existing between the surface and subliminal self is rent or abrogated altogether and a free and conscious flow of energies, powers and motives from the inner to the outer or from the depth to the surface self is made possible. Only then man can respond to the contact and vibrations of cosmic powers and realise his oneness with the universal being and consciousness. Thus the human being is not only constituted of a superficial, imperfect and limited consciousness, of a weak and unstable nervous organism or nerve-system and coarse physical organs, but is also possessed of an inner and wider consciousness, subtle senses and formidable life forces.

Thus there are three elements according to Sri Aurobindo in our personality. There is, "the submental and the subconscient which appears to us as if it were inconscient, comprising the material basis and good part of our life and body; there is the subliminal, which comprises the inner being, taken in its entirety of inner mind, inner life, inner physical with the soul or psychic entity supporting them; there is this waking consciousness which the subliminal and the subconscient throw upon the surface, a wave of their secret surge".[1]

But this is according to Sri Aurobindo not the whole truth of our being and of reality. There is also a higher and superconscious region above our normal waking self. This higher region includes the higher ranges of consciousness, namely the Higher Mind, Illumined Mind, Intuition, Overmind (as we will show in a subsequent chapter) and the Supermind and the supreme Spirit or Saccidānanda. It is only when the consciousness of man rises to these higher ranges that it begins to get rid of spatio-temporal limitations. For effecting a perfect integration in man's personality and establishing peace and harmony in the whole of his being, it is necessary that his mental consciousness is replaced by the supramental consciousness and his human personality is trånsformed by the descent of the supramental light and power into gnostic being or gnostic personality, as will be shown in a subsequent chapter.

Now we proceed to discuss the nature and characteristics of life which represents the next stage in the descent of Spirit after mind

---

1. *L.D.*, Vol. II, Part I, p. 324.

and show that life also like mind is not opposed to Spirit but is merely a mode or manifestation of Spirit and that it can manifest the light and power of spirit by its supramentalisation.

(2) Life

Life is, according to Sri Aurobindo, a form of Consciousness-Force. It is a mode of Saccidānanda. The divine principle manifests itself in the form of life as it does manifest itself in the forms of matter and mind. As matter is the final form of manifestation of the principle of Existence and mind is the manifestation of the Supermind, in the same way, life is a form of manifestation of Consciousness-Force. The Consciousness-Force assumes the form of life for proceeding ahead with the work of creation.

The Consciousness-Force assumes the aspect of life in order to create the individual forms in the world. It is the life-energy of the divine Being that creates the individualised forms and is responsible for their growth, maintenance and dissolution. In fact, the whole process of creation is carried on by the creative and dynamic knowledge-will of the Supermind. But the consciousness of Supermind is, as we know, integral and all-comprehensive. It creates the whole universe with all its forms but it comprehends them in an integral and all-embracing manner.

Supermind is the principle of unity and not of division and separation. So it cannot confine itself to different forms separately and look at different forms as separate entities. It cannot look at different forms as something quite distinct and separate from one another. It looks at all of them as merely the different forms of a single reality. It considers the diverse forms as the forms of a single reality. Hence there arises the necessity of some other principle or principles which may help in the process of individualisation or which may keep and hold different forms of the world separately and make them conscious of their separate individual existences. This work of individualisation is done by the principles of mind and life. Mind as a final operation of the all-comprehending and all-apprehending Supermind, confines itself to different forms separately and makes them conscious of their being distinct from each other and from the world. Thus it carries on the process of individualisation. In the same way, life is the final operation of the consciousness-force which unholds the individual forms as distinct from each other and enables the soul to act as an individual entity quite separate from and independent of other forms of the world. The force of Conscious-Being acting through the all-possessing and all-creative will of the universal Supermind assumes the forms of Life and "maintains and energises, constitutes and reconstitutes individual forms and acts in them as the basis of all the activities of the soul thus embodied".

It is the principle of Life which maintains the existence of organism and enables to adjust itself to its surrounding and to the world at large. It is due to the energy of Life that mind is able to influence the body and direct its operations. But for this principle of Life, mind would not have been able to keep in touch with body. Thus mind and body would have been condemned to eternal separation from each other. So the life-energy brings mind and body in touch with each other and thus gives the organism a distinct unity and enables it to carry on all its workings. It is the life-energy which provides force to Mind by which it "creates and relates itself no longer to ideas, but to motions of force and forms of substance". Thus it may be said to be the energy aspect of Mind. But this must be kept in mind that Life is not a separate and independent entity. It is merely an aspect of consciousness-force, its final operation which works behind each of the workings of Life in each and every form. Emphasising this point, Sri Aurobindo observes, "But it must immediately be added that just as Mind is not a separate entity, but has all Supermind behind it and it is Supermind that creates with Mind only as its final individualising operation, so Life also is not a separate entity or movement, but has all Conscious Force behind it in everyone of its workings and it is that Conscious Force alone which exists and acts in created things. Life is only its final operation intermediary between Mind and Body. All that we say of Life must be subject to the qualifications arising from this dependence."[1] Thus in order to know the real nature and working of Life we ought to know first of all the principle of consciousness-force that is working behind it and of which it is only the external aspect and instrument. We cannot have any idea of the aim or purpose of life, unless we pay attention to its divine aspect. If we consider this life as something undivine and evil, then we will not be able to realise the aim of life, its

---

1. *L.D.*, Vol. I, p. 239.

divine significance and cannot fulfil the will of God in this life. "Life is an evil; rings down the centuries the ancient cry, a delusion, a delirium, an insanity from which we have to flee into the repose of eternal being." This, in a nutshell, has been the well-recognised ascetic view of life for centuries. So if we consider life merely in its external aspect as something bereft of all divine element, we will have no other alternative but to acquiesce to this pessimistic view of life. Then the fulfilment of human life, its real goal and purpose will be attained not by enriching life more and more by the divine elements and qualities and moulding it into the image of the divine but by the negation of life and all its activities. So it is necessary that life should become conscious and aware of its divinity. It should unite and become one with the divine consciousness-force of which it is an external aspect and projection. We have to realise that not only there is divine principle within the body called soul which is eternal and whose aim is to realise its eternity in this life but the principle of life itself has to realise its divinity and eternity in the phenomenal world by becoming one with its original source and power. The divinity and eternity of existence has thus to be realised not only in the life beyond or in the repose of the Eternal transcending life and its activities but in the life itself, in its dynamic operations and workings. The divine has to be realised not only in the Being, but in the Becoming as well. And to realise it in the Becoming means realising it in the three principles of Life, Mind and Matter which apparently constitute the phenomenal world.

Now if Life is regarded, as we have seen above, as an external aspect of the divine consciousness-force, then whence come the limitation, division and incapacity in this life? It is, according to Sri Aurobindo, due to the darkened and dividing operation of mind. Life here acts as an intermediary between Mind and Matter. Thus it acts as an energy of mind and is thus subservient to it. It has also to undergo "all that subjection to death, limitation, weakness, suffering, ignorant functioning of which the bound and limited creature—Mind is the parent and cause". Thus human life is cut off from the overflowing stream of universal life and exists and acts as a separate life under all sorts of limitations and incapacity. But with the development of consciousness, life becomes aware more and more of its real nature. "To realise its own power and to master as well as to know its world," says Sri Aurobindo, "is therefore the increasing impulse of all individual life; that impulse is an essential feature of the growing self-manifestation of the Divine in cosmic existence".[1] Life can get rid of its limitations and incapacity only when it becomes one with the divine consciousness-force in the course of evolution and thus shares its freedom and power. Otherwise, the individual life in the individual form is, according to Sri Aurobindo, bound to remain subject to the three badges of its limitation, death, desire and incapacity.

Now we proceed to discuss Sri Aurobindo's conception of matter which represents the last stage in the descent of Spirit and show how matter also like life and mind, is not essentially opposed to Spirit but is only a mode or manifestation of Spirit or Brahman.

(3) Matter

Matter is a form of Spirit. To the common sense matter and spirit seem to be totally opposed to each other. They are regarded as incompatible and contradictory terms. But in reality, there is no fundamental opposition or incompatibility between these two. In essence matter is nothing else but spirit.[2] Spirit or Brahman is not only the underlying principle or substratum of matter, it is also its stuff, its constituting principle, its sole material. As Sri Aurobindo puts is, "As Mind is only a final action of Supermind in the descent towards creation and Life an action of conscious force working in the conditions of the ignorance created by this descent of Mind, so Matter, as we know it, is only the final form taken by conscious being as the result of that working. Matter is substance of the one conscious being phenomenally divided within itself by the action of a universal Mind—a division which the individual mind repeats and dwells in, but which does not abrogate or at all diminish the unity of Spirit or the unity of Energy or the real unity of Matter."[3]

But here a question arises as to why a phenomenal and pragmatic division has been introduced into the indivisible Existence. This division has been brought about by the mind. This has been done for the reason that mind has to carry the principle of multiplicity to its extreme limit and that can be done only by taking

1. L.D., Vol. I, p. 241.
2. अनं ब्रह्मेति व्यजानात् । (Tait. 111.2)
3. L.D., Vol. I, p. 298.

resort to separativeness and division. The very nature of creation is based on multiplicity. Without multiplicity there can be no creation. And this multiplicity, this diversity of beings and objects is possible only when the indivisible One divided itself into many by the operation of mind. But this division of the One into many does not mean that the One has ceased to be one, the indivisible and ultimate substance. The One maintains its Oneness in the same manner whether before or after creation. The creation of the world of multiplicity neither adds anything new to the unspeakable richness of the One nor takes away anything from it. Thus the mind gives to the "universal principle of Being the appearance of a gross and material substance instead of a pure and subtle substance". Mind suffers, as has been shown in the preceding chapters, from the inherent defect of division and separation. Through the senses it can only arrive at the knowledge of forms of things and not of their inner and deeper reality. It can only deal with appearance and not with the essence of objects. As the ultimate Being is indivisible and beyond any distinctions, it cannot be grasped by the dividing and limited mind. Hence there is the need of the appearance of the ultimate principle of Being as a gross and material substance. "Substance, then, as we know it, material substance," says Sri Aurobindo, "is the form in which Mind acting through sense contacts the conscious Being of which it is itself a movement of knowledge".[1] But Mind comes into contact with this form of the conscious Being not in its unity or totality but on the basis of the principle of division. It sees the substance of conscious Being in infinitesimal points and has to associate them together in order to arrive at a totality. "Thus the cosmic or universal Mind has to create atomic existences which by the very law of their being tend to associate themselves, to aggregate and form the world of objects. These atomic existences are instinct with the life that forms and hidden mind and will that actuate them." Not only that, in each atom all the principles of Existence are involved in an implicit manner. Thus each object, each aggregate carries with it an implicit or explicit notion of its separated individual existence. "Each such individual object or existence," says Sri Aurobindo, "is supported, according as the mind in it is implicit

---

1. *L.D.*, Vol I, p. 300.

or explicit, unmanifest or manifest, by its mechanical ego of force, in which the will-to-be is dumb and imprisoned but nonetheless powerful or by its self-aware mental ego in which the will-to-be is liberated, conscious, separately active".[1]

Thus the creation of Matter is not due to any eternal and original law of its own being. It is the cosmic Mind which is the creator of atomic existence. "Matter," says Sri Aurobindo, "is a creation, and for its creation the infinitesimal, an extreme fragmentation of the Infinite, was needed as the starting-point or basis".[2] So this atomic existence is the phenomenal basis of Matter. If Matter is divided into atoms and the aggregate of atoms or the formal atom is subdivided into essential atoms, we will even then arrive at some atomic existence. To whatever limit this division may be carried, even if the aggregate of atoms is broken up into the "most infinitesimal dust of being", we will still "arrive at some utmost atomic existence, unstable perhaps but always reconstituting itself in the eternal flux of force, phenomenally and not at a mere unatomic extension incapable of contents". Ether is regarded as an intangible support of matter but does not seem to be materially detectable as a phenomenon. So the ultimate atoms are regarded as the phenomenal basis of matter. In the realm of phenomena, we cannot arrive at a knowledge of the unatomic extension of substance. An extension which is not an aggregation of atoms is a reality of pure existence, pure substance. Our dividing finite mind cannot arrive at the unitary knowledge of the indivisible and unextended pure substance. This knowledge is possible only to Supermind which is the fundamental principle of unity and is always one with pure Existence. Mind, Life and Matter can be one with that pure existence and conscious extension in their static reality. As the pure Existence is the fundamental reality of Mind, Life and Matter, hence they can realise their oneness with it in their essence. In essence they are one with the ultimate Reality. But in their dynamic aspect, in their divided existence they cannot realise this oneness. The very action of Mind, Life and Matter is based, as we have seen above, on the principle of division and separation. They have to work under this necessary and phenomenal limitation. Hence in their dynamic aspect, they are not able to transcend the limitation

---

1. *L.D.*, Vol. I, p. 301.
2. *Ibid.*, p. 301.

of their phenomenal nature and realise the fundamental unity with the pure and indivisible Existence. But it must not be thought that all dynamic action, all the dynamic side of Existence is eternally and inherently condemned to this limitation and division. Supermind, even in its all embracing dynamic action does not lose touch with the essential and fundamental Oneness of the pure Existence.

Thus the truth of the matter is that "there is a conceptive self-extension of being which works itself in the universe as substance or object of consciousness and which cosmic Mind and Life in their creative action represent through atomic division and aggregation as the thing we call Matter. But this Matter, like Mind and Life is still Being or Brahman in its self-creative action".

Thus we find that there is no essential or fundamental difference between spirit and matter. The sharp division which has been created between spirit and matter is only due to the practical experience and long habit of mind and has no fundamental reality. "Spirit," according to Sri Aurobindo, "is the soul and reality of that which we sense as Matter; Matter is a form and body of that which we realise as Spirit".[1] Matter, as Sri Aurobindo puts it, "is the last stage known to us in the progress of pure substance towards a basis of cosmic relation in which the first word shall be not spirit but form, and form in its utmost possible development of concentration, resistance, durably gross image, mutual impenetrability—the culminating point of distinction, separation and division. This is the intention and character of the material universe; it is the formula of accomplished divisibility".[2] Thus the same reality which is matter at one end is spirit at the other.

Sri Aurobindo holds that matter like mind and life is destined to manifest in it the light and power of Spirit in the course of evolution. The opposition that the triple principle of mind, life and matter present to the Spirit will finally be removed only by the descent of the supramental consciousness and power. It is only then that mind will be finally united with the Supermind, life with Consciousness-Force, matter with Existence and soul with the Bliss of Brahman. Thus Saccidānanda will ultimately manifest itself in the world of Becoming. The world is not forever destined to suffer

1. L.D., Vol. I, p. 304.
2. Ibid., p. 319.

from darkness and inconscience. Human life is not destined to remain forever the abode of pain, evil and suffering. The imperfection of the world and of human life is destined to be removed in the course of evolution by the descent of the Supermind and Saccidānanda.

Now we proceed to discuss Sri Aurobindo's conception of evolution and show how Nature is to make an ascent to the status of Spirit and is to be transformed and transmuted by the descent of the light and power of the Spirit in the course of evolution.

PART IV

EVOLUTION OR ASCENT

CHAPTER IX

PROCESS OF EVOLUTION FROM MATTER TO MIND

Sri Aurobindo's Integral Advaitism is given a practical support by his theory of evolution. By means of this principle, he is able to resolve from a practical standpoint all the contradictions that seem to exist between the different aspects or grades of reality. As we have seen in our chapter on Ignorance, the supreme Being or Brahman manifests itself in the form of the world through the process of self-concentration or self-limitation of its consciousness-force. The principles of Mind, Life and Matter are nothing but the self-limited and self-concentrated forms of Brahman. Though outwardly they seem to be totally different from Brahman in nature, yet they are one with it in essence. This underlying presence of the supreme Reality or Brahman in the dense coating of matter indicates that matter is not always destined to remain in its original state of inconscience and inertia but it has the capacity and power in it to raise itself to and transform itself into the principle of Spirit. Sri Aurobindo holds that because there has already been an involution of Spirit into matter, so matter can rise again in the course of evolution to the status of spirit. This process of rising or ascent of matter to its essential and supreme level, viz., the principle of Spirit is known as the process of evolution. Hence there is, according to Sri Aurobindo, not only the involution or the descent of Spirit into the principles of ignorance and inconscience as manifested in the material world, but there is also an ascent or evolution of these principles or grades of existence into their highest or

312 THE INTEGRAL ADVAITISM OF SRI AUROBINDO

supreme status of Spirit. The double process of involution and
evolution explains the mystery of creation. The order of evolution
is just the reverse of that of involution. The process or order of
involution has been described in "The Life Divine" as follows:
Existence, Consciousness-Force, Bliss, Supermind, Mind, Psyche or
Soul, Life and Matter. The Process of evolution will therefore follow
the reverse order; that is, it will start with matter and reach its
culmination with the emergence of the Supermind and the three
principles of Bliss, Consciousness-Force and Existence. There is,
according to Sri Aurobindo, an evolution of the individual as well
as of the cosmos. The process of evolution is nothing but the
return of spirit to itself. In the stage of matter, spirit seems to have
lost in entirety its self-conscious character. There seems to have
been effected a total separation between its consciousness and
force. Thus if we look at matter in isolation, it seems to us nothing
but inert, static and unconscious. It reveals no trace of conscious-
ness in it. But when we turn our eyes towards the evolutionary
process, we find matter moving slowly but surely towards a higher
destiny.

(A) *The Process of Evolution: Its Triple Character*

The process of evolution follows, according to Sri Aurobindo, a
triple character, namely, a widening, a heightening and an inte-
gration. Now as the evolution starts from matter, there takes place
an evolution of the forms of matter proceeding from simple to
more and more complex ones which may admit the concentration
and action of a complex and subtle form of consciousness. This
is called by Sri Aurobindo the process of widening. Secondly, there
is a heightening or ascent from grade to grade, from the lower to
the higher grade. As, for example, when the principle of Life evolves
out of Matter, there is an ascent of the evolutionary process from
the grade of matter to that of life. The consciousness or spirit
present in a latent form in the stage of matter rises to a higher grade
of existence by the evolution of the principle of life. Thirdly, as
soon as the evolution reaches a higher grade, it takes up all the
lower grades and transforms them according to its own principles
and laws. Thus there is not merely an ascent from a lower to a
higher grade but a rising up and transformation of the lower grades
as well. This is called by Sri Aurobindo the process of integration.
As he puts it, "A taking up of what has already been evolved into

each higher grade as it is reached and a transformation more or less complete so as to admit of a total changed working of the whole being and nature, an integration must be also part of the process, if the evolution is to be effective."[1] It means that when a higher principle emerges, it effects a change according to its capacity in the principles of the lower grades also. The higher principle makes a descent into the lower principles and changes their order and working according to its own laws and capacity. Thus when life emerges out of the inconscience and inertia of matter, it not only marks an ascent to a higher grade in the evolutionary process but also effects a transformation in matter as well. The body of a living being presents quite different characteristics from that of pure material objects. In the same way when mind emerges, it descends into the lower grades of life and matter and changes them according to its laws and capacity.

The aim of this evolutionary process is to raise matter and all other principles present in a potential manner in the heart of matter to their divine status. Its aim is to change the principles of Inconscience and Ignorance into their supreme status of pure self-consciousness. The spirit which forms the substratum of matter and resides in it in a state of inertia and inconscience has to reveal itself more and more in the higher and higher grades of being and finally attain its pure self-luminous and self-conscious status. It demands a radical change in the nature and working of the principles of the material world. "The end of this triple process," says Sri Aurobindo, "must be a radical change of the action of the Ignorance into an action of knowledge, of our basis of inconscience into a basis of complete consciousness—a completeness which exists at present only in what is to us superconscience".[2] As he further observes, "An evolution in the inconscience is the beginning, an evolution in the Ignorance is the middle, but the end is the liberation of the spirit into its true consciousness and an evolution in the knowledge."[3]

But this liberation of spirit into its true consciousness cannot be attained by the emergence of the principles of life and mind. For,

---

1. *L.D.*, Vol. II, Part II, p. 500.
2. *Ibid.*, p. 500.
3. *Ibid.*, p. 500.

though these two principles effect a change in the nature and working of matter and modify it to some extent, they are also, on the other hand, effected and modified by matter. Life and mind evolve in matter. They do "transform its substance, first into living substance and then into conscious substance; they succeed in changing its inertia, immobility and inconscience into a movement of consciousness, feeling and life".[1] But they are not able to transform it altogether. They are not able to make it fully alive and completely conscious. The living being is subject to death and disintegration. The mind that evolves in living matter is controlled and subjugated by the subconscious and unconscious forces of nature. Thus it suffers from all-round ignorance. Thus it is clear that though matter is changed considerably by the emergence of life and mind, yet it also in its turn puts a serious limitation on their nature and working. It means that neither Mind nor Life can be taken as the original creative power. The original creative energy that manifests the world is, as we already know, neither material nor vital nor mental but is supramental in nature. So in order to effect an integral and total transformation in the nature and working of matter there must emerge the supramental principle. As Sri Aurobindo observes, "If there is to be an entire transformation, it can only be by the full emergence of the law of the spirit: its power of supermind or gnosis must have entered into Matter and it must evolve in Matter. It must change the mental into the supramental being, make the inconscient in us conscious, spiritualise our material substance, erect its law of gnostic consciousness in our whole evolutionary being and nature. This must be the culminating emergence or at least that stage in the emergence which first decisively changes the nature of the evolution by transforming its action of Ignorance and its basis of Inconscience."[2]

(B) *Sri Aurobindo's Theory of Emergent Evolution and Hegel's Theory of Continuity Compared*

Unlike Hegel, Sri Aurobindo does not regard reality as a coherent system. There are according to him decisive gaps between different grades of reality. Hegel has identified reality with thought. And

---

1. *L.D.*, Vol. II, Part II, p. 502.
2. *Ibid.*, p. 503.

as there are no gaps in thought so there are according to him no gaps in reality also. But Sri Aurobindo has not identified reality with any of the principles evolved so far. Reality is according to him Spirit which transcends all the principles known to man so far and which has manifested itself in the different grades of matter, life and mind. The world is moving on in a process of evolution. Matter has evolved life out of itself and mind has evolved out of life. So there is certainly a continuity between matter, life and mind. Sri Aurobindo does not deny the element of continuity altogether in evolution. But he does affirm that whereas, on the one hand, we find the element of continuity in evolution, on the other hand, we also find definite and decisive gaps between the different grades evolved so far. Thus, for example, though life has evolved out of matter, yet it is not the highest stage of matter. Similarly, mind, though it has evolved out of life, yet it cannot be called the highest stage of life. Thus whereas Hegel considers these different grades as differing only in degree, Sri Aurobindo regards them as different in kind also. There is no rigid separation between one grade and another grade but still there is a qualitative difference between them. As Sri Aurobindo puts it, "In the evolution, as it has been observed so far, although a continuity is there, for Life takes up Matter and Mind takes up submental Life, the Mind of intelligence takes up the mind of life and sensation— the leap from one grade of consciousness in the series to another grade seems to our eyes immense, the crossing of the gulf whether by bridge or by leap impossible; we fail to discover any concrete and satisfactory evidence of its accomplishment in the past or of the manner in which it was accomplished."[1] These gaps are felt not only on the side of evolution of consciousness but even in the outward evolution of physical forms. In the development of physical forms where one has the advantage of collecting and observing the data in a scientific manner, one comes across missing links that always remain missing. It is more so on the side of the evolution of consciousness. Here the gaps are found more glaring and decisive. Sri Aurobindo admits that it may be possible that on account of our inability to fathom the depth of our subconscious and submental life and to understand a lower mentality different

---

1. *L.D.*, Vol. II, Part II, p. 506.

from ours, we are unable to observe minute gradations not only between the different degrees of a single grade but also between different grades. The scientist who is concerned only with the study of the physical aspect of evolution believes in its continuity in spite of the presence of gaps and missing links. In the same way the philosopher could "discover the possibility and mode of these formidable transitions", if he could observe similarly the inner side of evolution, that is, the evolution of consciousness. But still there is, according to Sri Aurobindo, a vast difference between one grade and another grade. "But still there is a real, a radical difference," says Sri Aurobindo, "between grade and grade, so much so that the passage from one to another seems a new creation, a miracle of metamorphosis rather than a natural predictable development or quiet passing from one state of being to another with its well-marked steps arranged in an easy sequence".[1] Thus the principle of continuity ultimately breaks down as it fails to explain the real facts of evolution. In evolution we find the emergence of something new and not merely the continuation of something old.

The gaps or the gulfs between grade and grade become deeper but less wide as the evolution proceeds to higher and higher grades. We may take, for example, the case of a metal and a plant. The metal may show life-reaction like plant in a rudimentary way and it may be identical with life-reaction in plant in its essence, but the difference between them seems to us considerable. The former is merely a physical entity and seems to us inanimate. The other, though not apparently conscious might be called a living creature. In the same way the gulf between the highest plant life and the lowest animal life becomes deeper. The former is entirely devoid of any mental activity while the latter is possessed of mental consciousness though in a rudimentary form.[2] But though the gulf appears deeper yet it becomes narrower than what existed between metal and plant. As Sri Aurobindo puts it, "But the community of the phenomenon of life between plant and animal, however different their organisation, narrows the gulf even though it does not fill in its profundity."[3] In the same way there is a still deeper though narrower gulf visible between the highest animal

1. *L.D.*, Vol. II, Part II, p. 507.
2. *Ibid.*, p. 507.
3. *Ibid.*, pp. 507-08.

and the lowest human being—the gulf between sense-mind and intellect. The emergence of intellect makes a profound difference between the animal and human life. Even in the most primitive men, we find over and above the sense-knowledge, traces of emotional activity and practical intelligence. He has the capacity in him to think, to feel, to have some kind of moral and religious notions and to do some kind of skilful work. The light thrown by the sociologists on the savage life clearly shows that the life of savages also is governed by certain fundamental ideas and principles. The savage societies have as their guiding principles certain ethical and religious notions. They show their power of discrimination in a marked degree in their conception of taboos. They have the sense of right and wrong, good and evil. They have the sense of fellow feeling and share the joys and sorrows of life with their kinsmen. So we cannot say that the savages are devoid altogether of intellect. What we may say is that they are not possessed of as high degree of intellect as the civilised societies are. They are not familiar with the higher truths of science, philosophy and religion. Though they form a lower stage in the life of human evolution, yet they cannot be relegated to the animal order.

This phenomenon of gaps or gulfs in the evolutionary process presents a problem before the upholders of the emergent theory of evolution. The problem is, what is the cause or reason for these decisive gaps in evolution? That there are gaps or discontinuities in evolutionary process is a fact of experience. But the problem is, how it is to be explained? Sri Aurobindo tries to meet this problem squarely. According to him, the difference between one grade and another grade "consists in the rise of consciousness to another principle of being".[1] It is due to the ascent of consciousness to a higher principle of being that we find such gaping gulfs between the different grades of nature. It is the Spirit which is present even in the inconscience of matter. Now this Spirit or Consciousness hidden in the inconscience and inertia of matter is constantly engaged in revealing itself more and more through the higher and higher grades of nature. To serve this purpose, the Spirit has to leave one grade and to ascend to a higher or poise of being. This

---

1. *L.D.*, Vol. II, Part II, p. 509.

causes a chasm in the line of evolution. The difference between the higher and lower grades begins to appear immense. So the rise of consciousness to a higher principle of being is, according to Sri Aurobindo, the real cause of gaps or discontinuities in the evolutionary process. But this becomes clear to us only when we look not at the objective or physical aspect but at the subjective or psychological aspect of evolution. When we study the evolutionary process from the side of consciousness we find that consciousness assumes different forms or expresses itself in a different manner in different grades of being. In the stage of matter it does not reveal any sign of its existence. We find there neither the sign of life nor of consciousness. The metal does not show any sign of life or consciousness. The plant shows certain reactions of life but it is certainly not a mind-conscious being. Man and the animal are both possessed of consciousness. But the animal is possessed of vital and sense mind and is fixed in it. It cannot exceed its limitations. But man is possessed also of a higher principle of consciousness, the intellect, which makes the real difference between the animal and man. So it is clear that in each of these forms or grades of existence, the Spirit has fixed its action of consciousness in a different principle. "It is this stride from one principle of being to another quite different principle of being that creates the transitions, the furrows, the sharp lines of distance, and makes not all the difference but still a radical characteristic difference between being and being in their nature."[1]

(C) *Principle of Integration: Its Nature and Significance*
Now the problem arises, if there is no continuity in evolution, if there are apparently unbridgeable gulfs separating one grade from another grade in nature, then how the theory of evolution is to be supported at all? If the gaps separate the two grades of existence altogether, then it means that there is no connection between them and thus the theory of evolutionary process breaks down altogether. But Sri Aurobindo holds that the ascent to a higher grade does not mean the abandonment of the lower grades. When a higher principle emerges, it descends into the lower grades and transforms them according to its own values. "This heals the

---

1. *L.D.*, Vol. II, Part II, p. 510.

objection," observes Sri Aurobindo, "against the evolutionary theory created by these sharp lines of difference; for if the rudiments of the higher are present in the lower creation and the lower characters are taken up into the higher evolved being, that of itself constitutes an indubitable evolutionary process".[1] This process of transforming the lower grades by a higher principle, is, as has already been referred to, called by Sri Aurobindo, the process of integration. The conception of integration occupies a very important place in Sri Aurobindo's theory of evolution. This makes Sri Aurobindo's conception of evolution vitally different from the other theories of evolution both Eastern and Western. As Dr. Maitra puts it: "There is no Eastern or Western philosopher who has stressed this very essential feature of evolution, as Sri Aurobindo has done."[2] As he further says, "The usual view of evolution, which looks upon it as a mere ascent from the lower grade to the higher grade may be compared to the march of an army which advances without keeping its lines of communication with the base intact. And we may compare Sri Aurobindo's conception of evolution with the march of an army which advances with the whole force, keeping all its lines of communication perfectly intact."[3] Sri Aurobindo does not favour the evolution or development of only a part of our being. The one-sided development of our personality may have some importance from the individual standpoint but it has not got any cosmic significance. Sri Aurobindo wants the evolution or development of both subjective as well as the objective sides of our being. We have, according to him, not only to make efforts to realise Brahman in the subjective part of our being or in consciousness only, but also in the objective side or in matter as well. Not only the eternal soul in us has to realise its identity with Brahman, but matter or the physical part of our being has also to realise itself as one with Brahman or as merely a form of Brahman. Our personality is complex in nature. The human organism is constituted of body, life, mind, intellect and spirit. Now the general rule for the aspirants for liberation has been not only to detach themselves from the world but also to realise themselves as separate from the body, life, mind and intellect. Thus they were merely

---

1. *L.D.*, Vol. II, Part II, p. 510.
2. Dr. S.K. Maitra, *An Introduction to the Philosophy of Sri Aurobindo*, p. 66.
3. *Ibid.*, pp. 66-67.

concerned with the realisation of their spirit or self and not with the transformation of other parts of our personality—the body, life, mind and intellect. The realisation of spirit does have some effect on our mind and intellect but it does not make any radical change in our personality, especially in the physical parts of one's being. The result is that though the individual attains liberation of spirit, his psycho-physical organism is left to the care of the blind, inconscient mechanical nature. His spirit enjoys freedom but his body is ruled by necessity. The same individual lives simultaneously in two different worlds in a way—the noumenal and the phenomenal world or the world of freedom and the world of necessity. The liberated spirit does not find itself at home in the world of matter. It finds itself alien in it. After attaining liberation or realisation, the individual sees no purpose in living in this world. In reality he does not live in this world but only suffers to live. The result of this one-sided development is that though the spirit ascends to a higher plane, the physical or the material organism is left in the lower plane of existence. The individual gets liberation but the world is left where it was. It does not show any sign of breaking its bondage. But Sri Aurobindo does not only aim at the liberation of spirit but of body also. The rule of necessity is to be transformed into that of freedom. The mechanical order is to transform itself into the spiritual order. Unlike Kant, Sri Aurobindo does not think of any unbridgeable opposition or separation between the noumenal and the phenomenal world. According to Kant, spirit cannot enjoy its real freedom in the world of necessity. But according to Sri Aurobindo, not only the spirit is to realise its freedom in the world of necessity but the world of necessity itself is to evolve and transform itself ultimately into the world of freedom. What appears at one stage as the mechanical world or the world of necessity will appear at a higher stage, at the supramental stage, as the world of freedom. The world of matter is not destined to remain always where it is at present. It has evolved out of itself the principles of life and mind and has undergone considerable changes by their evolution. Now the next emergence will be that of the gnostic being. It will require the descent of Supermind. When the supermind will descend, the world of necessity will for the first time give way to the world of freedom. It is only then that the physical side of our being will also like spirit enjoy its perfect and unfettered freedom and will consider itself as one with

Brahman. If matter is in reality nothing but spirit, it must transform itself in the course of evolution into spirit. Thus, unlike Śankara, Sri Aurobindo does not feel constrained to call the world unreal or illusory. The recognition of the reality of the world does not endanger in any way the Advaitic conception. Śankara's identification of Brahman with immutable and differenceless Being left him no option but to call the world unreal or illusory. But Brahman, according to Sri Aurobindo, is not only Being but Becoming as well. It is not only consciousness but force also. Śankara could not reconcile consciousness with force. The force according to him was not the real force of consciousness. It was neither real nor unreal, nor real and unreal both. It was something indescribable, Māyā. Now as this force was called Māyā, the world which was nothing but the creation of force was also called Māyā or unreal in nature. Sri Aurobindo is saved from this conception on account of his realisation of the integral nature of reality and of his theory of evolution. It is due to the principle of integration that he could conceive of matter as transforming itself in the course of evolution into spirit. Thus unlike Śankara, he does not advocate the disappearance of the world on the realisation of Brahman. On the other hand the world itself has, according to him, to be transformed into Brahman or spirit through the descent of supermind. In this conception Sri Aurobindo does not only differ from Śankara and the other Māyāvādins but also from the Vedāntins of other schools as well. The theistic philosophers, like Rāmānuja, Vallabha, Madhva and others, also aim at the liberation of spirit only and not of the other parts of our being. And the bliss of Brahman is, according to them, to be enjoyed not in this world but in the higher plane of Brahman itself. The bliss of the Divine Līlā is not to be enjoyed in this mortal world of dire necessity but in the immortal world of utter freedom. Thus the material world is given no chance in their systems to rid itself of the bondage of mechanism, necessity and inconscience and raise itself to the spiritual plane of infinite freedom and bliss. The Sāṁkhya system conceives of an opposition between Puruṣa and Prakṛti or Spirit and matter. If one considers them identical, it is due to ignorance. The liberation of Puruṣa consists in realising himself as completely separate from Prakṛti and its products. So it is ignorance which effects a temporary identification of spirit and matter according to the Sāṁkhya and the Vedānta. Knowledge consists in realising oneself as separate from matter or from the physical side of our nature. But according to Sri Aurobindo, it is only a partial knowledge. The true knowledge consists in not only realising oneself as one with Brahman but matter also as one with Brahman and as capable of raising itself to the status of Brahman. This will be called the integral realisation of Reality as against its partial and one-sided realisation. Thus Sri Aurobindo follows the integral method in his conception of Yoga and evolution. Not only has the individual to perform Yoga in order to attain the divine status, but the whole nature or cosmos has to attain that supreme status through the performance of Yoga. Thus along with the individual, the cosmos is also engaged in performing Mahāyoga. Like man, nature also is not satisfied with its present status. It is also full of discontent. It continuously aspires for a higher status. So, it is continuously engaged in making mighty efforts to make the ascent to a higher status.

(D) *Process of Cosmic Evolution from Matter to Mind*

Now the problem is, how nature makes an ascent from one status to a higher status? What is the process of ascent from grade to grade? Sri Aurobindo's reply is that the ascent from one grade to another grade takes place by the heightening and intensification of consciousness-force present in an occult way in the material nature. Matter goes on evolving into higher and higher forms until a stage is reached when the consciousness-force present in a latent way in matter is so much heightened and intensified that it seeks a new channel of expression with the result that the principle of Life evolves or emerges out of matter. Not only that; there is also a pressure from the higher plane, where the evolving principle has already a dominant status, on the physical world. This pressure from the higher planes enables the hidden principle to emerge and establish itself in the world. So two factors play their part in the emergence of a new principle in terrestrial nature. One is the heightening and intensification of consciousness from below and the other is the pressure from a plane above that of material nature. As Sri Aurobindo puts it, "What is necessary is a working that brings the lower gradation of being to a point at which the higher can manifest in it; at that point a pressure from some superior plane where the new power is dominant may assist towards a more or less rapid and decisive transition by a bound or a series of bounds—a slow creeping, imperceptible or even occult action is followed by a run and an evolutionary saltus across the border. It is in some such way that the transition from the lower to higher grades of consciousness seems to have been made in Nature.[1]

It has already been said that before the starting of the process of evolution, there had already taken place a process of involution or the descent of the Spirit in the different grades of existence. All the principles that are to evolve in the physical or terrestrial nature are already present in matter in a latent form. Matter is the lowest or the last stage in involution and it is the first stage in evolution. The atom and electron contain in them in a latent form the principles of Life, Mind, Supermind and Spirit. But outwardly their existence is not felt. The atom and electron are called by Sri Aurobindo eternal somnambulists. They seem to be driven by an unconscious force. The consciousness of Spirit seems to have gone to sleep in the state of matter. But it is so only in its outward appearance. In itself the consciousness of spirit is fully awake. In reality it is the Spirit which is guiding quite consciously the evolution of nature. But in its outward form it does not show any signs of consciousness. It assumes the garb of inconscience. So the spirit is said to have in a way gone to sleep in the form of matter. In the plant, this outer form-consciousness is still in a state of sleep, "but a sleep full of nervous dream, always on the point of waking, but never waking".[2] Nature is still in the state of inconscience. But nature does not stop here. The consciousness-force present in an occult way in the material world is so much intensified, raises itself to such a height of power as to develop itself and emerge in the form of a higher principle, namely, the vitality or life-force. But along with this heightening and intensification of consciousness-force from below, there also takes place a pressure from the higher plane of life. "It is the pressure of the life-world which enables life to evolve and develop here in the forms we already know; it is that increasing pressure which drives it to aspire in us to a greater revelation of itself and will one day deliver the mortal from his subjection to the narrow limitations of his present incompetent

---

1. *L.D.*, Vol. II, Part II, p. 510.
2. *Ibid.*, p. 511.

and restricting physicality.[1] Now the emergence of life makes a significant change in the status of the world. A living creature is able to make response to the objective stimulus. It affects the environment and is affected by it. Its actions possess a higher and subtler value than the purely mechanical and physical action. It turns all contacts and stimulus from the physical world and other living creatures into the new life-value. This is a thing which forms of mere matter cannot do; they cannot turn contacts into life-values or any kind of value, partly because their power of reception—although it exists if occult evidence is to be trusted—is not sufficiently awake to do anything but dumbly receive and imperceptibly react, partly because the energies transmitted by the contacts are too subtle to be utilised by the crude inorganic density of formed Matter. Life in the tree is determined by its physical body, but it takes up the physical existence and gives it a new value or system of values—the life-value.[2] Thus it is clear that matter and life are different in nature. Life is not the highest form of matter. It is a different principle altogether.

But even in the stage of vegetable life, nature has not come to consciousness. So the evolution of nature does not stop there. There is again an upward movement of consciousness-force. ''The force of being,'' observes Sri Aurobindo, "is so much intensified, rises to such a height as to admit or develop a new principle of existence—apparently new at least in the world of Matter—mentality.[3] But again, there has not only been an upward thrust of consciousness-force from below but also a downward pressure from above for the emergence of mental principle. "It is the pressure of the mind-world which evolves and develops mind here and helps us to find a leverage for our mental self-uplifting and expansion, so that we may hope to enlarge continually ourself of intelligence and even to break the prison walls of our matter—bound physical mentality."[4] This is with regard to the evolution of the human being. But at present we are dealing with the stage of animal life. The animal is possessed of a sort of mentality. Sri Aurobindo says, "Animal being is mentally aware of existence, its own and others,

1. *L.D.*, Vol. II, Part II, p. 595.
2. *Ibid.*, p. 511.
3. *Ibid.*, p. 512.
4. *Ibid.*, p. 595.

puts forth a higher and subtler grade of activities, receives a wider range of contacts, mental, vital, physical, from forms other than its own, takes up the physical and vital existence and turns all it can get from them into sense values and vital mind values. It senses body, it senses life, but it senses also mind; for it has not only blind nervous reactions but conscious sensations, memories, impulses, volitions, emotions, mental associations, the stuff of feeling and thought and will. It has even a practical intelligence, founded on memory, association, stimulating need, observation, a power of device; it is capable of cunning, strategy, planning, it can invent, adapt to some extent its inventions, meet in this or that detail the demand of new circumstance. All is not in it a half-conscious instinct; the animal prepares human intelligence.[1] The modern researches in animal psychology bear a clear testimony to the presence in animals of sensations, memories, impulses, volitions, emotions, mental association etc. They seem to be possessed of practical intelligence. Thus we find a deep gulf between the vegetable and animal kingdom. The life-force in plant is outwardly utterly devoid of consciousness. But the life-force in the animal is possessed of quite a new principle altogether. It is that of mind. The presence of mind makes all the difference between the vegetable and the animal kingdom.

The next stage of evolution is that of man. Here nature seems to come to a fuller realisation of itself. The animal, though it is possessed of consciousness, has a limited waking mind which is capable of adapting itself to the environment for preserving its vital existence. In man, the conscious mentality develops to a far greater extent, and though he is at first not fully self-consciousness, yet he is capable of rising higher and higher in the range of self-consciousness. The ascent from the stage of animal to that of man takes place in the same way. There is a heightening of the force of consciousness latent in the principle of vital and sense mind and a consequent pressure from the plane of intellect above and the result is the emergence of intellect.

When the stage of man is reached by an ascent from the plane of life-mind or sense-mind to that of intellect there begins like the two lower stages also a widening of the range of consciousness. Man begins to know more and more of the world. The horizon of man's knowledge grows wider and wider till it tries to take the

1. *L.D.*, Vol. II, Part II, p. 512.

whole of the cosmos in its embrace. His knowledge grows more and more both in the objective as well as in the subjective spheres. Not only there is a heightening and widening of consciousness but there also follows the process of integration. Mind takes up the lower grades of vital mind, life and matter and gives to their action and reaction intelligent values. Man looks at his sensations, volitions, emotions, impulses, mental associations from a higher standpoint. He is not merely concerned with preserving his vital existence at all costs. Unlike animals, his thoughts, feelings, emotions and willing are not merely directed towards maintaining life but are also meant for the realisation of higher ideals. What is present as a crude stuff of thought and feeling and will in the animal, man "turns into the finished work and artistry of these things". The animal also thinks, but his thoughts are not self-conscious. They are more or less based on a "mechanical series of memories and mental associations, accepting quickly or slowly the suggestions of Nature and only awakened to a more conscious personal action when there is need of close observation and device; it has some first crude stuff of practical reason, but not the formed ideative and reflective faculty".[1] The awakening consciousness in the animal, observes Sri Aurobindo further, "is the unskilled primitive artisan of mind, in man it is the skilled craftsman and can become—but this he does not attempt sufficiently—not only the artist but master and adept".[2]

(i) *Two Developments in Evolution at the Stage of Man*
We find two significant developments in the course of evolution when it reaches the stage of man. Firstly, the universal spirit in man turns its gaze downwards on the lower grades of existence and transforms them according to its own laws and gives them its own values. Man is possessed of the power of knowledge and action, has in him the twin principle of knowledge and will, and he tries to make full use of them to transform his physical, vital and lower mental nature. He aspires to mould his whole life and personality according to social, moral, religious, cultural and spiritual ideals and values. It means that he does not reject his physical and vital

---

1. *L.D.*, Vol. II, Part II, p. 513.
2. *Ibid.*, p. 513.

life but he raises them to a higher level. So the evolution to a higher stage does not mean the suicide of the lower principle. The lower principles are not rejected but transformed according to a higher pattern. All his ethical, social, and spiritual disciplines are meant "to lessen and tame, purify and prepare to be fit instruments the vital and physical and lower mental life so that they may be transformed into notes of the higher mental and eventually the supramental harmony, but not to mutilate and destroy them. Ascent is the first necessity, but an integration is an accompanying intention of the spirit in Nature".[1] It is true that this downward gaze and integration is not a factor peculiar to man. The process of integration has been taking place at all the stages of evolution. The plant soul takes a nervous material view of its whole physical existence. The animal, as has been said above, takes a mentalised sense-view of its vital and physical existence. Thus integration takes place at all the levels of existence. But the difference between the downward gaze of the universal spirit in the stage of man and those of animal and plant is that in man it is conscious, whereas in the plant and animal it does not become conscious. Unlike man, the animal does not make conscious efforts to improve its nature, its conditions or to exceed its limitations. It is the universal spirit in it that impels it subconsciously to adapt itself to its environment in order to maintain its existence. But with man, the case is different. He makes conscious efforts to break the bounds of his limitations, to exceed his present status.

The second development that takes place in the course of evolution in man is that he turns his gaze consciously not only downward and around him but also upward towards what is above him and inward towards what is within him. "In him," says Sri Aurobindo, "not only the downward gaze of the universal Being in the evolution has become conscious, but its conscious upward and inward gaze also develops".[2] In the stage of the animal, the universal Being present occultly within it, does look upwards to attain the human status. But that upward gaze is not shared by the animal. It is not conscious of the working of spirit within it. As Sri Aurobindo puts it, "The animal lives as if satisfied with what Nature has done for it; if there is any upward gaze of the secret spirit within its animal being, it has nothing consciously to do with it, that is still

---

1. *L.D.*, Vol. II, Part II, p. 514.
2. *Ibid.*, p. 515.

Nature's business: it is man who first makes this upward gaze consciously his own business."[1] The animal is possessed only of an undeveloped consciousness and is entirely driven by Prakṛti, by the mechanical energies of Nature. It has no say in the working of nature. But man, unlike animal, is not an utter slave of nature. Though he is also normally very much under the bondage of nature, yet he is not under perfect subjection to her. At least man is conscious of his limitations and has the capacity to get rid of them. He begins to feel very keenly the sufferings that overcome him due to his living under the subjection of nature. The Puruṣa in man aspires to rise above the bondage of Prakṛti. He has a deep longing in his heart not only to get rid of the limitations and subjection of nature but also to become her master and lord. "To climb to higher altitudes, to get a greater scope, to transform his lower nature," says Sri Aurobindo, "this is always a natural impulse of man as soon as he has made his place for himself in the physical and vital world of earth and has a little leisure to consider his farther possibilities".[2] "It is in his human nature, in all human nature," further says Sri Aurobindo, "to exceed itself by conscious evolution, to climb beyond what he is".[3] It is not only true of the individuals but to a very great extent true of the human race also. The human race can rise beyond the imperfections of its present very undivine nature and ascend to a higher and superior status of humanity, "if it cannot absolutely reach to a divine manhood or supermanhood".

(ii) *Evolution through the Three Planes of Human Mind*
The human phase of evolution also takes a sufficiently long period to attain its maturity. There is not a sudden jump from the higher animal to man—the thinker, the sage, the philosopher. The intellect in man does not attain its highest status by a sudden jump but has to evolve itself in a gradual manner. Thus we come across three distinct grades of human mind or human beings—the physical man, the vital man and the intellectual or mental man. There takes place first of all the evolution of physical mind or physical

1. *L.D.* Vol. II, Part II, pp. 515-16.
2. *Ibid.*, p. 516.
3. *Ibid.*, p. 516.

man. The physical mind attaches utmost importance to objective things and to his external life and has little or no sensibility for his subjective experience and existence. His sensations, desires, hopes, feelings and satisfactions are dependent on external things and external contacts. The physical mind "takes its stand on matter and the material world, on the body and the bodily life, on sense-experience, and on a normal practical mentality and its experience".[1] Normally man takes his first stand on the physical mind. He is first of all concerned only with his material or bodily existence. All his desires, feelings and actions are centred round the comforts and maintenance of his bodily existence. The terrestrial evolution takes its first stand on matter. In man also it is his body which forms the basis of his higher development. So it is in order to ensure the safety and integrity of body that nature evolves first of all the physical man, whose main business is to look after the well-being and comforts of his physical existence. As Sri Aurobindo puts it, "It is inevitable that the human being should thus take his first stand on Matter and give the external fact and external existence its due importance; for this is Nature's first provision for our existence, on which she insists greatly: the physical man is emphasised in us and is multiplied abundantly in the world by her as her force for conservation of the secure, if somewhat inert, material basis on which she can maintain herself while she attempts her higher human developments, but in this mental formation there is no power for progress or only for a material progress. It is our first mental status, but the mental being cannot remain always at this lowest rung of the human evolutionary ladder."[2]

So nature pushes forward and upward and there emerges the vital or life-mind in man. The life-mind attaches the utmost importance to the satisfaction of vital nature and existence. The physical or bodily existence is to it a field for the satisfaction of life's impulses and for all kinds of new life-experience. The physical existence gives an opportunity to the life-mind to show its strength, character, power, love, passion, adventure and thus to satisfy all sorts of ambitions. Unlike physical mind, the vital mind is not concerned only with the preservation of body but it utilises body

---

1. *L.D.* Vol. II, Part II, p. 518.
2. *Ibid.*, p. 518.

for the satisfaction and fulfilment of its higher ambitions and ideals. The vital man, according to Sri Aurobindo, "is the man of desire and sensation, the man of force and action, the man of passion and emotion, the kinetic individual: he may and does lay great emphasis on the material existence, but he gives it, even when most preoccupied with its present actualities, a push for life-experience, for force of realisation, for life-extension, for life-power, for life-affirmation and life-expansion which is Nature's first impetus towards enlargement of the being; at a highest intensity of this life impetus, he becomes the breaker of bonds, the seeker of new horizons, the disturber of the past and present in the interest of the future".[1] "His mental life is directed to serve the purpose of his desires and passions. When he takes strong interest in mental things, "he can become the mental adventurer, the opener of the way to new mind formations or the fighter for an idea, the sensitive type of artist, the dynamic poet of life or the prophet or champion of a cause. The vital mind is kinetic and therefore a great force in the working of evolutionary Nature".[2]

Above the level of vital mentality, there is the mental or intellectual plane. It is a plane of pure thought and intelligence to which the things of the mental world are not fictions of imagination but the most important realities. It is the highest level of human mind and constitutes the class of "the philosopher, thinker, scientist, intellectual creator, the man of the idea, the man of the written or spoken word, the idealist and dreamer".[3] The mental man is not only possessed of mind but also has physical and vital interests. He has also the life of feelings, desires and passions and is sometimes also dominated by them. But his constant effort and ambition is to dominate his desires, passions and will and not to be dominated by them. "The mental man," observes Sri Aurobindo, "cannot transform his nature, but he can control and harmonise it and lay on it the law of a mental ideal, impose a balance or a sublimating and refining influence, and give a high consistency to the multipersonal confusion and conflict or the summary patch-work of our divided and half-constructed being".[4] Thus the intellectual plane is the highest summit of human mind short of spirituality.

---

1. *L.D.*, Vol. II, Part II, pp. 519-20.
2. *Ibid.*, p. 520.
3. *Ibid.*, p. 520.
4. *Ibid.*, p. 521.

The physical, the vital and the mental planes are not the three separate planes of human mind but they are the different degrees through which nature has evolved herself to the intellectual status. From her apparently inconscient or half-conscient status, nature has come to her consciousness through these different degrees of mind. Thus they have a great significance from the standpoint of human evolution. As Sri Aurobindo puts it, "These three degrees of mentality, clear in themselves, but most often mixed in our composition, are to our ordinary intelligence only psychological types that happen to have developed, and we do not discover any other significance in them; but in fact they are full of significance, for they are the steps of Nature's evolution of mental being towards its self-exceeding, and, as the thinking mind is the highest step she can now attain, the perfected mental man is the rarest and highest of her normal creatures. To go further she has to bring into the mind and make active in mind, life and body the spiritual principle."[1]

The journey of evolutionary nature does not end with the emergence of man. The real aim of the universal spirit, as has been said above, is to effect a radical transformation of nature. Now this cannot be done even by the highest type of mental or intellectual man. Outwardly, such a man appears to have a well-integrated personality. But this integration is only on the surface. He is not aware of the subconscious, the subliminal, the spiritual and the supramental planes of his being. His surface mentality is only a small fraction of his whole personality. He does not enjoy perfect control over the physical and vital parts of his being. Though the evolution of mental or intellectual man makes a considerable change in the status of nature and gives mental values to it, yet this change is only partial and fragmentary and not integral. Man, as Sri Aurobindo observes, "carries along with him even at his highest elevation the mould of his original animality, the dead weight of subconscience of body, the downward pull of gravitation towards the original Inertia and Nescience, the control of an inconscient material Nature over his conscious evolution, its power of limitation, its law of difficult development, its immense force for retardation and frustration".[2] Thus the mental man presents a strange

---

1. *L.D.*, Vol. II, Part II, pp. 521-22.
2. *Ibid.*, p. 649.

contradiction in his personality. He is possessed of knowledge but he is also possessed of a far greater degree of ignorance. He is able to attain a great deal of control over his mental life, his thoughts, feelings, desires, will and so on. But he has little control over the physical, physiological and vital parts of his being. His mind, life and body are always at war with one another. Thus his personality suffers from inner conflict and contradictions. It is this distressing fact which compels and induces man to aspire for a higher destiny, to exceed his present status. This is possible only when man is able to realise the spiritual principle in his being. He has to evolve out of himself the spiritual man who may effect a radical transformation in his whole being. As Sri Aurobindo puts it, "Thus hampered and burdened mental man has still to evolve out of himself the fully conscious being, a divine manhood or a spiritual and supramental supermanhood which shall be the next product of evolution. That transition will mark the passage from the evolution in the Ignorance to a greater evolution in the Knowledge, founded and proceeding in the light of the Superconscient and no longer in the darkness of the Ignorance and Inconscience."[1]

So far we have discussed only one aspect of evolution—its physical, outward or cosmic aspect. But there is one other aspect of evolution, the evolution of consciousness or the individual soul. In fact it is the evolution of consciousness that is the real aim of nature or of the spirit hidden in nature. The physical evolution is merely an instrument for the evolution of consciousness. But until the emergence of man, the mental or intellectual being, this truth of evolution does not become so clear. As Sri Aurobindo puts it: "In the inner reality of things a change of consciousness was always the major fact, the evolution has always had a spiritual significance and the physical change was only instrumental; but this relation was concealed by the first abnormal balance of the two factors, the body of the external Inconscience outweighing and obscuring in importance the spiritual element, the conscious being. But once the balance has been righted, it is no longer the change of body that must precede the change of consciousness; the consciousness itself by its mutation will necessitate and operate whatever mutation is needed for the body."[2] The evolution of consciousness has

---

1. *L.D.*, Vol. II, Part II, p. 649-50.
2. *Ibid.*, p. 672.

been going on from the very beginning. Thus there takes place a double process in the evolution of cosmos or terrestrial evolution. As Sri Aurobindo observes, "This terrestrial evolutionary working of Nature from Matter to Mind and beyond it has a double process; there is an outward visible process of physical evolution with birth as its machinery—for each evolved form of body housing its own evolved power of consciousness is maintained and kept in continuity by heredity; there is at the same time, an invisible process of soul evolution with rebirth into ascending grade of form and consciousness as its machinery. The first by itself would mean only a cosmic evolution; for the individual would be a quickly perishing instrument, and the race, a more abiding collective formulation, would be the real step in the progressive manifestation of the cosmic Inhabitant, the universal Spirit: rebirth is an indispensable condition for any long duration and evolution of the individual being in the earth existence."[1]

Thus the whole question of individual evolution or soul-evolution centres round the problem of rebirth. If there is merely the evolution of species in nature, then the individual evolution or soul-evolution has got no place at all. The evolution will have only a cosmic significance. Thus the problem of rebirth assumes a considerable importance in Sri Aurobindo's philosophy as the whole question of soul-evolution depends on the solution of this knotty problem. So before proceeding with the question of evolution from the mental to the supramental and the spiritual status, we have first of all to deal with the problem of rebirth and its bearing on the evolution of the individual soul.

(E) *The Problem of Rebirth: Its Bearing on the Evolution of the Individual Soul*

The doctrine of rebirth or transmigration or reincarnation has a long history behind it. It is one of the most ancient and widespread beliefs that has been prevalent among the different peoples belonging to different stages of culture and progress. It was not only a crude, superstitious and animistic belief of the primitive tribes of Asia, Africa and Australia but was also held in common by the

---

1. *L.D.*, Vol. II, Part II, p. 650.

ancient and semi-civilised peoples of Europe and the enlightened philosophers and sages of India and Greece. By rebirth or reincarnation is meant the passage of soul from one body to another body belonging usually to the same species or even to the lower as well as higher species. It means, firstly, that the individual does not disappear altogether with the death of the body. There is something in him called soul or essential substance which survives the death of the body. Secondly, the soul, or essential substance surviving the death of the body is reincarnated or reborn with a different body on earth. The same soul passes from one body to another and thus there remains a continuity between the different lives passed by the soul on earth. It will be interesting to note the different conceptions of rebirth as found in the different philosophical systems of India as well as in the writings of the great Greek philosophers, namely, Pythagoras, Empedocles, Plato, etc.

(i) Rebirth and Greek Philosophy

In Greece, the doctrine of rebirth or transmigration is said to have been first introduced by Pherecydes, who was born about 600 B.C. and is reputed to have been the teacher of Pythagoras. On the other hand, Herodotus declared that this doctrine was not native to Greece but was borrowed from the Egyptians. There are some scholars who hold that this doctrine passed from India to Greece. But the Western scholars generally do not agree to the view of any kind of influence of Indian philosophy on the Greek mind. They think it to have been inherited from the primitive peoples of ancient Europe. "The truth seems to be that a belief in the transmigration of human souls into other bodies after death was a relic inherited from the primitive or savage ancestors of the European peoples. It is expressly attributed to the Gauls and less explicitly to the Thracians and Scythians."[1] But at that time it was confined to particular groups and was not a widespread doctrine. But "it was brought into prominence by the religious upheavel which undoubtedly took place in the 6th cent., and became associated with the worship of Dionysus and the Orphic cults".[2] The concept of rebirth was deeply rooted and attained a great prominence in the

---

1. *Encyclopaedia of Religion and Ethics*, Vol. XII, p. 432.
2. *Ibid.*, p. 432.

Orphic cults. The Orphic mystics believed in the human soul undergoing the cycle of birth and death repeatedly till it attained final release.

But popularly the doctrine of rebirth is associated with Pythagoras. "Much of what has been established as belonging to the Orphics, the imprisonment of the soul in the body as retribution for the past ill deeds, the undeviating recurrence of the cycle of existence, the prospect offered of ultimate escape after purification, and the abstinence from a flesh diet—limited, however, by the reservation that it did not apply to the flesh of such animals as are offered in sacrifice to the Olympian gods—is established for the Pythagorians by not less convincing testimony. It would seem, therefore, that, when founding his brotherhood, Pythagoras appropriated much that was characteristic of contemporary religious asceticism. Nevertheless, the reincarnation of souls in various bodily shapes is so closely associated with the person of Pythagoras that he must be held to have inculcated it with peculiar vigour."[1] Xenophanes in his poems describes Pythagoras as seriously teaching the doctrine of transmigration. Pythagoras did not hesitate to ascribe even reasonable or rational souls to animals but held that the rational element in them could not express itself on account of their deficient organic structure. He believed that the same soul could dwell in the animals as well as in man and that there was a kinship between all living beings. "The punishment of souls for their misdeeds by successive incarnations in corporeal dungeons was a theme developed by the Pythagoreans in a manner hardly separated from the Orphic, and the results of their joint influence are to be found in the Platonic myths."[2]

Empedocles borrowed the doctrine of transmigration from the Orphic-Pythagorean school and deals with it in his poem, entitled-*Purifications*. He tells us of demons, who on account of their evil deeds, "are condemned to wander for thrice ten thousand seasons in all manner of mortal forms through the universe until their sin is expiated; and one of these", he says, 'I now am,' an exile and a wanderer from the gods,....Here is the doctrine of retribution for guilt, and here, too, that of metempsychosis."[3] According to

---

1. *Encyclopaedia of Religion and Ethics*, Vol. XII, p. 433.
2. *Ibid.*, p. 433.
3. *Ibid.*, Vol. V, pp. 293-94.

him, the less base souls among human beings appear in the form of higher animals and plant after death. The best of them become "prophets, bards, physicians and chieftains, and at last return as divine beings to the company of gods".[1] Plato deals with the doctrine of the immortality of souls and their transmigration in several of his dialogues, particularly in the *Phaedo, Phaedrus, Republic* and *Timaeus*. According to him, the souls which have not got rid of the carnal desires and lower passions in the present life are reborn as animals, birds, plants etc. According to the *Phaedo*, "those who in this life have failed to emancipate themselves from the burden of the corporeal element cannot rise to the purer element above, but being dragged down into the visible world haunt burial grounds as ghostly apparitions until they are again imprisoned in another body. Of these the sensual become asses or similar animals, the violent and unjust wolves or kites, but those, who, though lacking the philosophic impulse to virtue, have lived an ordinary respectable life may become bees or ants, or even men who in their next incarnation prove themselves just and moderate".[2] As regards those who devote themselves to philosophy, he states, "Only those who have devoted themselves in this life to philosophy are entirely exempt from any further incarnation and pass to the pure ethereal homes destined for them in the upper world".[3] The souls are also punished for their misdeeds after death and before they are reborn in some other form. In the *Phaedrus,* he says, "the souls of the dead are punished or otherwise treated according to the measure of their human actions for 1000 years, until the period of reincarnation arrives, when they are allowed a limited area of choice, so that it often happens that the soul of a man comes into life as a beast, and that of a beast which had formerly been human again enters into the body of man".[4] In the Timaeus, Plato says, "the creator fashions as many souls as there are stars, and distributes one to each star, in order that later, after a period of contemplation, they may be embodied in human form. If during the time of probation, the soul lived well, he would return to his ethereal habitation, but, if he failed, he would suffer a new incarnation as

---

1. *Encyclopaedia of Religion and Ethics,* Vol. XII, p. 433.
2. *Ibid.,* p. 433.
3. *Ibid.,* p. 433.
4. *Ibid.,* p. 433.

a woman; and, if his wickedness continued, he would sink down among the beasts until his corporeal taints had been thoroughly purged away. In the same dialogue Plato explains the evolution of birds and other animals as arising from the deterioration of human souls".[1] The harmless but light-minded men are born as birds with feathers. In the same way men who never practised virtue and indulged in all sorts of passions and prejudices were reborn as four-footed beasts.

According to Plotinus, the future destiny of the soul depends on its actions in each particular incarnation. The souls which yield to the passions and lower desires go down in the scale of evolution while those which are engaged in the higher pursuits of life rise upward. "Thus he who has exercised his human capacities again becomes a man, but those who have lived by sensation alone become animals. If, without yielding to active passions, they have remained immersed in sluggish perversity, they may even become plants. There is always retribution for an ill-spent life: the bad master becomes a slave, the abuser of wealth a poor man; the man who has murdered his mother becomes a woman and is murdered by a son. On the other hand, those souls which are pure and have lost their attraction to the corporeal will cease to be dependent upon the body. So detached, they will pass to the region of being and the divinity, which cannot be apprehended by a human vision as if it were akin to the corporeal."[2]

Thus it is clear that some of the great Greek philosophers looked upon the doctrine of reincarnation or rebirth as an integral part of the evolution of the immortal souls. Plotinus and the Neo-Platonists also hold the same view. "The doctrine of rebirth," says Dr. Radhakrishnan, "has had a long and influential history. It is cardinal belief of the Orphic religion that the wheel of birth revolves inexorably. Phythagoras, Plato and Empedocles regard rebirth as axiomatic. For them pre-existence and survival stand or fall together. It persists down to the later classical thinkers, Plotinus and the Neo-Platonists."[3]

---

1. *Encyclopaedia of Religion and Ethics*, Vol. XII, p. 433.
2. *Ibid.*, p. 434.
3. *An Idealist View of Life*, p. 286.

(ii) Rebirth and Indian Philosophy

The doctrine of rebirth has been considered as an integral part of Indian Philosophy. This doctrine has been accepted not only by the orthodox schools of Indian Philosophy but also by the Buddhist and the Jain schools. But curiously enough we do not find it mentioned in the Vedas. As Dr. Radhakrishnan says, "The Vedic Aryans entered India in the pride of strength and joy of conquest. They loved life in its fullness. They therefore showed no great interest in the future of the soul. Life to them was bright and joyous, free from all the vexations of a fretful spirit. They were not enamoured of death. They wished for themselves and their posterity a life of a hundred autumns. They had no special doctrines about life after death, though some vague conceptions about heaven and hell could not be avoided by reflective minds. Rebirth is still at a distance."[1] Thus it is clear that though the doctrine of rebirth forms one of the basic tenets of all the schools of Indian Philosophy, yet it did not develop in the Vedas. "The doctrine of the transmigration of souls is in India the presumption which underlies not only Buddhism and Jainism, but also the philosophical systems of the Brāhmaṇas and the whole of Hinduism. In the ancient Vedic period it had as yet no existence. At that time the Indian people were still filled with a keen delight in life and the righteous man looked forward to eternal continuance of existence after death. They believed that good men ascended to heaven to the companionship of gods, and there led a painless existence, free from all earthly imperfections—a happy life which was usually depicted as an enjoyment of sensual pleasures, but was yet occasionally conceived in a higher spiritual sense. The necessary consequence of this belief was the view (very rarely expressed in the Veda) that the souls of the wicked sank down in the abyss of hell. This naive representation of the soul's fate after death experienced a real change when suddenly and without any transitional stages that we can perceive, the Indian people was seized by the oppressive belief in transmigration, which holds it captive to the present day."[2] Whether the "Indian people was seized by the oppressive belief in transmigration" or whether it was a fundamental and momentous discovery made by the Indian mind in the course of evolution,

1. *Indian Philosophy*, Vol. I, pp. 113-14.
2. *Encyclopaedia of Religion and Ethics*, Vol. XII, p. 434.

on the solid foundations of experience and reason, will be made clear when we come to deal with Sri Aurobindo's view of rebirth or transmigration. In the Brāhmaṇas, we find some glimpses of the doctrine of rebirth. "In the Brāhmaṇas," observes Dr. Radhakrishnan, "we do not find any one view about the future life. The distinction between the path of the fathers and that of the devas is given. Rebirth on earth is sometimes looked upon as blessing and not an evil to be escaped from. It is promised as a reward for knowing some divine mystery. But the most dominant view is that of immortality in heaven, the abode of the gods".[1] The Brāhmaṇas hold that the souls are rewarded or punished in the other world according to their actions done in the earthly life. But the wicked neither suffer eternal punishment nor the good enjoy eternal bliss. When the soul completes its period of reward or punishment, it is born again on earth. "The natural rhythm by which life gives birth to death and death to life leads us to the conception of a beginningless and endless circuit."[2] Now the true ideal is regarded as redemption from the bondage of birth and death. Those who study Vedas are said to be freed from the cycle of birth and death. "The Brāhmaṇas," says Dr. Radhakrishnan, "contain all the suggestions necessary for the development of the doctrine of rebirth. They are, however, only suggestions, while individual immortality is the main tendency. It is left for the Upaniṣads to systematise these suggestions into the doctrine of rebirth".[3]

The Upaniṣads specially the two great Upaniṣads, namely, the *Chāndogya* and the *Bṛhadāraṇyaka,* give a vivid description of the souls after death and of their rebirth in the world. They take their stand on the Vedas but make a definite advancement in their different conceptions regarding the nature of man, the world and gods or Godhead. This we find true in the case of the doctrine of rebirth also. "No philosophy" as Dr. Radhakrishnan puts it, "could discard its past. The Upaniṣad theory of future life had to reckon with the old Vedic doctrine of rewards and punishments in another world. The conservative spirit of man tried to combine the new idea of rebirth with the earlier eschatology, which spoke

---

1. *Indian Philosophy*, Vol. I, p. 133.
2. *Ibid.*, p. 135 (*Ait.* iii, 44)
3. *Ibid.*, pp. 135-36.

of the joyous world of the spirits of the dead where Yama presided and the joyless regions of darkness. This led to a complication of the Upaniṣad theory which had to distinguish three ways after death".[1] The two ways mentioned in the Upaniṣad by which a departed soul proceeds to enjoy the fruits of *karma* done in its lifetime on earth are called the *devayāna* or the *arcirmārga* or the path of light and the other *pitryāna* or the *dhūmamārga*, the path of smoke and darkness. He who goes by the *devayāna* does not return to this world but he who goes by the *pitryāna*, comes back to the earth after enjoying the fruits of his acts. "The *devayāna* and *pitryāna*," observes Dr. Radhakrishnan, "correspond to the kingdom of light and the kingdom of darkness or *ajñāna*, which involves us in *Saṅsāra*."[2] But those souls who do not follow either the path of gods or that of fathers have to undergo the process of birth and death repeatedly."[3] But the liberated souls who realise perfect identity with Brahmana do not have to go anywhere. They become Brahman in reality. The soul which is without desires, which is free from desires, has obtained the objects of its desire, and to which all the objects of desire are but the self—the vital force or the organs of such a soul do not depart. Being Brahman, it is merged or identified with Brahman.[4] But the soul which is not free from desires and attachment has to transmigrate and undergo the process of birth and death. After enjoying the fruits of *karma* or action done in its life on earth it comes back again to this world to engage itself in new and fresh activities.[5] The birth of a soul in a higher or lower order of society or the scale of evolution depends on its actions done in the previous life. Those whose conduct has been good will quickly attain good birth in a higher order of Brāhmaṇa, Kṣatriya or Vaiśya. But those who perform evil deeds quickly attain an evil birth, the birth of a dog, a hog, or a *caṇḍāla*.[6]

---

1. *Indian Philosophy*, Vol. I, p. 252.
2. *Ibid.*, Vol. I, p. 253.
3. अथैतयो: पथोर्न कतरेण च न तानीमानि क्षुद्राण्यसकृदावर्तीनि भूतानि भवन्ति जायस्व
   म्रियस्वेत्येतत्तृतीयं स्थानम्... । (*Chān*. V.10.8)
4. योऽकामो निष्काम आप्तकाम आत्मकामो न तस्य प्राणा उत्क्रामन्ति, ब्रह्मैव सन्ब्रह्माप्येति।
   (*Bṛh*. 4.46)
5. *Bṛh*. 4.46.
6. *Chān*. V.10.7.

Thus we find that the doctrine of rebirth attained sufficient development in the Upaniṣads. The Upaniṣads show the cause of rebirth and also show the way of getting release from the cycle of birth and death. Now from this time on, we find this doctrine given a place of supreme importance by all the schools of Indian Philosophy with a single exception of the materialist or Cārvāka school. In Jainism we find a great emphasis laid on the doctrine of *karma* and rebirth. There is a continuous influx (*āsrava*) of *karma* into the soul. In the ordinary state, a soul harbours passions (*kaṣāya*) and this passion leads to the influx of *karma*. Each action done by the soul 'produces some *karma*, good, bad or indifferent'. This *karma* produces certain painful, or pleasant or indifferent conditions and events which the individual in question has to experience. Now when a particular *karma* has produced its effect, it vanishes from the soul. The soul which is on the path of liberation gets rid of all *karmas* in this way and does not allow new *karmas* to arise. Thus when all the *karmas* are purged out from the soul, when all passions cease, the individual gets liberation. Then he is no more born in this world. But this highest state of spirit is attained only by the few. In the usual course of things the purging of old *karmas* and the influx of new *karmas* go on simultaneously and thus the individual is never able to get rid of the bondage of matter and has to undergo the cycle of birth and death. This is the process of *saṁsāra*. This cycle of birth and death goes on till the individual attains liberation.

In Buddhism also we find the doctrine of rebirth given a place of great importance. Though Buddhism does not believe in any such permanent entity called soul or spirit, yet it believes in the doctrine of rebirth. What is ordinarily called soul or spirit is, according to Buddhism, nothing but the stream or flux of conscious states. This stream of conscious mental states constitutes the personality or individuality of man. Now this flux or stream of conscious states is carried on in accordance with the law of *karma*. When a man dies, it is not the soul that migrates from one body to another. The only continuity that Buddhism admits is that of character or disposition. "There is no such thing in Buddhism," says Dr. Radhakrishnan, "as the migration of soul or the passage of an individual from life to life. When a man dies, his physical organism, which is the basis of his psychical dissolves, and so the physical life comes to an end. It is not the dead man who comes to rebirth but another. There is no soul to migrate. It is the character that continues".[1] Now it is this character or disposition left as a residue after death, that becomes the cause of rebirth. "Buddhism," observes Dr. Radhakrishnan, "does not explain the mechanism by which the continuity of *karma* is maintained between two lives separated by the phenomenon of death. It simply assumes it. We are told that the successive lives are linked by a chain of natural causation. The resulting character builds up a new individuality which gravitates automatically to the state of life for which it is fitted".[2] This resulting character is due to the attachment of the individual. This desire or clinging to existence goes on creating new *karmas*. So as long as the desires and *karmas* continue, the cycle of birth also goes on. "The man who is reborn," says Dr. Radhakrishnan, "is the heir of the action of the dead man. Yet he is a new being. While there is no permanent identity there is at the same time no annihilation or cutting off. The new being is what its acts have made it".[3] Thus it is clear that the doctrine of rebirth forms an integral part of Buddhist philosophy and religion. The whole history of the individual is not exhausted in a single birth. As Dr. Radhakrishnan characteristically puts it, "The history of an individual does not begin at his birth, but has been for ages in the making."[4] The wheel of *saṁsāra* consisting of repeated births according to Buddhism goes on till the *nirvāṇa* or liberation is attained.

The doctrine of rebirth has been accepted in no uncertain terms by all the schools of Vedānta. The journey of the individual soul does not stop with the end of body. The soul is considered as different from body and mind. Unlike Buddhism, the Vedānta does not consider soul as a conglomeration of mental states. The soul according to the Vedāntins survives the death of the body, and, due to the force of the desires and *karmas*, is born in other bodies. The wheel of birth and death goes on till the individual attains liberation. The Advaita Vedānta does not regard the individual soul as ultimately real. The individual soul is, according to it, nothing but Brahman in reality. It assumes the form of individuality on

---

1. *Indian Philosophy*, Vol. I, p. 444.
2. *Ibid.*, p. 444.
3. *Ibid.*, p. 446.
4.. *Ibid.*, p. 441.

account of its false identification with the body-mind organism. The soul has to suffer repeated birth and death so long as it remains attached to the organism and is bound by desires and actions. But the moment it realises its real nature and considers itself as separate from the psycho-physical organism, it is freed forever from the wheel of births or *saṁsāra*.

In the same way, the doctrine of rebirth, as has been already said, has been accepted without question by all other schools of Indian philosophy such as the Nyāya, Sāṁkhya, Mīmāṁsā etc. It is for them in a way an article of faith. They do not feel even the need of advancing cogent arguments in support of this theory or doctrine. The survival of the individual soul of the death of the body and its rebirth in other bodies has been regarded as necessary and inevitable for the evolution of the individual soul. The goal of man's destiny is not attained in a single flight. The soul has to fly many times from the cage of the body before it attains liberation and reaches its destination. So the evolution of the individual soul and consciousness mainly depends on the doctrine of rebirth. If this doctrine is not accepted, the conception of the evolution of the individual soul will become meaningless. Thus the problem of the evolution of the individual soul stands or falls with the doctrine of rebirth. It is for this very reason that we find Sri Aurobindo laying a very great emphasis on the problem of rebirth and giving cogent arguments in support of this ancient doctrine.

(iii) *Sri Aurobindo's Conception of Rebirth*

"Rebirth," observes Sri Aurobindo, "is an indispensable machinery for the working out of a spiritual evolution; it is the only possible effective condition, the obvious dynamic process of such a manifestation in the material universe".[1] The universe is, according to Sri Aurobindo, the manifestation of Saccidānanda. By a process of self-concentration, Saccidānanda has manifested itself in an apparent inconscient. Thus the stage of inconscient or that of matter is the stage of self-forgetfulness of Saccidānanda. The spirit hidden in matter has to come to its self-awareness through the process of evolution. Whereas the process of involution was followed by the

---

1. *L.D.*, Vol. II, Part II, p. 563.

limitation and attenuation of consciousness of spirit, the process of evolution follows the reverse process of self-expansion of spiritual consciousness. Thus the process of evolution, as has been pointed out above, is nothing but the coming to self-awareness of spirit hidden in matter. It is the evolution of matter into spirit, of inconscience into consciousness and of ignorance into knowledge. The inconscient nature or cosmos has to release the higher powers of consciousness hidden within it in order to rise to the spiritual status. Now this rediscovery by nature of its lost self or consciousness is possible only through an individual being. "It is through the conscious individual," says Sri Aurobindo, "that this rediscovery is possible; it is in him that the evolving consciousness becomes organised and capable of awaking to its own reality".[1] It means that the universe or universal nature comes to its self-consciousness only through the individuals. It is the individual who gives real and higher values to universe or nature. Hence the individuality has a great significance. As Sri Aurobindo puts it, "The immense importance of the individual being, which increases as he rises in the scale, is the most remarkable and significant fact of a universe which started without consciousness and without individuality in an undifferentiated Nescience."[2] Thus the individual is no less real than the cosmos. Both the individual as well as the cosmos are to be regarded as the power of the eternal Being. Now this immense importance of the individual makes the conception of rebirth also necessary. The rebirth, according to Sri Aurobindo, "is no longer a possible machinery which may or may not be accepted; it becomes a necessity, an inevitable outcome of the root nature of our existence".[3]

Individuality, according to Sri Aurobindo, cannot be supported as an illusory phenomenon created on account of the false identification of spirit or Ātman with the psychophysical organism, as the Māyāvādins would have us believe. The individual is, according to Sri Aurobindo, a persistent reality, an eternal portion or power of the Eternal. It is through the growth of individual's consciousness that the supreme Spirit discloses its being and nature

---

1. *L.D.*, Vol. II, Part II, p. 564.
2. *Ibid.*, p. 564.
3. *Ibid.*, p. 565.

comes to its self-consciousness. "Then, secure behind all the changings of our personality," says Sri Aurobindo, "upholding the stream of its mutations, there must be a true Person, a real spiritual individual, a true Purusha."[1] If there were no need of the self-finding or self-discovery by the spirit hidden in matter of its own essential nature, then evolution and rebirth need not have come into operation. But the spirit, as we know, has lost its original unity in its play of multiplicity and finds itself in the state of utter forgetfulness and inconscience in the stage of matter. Hence it is only by means of evolution that the spirit hidden in nature is able to transform its inconscience into consciousness and it is by means of birth in the body that the spirit is able to develop its consciousness and attain unity with the cosmos and the supreme reality.

"Birth," as Sri Aurobindo puts it, "is a necessity of the manifestation of the Purusha on the physical plane; but his birth, whether the human or any other, cannot be in this world-order an isolated accident or a sudden excursion of a soul into physicality without any preparing past to it or any fulfilling hereafter".[2] "In a world of involution and evolution," further observes Sri Aurobindo, "not of physical form only, but of conscious being through life and mind to spirit, such an isolated assumption of life in the human body could not be the rule of the individual soul's existence; it would be a quite meaningless and inconsequential arrangement, a freak for which the nature and system of things here have no place, a contrary violence which would break the rhythm of the Spirit's self-manifestation. The intrusion of such a rule of individual soul life into an evolutionary spiritual progression would make it an effect without cause and a cause without effect; it would be a fragmentary present without a past or a future".[3] It means that the emergence of a soul in a physical form does not take place all of a sudden. It must have had a past history of development and a possibility of further development in future. The life of the individual must have the same law of progression as the cosmic life. It cannot also be admitted that the soul assumes birth in the human form only once and that it was living in some other world

---

1. *L.D.*, Vol. II, Part II, p. 565.
2. *Ibid.*, p. 567.
3. *Ibid.*, p. 567.

THE INTEGRAL ADVAITISM OF SRI AUROBINDO

or plane prior to its birth and will go to some other plane or world after death. "For here life upon earth, life in the physical universe," observes Sri Aurobindo, "is not and cannot be a casual perch for the wanderings of the soul from world to world; it is a great and slow development needing, as we know now, incalculable spaces of Time for its evolution".[1] The evolution of soul in the world takes place gradually from one grade to another grade. The soul does not begin its existence in human life. It was present in the grades below the human level and it rises to the grades of existence and consciousness above the human level. It means that the journey of the soul in the world does not come to an end with a single birth in human form but that it undergoes the process of rebirth all along its progress to the higher grades of existence. As Sri Aurobindo puts it, "This ascent can only take place by rebirth within the ascending order; an individual visit coming across it and progressing on some other line elsewhere could not fit into the system of this evolutionery existence."[2]

"The human birth in this world is," as Sri Aurobindo puts it, "on its spiritual side a complex of two elements, a spiritual person and soul of personality; the former is man's eternal being, the latter is his cosmic and mutable being".[3] With this two-fold spiritual nature, man is able to maintain his identity and contact both with the Absolute and the world. As Sri Aurobindo says, "As a spirit he is one with the Transcendence which is immanent in the world and comprehensive of it; as a soul he is at once one with and part of the universality of Sachchidananda self-expressed in the world; his self-expression must go through the stages of the cosmic expression, his soul-experience follow the revolutions of the wheel of Brahman in the universe."[4] The cosmic self-expression and the individual self-expression are the two aspects of the evolutionary process. The individual soul-experience and self-development follows the process of cosmic evolution. It means that as the spirit hidden in the cosmos has revealed itself through the various grades and sub-grades of matter, life, mind and intellect, so the individual soul also must have presided over the lower forms of life before it took up the human evolution.

1. *L.D.*, Vol. II, Part II, p. 568.
2. *Ibid.*, p. 568.
3. *Ibid.*, p. 568.
4. *Ibid.*, p. 569.

"To suppose otherwise," says Sri Aurobindo, "would be to suppose that the spirit which now presides over the human soul-experience was originally formed by a human mentality and the human body, exists by that and cannot exist apart from it, cannot ever go below or above it. In fact it would then be reasonable to suppose that it is not immortal but has come into existence by the appearance of the human mind and body in the evolution and would disappear by their disappearance".[1] "But body and mind," further observes Sri Aurobindo, "are not the creators of the spirit; the spirit is the creator of the mind and body; it develops these principles out of its being, it is not developed into being out of them, it is not a compound of their elements or a resultant of their meeting".[2] The spirit manifests itself into different forms and grades in the course of its evolutionary development. It is not fixed to humanity. "The soul" says Sri Aurobindo, "is not bound by the formula of mental humanity; it did not begin with that and will not end with it; it had a prehuman past, it has a superhuman future".[3]

Now the question is, whether the soul when it attains the human status after a long succession of rebirths in the lower grades of life can again revert to the animal life and body as the old popular theories of transmigration believed? Sri Aurobindo answers this question in the negative. "It seems impossible," he observes, "that it should go back with any entirety, and for this reason that the transit from animal to human life means a decisive conversion of consciousness, quite as decisive as the conversion of the vital consciousness of the plant into the mental consciousness of the animal. It is surely impossible that a conversion so decisive made by Nature should be reversed by the soul and the decision of the spirit within her come, as it were, to naught."[4] This reversion to the lower grades of life may be possible in the case of those souls in whom the conversion was not decisive and who had developed so far as to attain the human status but had not evolved far enough to maintain their existence in human form, to adapt themselves to the human type of consciousness or in another case, the human soul may revert to animal status for a temporary period if it is

---

1. *L.D.*, Vol. II, Part II, p. 570.
2. *Ibid.*, p. 570.
3. *Ibid.*, p. 571.
4. *Ibid.*, p. 572.

overpowered by certain animal propensities and has to satisfy them in entirety in a separate manner. "The movement of Nature," observes Sri Aurobindo, "is always sufficiently complex for us to deny dogmatically such a possibility, and, if it be a fact, then there may exist this modicum of truth behind the exaggerated popular belief which assumes an animal rebirth of the soul once lodged in man to be quite as normal and possible as a human reincarnation. But whether the animal reversion is possible or not, the normal law must be the recurrence of birth in new human forms for a soul that has once become capable of humanity".[1]

But now the question is, why should we believe in a succession of human births and not in one alone? The answer is that "the soul has not finished what it has to do by merely developing into humanity; it has still to develop that humanity into its higher possibilities".[2] The same reasons which made the soul pass through a succession of births in the lower grades of existence before reaching the human status, make the human soul pass through a further succession of human births in order to attain a higher status of consciousness. The soul of a primitive man, or of a vitalistic European or of an Asiatic peasant cannot be said to have developed and exhausted all the possibilities of human development. The soul of even a Plato or a Śaṅkara cannot be said to "mark the crown and therefore the end of the outflowering of the spirit in man". "There may be a higher or at least a larger possibility, says Sri Aurobindo, 'which the Divine intends yet to realise in man, and if so, it is the steps built by these highest souls which were needed to compose the way up to it and to open the gates. At any rate this present highest status at least must be reached before we can write finish on the recurrence of the human birth for the individual".[3] At present, mind outwardly represents the highest status of consciousness in man. Even the spirit of man when realised by him, manifests itself through the mind. But there are other and higher dynamic grades of consciousness present in a latent way in man. They have also to evolve and manifest themselves in man. Hence the evolution of soul cannot stop by attaining to the highest status of mental or intellectual development or realising the spirit

1. *L.D.*, Vol. II, Part II, p. 573.
2. *Ibid.*, p. 573.
3. *Ibid.*, p. 574.

within. The successions of rebirths of human soul through higher and higher forms will continue till the supramental status is reached and mind is transformed, transmuted and replaced by the supermind. As Sri Aurobindo puts it, "If supermind also is a power of consciousness concealed here in the evolution, the line of rebirth cannot stop even there; it cannot cease in its ascent before the mental has been replaced by the supramental nature and an embodied supramental being becomes the leader of terrestrial existence."[1]

This is, according to Sri Aurobindo, the rational and philosophical foundation for a belief in rebirth. We can now see that the belief in rebirth is not based on a flight of imagination but on the solid foundations of reason. It is an inevitable logical conclusion "if there exists at the same time an evolutionary principle in the Earth-Nature and a reality of the individual soul born into evolutionary Nature".[2] Though the doctrine of rebirth is upheld by all the schools of Indian Philosophy excepting the materialists, yet its purpose has not been explained so well in other systems as it has been done by Sri Aurobindo. Māyāvāda and Buddhism do not believe in the reality and immortality of the individual soul, hence the doctrine of rebirth seems to have no real justification in their systems. The liberation of the individual soul loses all meaning if the soul itself is ultimately called unreal or a mere flux of conscious states. "There can be no theory of rebirth without a theory of immortality of the individual soul and the acceptance of rebirth in their systems (such as Māyāvāda, Buddhism etc.) is unwarranted."[3] The realistic systems of Vedānta which believe in the reality of the individual souls have also not been able to explain satisfactorily the purpose of rebirth. "The purpose of the individual atomic soul in trying to achieve its real nature of immortality and through the process of rebirths into matter and other lower forms of life is not explained as adequately as may be desired in the philosophies of realistic Vedānta. If Māyā had been inexplicable in Māyāvāda, it is no less true of the Karma."[4]

1. *L.D.*, Vol. II, Part II, p. 574.
2. *Ibid.*, p. 575.
3. Dr. K.C Varadachari, *The Individual Self in the Philosophy of Sri Aurobindo*, Sri Aurobindo Mandir Annual (1943), p. 24.
4. *Ibid.*, p. 25.

Sri Aurobindo has been able to explain the purpose of rebirth in a better way than others due to the fact that he believes in the evolution of not only the individual but of the whole of cosmos towards a spiritual status. Nature is able to discover, as has been stated above, its lost self-consciousness only through the individual. "It is only through the conscious individual," to quote again Sri Aurobindo, that this rediscovery is possible; it is in him that the evolving consciousness becomes organised and capable of awaking to its own reality.[1] The individual consciousness cannot attain its highest status in a single birth. Hence the conception of rebirth becomes a logical necessity. Rebirth "is as necessary as birth itself; for without it birth would be an initial step without sequel, the starting of a journey without its farther steps and arrival. It is rebirth that gives to the birth of an incomplete being in a body its promise of completeness and its spiritual significance".[2]

The evolution of nature from matter to mind does not mark the apex of evolutionary process. It is an evolution in and through ignorance. In order to attain culmination, evolution has to proceed upwards to attain the supramental status. It can be done only when the supermind makes a descent into earth-consciousness and effects a radical transformation by its consciousness and power. So now we proceed to trace the course of evolution from mind to supermind, and show what stages nature has still to cross before the descent of the Supermind takes place.

---

1. *L.D.*, Vol. II, Part II, p. 564.
2. *Ibid.*, p. 575.

CHAPTER X

EVOLUTION FROM MIND TO SUPERMIND AND SACCIDĀNANDA: THE TRIPLE TRANSFORMATION

We have so far traced the evolution of the cosmos from matter to mind. We have also seen that along with the cosmic evolution there also takes place an evolution of the individual soul through the process of rebirth. But this process takes place in a latent manner. We are generally aware only of the cosmic evolution and not of the evolution of the individual soul. Upto the stage of mind, our attention is directed more towards the external side of evolution rather than to the internal one. The physical change, the evolution of the higher and better types of objects commands greater attention at this stage than the evolution of consciousness. But the real aim of evolutionary nature is, according to Sri Aurobindo, the evolution of consciousness. So when the stage of mind has been reached and the evolution of mental consciousness in man has attained a sufficient development, the attention of evolutionary nature is directed towards a major change in consciousness latent in man and greater than the mental consciousness. Man, as has been shown above, is not able to effect a perfect integration of his personality even at the highest development of his intellect. He is faced with discords and contradictions in his own personality. He feels constantly the unbearable weight of ignorance, incapacity and evil. So he becomes discontented with his present mental or intellectual status and wants to exceed his limitations. Man becomes acutely conscious of his limitations and so wants to get rid of them at any cost. He attains freedom from these limitations by the realisation of his self or spirit. But in this way, though his spirit is liberated and rises beyond the limitations of his physical nature, yet the physical side of his being, his psycho-physical organism still suffers from bondage and limitations of external nature. So the liberation of spirit in this respect is partial. This is not the whole aim of evolutionary nature according to Sri Aurobindo. The aim of evolution is to effect a radical and integral transformation of the whole personality of man. This is not possible by the realisation of spirit by itself but by the descent of the supramental principle in man. But the mental man cannot make an ascent to the Supermind and bring down its light and powers into the terrestrial existence in a single jump. For the gulf between mind and supermind has to be bridged and the lines of ascent and descent have to be created before the supramental descent takes place. This can be done according to Sri Aurobindo only by the triple transformation, namely, the psychic, the spiritual and the supramental transformation. As he puts it, "there must first be the psychic change, the conversion of our whole present nature into a soul-instrumentation; on that or along with that there must be the spiritual change, the descent of a higher light, knowledge, Power, Force, Bliss, Purity into the whole being, even into the lowest recesses of the life and body, even into the darkness of our subconscience; last, there must supervene the supramental trans-mutation—there must take place as the crowning movement the ascent into the supermind and the transforming descent of the supramental consciousness into our entire being and nature".[1]

So we now proceed to discuss the nature of the triple trans-formation. First of all, we take up the psychic change or psychic transformation.

(A) *The Psychic Transformation*
Man is not ordinarily aware of his soul. There is a peculiar paradox that the individual exists by the soul but he is not normally aware of it. He considers himself an embodied being, a psycho-physical

---

1. *L.D.*, Vol. II, Part II, p. 729.

organism. The soul remains hidden beneath his personality. The soul constitutes the real essence of our personality. The other parts of our personality are not only mutable but perishable; and the soul or psychic entity in us persists and is fundamentally the same always. It contains in a potential manner all the essential possibilities of our manifestation but is not constituted by them. It is according to Sri Aurobindo, "the permanent being in us, puts forth and uses mind, life and body as its instruments, undergoes the envelopment of their conditions, but it is the other and greater than its members".[1] It is "not limited by what it manifests, not contained by the incomplete forms of the manifestation, not tarnished by the imperfections and impurities, the defects and depravations of the surface being. It is an ever-pure flame of the divinity in things and nothing that comes to it, nothing that enters into our experience can pollute its purity or extinguish the flame".[2] The soul is perfectly luminous and so, unlike our mind, it is immediately, intimately and directly aware of truth, good and beauty. Sri Aurobindo divides the central being of man into two forms. The upper which he calls the Jīvātman is our true being and is a portion of the divine Being or Paramātman. Its chief characteristic is that it stands above the empirical existence and presides over it. It is a transcendent principle and is not affected by the evolutionary process. The lower form is the soul or psychic being which acts as a representative of the Jīvātman in the psycho-physical organism and supports its activity. "The phrase central being in our Yoga is," observes Sri Aurobindo, "usually applied to the portion of the Divine in us which supports all the rest and survives through death and birth. This central being has two forms—above, it is Jivatman, our true being, of which we become aware when the higher knowledge comes—below, it is the psychic being which stands behind mind, body and life. The Jivatman is above the manifestation in life and presides over it; the psychic being stands behind the manifestation in life and supports it".[3] The soul or the psychic being, according to Sri Aurobindo, "is a flame born out of the Divine and, luminous inhabitant of the Ignorance, grows in it till it is able to turn it towards the knowledge. It is the concealed witness and control, the hidden Guide, the Daemon of Socrates,

---

1. *L.D.*, Vol. II, Part II, p. 730.
2. *Ibid.*, p. 730.
3. *Lights on Yoga*, p. 16.

the inner light or inner voice of the mystic. It is that which endures and is imperishable in us from birth to birth, untouched by death, decay or corruption, an indestructible spark of the Divine. Not the unborn Self or Atman, for the Self even in presiding over the existence of the individual is aware always of its universality and transcendence, it is yet its deputy in the forms of Nature, the individual soul, *caitya puruṣa,* supporting mind, life and body, standing behind the mental, the vital, the subtle physical being in us and watching and profiting by their development and experience".[1]

The first step towards an integral transformation and complete dynamisation of Nature consists in bringing the veiled psychic entity to our surface consciousness and making it an active principle of our life and existence. Psychicisation means the illumination of the surface mind, life and body by the light from within. "Psychicisation means psychic change of the lower nature, bringing right vision into the mind, right impulse and feeling into the vital, right movement and habit into the physical—all turned towards the Divine, all based on love, devotion and adoration—and finally, the true vision and sense of the dynamic Divine (the Mother) everywhere in the world as well as in the heart. When the psychic comes to the front and assumes the reins of administration, progress in Integral Yoga is enormously accelerated and there is a sure and quick movement towards the dynamic realisation of the Truth. It is the psychicisation which can effectuate a true integration or harmonisation of our being because the psychic entity is the central principle of integration within us."[2]

If the soul had not been a veiled part of ourselves, then the human evolution would have been rapid and smooth and not the difficult, chequered and disfigured development it now is. But the soul at first supports the natural evolution keeping itself behind the surface personality. It supports the evolution of body and mind and gathers the essence of all our mental, vital and bodily experience. The evolution of soul goes on from birth to birth. But in the early material and vital stages of the evolution of being, there is no consciousness of the soul. Even the mind so long as it is primitive and not properly developed does not have any

1. *L.D.,* Vol. I, p. 284.
2. Haridas Chaudhary, *Sri Aurobindo: The Prophet of Life Divine,* pp. 88-89.

consciousness of the soul. It does not mean that the soul does not exist in men of undeveloped minds or primitive men and animals. The soul exists and forms the substratum of even what we call inanimate objects or matter. The soul does not reveal its existence in matter. Similarly it does not manifest itself outwardly in the animals and undeveloped men. But as the evolution proceeds, the soul or psychic entity begins to exert its influence on our personality. It begins to take form and puts forward or develops a soul personality called by Sri Aurobindo the psychic being or *Caitya Puruṣa*. As the psychic being grows and develops, it begins to influence man's thoughts, feelings and actions. Though it still exists behind the veil of the surface mind, yet it begins to exert an influence on the outer or surface consciousness. Now man begins to be dimly aware of something that can be called a soul as distinct from mind, life and body. "A certain sensitive feeling for all that is true and good and beautiful, fine and pure and noble, a response to it, a demand for it, a pressure on mind and life to accept and formulate it in our thought, feelings, conduct, character is the most usually recognised, the most general and characteristic, though not the sole sign of this influence of the psyche. Of the man who has not this element in him or does not respond at all to this urge, we say that he has no soul. For it is this influence that we can most easily recognise as a finer or even a diviner part in us and the most powerful for the slow turning towards some aim at perfection in our nature."[1]

The psychic being or soul personality does not emerge full grown and luminous. It grows and develops, as has been said above, through the process of evolution. At first its influence on the external or surface mind and personality is very much hampered and diminished by the obstructions put by our vital desires, cravings and instincts—the products of ignorance. Man is generally a slave to his habits, desires, passions, his narrow and imperfect ideals etc. So naturally he is not at first inclined to accept any new thought, any higher ideals however enobbling and perfect they may be. So whatever new light or higher thoughts, feelings and ideals our surface consciousness gets from the psychic being, it twists in its own pattern and thus forms a very limited, distorted and imperfect view of it. Thus the true psychic light is "diminished

---

1. *L.D.*, Vol. II, Part II, p. 732.

or distorted in the mind into a mere idea or opinion, the psychic
feeling in the heart into a fallible emotion or mere sentiment, the
psychic will to action in the life parts into a blind vital enthusiasm
or a fervid excitement....".[1] But as the psychic personality develops
more and grows stronger, it transmits its intimations to the surface
personality with a greater purity and force. It begins to mould our
whole personality in its own pattern, that is, in accordance with
its own light, knowledge and force.

Ordinarily man is not aware of his soul. He enjoys a more or
less integration of his personality in his surface consciousness. But
this integration of our normal personality is, according to Sri
Aurobindo, far from being perfect and real integration. Even the
highest type of integration effected by mind proves to be only a
partial and limited one. Mind is not able to integrate and harmonise
all the parts of one's being in a sound and perfect manner. "Mind
in spite of its power," observes Sri Aurobindo, "is often impotent
before the inconscient and subconscient which obscure its clarity
and carry it away on the tide of instinct or impulse; in spite of its
clarity it is fooled by vital and emotional suggestions into giving
sanction to ignorance and error, to wrong thought and to wrong
action, or it is obliged to look on while the nature follows what
it knows to be wrong, dangerous or evil. Even when it is strong,
clear and dominant, Mind though it imposes a certain, a consid-
erable mentalised harmony cannot integrate the whole being and
nature".[2] The fundamental discoveries of modern psychology like
those of Freud, Jung and others have proved beyond any shadow
of doubt that our mind or surface consciousness is merely a frac-
tion of our total consciousness and is merely a tool in the hands
of the subsconscious or the unconscious parts of our being. The
first step towards a true integration or harmonisation, according to
Sri Aurobindo, is achieved by finding the real centre of our being,
our soul or psychic entity. "For the true central being," says Sri
Aurobindo, "is the soul, but this being stands back and in most
human nature is only the secret witness or one might say, a
constitutional ruler who allows his ministers to rule for him,

1. *L.D.*, Vol. II, Part II, p. 734.
2. *Ibid.*, p. 740.

delegates to them his empire, silently assents to their decisions and only now and then puts in a word which they at any moment override and act otherwise. But this is so long as the soul personality put forward by the psychic entity is not yet sufficiently developed; when this is strong enough for the inner entity to impose itself through it, then the soul can come forward and control the nature. It is by the coming forward of this true monarch and his taking up of the reins of government that there can take place a real harmonisation of our being and our life".[1]

Sri Aurobindo lays great stress on the necessity of self-surrender to the Divine. The path of spirituality is attended by numerous dangers. The dangers can be surmounted only "if there is or there grows up a complete sincerity, a will for purity, a readiness for obedience to the Truth, for surrender to the Highest, a readiness to lose or to subject to a divine yoke the limiting and self-affirming ego".[2] He says elsewhere, "It is necessary if you want to progress in your sadhana that you should make the submission and surrender of which you speak sincere, real and complete. This cannot be as long as you mix up your desires with your spiritual aspiration. It cannot be as long as you cherish vital attachment to family, child or anybody else. If you are to do this Yoga, you must have only one desire and aspiration, to receive the spiritual Truth and manifest it in all your thoughts, feelings, actions and nature."[3] "In the practice of Yoga," says Sri Aurobindo, "what you aim at can only come by the opening of the being to the Mother's force and the persistent rejection of all egoism and demand and desire, all motives except the aspiration for the Divine Truth".[4]

So the emergence of the psychic being or soul takes place when the surface personality of man gets rid of all kinds of egoistic desires, passions, prejudices, deficiencies and weakness by making a self-surrender to the Divine and by making an approach to the Divine through mind, heart and will. The surface consciousness or the ego-consciousness is now totally replaced by the self-consciousness of the soul or the psychic being. The soul now

1. *L.D.*, Vol. II, Part II, p. 741.
2. *Ibid.*, p. 747.
3. *More Lights on Yoga*, pp. 58-59.
4. *Bases of Yoga*, p. 39.

manifests itself as the central being which consciously supports life, mind and body and serves as the guide and ruler of the nature. Now the human actions are not directed simply by the mind but by the soul. The human personality is not now a mental prsonality but a psychic personality. Now it is not the mind that receives the stimulus from the outer world and makes a response to it, but it is the soul that is directly connected in all our thoughts, feelings and actions. The soul now repels all that is false, obscure and opposed to the divine realisation. Now "every region of the being, every nook and corner of it, every movement, formation, direction, inclination of thought, will, emotion, sensation, action, reaction, motive, disposition, propensity, desire, habit of the conscious or the subconscious physical, even the most concealed, camouflaged, mute, recondite is lighted up with the unerring psychic light, their confusions dissipated, their tangles disentangled, their obscurities, deceptions, self-deceptions precisely indicated and removed; all is purified, set-right, the whole nature harmonised, modulated in the psychic key, put in spiritual order".[1] This process of purification and enlightenment of the whole organism goes on unalteringly till it is ready to receive all kinds of spiritual experiences and mould itself in their light and truth. The human organism is finally delivered from "the darkness and stubbornness of the tamasic inertia, the turbidities and turbulences and impurities of the rajasic passion and restless unharmonised kinetism, the enlightened rigidities and sattwic limitations or poised balancements of constructed equilibrium which are the character of the ignorance".[2] But this is not all. This is only the first result of soul's emergence. The second and the positive result is, according to Sri Aurobindo, "a free inflow of all kinds of spiritual experience, experience of the Self, experience of the Ishwara and the Divine Shakti, experience of cosmic consciousness, a direct touch with cosmic forces and with the occult movements of universal Nature, a psychic sympathy and unity and inner communication and interchanges of all kinds with other beings and with Nature, illuminations of the mind by knowledge, illuminations of the heart by love and devotion and spiritual joy and ecstasy, illuminations of

1. L.D., Vol. II, Part II, pp. 749-50.
2. Ibid., p. 750.

the sense and the body by higher experience, illuminations of dynamic action in the truth and largeness of a purified mind and heart and soul, the certitudes of the divine light and guidance, the joy and power of the divine force working in the will and the conduct".[1]

(B) *The Spiritual Transformation*

The emergence of soul and psychic transformation, as has been indicated above, is merely the first decisive step of the integral Yoga or integral evolution. It is the first step of the spiritual and supramental transformation. It is due to the fact that the psychic or soul-personality has still to work through the instrumentation of mind, life and body and is thus very much limited and hampered by them in its actions. Though the psycho-physical parts of man's personality, namely, mind, life and body undergo a decisive change during the process of the emergence of the soul, yet they are not radically changed. Though the body is very much freed from "the darkness and stubbornness of the tamasic inertia", the life-force from "the turbidities and turbulences and impurities of the rajasic passion and restless unharmonised kinetism" and the mind from "the enlightened rigidities and sattwic limitations or poised balancements of constructed equilibriums" yet they have not attained their original status—the status of the Supermind and Brahman or Saccidānanda. The realisation of the soul of its original status is according to Sri Aurobindo not enough. What is also necessary is that the body, life and mind that constitute the external aspect of man's personality must realise their original and fundamental status and must be radically transformed and transmuted by the power and consciousness of Supermind and Saccidānanda. It is in this respect that Sri Aurobindo differs fundamentally from the other schools of Vedānta and other Yogic or spiritual disciplines. In the other schools of Vedānta and other Yogas—the Sāṁkhya Yoga, the Yoga of Patañjali and others, the realisation of the soul or the realisation of the identity of the soul with Brahman or Īśvara in some way or other is considered to be the highest attainment of man and the fulfilment of his destiny. But it is not so in the integral Yoga of Sri Aurobindo. The realisation

---

1. *L.D.*, Vol. II, Part II, p. 750.

of the soul or of its essential nature is of very great importance, but no less important according to him is the realisation of Prakṛti or nature of its oneness with the supreme Reality. If the soul is one with the Spirit or Brahman, matter also, according to Sri Aurobindo, is ultimately one with Brahman. It is due to this fact that Sri Aurobindo calls his Yoga integral and thus differentiates it from the other partial Yogas. Sri Aurobindo, of course, never asserts that the liberation of spirit is not possible without the liberation of nature or the natural parts of man's personality. But he does say that the liberation of spirit is not enough or sufficient and thus cannot mark the acme of man's spiritual realisation.

So in order that the nature may also realise its essential and fundamental status—its oneness with the supreme Reality, it is necessary that it must rise from its present level. It means the evolution of nature from mind—its present highest status—to the higher levels of existence and consciousness or the higher grades of spirit or Brahman. For the attainment of psychic transformation, the evolution had to proceed inwards to the inner depths of man's being. Now the evolutionary process has to proceed upwards. The psychic transformation is now to be completed by the spiritual and supramental transformation. As Sri Aurobindo observes, "A highest spiritual transformation must intervene on the psychic or psycho-spiritual change; the psychic movement inward to the inner being, the self or Divinity within us, must be completed by an opening upward to a supreme spiritual status or a higher existence. This can be done by our opening upward into what is above us, by an ascent of consciousness into the ranges of overmind and supramental nature in which the sense of self and spirit is ever unveiled and permanent and in which the sense of self-luminous instrumentation of the self and spirit is not restricted or divided as in our mind-nature, life-nature, body-nature."[1]

Now we will trace the ascent of the evolutionary process from the stage of mind to the higher grades of consciousness and existence that lie between mind and the Supermind. "It is not to be supposed," observes Sri Aurobindo, "that the circumstances and the lines of the transition would be the same for all, for here we enter into the domain of the infinite; but, since there is behind

---

1. *L.D.*, Vol. II, Part II, p. 752.

all of them the unity of a fundamental truth, the scrutiny of a given line of ascent may be expected to throw light on the principle of all ascending possibilities. Such a scrutiny of one line is all that can be attempted. This line is, as all must be, governed by the natural configuration of the stair of ascent: there are in it many steps, for it is an incessant gradation and there is no gap anywhere; but, from the point of view of the ascent of consciousness from our mind upwards through a rising series of dynamic powers by which it can sublimate itself, the gradation can be resolved into a stairway of four ascents, each with its high level of fulfilment".[1] These four grades of ascent are called by Sri Aurobindo, Higher Mind, Illumined Mind, Intuition and Overmind respectively. These grades are not simply ways of knowing the reality or modes of cognition. They are "domains of being, grades of the substance and energy of the spiritual being, fields of existence which are each a level of the universal Consciousness-Force constituting and organising itself into a higher status".[2] The human personality is transformed and transmuted by the descent of knowledge and power of these higher grades before it is ultimately transformed by the descent of the Supermind. As Sri Aurobindo puts it, "when the powers of any grade descend completely into us, it is not only our thought and knowledge that are affected, the substance and very grain of our being and consciousness, all its states and activities are touched and penetrated and can be remoulded and wholly transmuted. Each stage of this ascent is therefore a general, if not a total, conversion of the being into a new light and power of a greater existence".[3]

The Higher Mind

The first step that the evolutionary process takes in its upward march beyond mind is its ascent to a higher grade of Spirit called by Sri Aurobindo, the Higher Mind. It is "a luminous thought-mind, a mind of spirit-born conceptual knowledge".[4] But the thought processes of the higher mind differ greatly from that of the normal mind. The normal mind depends for its knowledge on sense-

---

1. *L.D.*, Vol. II, Part II, pp. 785-86.
2. *Ibid.*, p. 786.
3. *Ibid.*, pp. 786-87.
4. *Ibid.*, p. 788.

experience, inference and other sources of knowledge. But the Higher Mind and other higher grades of consciousness or spirit are not dependent on these limited sources of knowledge. The higher Mind, according to Sri Aurobindo, "can freely express itself in single ideas, but its most characteristic movement is a mass ideation, a system or totality of truth seeing at a single view; the relations of idea with idea, of truth with truth are not established by logic but pre-exist and emerge already self-seen in the integral whole. There is an initiation into forms of an ever present but now inactive knowledge, not a system of conclusions from premises or data; this thought is a self-revelation of eternal Wisdom, not an acquired knowledge".[1] But the Higher Mind by its descent is not able to effect a complete and integral transformation or integration of human personality because it does not eliminate altogether the ignorance, inconscience and inertia prevailing in it. Its light, knowledge and power are diminished, distorted and modified to a considerable extent by the mind, life and body. But it does raise man to a higher status. "The power of the spiritual Higher Mind and its idea-force," observes Sri Aurobindo, "modified and diminished as it must be by its entrance into our mentality, is not sufficient to sweep out all these obstacles and create the gnostic being, but it can make a first change, a modification that will capacitate a higher ascent and a more powerful descent and further prepare an integration of the being in a greater force of consciousness and knowledge".[2]

Illumined Mind

From the Higher Mind, the evolutionary process makes an upward ascent to the next higher stage, called by Sri Aurobindo, the Illumined Mind. Unlike the Higher Mind, the Illumined Mind is no longer a mind of higher thought but of spiritual light. "The Illumined Mind," observes Sri Aurobindo, "does not work primarily by thought, but by vision; thought is here only a subordinate movement expressive of sight. The human mind which relies mainly on thought, conceives that to be the highest or the main process of knowledge, but in the spiritual order thought is a secondary and

---

1   L.D., Vol. II, Part II, p. 789.
2   Ibid., p. 793.

a not indispensable process".[1] The ascent to the Illumined Mind also is followed by the descent of knowledge, power and joy or bliss from it and an integration of human personality in its own pattern. The human organism is now remoulded and integrated into a still higher order. It is now possessed of a greater and a higher consciousness and superior power or dynamism. But the knowledge and power of the Illumined Mind also undergo a modification, diminution and distortion in the process of descent on account of the resistance offered by the lower nature. As the integration of human personality is not yet complete, the evolutionary nature makes an ascent upwards to a higher spiritual plane, called by Sri Aurobindo, Intuition.

Intuition

Intuition is a direct outcome of the meeting of the subject-consciousness with object-consciousness. As Sri Aurobindo puts it, "it is when the consciousness of the subject meets with the consciousness in the object, penetrates it and sees, feels or vibrates with the truth of what it contacts, that the intuition leaps out like a spark or lightening flash from the shock of the meeting;...."[2] But the relationship between the subject and the object is quite different on the plane of intuition from what it is at the lower plane. At the mental level, the knowledge of the external world is obtained mainly by perception and reflection or by senses and intellect. But, the perception at that level is merely an external contact of the consciousness of the subject with that of the object. The senses as well as the intellect grasp only the forms or appearances of things and not reality as such, as Kant, Śaṅkara as well as Sri Aurobindo all clearly state. But at the level of Intuition, the consciousness of the subject penetrates into the object and comes in contact with the realities underlying the appearances. "This close perception," says Sri Aurobindo, "is more than sight, more than conception: it is the result of a penetrating and revealing touch which carries in it sight and conception as part of itself or as its natural consequence".[3]

The human mind often gets the glimpses of intuitions coming from the higher level. But it fails to experience intuitions in their

1. L.D., Vol. II, Part II, p. 794.
2. Ibid., pp. 796-97.
3. Ibid., p. 797.

pure and unadulterated form. A pure intuition, according to Sri Aurobindo, "is a rare occurrence in our mental activity....".[1] Whatever intuitions are projected in the mind are modified by our mental consciousness. The mind has its own laws of perception and thought. So whatever experiences come to the mind, it views them in accordance with its own laws, principles or categories. Thus even the knowledge coming from the higher sources is characterised and modified by mind in accordance with its own limited categories and thus loses its purity and essence during such modification. Sri Aurobindo does contend that at the ordinary mental level, it is quite essential for reason to make a strict scrutiny of intuitions. The intuitions may come from the higher as well as the lower sources, from the subconscient or the conscient and such intuitions may lead the mind into a wrong direction. So reason is perfectly justified at its own level to make a proper discrimination between the truth and the falsehood and between superstition and true spirituality. But in this process of verification, mind also fails to realise the true significance of the intuitions coming from the higher planes of consciousness and takes them as its own creations or projections. And such an intuition ceases to have any significance or importance. But when the mind rises to the planes of Higher Mind and the Illumined Mind and is transformed by their knowledge and power, it gets rid of the limitations of space, time and categories to a considerable extent and becomes fit enough to receive directly the pure spiritual truths descending from the spiritual plane.

"Intuition," remarks Sri Aurobindo, "has a fourfold power. A power of revelatory truth-seeing, a power of inspiration or truth hearing, a power of truth touch or immediate seizing of significance, which is akin to the ordinary nature of its intervention in the mental intelligence, a power of true and automatic discrimination of the orderly and exact relation of truth to truth—these are the fourfold potencies of Intuition".[2] The ascent to the plane of Intuition is followed by the descent of the consciousness and power of Intuition into the human organism and thus there results an integration of human personality in a higher pattern of consciousness, and power. As Sri Aurobindo puts it, "It can thus change

1. *L.D.*, Vol. I, p. 345.
2. *L.D.*, Vol. II, p. 799.

the whole consciousness into the stuff of intuition; for it brings its own greater radiant movement into the will, into the feelings and emotions, the life-impulses, the action of sense and sensation, the very workings of the body consciousness; it recasts them into the light and power of truth and illumines their knowledge and their ignorance."[1]

The next step of the evolutionary process is its upward ascent to a still higher spiritual plane, called by Sri Aurobindo, the Overmind.

The Overmind

Overmind is, according to Sri Aurobindo, in its nature and law a delegate of the Supermind to the ignorance. The Supermind acts on the world of ignorance through the Overmind. As the ignorance cannot bear the direct impact of the supramental consciousness, therefore it has to act through the screen of Overmind to give a secret dynamism to the energies and potentialities hidden in the lap of ignorance. Overmind does not enjoy the integral unity of the Supermind. The whole tendency of the Overmind is towards separation. It enables one to manifest itself as many keeping the fundamental principle of unity in the background. "Purusha and Prakriti, Conscious Soul and executive Force of Nature," says Sri Aurobindo, "are in the supramental harmony a two-aspected single truth, being and dynamics of the Reality; there can be no disequilibrium or predominance of one over the other. In Overmind, we have the cleavage, the distinction made by the philosophy of the Sankhya in which they appear as two independent entities, Prakriti able to dominate Purusha and cloud its freedom and power, reducing it to a witness and recipient of her forms and action, Purusha able to return to its separate existence and abide in a free self-sovereignty by rejection of her original overclouding material principle".[2] Sri Aurobindo regards overmental consciousness as global in character. "Overmind consciousness is global in its cognition and can hold any number of seemingly fundamental differences together in reconciling vision."[3]

---

1. *L.D.*, Vol. II, Part II, p. 800.
2. *L.D.*, Vol. I, pp. 351-52.
3. *Ibid.*, p. 353.

The Overmind also, like other mental grades, is not able to effect an integral transformation of nature by its descent into the human organism. It is not able to transform wholly the ignorance and inconscience. A basis of Nescience would remain; "it would be as if a sun and its system were to shine in an original darkness of Space and illumine everything as far as its rays could reach so that all that dwelt in the light would feel as if no darkness were there at all in their experience of existence. But outside that sphere or expanse of experience the original darkness would still be there and since all things are possible in an Overmind structure, could reinvade the island of light created within its empire".[1] So the descent of the Overmind does not change the basis of terrestrial nature. The terrestrial evolution still proceeds on the basis of ignorance. And as the original basis of the terrestrial evolution is not changed, there is always a possibility of regression or total disintegration of terrestrial process due to an irresistible pull from below, the inconscient. The descent of the Supermind into the earth-consciousness can alone be a safeguard against this constant danger threatening the evolutionary nature. "The liberation from this pull of the Inconscience and a secured basis for a continuous divine or gnostic evolution would only be achieved by a descent of the Supermind into the terrestrial formula bringing into it the supreme law and light and dynamics of the spirit and penetrating with it and transforming the inconscience of the material basis. A last transition from Overmind to Supermind and a descent of Supermind must therefore intervene at this stage of evolutionary nature."[2]

(C) *The Supramental Transformation and the Emergence of Gnostic Being*

The evolutionary process in its ascent from the Overmind to the Supermind follows the same principle as it does in the lower stages. The Supermind present in a potential form in nature emerges on account of a push or dynamism in the evolutionary nature itself and on account of pressure from the plane of the Supermind. The

---

1. *L.D.*, Vol. II, Part II, p. 805.
2. *Ibid.*, p. 806.

descent of the Supermind into earth-consciousness effects a radical change in the evolutionary process. Upto the stage of the Overmind, the evolution proceeds through ignorance and through imperfect knowledge. But the descent of the Supermind effects a radical change in this original law of Nature. The basis of ignorance is now changed into that of knowledge. The evolution now passes from the lower nature or Aparā Prakṛti to the higher nature or Parā Prakṛti. So the result of this supramental descent is that the spiritual being is transformed into the gnostic being and the lower nature or Aparā Prakṛti is transformed into the higher nature or Parā Prakṛti or Cit-Śakti.

As a result of the supramental transformation of human personality, there will be a radical change in the working of mind, life and body. "The supramental transformation, the supramental evolution," observes Sri Aurobindo, "must carry with it a lifting of mind, life and body out of themselves into a greater way of being in which yet their own ways and powers would be not suppressed or abolished, but perfected and fulfilled by the self-exceeding".[1]

In the gnostic being or the gnostic personality, the process of knowledge undergoes a fundamental change. In the ordinary human personality, the senses and the mind are the chief sources of knowledge. But in the gnostic personality, mind is replaced by a fundamental consciousness of unity or identity. To mind, the world of objects is the not-self which is totally different from and independent of the self. But to the gnostic consciousness, the so-called not-self is not really opposed to the self but is only a part of the self or a projection of it in the order of space and time. As Sri Aurobindo remarks, "the gnostic consciousness will at once intimately and exactly know its object by a comprehending and penetrating identification with it. It will overpass what it has to know but it will include it in itself; it will know the object as part of itself as it might know any part or movement of its own being without any narrowing of itself by the identification or snaring of its thought in it so as to be bound or limited in knowledge".[2]

Like mind, life also will undergo a radical change in the personality of the gnostic being. Life is in reality nothing but the projection of consciousness-force of spirit. But it is encircled

---

1. *L.D.*, Vol. II, Part II, pp. 839-40.
2. *Ibid.*, p. 841.

368 THE INTEGRAL ADVAITISM OF SRI AUROBINDO

everywhere by the triple principle of death, desire and incapacity due to the limiting, dividing and ignorant mind. But when mind gets rid of its limitations and is transformed into the integral consciousness of the gnostic being, life also gets rid of its limitations of death, desire and incapacity and is energised by the light and power of the spirit. The quest of life is, according to Sri Aurobindo, "for growth, power, conquest, possession, satisfaction, creation, joy, love, beauty, its joy of existence is in a constant self-expression, development, diverse manifoldness of action, creation, enjoyment, and abundant and strong intensity of itself and its power".[1] All these ideals and aspirations of life are realised to the fullest extent in the gnostic personality.

In the gnostic personality, the relation between the Spirit and body also undergoes a radical change. Ordinarily, the body is governed by the laws of the subconscious and the unconscious. But in the gnostic being, the will of the spirit controls and determines the movements and workings of the body. In him, the "subconscient will have become conscious and subject to supramental control, penetrated with its light and action; the basis of inconscience with its obscurity and ambiguity, its obstruction or tardy responses will have been transformed into a lower or supporting superconscience by the supramental emergence".[2] Now the physical, vital and mental laws that governed the body so long are replaced by the gnostic law of freedom. Instead of a blind inconscient nature or the subconscious or partially conscious mind, it is the Real-Idea "which will rule the existence with an entire knowledge and power and include in its rule the functioning and action of the body. The body will be turned by the power of the spiritual consciousness into a true and fit and perfectly responsive instrument of the spirit".[3]

This makes a decisive change in our attitude towards spiritual life. The spiritual life will no longer necessitate a rejection of the world. On the other hand, it will mean a free acceptance of it. The gnostic being will realise matter also as Brahman, a self-energy put

---

1. *L.D.*, Vol. II, Part II, p. 842.
2. *Ibid.*, p. 844.
3. *Ibid.*, pp. 844-45.

forth by Brahman, or a form and substance of Brahman. "The gnostic being," observes Sri Aurobindo "using matter but using it without material or vital attachment or desire, will feel that he is using the spirit in this form of itself with its consent and sanction for its own purpose. There will be in him a certain respect for physical things, an awareness of the occult consciousness in them, of its dumb will of utility and service, a worship of the Divine, the Brahman in what he uses, a care for a perfect and faultless use of his divine material, for a true rhythm, ordered harmony, beauty in the life of Matter, in the utilisation of Matter".[1]

The evolutionary process does not come to a halt with the emergence of gnostic beings. Prior to the supramental transformation, the evolutionary process has to work through ignorance, but after the emergence of the supramental or gnostic consciousness, it will continue through knowledge. After supramental transformation, the evolutionary process has to manifest the bliss of Saccidānanda in the earth-consciousness. The supermind itself in the involution or descent emerges from the Ānanda or bliss and in the evolution or ascent merges into the Ānanda. "A supramental manifestation in its ascent," observes Sri Aurobindo, "would have as a next sequence and culmination of self-result a manifestation of the bliss of Brahman: the evolution of the being of gnosis would be followed by an evolution of the being of bliss; an embodiment of gnostic existence would have as its consequence an embodiment of the beatific existence".[2] Now nature or becoming will no more appear as something undivine and will no more suffer from darkness, ignorance and inconscience. On the other hand, it will shine with the light and consciousness of the Divine and will permanently enjoy in its movement and further evolution in knowledge the powers and bliss of Saccidānanda.

(D) Place of Personality in the Gnostic Being

Now a question may be asked: what is the place of personality in the gnostic being? Is gnostic being similar to other human beings in the form and appearance or quite different from them? Or as

---

1. *L.D.*, Vol. II, Part II, p. 846.
2. *Ibid.*, pp. 849-50.

Sri Aurobindo puts it: "whether the status, the building of the being will be quite other than what we experience as the form and life of the person or similar".[1] In the Advaita Vedānta of Śaṅkara, we find, that there is no place for individuality and personality after the attainment of liberation. The individuality and personality are supposed to the constituted by the limited and separative ego and so, when the consciousness of the Transcendent dawns and the ego is cancelled, the individuality and personality of the individual also cease to exist altogether. But according to Rāmānuja, the notion of individuality is not incompatible with that of salvation. The individual remains in bondage on account of his being limited by the ego. So it is the ego which keeps the individual in bondage and not his spiritual self or individuality. As Dr. Radhakrishnan observes concerning Rāmānuja's view of salvation, "It is egoity that is opposed to salvation and not individuality."[2] In this respect, Sri Aurobindo agrees with Rāmānuja. According to both, liberation means only the annihilation of the ego and not that of the individuality itself. Sri Aurobindo does not agree with Rāmānuja in his view that the full liberation can be attained only when the individual throws off his body after exhausting all *karmas*. According to Sri Aurobindo, the liberation is attained by the individual in the present life and on this earth. According to Rāmānuja, though the individuality remains even after liberation, yet there no more remains any personality. The individual soul does not possess any personality after liberation. As the individual souls are not possessed of their particular organisms, so they cannot be said to have any personality. "In the state of release the souls are all of the same type. There are no distinctions there of gods, men, animals and plants. In the world or *sansāra* these distinctions have a meaning. It is the connection with matter that gives uniqueness to the soul. But the souls can get rid of this connection, which is not a natural one."[3] Now the question is, is the gnostic being as viewed by Sri Aurobindo, possessed of individuality like the liberated soul in Rāmānujā or of personality also? "It might be deduced," says Sri Aurobindo, "that this gnostic or supramental individual is a self

1. *L.D.*, Vol. II, Part II, p. 852.
2. *Indian Philosophy*, Vol. II, p. 710.
3. *Ibid.*, p. 710.

without personality, an impersonal Purusha. There would be many gnostic individuals but there would be no personality, all would be the same in being and nature".[1] But, as the gnostic being in Sri Aurobindo's view, is not devoid of body, so he can be said to be necessarily possessed of personality. But the personality of the gnostic being will not be limited and restricted like that of an ordinary individual. "A supramental gnostic individual," observes Sri Aurobindo, "will be a spiritual Person, but not a personality in the sense of a pattern of being marked out by a settled combination of fixed qualities, a determined character; he cannot be that since he is a conscious expression of the universal and the transcendent."[2] The ordinary restricted personality can be grasped by an observation of the behaviour of the individual and by a description of the working of his inner mental processes. But such a description would be pitifully inadequate to express the character and personality of the gnostic being who has attained oneness in consciousness and power with the universal and the transcendent. As Sri Aurobindo puts it: "We feel ourselves in presence of light of consciousness, a potency, a sea of energy, can distinguish and describe its free waves of action and quality, but not fix itself; and yet there is an impression of personality, the presence of a powerful being, a strong, high or beautiful recognisable Someone, a Person, not a limited creature of Nature but a Self or Soul or a Purusha. The gnostic Individual would be such an inner Person unveiled, occupying both the depths—no longer self-hidden—and the surface in a unified self-awareness; he would not be a surface personality partly expressive of a larger secret being, he would be not the wave but the ocean; he would be the Purusha, the inner conscious Existence self-revealed, and would have no need of a carved expressive mask or persona."[3]

Thus it is clear that, according to Sri Aurobindo, the individuality and personality are not opposed to salvation or liberation and that they do not stand in the way of realisation of the highest destiny of man. On the other hand, the individuality and personality attain their highest status in the life of the gnostic being.

1. *L.D.*, Vol. II, Part II, p. 852.
2. *Ibid.*, p. 854.
3. *Ibid.*, p. 856.

(E) *Place of the Ethical Element in the Gnostic Personality*
As the gnostic being is possessed of an individuality and person-
ality, the question that arises next is with regard to the place of
the ethical element in the life of a gnostic being. "If there is a
personality and it is in any way responsible for its action," observes
Sri Aurobindo, "there intervenes, next, the question of the place
of the ethical element and its perfection and fulfilment in the
gnostic nature".[1] But the gnostic being, as we have seen above,
is a self-conscious and self-illuminated personality. It is not subject
to ignorance and incapacity. The gnostic being is a self-conscious
and self-determined personality. The consciousness and behaviour
of the gnostic personality are determined and directed by its own
inherent spiritual principles. And as it does not suffer from igno-
rance, error and evil, it does not stand in need of ethical principles
to guide its action and enable it to attain perfection. As Sri Aurobindo
puts it, "there could be in it no separate problem of an ethical or
any similar content, any conflict of good and evil. There could
indeed be no problem at all, for problems are the creations of
mental ignorance seeking for knowledge and they cannot exist in
consciousness in which knowledge arises self-born and the act is
self-born out of the knowledge, out of a pre-existent truth of being
conscious and self-aware".[2] "The purity of the eternal self-exist-
ence," further says Sri Aurobindo, "would pour itself into all the
activities, marking and keeping all things pure; there could be no
ignorance leading to wrong will and falsehood of the steps, no
separative egoism inflicting by its ignorance and separate contrary
will harm on oneself or harm on others, self-driven to a wrong
dealing with one's own soul, mind, life or body or a wrong dealing
with the soul, mind, life, body of others, which is the practical
sense of all human evil."[3] To rise beyond virtue and sin, good and
evil is the real aim of all Yoga and spiritual disciplines. It is the
real goal inherent in the Vedāntic idea of liberation. The clash
between the opposite forces of virtue and sin, good and evil, is
experienced in the ordinary human nature. The forces of darkness,
ignorance, evil, the *rājasic* and *tāmasic* forces, continually strive

---

1. *L.D.*, Vol. II, Part II, p. 852
2. *Ibid.*, p. 857.
3. *Ibid.*, pp. 857-58.

to take man down to the depth of degradation. So the ordinary or ignorant human being requires some standard of conduct, some noble principles to guide his thought and actions in order to save himself from the onslaught of ignorance, evil and other forces akin to them and raise himself to a higher status. But when the individual attains his real status, real consciousness and power of the spirit and is guided in his thought, action and behaviour by the truth-consciousness or real-idea of the spirit, the problems of virtue and sin, good and evil, merit and demerit do not exist for him. Once the individual soul realises its essential nature and becomes one with the spirit, it goes beyond all mental or ethical laws. Plato's cardinal virtues, Aristotle's doctrine of the mean and Kant's categorical imperative have no value and necessity for it. In the case of ordinary human beings, these laws or values seem to be imposed from without. The ignorant individual does not consider them as an essential part of his own nature. But the liberated man, the gnostic being considers these values as the manifestations of his own nature. Instead of being guided by these ethical laws or values, it is the gnostic being who gives value and significance to them. Without any underlying self-conscious spiritual principle, these laws seem to be merely abstract in nature having no integral connection with the human being of flesh and blood. But these laws gain meaning and value when one attains the truth of spirit and realises them as the essential steps in the realisation of the real destiny of man. "To grow into this nature of our true being, a nature of spiritual truth and oneness," observes Sri Aurobindo, "is the liberation attained by an evolution of the spiritual being: the gnostic evolution gives us the complete dynamism of that return to ourselves. Once that is done, the need of standards of virtue, *dharmas* disappears; there is the law and self-order of the liberty of the spirit, there can be no imposed or constructed law of conduct, *dharma*. All becomes a self-flow of spiritual self-nature, *Swadharma* of *swabhava*".[1]

(F) *Gnostic Race of Beings not of a Single Type*
It must not be thought that the supramental or gnostic beings will be all alike in form and nature. As we find differences in the

---

1. *L.D.*, Vol. II, Part II, pp. 858-59.

individuality and personality of mental beings, so there will be differences in the case of gnostic beings also. The principle of diversity will in no way be abolished by the emergence of the gnostic being. The descent of the Supermind in earth-consciousness does not abolish the diversity but fulfils it and carries it to the highest consummation of its destiny. But unlike mental beings, there will be no ignorance in the case of gnostic being or superman. The gnostic beings will be aware of their individuality, universality and transcendence at the same time. They will be aware of their outward differences as well as of the basic unity existing between them. "A supramental or gnostic race of beings," observes Sri Aurobindo, "would not be a race made according to a single type, moulded in a single fixed pattern; for the law of the supermind is unity fulfilled in diversity, and therefore there would be an infinite diversity in the manifestation of the gnostic consciousness".[1] Unlike Śaṅkara, Sri Aurobindo does not contend that unity can be established only by effacing or abolishing diversity altogether. The diversity cannot be reconciled with unity so long as it is subject to ignorance and limitation. When the ignorance is cancelled, the diversity is seen as nothing else but the manifestation of unity. So man according to Sri Aurobindo realises his highest destiny not by sacrificing his individuality and personality at the altar of bare and abstract unity but by raising them to their highest status of development by the realisation of his universal and transcendent nature. The gnostic being realises the highest status or destiny when he becomes one with the Absolute in both status and dynamis. So the diversity exists side by side of the principle of unity and there is no opposition felt between them in supramental or gnostic consciousness. "But in the supramental race itself, in the variation of its degrees," observes Sri Aurobindo, "the individuals would not be cast according to a single type of individuality; each would be different from the other, a unique formation of the Being, although one with all the rest in foundation of self and sense of oneness and in the principle of his being. It is only this general principle of the supramental existence of which we can attempt to form an idea however diminished by the limitations of mental thought and mental language. A more living

---

1. *L.D.*, Vol. II, Part II, p. 826.

picture of the gnostic being supermind alone could make; for the mind some abstract outlines of it are alone possible".[1]

(G) The Gnostic Being and the Jīvanmukta

The *jīvanmukta* according to the Vedānta is one who has realised Brahman even in the embodied state. Liberation according to the Advaitins is possible even in this life and not only after death. Liberation causes the destruction of ignorance and the *karmas* or past actions that act as fetters to the soul. "The fetters of the heart are cut asunder, all doubts are dispelled, and all *karmas* are destroyed when the Reality or Brahman is seen."[2] But all *karmas* are not destroyed altogether on the attainment of Brahman knowledge. The Vedānta makes a distinction between two kinds of *karma*, called respectively, *sañcita karma* and *prārabdha karma*. *Sañcita karmas* are those which are accumulated in the unconscious of the individual and have not yet begun to produce results; while *prārabdha karmas* are those which are not only stored up in the safe custody of the unconscious but have already begun to operate on the individual and have also produced the organism through which man attains Brahman-knowledge or Brahman-bliss. It is the *sañcita karmas* which are destroyed completely on the attainment of liberation and not the *prārabdha karmas*. The *prārabdha karmas* have already gained a momentum and so long as it lasts, the liberated man or the *Jīvanmukta* has to remain in the body. When they are destroyed, the body is cast off and the individual spirit which has already attained unity with the Divine passes forever beyond the clash and struggle, the joys and sorrows of the empirical world to the abode of the Transcendent.

It must not be thought that the individual will have to reap the fruits of the *Karmas* or actions which are done in the state of liberation or *jīvanmukti* The actions which are performed after the attainment of liberation cease to affect the liberated soul. The *jīvanmukta* or the liberated individual ceases to consider himself the agent or the enjoyer of actions. He ceases to identify himself with his body and with the resulting actions. As the lotus remains

---

1. *L.D.*, Vol. II, Part II, p. 827.
2. *Muṇḍ.* 2.2.8.

unaffected by water, even so no *karmas* or no *sins* cling to him who knows Reality.[1]

So it is clear that the spirit of the liberated individual or the *jīvanmukta* is not affected in any way by the actions of life even though the body has still to act in accordance with the laws laid down by the *prārabdha karmas* and to experience the resulting joys and sorrows of life till death. The difference between the ordinary man and the *jīvanmukta* consists in the fact that while the former labours under the misapprehension of being the agent or doer of actions and has thus to reap the resulting fruits in terms of the shocks and sufferings of life, the latter remains completely unaffected by the varying experience of bodily life and enjoys in his spirit the complete freedom and bliss of the divine existence. The ordinary man has no awareness of his soul or spirit and is thus under the complete subjection of Prakṛti, the lower nature, but the *jīvanmukta* enjoys complete freedom in spirit, though his body continues to function under the yoke of past *karmas* which have produced the body. The spirit of the ordinary or the unenlightened man is completely conditioned by the body and the *karmas* which produce it and are also its results, but the spirit of the enlightened man is conditioned not by the body and the *karmas* but by the Divine. The process of liberation consists chiefly in being completely unconditioned by nature and being conditioned by the Divine. The life of *jīvanmukta* bears evidence of the supremacy of knowledge over ignorance, of freedom over necessity and of Spirit over Nature.

But though the attainment of the state of *jīvanmukta* is in itself a great and mighty achievement on the part of the spiritual aspirant, yet it cannot be called the ultimate goal or the *summum bonum* of spiritual life. Sri Aurobindo aims not only at the liberation of spirit but also at the liberation of psycho-physical organism from the mechanical rule of nature. In the personality of the gnostic being, not only is the spirit freed from the thraldom of the mechanical rule of nature but the bodily organism also transcends all sorts of natural limitations and ceases to work in accordance with the laws of ignorance and inconscience. It does not mean that the body ceases to work altogether. But now it obeys a higher law,

---

1. *Chān.* 4.14.3.

the divine law. The consciousness, force and bliss of Saccidānanda are now manifested in the becoming also. All the actions and movements of the gnostic being are propelled by the self-conscious will of the Divine and are done for the Divine. The bodily organism of the gnostic being works perfectly not only in accordance with the will of the spirit but it manifests the force and bliss of the spirit as well. It now becomes the true abode of the spirit.

Thus we find that in the *jīvanmukta*, the spirit alone enjoys complete freedom from the bondage of ignorance and inconscience, but in the gnostic being, the spirit as well as the body are freed from them. The body of the *jīvanmukta* has to work under the control and guidance of the *prārabdha karmas* till death and has to bear the resulting consequences, but the body of the gnostic being is freed forever from the limitations and subjection of all kinds of *karmas* or actions, ignorance and inconscience and works in perfect freedom and harmony under the luminous and unfailing light of the Divine. Not only that; the very basis of ignorance and inconscience is destroyed in the personality of the gnostic being. The rule of the spirit is perfectly established in the realm of the becoming also. As Sri Aurobindo observes, "The spiritual man is one who has discovered his soul: he has found his self and lives in that, is conscious of it, has the joy of it; he needs nothing external for his completeness of existence. The gnostic being starting from this new basis takes up our ignorant becoming and turns it into a luminous becoming of knowledge and a realised power of being. All therefore that is our attempt to be in the ignorance, he will fulfil in the knowledge."[1]

The *jīvanmukta* marks the liberation of the individual but the gnostic being signifies the liberation of the cosmos as well. Nature is raised to a higher status with the emergence of the gnostic being. As has been stated above, the light of the supermind will make a permanent abode in the earth-consciousness and there will emerge a race of gnostic beings as there is at present the race of mental beings. The *jīvanmukta* attains his individual salvation and sets a shining example to other spiritual aspirants also. But this liberation does not attain any victory for the blind and inconscient nature.

---

1. *L.D.*, Vol. II, Part II, p. 839.

Individuals attain liberation but nature goes on in its own way. The *jīvanmukta* remains well-stationed in his spirit and is not disturbed in any way by the mighty changes, movements and upheavals of nature. Thus, there is no interference of nature in the freedom of the *jīvanmukta*. But the *jīvanmukta* also does not interfere with the workings of nature. The workings of nature are interfered with only to the extent that they do not affect his freedom of spirit and not beyond that. Otherwise, the *jīvanmukta* remains a detached and disinterested spectator of the world-show which to him has no reality in it.

But such is not the case with the gnostic being. With his emergence, the old order of the world changes yielding place to the new. He heralds the dawn of a new era in the history of the evolutionary process. Now a new and fundamental principle of divine knowledge and will will be established in earth-consciousness and will effect a reorganisation of nature. This new principle of knowledge-will will henceforth guide the destiny of evolutionary nature. Instead of being guided by the laws of ignorance and inconscience, the evolutionary process of nature will now receive the direct guidance and direction of the divine knowledge and will. The evolution will now proceed not on the basis of ignorance and inconscience but on the basis of knowledge. Spirit will now reign supreme not only beyond the becoming but in the becoming or the spatio-temporal order as well.

Thus it is clear that Sri Aurobindo's conception of liberation is far superior to that of the Vedānta. In the other schools of Vedānta and the other Yogas also, liberation signifies the attainment of freedom of spirit in the embodied state, or after death, but in Sri Aurobindo's view, liberation means not only the freedom of spirit from spatio-temporal limitations but the freedom of nature or the spatio-temporal order itself from the present limitations, from the blind and mechanical rule of ignorance and inconscience.

(H) *The Gnostic Being and the Avatāra Compared*
The doctrine of *Avatāra* has been discussed by Sri Aurobindo very elaborately in his *Essays on the Gītā*. The *Avatāra* is said to be a descent of Godhead into humanity. It is the direct manifestation of the Divine Being in human form, of the Divine consciousness in human consciousness. In *Avatāra*, the Divine Personality is revealed in the human form. The Divine is undoubtedly supporting all the

manifold existences as the One immutable, imperishable and impersonal Self or Spirit. He is also present in each individual as the eternal soul or *jīva* and directs the whole course of his phenomenal becoming. He directs the whole course of human life and action in a secret and unknown manner. The human being is not at all aware of the existence of the Supreme Being within him. The eternal lamp of the Divine Light is continuously burning in the deep sanctuary of human heart but the poor human being, the transient, the phenomenal and ephemeral human creature is totally ignorant of it. The phenomenal consciousness of the individual is thus totally cut off and separated from the eternal and real consciousness of the Divine. Thus though the Divine and the Individual live so close to each other, are in reality eternally united or even identified with each other, yet in this domain of Nature, they find themselves totally separate from each other. The gulf of ignorance or the wall of darkness apparently separates the individual from the Divine, from his eternal friend, his helper and his guide and keeps him groping in the dark. The main cause of this ignorance is the identification of the individual self with the ego, the physical sense, constituted of psycho-physical organism.

It is to remove this barrier of separation existing between the human being and the Divine, it is to rend this veil of ignorance that there is a descent of the Godhead into humanity in the form of *Avatāra*. The main function of *Avatāra* is to raise man from the status of animality to that of divinity and from the state of abject ignorance into that of perfect knowledge. It is the birth of man into Godhead as is expressed very beautifully by Sri Aurobindo.

Sri Aurobindo says that the upholding of *dharma*[1] is not the only object of the descent of the *Avatāra*: "the upholding of the *Dharma* is not an all-sufficient object in itself, not the supreme possible aim for the manifestation of a Christ, a Krishna, a Buddha, but is only the general condition of a higher aim and more supreme and divine utility".[2] Further, Sri Aurobindo gives a very vivid description of the double aspect of the divine birth and this shows its real significance. As he says, "there are two aspects of the divine birth; one is a descent, the birth of God in humanity, the Godhead

---

1. धर्मसंस्थापनार्थाय सम्भवामि युगे युगे । (*B.G.* 4.7)
2. *Essays on the Gītā*, First Series, Fourth Ed., 1944, p. 204.

manifesting itself in the human form and nature, the eternal *Avatāra;* the other is an ascent, the birth of man into the Godhead, man rising into the divine nature and consciousness, *madbhāvam āgataḥ;* it is the being born anew in a second birth of the soul".[1] The upholding of the *Dharma* has a deeper significance according to Sri Aurobindo and signifies this new birth of the soul. If *Avatāra* was not meant to raise man into the Godhead, then it would be in the words of Sri Aurobindo simply "an otiose phenomenon, since mere right, mere justice or standards of virtue can always be upheld by the divine omnipotence through its ordinary means, by great men or great movements, by the light and works of sages and kings and religious teachers, without any actual incarnations".[2] He further says, "the *Avatara* comes as the manifestation of the divine nature in the human nature, the apocalypse of its Christhood, Krishnahood, Buddhahood, in order that the human nature may by moulding its principle, thought, feeling, action, being on the lines of that Christhood, Krishnahood, Buddhahood transfigure itself into the Divine".[3]

The birth of the Divine is of a special kind. He descends into the human organism in the form of *Avatāra* by the help of his own Māyā, the Yoga Māyā, as the Gītā calls it.[4] In this respect the birth of the Divine differs from that of the ordinary mortals. The birth of the ordinary human beings, takes place in ignorance. But the Divine comes into birth in perfect self-consciousness. It is the birth into knowledge. The human beings are from the very moment of their birth under the subjection of the threefold modes of Nature, the lower Prakṛti. But the Divine descends not only in perfect self-consciousness but in full freedom. He is in no way subjected to the operations of the triple guṇas. On the other hand he directs the operations of the triple mode of Nature according to his free-will. The human beings in general are not aware of their past lives, remember nothing of their previous earthly existences. But the *Avatāra* remembers all his previous births.[5] The divine birth is thus according to Sri Aurobindo, the opposite of human birth, the

---

1. *Essays on the Gītā,* First Series, Fourth Ed., 1944, p. 204
2. *Ibid.,* p. 205.
3. *Ibid.,* p. 205.
4. अजोऽपि सन्नव्ययात्मा भूतानामीश्वरोऽपि सन्। प्रकृतिं स्वामधिष्ठाय सम्भवाभ्यात्ममाययया।
(*B.G.* 4.6)
5. बहूनि मे व्यतीतानि जन्मानि तव चार्जुन! तान्यहं वेद सर्वाणि न त्वं वेत्थ परमतप॥ (*B.G.* 4.5)

ordinary birth, even though the same means are used. "It is,"
in the words of Sri Aurobindo, "the Soul's coming into birth as the
self-existent Being controlling consciously its becoming and not
lost to self-knowledge in the cloud of ignorance. It is the Soul born
into the body as Lord of Nature, standing above and operating in
her freely by its will, not entangled and helplessly driven round
and round in the mechanism, for it works in the knowledge and
not, as most do, in the ignorance".

And the Divine comes forward into the frontal, the phenomenal
consciousness mainly to break the veil between himself and hu-
manity which man limited in his own nature could never lift. Sri
Aurobindo contends that by manifesting in the human form, the
Divine throws open all the gates for man's ascent or upward jour-
ney. By His birth, man also sees the possibility of making an ascent
into the Divine and becoming the Divine himself. But for this
descent of the Divine into humanity man would never have thought
it possible to exceed himself and become something totally dif-
ferent from what he is.

Moreover, the spiritual influence of the *Avatāra* outlasts his
temporal existence. He gives such a mighty and dynamic push to
the upward human evolution that it continues to evolve further
and further long after the passing away of the *Avatāra* from the
terrestrial existence.

The *Avatāra* gives a *dharma*, a religion—not a mere creed but
a method of inner and outer living. He establishes an eternal and
spiritual law which may enable man to grow into divinity. This law
enables man not only to attain a perfect equilibrium and adjust-
ment in his phenomenal being but also in his real, the permanent
and spiritual being. This adjustment and spiritual equilibrium can
be made possible only by a perfect unfoldment of spiritual vision
and consciousness. Moreover the *Avatāra* is the helper of the
forces of the good and the divine and the destroyer of the forces
of evil.[1] The *Avatāra*, says Sri Aurobindo, "does not come as a
thaumaturgic magician, but as the divine leader of humanity and
the exemplar of a divine humanity".

The Divine thus comes in the form of *Avatāra* to break the veil
of ignorance that exists between the human and the Divine nature
and enables humanity to make an ascent to the Divine status. But

1. परित्राणाय साधूनां विनाशाय च दुष्कृताम्। धर्मसंस्थापनार्थाय सम्भवामि युगे युगे ॥ (*B.G.* 4.8)

when his mission is completed, he withdraws from the world leaving the world to proceed on its evolutionary journey in accordance with the new light, truth and law revealed by him. But though the *Avatāra* enables humanity to get the light of the divine, to raise itself to a higher status, yet he does not effect any radical change in the nature and working of the universe. By his descent into humanity, the *Avatāra* fully justifies the innate aspirations of man to rise above his present status, but he does not give any higher and permanent principle to the universe.

Unlike the *Avatāra*, the gnostic being or superman does not pass away from the world. The Supermind or the Divine Being makes a descent in the world and raises humanity to a higher and divine status, the status of gnostic consciousness. The *Avatāra* gives the divine light to the world to enable it to make an ascent to the higher status, but the gnostic beings represent the decisive ascent of the world to the divine status. Unlike the *Avatāra*, the gnostic being enjoys a higher psychophysical organism and is possessed of a higher dynamism. Outwardly the *Avatāra* has to manifest himself and act through the mind-body organism. But the Gnostic Being is possessed of a higher organism which is not governed by the laws of the lower nature but of the higher nature. The body of the *Avatāra* is subject to decay and death, but that of the gnostic being is freed from such natural limitations. The *Avatāra* is an isolated being in the world but there is a race of gnostic beings. The light given by *Avatāra* may in the course of time begin to flicker and even pass away but the gnostic consciousness will never be extinguished from the world. The gnostic being may in a way be said to represent the consummation of the *Avatāra*, the permanent descent of the Divine in the world.

(I) *Sri Aurobindo's Gnostic Being and Alexander's Deity Compared*

Like Sri Aurobindo, Alexander also considers the evolutionary nature as engaged in producing a higher world order, radically different from what it is at present. According to Alexander, three principles, namely, matter, life and mind have emerged so far in the present world out of the primordial stuff of space-time. But the present world consisting of matter, life and mind cannot be considered as the highest formation of evolutionary nature. The evolutionary nature is still, according to him, proceeding towards a higher status and a fourth principle, namely deity, which is higher and radically different from the other three principles is bound to emerge out of the stuff of space-time. By deity, Alexander does not mean any specific principle. It is a general term indicating the next higher principle. So, when the principle of matter had emerged, deity was the principle of life. On the emergence of life, deity was the principle of mind. "For any level of existence," observes Alexander, "deity is the next higher empirical quality. It is therefore a variable quality, and as the world goes in time, deity changes with it".[1] But now the problem is, what is the deity? What will be the next higher status which the evolutionary process has to attain? Here Alexander fails to give us any definite idea of the next higher principle or deity which is to envolve in the world. He only says that it is not mind and it is not only quantitatively but qualitatively different from mind. As he puts it, "we cannot tell what is the nature of deity, of our deity, but we can be certain that it is not mind, or if we use the term spirit as equivalent to mind, deity is not spirit, but something different from it in kind".[2]

Now the question arises, can man who is at present possessed of the three qualities of matter, life and mind rise to a higher status according to Alexander and possess the quality of the deity? Will the next higher deity be a higher or superman or some being entirely different from man? According to him, the next higher deity cannot be called a higher or a superman.

In this respect, Sri Aurobindo's view of the gnostic being is entirely different from Alexander's deity. The gnostic being is not some being quite different from man but it is a higher man or a superman. Though the gnostic consciousness is radically different from mental consciousness, yet it makes a descent in the mind, life and body and transforms them in accordance with its own light and power. In Alexander we do not find this conception of the transformation of the lower principles by the emergence of the higher principle or deity. The world of matter, life and mind will not be transformed by the emergence of the deity. So the emergence of the deity will not raise man to a higher status. He may be reduced to a subordinate position in the world by the emergence of a higher being but he cannot himself rise to a higher status. But according to Sri Aurobindo, there is no limit to the

1. *Space, Time and Deity*, Vol. II, p. 348.
2. *Ibid.*, p. 349.

progress and evolution of man. He has to rise to the divine status and manifest in him all the powers and light of the spirit. His evolution is not stopped by the descent of the supermind and the emergence of the gnostic being. Whereas formerly, he was undergoing the process of evolution in ignorance, now as a gnostic being he will proceed towards the next higher status of Saccidānanda in perfect knowledge. His evolution will no more be governed by the laws of the lower nature, of Aparā-Prakṛti, but by the higher nature or Parā-Prakṛti. Thus it is clear that Sri Aurobindo's, conception of the destiny of man is infinitely higher than that of Alexander. Sri Aurobindo agrees with Alexander insofar as he thinks that the emergence of a higher principle is necessary to raise the world to a higher status. The real peace and harmony cannot be maintained in the world by the principle of mind. But unlike Alexander, Sri Aurobindo thinks that it is man who has to evolve the next higher principle out of himself or in other words it is man who has to transform himself in the light of spirit and to rise to a higher status of personality. All the ills of man are due to the fact that man is not possessed of a fully integrated personality. No amount of external devices or mental manipulations can enable man to adjust himself to the world. It is only when he receives the unobstructed light and power of the spirit that he is transformed into the superman or the perfect man and is thus able to make a perfect adjustment to the world. The only way of raising the world to a higher moral and spiritual status is to raise man first of all. "A perfected human world," says Sri Aurobindo, "cannot be created by men or composed of men who are themselves imperfect."[1] "Even if all our actions," further says Sri Aurobindo, "are scrupulously regulated by education or law or social or political machinery, what will be achieved is a regulated pattern of minds, a fabricated pattern of lives, a cultivated pattern of conduct; but a conformity of this kind cannot change, cannot recreate the man within, it cannot carve or cut out a perfect soul or a perfect thinking man or a perfect or growing living being".[2]

(J) *Gnostic Being and Nietzsche's Superman Compared*
Sri Aurobindo's conception of the gnostic being differs from

---

1. *L. D.*, Vol. II, Part II, p. 887.
2. *Ibid.*, pp. 887-88.

Nietzsche's conception of the Superman. Though Sri Aurobindo's
gnostic being and Nietzsche's superman resemble in the sense that
both rise above the hold of traditional morality, they are com-
pletely different in the sense that whereas the gnostic being is a
divine man, possessed of the higher qualities of goodness, beauty,
love, bliss, divine strength etc., the superman is an embodiment
of a titan or *asura* and is possessed of the qualities of physical
strength, indomitable will, ruthlessness, egoism and so on. The
morality of the Superman which Nietzsche calls the master-moral-
ity, exalts the qualities which enable men to attain the lordship of
the world e.g. the brute force, recklessness etc., and does not give
any place to the divine qualities or values like sympathy, benevo-
lence, love etc. But Sri Aurobindo's gnostic being represents the
consummation of all that is good, noble and true in man. But both
Nietzsche and Sri Aurobindo are agreed in the view that the world
can be raised to a higher status only by the emergence of a new
and higher race of men. The salvation of humanity according to
Sri Aurobindo lies in rising to a status higher than the human. It
lies in exceeding the limits of the present status. The individual
salvation attained by following the traditional principles and paths
of morality, religion and asceticism cannot enable humanity to
attain a higher or divine status. It cannot establish lasting peace,
harmony and joy in the world. So, unlike the view of the individual
liberation favoured by the ancient philosophers of both the East
and the West, Sri Aurobindo stands for the liberation of the whole
world. The destiny of man, according to him, can be fulfilled only
when the world rises to a higher status, the status of gnostic or
divine consciousness. The advancement of not only the individu-
als but of the race as a whole is needed to bring a higher order
in the world. As Sri Aurobindo says "for it is only if the race
advances that, for it, the victories of the Spirit can be secure".[1] Sri
Aurobindo admits that the advancement of the race to a higher or
divine status does not mean that the whole human race will become
divine and there will be no human beings or mental men left in
the world. "It is not indeed necessary or possible," says Sri
Aurobindo, "that the whole race would transform itself from mental

---

1. *L.D.*, Vol. II, Part II, p. 525.

into spiritual beings, but a general admission of the ideal, a widespread endeavour, a conscious concentration are needed to carry the stream of tendency to its definitive achievement. Otherwise what will be ultimately accomplished is an achievement by the few initiating a new order of beings, while humanity will have passed sentence of unfitness on itself and may fall back into an evolutionary decline for a stationary immobility; for it is the constant upward effort that has kept humanity alive and maintained for it its place in the front of creation".[1]

The gnostic being or the divine man represents the culmination of the evolutionary process. The process of evolution consists in the return of spirit embodied in matter to itself. It is the ascent of matter to the status of spirit. Matter which is essentially nothing but spirit seems outwardly to be quite opposed to spirit. Thus mind or finite reason considers matter and spirit as opposed to each other. The "Materialist denial" and the "Refusal of the ascetic" are based on this very so-called opposition between Spirit and Matter. But Sri Aurobindo on account of his conception of integration has succeeded in effecting a reconciliation between spirit and matter. This reconciliation finally takes place in the personality of the gnostic being. In the lower grades of being, spirit does not manifest itself fully in the external forms of matter. In the ordinary human being or mental man, spirit remains hidden behind the surface consciousness. The body-mind organism is considered as the not-self and as opposed to the self or spirit. But in the gnostic personality this opposition between the self and the not-self or spirit and matter is abolished altogether. Matter is now no more matter but a mode or power of spirit. The organism of the gnostic being is not considered as something opposed to the self or spirit but is regarded as the mode or power or garb of the spirit and itself nothing but spirit. The dynamic parts of the gnostic personality are considered as different powers of the divine. There will now no more be the opposition between the inner and outer or substance and form. The opposition between matter and spirit, Being and Becoming, status and dynamis is resolved not only theoretically but even practically in the gnostic personality. Unlike Mind, these are not regarded by gnostic consciousness as opposed

1. *L.D.*, Vol. II, Part II, pp. 525-26.

to or contradictory of each other but as the complementary aspects of the same personality. The gnostic being, as we have seen above, represents in himself both the personal and the impersonal aspects. He is individual, universal and transcendent at one and the same time. These terms represent merely the three states or aspects of the same personality. The gnostic being cannot be characterised by a single term. These terms when separated from each other become the source of limitation. The gnostic being is an individual but he is also the universal spirit embracing all existence and at the same time transcends all existence. While the mental or finite consciousness considers these aspects as contradictory of each other, the gnostic consciousness realises them as different but complementary aspects of the same personality.

The gnostic personality represents the fullest integration of the diverse elements of reality. The destiny of man is, according to the sages of Upaniṣads, fulfilled by the realisation of the Divine. The fullest or the integral realisation of the Divine consists, according to the sages of the Upaniṣads and according to Sri Aurobindo, not only in the realisation of the individual self or spirit as absolutely identical with Brahman or as a portion of Brahman, but in the realisation of nature or Prakṛti also as nothing but Brahman. This integral nature of reality or integral Advaitism is fully and perfectly realised and represented by the gnostic being or superman.

PART V

CONCLUSION

CHAPTER XI

A CRITICAL ESTIMATE OF SRI AUROBINDO'S INTEGRAL ADVAITISM

In the preceding chapters we have given a critical and comparative exposition of Sri Aurobindo's Integral Advaitism. We have also endeavoured to give a fair and satisfactory answer to many of the important criticisms that are made or can possibly be made against Sri Aurobindo's system. Our treatment of Sri Aurobindo's system has been critical as well as sympathetic. We think that a certain amount of sympathy is required for a true understanding of a philosophical system. But though we have been sympathetic towards Sri Aurobindo's system and have found ourselves in agreement with most of the views propounded in it, yet we have not accepted any of these in a dogmatic manner. We have everywhere tried to put forward logical arguments in support of the views which have appeared to us to be right and valid in Sri Aurobindo's system.

Now we will proceed to make a critical estimate of Sri Aurobindo's system and express our views regarding the merits and shortcomings of his integral Advaitism. First of all we proceed to give a critical estimate of Sri Aurobindo's conception of the Absolute.

(A) *Conception of the Absolute*
The special feature of Sri Aurobindo's Integral Advaitism is that it establishes the oneness of the Absolute or Brahman without denying

the reality of the world. The Advaitism of Śaṅkara is, as we have pointed out in the preceding chapters, based on the denial of the reality of the world. But Sri Aurobindo's system throws a direct challenge to this contention. According to Sri Aurobindo, Advaitism can be maintained even while we admit the reality of the world. And we have seen in the preceding chapters that Sri Aurobindo has achieved admirable success in establishing Advaitism without denying the reality of the world. Sri Aurobindo looks at the Absolute from an integral standpoint. To him the Absolute is both Being and Becoming, One and Many, Infinite and Finite etc., and at the same time it transcends them all. The Absolute, as we have fully shown in the preceding chapters, cannot be confined within the limits of any of our mental categories or of all the categories taken together. It cannot be called either a pure identity or an identity-in-difference. It is both as well as beyond both. The integral view of the Absolute consists in recognising the truth of all the aspects of Existence—the individual, the universal and the transcendent. It sees the Absolute as both transcendent and immanent.

Sri Aurobindo has proved beyond any shadow of doubt the futility of our making an approach to the Absolute through the finite or abstract reason. The abstract and analytic reason can be applied *a priori* and unconditionally only in formal logic, mathematics etc., but not in respect of the relational categories and propositions which express the nature of the Absolute. We have seen that the contradictions which we find between Indeterminate and Determinate, One and Many, Infinite and Finite appear to be irreconcilable only to our finite or abstract reason. But these contradictions can be resolved by our higher reason or Logic of the Infinite, as we have fully shown in our chapter, entitled 'The Logic of the Infinite' and in the other chapters on the Absolute. It is true that all the systems of the Vedānta hold the view that the Absolute cannot be grasped and realised by our mind or finite reason. We have seen that this view was held even by the sages of the Upaniṣads. But the main defect of the Vedāntic systems is, as we have pointed out in some of the preceding chapters, that they try to determine the nature of the Absolute and its relationship with the world generally through the finite or abstract reason. We find a perfect demonstration of it in the system of Śaṅkara. The result is that he is confronted everywhere with all sorts of contradictions. He finds the Indeterminate and the Determinate, One and

Many, Being and Becoming, Subject and Object, Knowledge and Ignorance etc., as opposed to and contradictory to each other. Śaṅkara and the Śaṅkarites make a critical examination of all the realistic categories and show their self-contradictory nature. And their failure to determine the nature of the relational categories leads them to deny their reality altogether. Because they fail to determine the relationship between the Absolute and the world, therefore they are forced to deny the reality of the latter in order to establish their Advaitic position. The Advaita Vedānta commits a grave error in judging the relationship between the Absolute and the world on the basis of an *a priori* application of the law of Contradiction. Thus it destroys the conditions which make their relationship intelligible.

Sri Aurobindo agrees with Śaṅkara in that he also considers the Absolute as essentially beyond all categories and incapable of being confined within the limits of any of the categories or of all the categories taken together. But he does not call the relations unreal or false as Śaṅkara does. He does hold that the full truth of the Absolute cannot be expressed by our relational categories, like Being and Becoming, Substance and Attributes, etc. but he does not call them unreal or false. All these relational categories, according to him, express the nature of the Absolute though in an imperfect and partial manner. The Absolute, according to him, transcends all sorts of relationships and at the same time manifests itself in different relations. Thus it is both relational as well as supra-relational, immanent as well as transcendent in nature. It can be determined neither by our affirmations nor by our negations. To say that the Absolute is simply relationless and hence incapable of manifesting itself in relational aspect is to put a limitation upon it. The perfect freedom of the Absolute means its freedom from all relations and determinations and at the same time its freedom to manifest relations and determinations out of its being. To say that the Absolute is indeterminate and relationless does not mean, as we have pointed out repeatedly, that it is devoid of all determinations and relations but that it cannot be limited by any determination and relation or any sum of determinations and relations. Śaṅkara and the Śaṅkarites commit the error of determining the Absolute by negations. They establish the relationlessness of the Absolute by denying the reality of determinations and relations. But this gives us only a partial view of the Absolute and not an integral view of it. Sri Aurobindo rightly argues that in order to have an integral view of Reality, we are not to take into account only the relationless or transcendent aspect of the Absolute but we have to include its immanent aspect, its universal and individual aspects also. Thus Sri Aurobindo rightly holds that the Absolute cannot be limited or determined either by our affirmations or negations. We regard this as a major contribution of Sri Aurobindo to the theory of Reality or the Absolute. And the merit of this integral view of the Absolute is enhanced by the fact that it is strongly supported by our higher reason or the logic of the Infinite.

It is true that Sri Aurobindo's integral view of Reality cannot be said to be perfectly original. The transcendence and immanence of the Absolute or Brahman has been advocated in the Upaniṣads and the different systems of the Vedānta. While Śaṅkara and his followers do not concede reality to the immanent aspect from the ultimate or ontological standpoint, Rāmānuja, Vallabha, Nimbārka etc., regard both the transcendent and the immanent aspects as real and establish relationship between these two aspects in different ways. But the difficulty with the theistic systems of the Vedānta lies in the fact that they have not generally been able to give a strong and sound logical foundation to their systems. They have not been able to meet squarely the criticism made by Śaṅkara and his followers against the immanent or relational aspect of the Absolute. The originality of Sri Aurobindo lies not in admitting the reality of both the immanent and the transcendent aspects of the Absolute but in showing us the way to reconcile these apparently opposed aspects. It lies in his pointing out in a clear-cut manner the futility of our attempts to reconcile these apparently opposed aspects through our finite or abstract reason. Śaṅkara and his followers also show the impossibility and the futility of our trying to determine the relationship between the Absolute and the world through reason. But they signally fail to grasp the essential significance of this truth and draw a wrong conclusion from it. Because they fail to establish a relationship between the Absolute and the world through reason, therefore they call the latter unreal. Sri Aurobindo does not follow this course. He shows us in unmistakable terms that the reason for our inability to determine the relationship between the Absolute and the world is not that the latter is false but that our way of dealing with this problem is defective. Our reason fails to grasp the nature of the Absolute and the world owing to its abstract and analytic nature. Sri Aurobindo hits at the very root of the Advaita dialectic of Śaṅkara and the Śaṅkarites by showing its inability to determine the truths of reality on account of its abstract and formal character. It operates by an *a priori* and unconditional application of the principles of Formal Logic, Identity, Contradiction etc. to relational categories which is not rationally justified, as has been discussed before. Thus Sri Aurobindo is not merely satisfied by giving a trenchant criticism of the doctrine of the unreality of the world or Māyā but he questions the very logic on which this system is based. A clear awareness of the limitations of the principles of Formal Logic and the shortcomings of dialectical reasoning enables one to have a full appreciation of the necessity of the Logic of the Infinite to comprehend the Absolute.

The system of Śaṅkara has been criticised by all the schools of the Vedānta. Many of the criticisms that Sri Aurobindo has made against the system of Śaṅkara are undoubtedly merely the repetitions of what Rāmānuja and others have made already in an elaborate and exhaustive manner. But no other school of Vedānta has challenged so successfully the very logic on which this system is based. The views of the theistic schools of Vedānta have been shattered to pieces by the relentless attack of the Advaita dialectic. But though they have also made equally devastating criticism of Māyāvāda and have shown the contradictions inherent in it, yet they have not been able to strike it at its very root. In this respect Sri Aurobindo's Integral Advaitism has presented a most formidable challenge to the abstract Advaitism of Śaṅkara and the Śaṅkarites. Sri Aurobindo has rightly shown that the nature of reality can be determined only by the higher reason or the logic of the Infinite and not by our formal and abstract reason.

So far we have seen that the chief merit of Sri Aurobindo's view of the Absolute lies in its being integral in nature and its being based on the higher reason or logic of the Infinite. The next important contribution of Sri Aurobindo's integral Advaitism is that it regards the creative force as conscious in nature. The creative force or Cit-Śakti is regarded by Sri Aurobindo, as we have shown in a preceding chapter, as one with the Absolute. So there is no opposition between the Absolute and its creative force in Sri Aurobindo's system. In the Sāṃkhya system we find a complete opposition between Puruṣa and Prakṛti. Puruṣa is conscious but inactive while Prakṛti is active but unconscious. Thus they are looked upon as completely opposed to each other. But this rank dualism of the Sāṁkhya does not satisfy the logical quest which seeks unity behind diversity. In Rāmānuja we find reason attaining this goal. He tries to reconcile the opposition between Puruṣa and Prakṛti by regarding them as the modes of the Absolute or Brahman. Prakṛti is not regarded as independent of Brahman and opposed to it but as dependent on it and forming an essential and integral part of it. But he nevertheless regards force as unconscious. It is *acit* for him. Now his conception of force as *acit* or unconscious in nature lands him in serious logical difficulties. He fails to reconcile in a satisfactory manner an unconscious force and the conscious Brahman. If the unconscious force forms an integral part of the Absolute, then it is sure to affect its absoluteness. Śaṅkara also regards the creative force or Māyā as unconscious. But he calls it unreal in order to maintain his Advaitism. But this is only an escape from the problem and not its solution. Our criticism of the doctrine of Māyā in a preceding chapter has clearly shown that it does not solve the problem of reality but renders it for ever insoluble. Sri Aurobindo escapes the difficulties inherent in the systems of Rāmānuja and Śaṅkara by conceiving force as conscious in nature. The Conscious Force or Cit-Śakti, according to him, assumes the garb of unconscious Prakṛti by a process of self-concentration in order to manifest the spatio-temporal world. Thus there is no real opposition between Cit-śakti and Prakṛti. Prakṛti is merely the external aspect of Conscious Force or Cit-Śakti. Thus Sri Aurobindo's conception of creative force as conscious in nature enables him to establish his integral Advaitism. It enables him to regard matter also as Brahman because the former is, according to him, nothing but the self-concentrated form of the latter. It is the Conscious Force of Brahman that manifests itself in the forms of matter, life and mind through the process of self-concentration. Thus Sri Aurobindo is able to give to the object also the status of Brahman. In the system of Śaṅkara the object is given only an epistemic and not an ontological status. In the system of Rāmānuja, though the reality of the object is admitted, yet it is treated as unconscious. It retains its unconscious and inert status, even when looked at from the transcendental standpoint. But in Sri Aurobindo, we find object also given unreservedly the status of Brahman. Thus we find that the integral Advaitism of Sri Aurobindo is a decisive improvement on the systems of Śaṅkara and Rāmānuja.

The most important and fundamental contribution that Sri Aurobindo has made to the theory of the Absolute lies, as we have elaborately shown in a preceding chapter, in his conception of the Supermind. It is the Supermind that gives us an integral view of the Absolute. It reconciles the apparent opposition between the Absolute and the world. The Absolute in itself is a timeless and spaceless Reality and the world is an extension in Time and Space and is a movement. So the Absolute by itself can have no connection with the world. A principle is required which may connect the two and reconcile their apparent opposition. This connecting link is provided by the Supermind. For this very reason Sri Aurobindo regards the existence of the Supermind, as a logical necessity. But it must not be thought that the Supermind is different from the Absolute or Saccidānanda. It is the Absolute itself in its creative aspect. Saccidānanda is an undifferentiated unity. Supermind is a differentiated unity. And as Supermind is nothing else than the creative or dynamic aspect of Saccidānanda, so the latter may be said to be both an undifferentiated unity and a differentiated unity. Saccidānanda exceeds all determinations and at the same time is the centre of all determinations. Thus it is both unqualified as well as qualified, indeterminate as well as determinate, passive as well as active simultaneously.

There is no real opposition between the active and passive consciousness of Brahman. As Sri Aurobindo rightly remarks, "The passive consciousness of Brahman and its active consciousness are not two different, conflicting and incompatible things; they are the same consciousness, the same energy, at one end in a state of self-reservation, at the other cast into a motion of self-giving and self-deploying, like the stillness of a reservoir and the coursing of the channels which flow from it. In fact, behind every activity there is and must be a passive power of being from which it arises, by which it is supported which even, we see in the end, governs it from behind without being totally identified with it—in the sense at least of being itself all poured out into the action and indistinguishable from it. Such a self-exhausting identification is impossible; for no action, however vast, exhausts the original power from which it proceeds leaving nothing behind it in reserve. When we get back into our own conscious being, when we stand back from our own action and see how it is done, we discover that it is our whole being which stands behind any particular act or sum of activities, passive in the rest of its integrality, active in its limited dispensation of energy, but that passivity is not an incapable inertia, it is a poise of self-reserved energy. A similar truth must apply still more completely to the conscious being of the Infinite whose power, in silence of status as in creation, must also be infinite."[1]

So we cannot regard the active and passive Brahman as two realities and as mutually opposed to each other. In fact this distinction is made for the convenience of our mind and so far it holds good. But in reality "there is not a passive Brahman and an active Brahman, but one Brahman, an Existence which reserves its Tapas in what we call passivity and gives itself in what we call its activity".

According to Sri Aurobindo, the individual consciousness in spiritual experience is forced to deny the reality of one aspect or other of the Absolute due to the fact that it identifies itself exclusively with some particular aspect and fails to have an integral view of Reality. As in sleep we have no consciousness of the waking state, in the same way when one gets identified with the passive state of Brahman's consciousness, one becomes forgetful of the active state. So also, the identification with the active state of Brahman's consciousness makes one forgetful of its passive state. So this is also a kind of ignorance and limitation. But Brahman does not suffer from ignorance and limitation, like our individual consciousness. "Integral Brahman possesses both the passivity and the activity simultaneously and does not pass alternately from one to the other as from a sleep to a waking: it is only some partial activity in us which seems to do that and we, by identifying ourselves with that partial activity, have the appearance of this alternation from one nescience to another nescience; but our true, our integral being is not subject to these opposites and it does not need to become unaware of its dynamic self in order to possess its self of silence. When we get the integral knowledge and the integral liberation of both soul and nature, free from the disabilities of the restricted, partial and ignorant being, we too can possess the passivity and the activity with a simultaneous possession, exceeding both these poles of the universality, limited by neither of these powers of the Self in its relation or non-relation to Nature."[2]

1. *L.D.*,Vol. II, Part I, pp. 339-40.
2. *Ibid.*, p. 343.

So the integral reality of Brahman can be expressed fully neither by our active Self nor by our passive Self nor by a combination of both these aspects of Brahman. Brahman is all these and at the same time transcends them all. As the states of waking, dream and deep sleep form the different poises of individual consciousness but do not exhaust the whole truth of human personality, whether taken singly or when put together, in the same way Brahman also cannot be exhausted by its different states whether taken singly or when put together. "For obviously we do not mean, when we speak of his possessing them (the active and passive states) simultaneously, that he is the sum of a passivity and an activity, an integer made of those two fractions, passive with threefourths of himself, active with one fourth of his existence. In that case, Brahman might be a sum of nesciences, the passive threefourths not only indifferent to but quite ignorant of all that the activity is doing, the active one fourth quite unaware of the passivity and unable to possess it except by ceasing from action. Even Brahman the sum might amount to something quite different from his two fractions, something, as it were, up and aloof, ignorant of and irresponsible for anything which some mystic Maya was at once obstinately doing and rigidly abstaining from doing in the two fractions of his existence. But it is clear that Brahman the Supreme Being must be aware both of the passivity and the activity and regard them not as his absolute being, but as opposite, yet mutually satisfying terms of his universalities."[1] So from what we have discussed above and in the chapters on the Absolute, it is clear that Sri Aurobindo does not commit any self-contradiction in regarding the Absolute as indeterminate and determinate or passive and active simultaneously as well as transcending them both. In fact this is the only way to have an integral view of Reality. The attempt on the part of the human mind to confine the Absolute exclusively to some particular poise or status may have some justification from the standpoint of our formal and abstract logic but it has no justification at all from the standpoint of higher reason and experience.

But it might be objected from the side of the Śankarites that Brahman as Brahman transcends all knowledge and hence it cannot be said to be possessed of integral knowledge from the ultimate

---

1. *L.D.*, Vol. II, Part I. pp. 343-44.

standpoint. All knowledge involves some form of dualism. If there is any knowledge which does not involve this dualism it would become identical with being and hence can no more possess the characteristic of integrality. It would then be simply pure knowledge or pure consciousness. If Brahman is said to be possessed of integral knowledge then it means that it contains an element of duality in it which is sure to affect its absoluteness.

To answer this question satisfactorily, it is necessary to take into account Sri Aurobindo's Theory of Knowledge.

(B) *Theory of Knowledge*

Knowledge, according to Sri Aurobindo, is relational as well as supra-relational. It expresses itself both in identity and in relations. But the knowledge by identity does not, according to Sri Aurobindo, mean that is devoid of relations altogether, but that it exceeds all relations and cannot be exhausted by any relation or any sum of relations. Thus the knowledge by identity or supra-relational knowledge does not negate or reject relations but it only exceeds their limitations. The same knowledge which expresses itself at one end in the form of identity, does express itself at the other end in the form of relations. The knowledge by identity or supra-relational knowledge and the relational knowledge are thus not exclusive of and mutually opposed to each other but they are complementary in nature. Both of them express the truth of the absolute or integral knowledge in their own ways and there is no real opposition between them.

Thus, it is clear that the integral knowledge of Sri Aurobindo does not deny the fact of identity of consciousness and being but it does hold that this identity does not reject or deny relational knowledge but only exceeds its limitations. In this respect Sri Aurobindo's theory of knowledge differs from that of Śaṅkara and Rāmānuja.

Śaṅkara regards knowledge as of two kinds—supra-relational and relational. The supra-relational knowledge is real and essential knowledge and the relational knowledge is simply a kind of ignorance. The Absolute, according to Śaṅkara, is of the nature of non-relational or supra-relational knowledge. It represents the perfect identity of consciousness and being. It is pure consciousness. It is what is called intuition. Intuition is of the nature of pure consciousness. It is not conscious of itself or the world. Relational knowledge is of the nature of thought. It is logical in nature. It is a unity which expresses itself in different relations. The very life of thought is based on relations. It is aware of itself as well as of all the relations and determinations that form a part of its being. But intuition does not depend on relations. On the other hand, it rejects all relations and differences. It not only exceeds differences but also negates them. Thus relational knowledge is relegated by Śaṅkara to the domain of ignorance. Śaṅkara does not find a way to synthesise relational and supra-relational knowledge or thought and intuition. The two are considered diametrically opposed to each other and hence no synthesis between them is possible.

Rāmānuja denies the non-relational character of knowledge. All knowledge, according to him, connotes relation. It is the unit of judgment. It expresses a relation between the subject and the predicate. The predicate is the concrete expression of the subject. "It helps to draw out the connotation of the subject term or in other words an abstract notion makes itself concrete through the concrete expression of a predicate. A judgment is, therefore, a subjectfully developed and this development is an inner growth and an inherent necessity. Knowledge is dynamic; it has a constant tendency to fully affirm its concreteness through all the qualities it possesses. Knowledge is essentially then judgment. This is the decided opinion of Rāmānuja and other theistic teachers."[1] Thus Rāmānuja does not, unlike Śaṅkara, raise any opposition between intuition and thought. Though the knowledge of the Absolute is attained through intuition, yet intuition is not opposed to thought. "In Rāmānuja the apparent discord between reason and intuition has been set aside and it has been possible for him to show that intuition and reason give us the same truth. The fundamental points of difference between Śaṅkara and Rāmānuja arise out of the relation between reason and intuition. Rāmānuja does not find any conflict between the two, for in his case reason and intuition function in the same way: they are relational consciousness. Reason conceives, intuition perceives. Reason conceives relations, intuition perceives them. Both of them work in the same way. We may go far and say that intuition is a form of judgment, since intuition intuits."[2]

---

1. A.B. Shastri, *Studies in Post-Śaṅkara Dialectics*, p. 13.
2. *Ibid.*, p. 22.

All knowledge according to Rāmānuja is qualified and differenti-
ated. According to Śankara, it is unqualified and undifferentiated.
Śankara and the Śankarites make a critical examination of all the
relational categories and show their self-discrepant and self-con-
tradictory nature. They try to prove the impossibility of making any
reconciliation between them. And as all relational categories are
found to be riddled with self-contradictions, so they are denied
any place in the transcendent Absolute. Identity and relation cannot
go together. "If there is identity there can be no relations, and if
there is relation there must be some difference and unity cannot
be established. The conception of unity embracing difference seems
to be a hopeless one. In unity either there is difference or there
is no difference. If there is difference there can be no unity and
if there is no difference, there can be no relation. The conception
of unity does not admit of a relation without difference."[1]

Sri Aurobindo's theory of knowledge tries to steer clear of the
extremes of Śankara and Rāmānuja. He does not call knowledge
simply relationless and unqualified or simply relational and quali-
fied. Knowledge, according to him, is integral in nature. The re-
lational and supra-relational aspects of knowledge form, according
to him, the two poises of integral knowledge. Integral knowledge
expresses itself, as has been pointed out above, in non-relational
and relational aspects or poises. It cannot be identified exclusively
either with non-relational knowledge or with relational knowl-
edge. Nor is it a sum of these two poises of knowledge. It ex-
presses itself in both. But Sri Aurobindo does not make merely an
artificial synthesis between the relational and non-relational knowl-
edge. Non-relational knowledge does not mean, as we have pointed
out above, that it is devoid of all relations, as Śankara would have
us believe, but it means that it exceeds or transcends all relations
and cannot be limited by any relation or any sum of relations. He
believes in the identity of consciousness and being. The identity
of consciousness and being is expressed both in the timeless status
as well as in Time. In the supreme timeless Existence, existence
and consciousness are one. As Sri Aurobindo puts it, "In the supreme
timeless status where consciousness is one with being and immo-
bile, it is not a separate reality, but simply and purely the self-

1. A.B. Shastri op. cit., p. 13.

awareness inherent in existence. There is no need of knowledge nor is there any operation of knowledge. Being is self-evident to itself: it does not need to look at itself in order to know itself or learn that it is."[1]

Thus it is clear that Sri Aurobindo believes in the identity of consciousness and being, but this identity is not of the nature of pure awareness or pure consciousness, as Śaṅkara would have us believe, but it is of the nature of self-awareness or self-consciousness. It is not a pure awareness which is neither aware of itself nor of what it becomes. The category of self-consciousness according to the Śaṅkarites involves a duality of subject and object. Self-consciousness is not possible without the consciousness of the object. Consciousness is aware of itself only when it is confronted by an object whether that object lies outside it or in it. As the category of self-consciousness is mediated by the object and depends on it, so it cannot be called the ultimate nature of the absolute knowledge which must be independent and unconditioned. So the ultimate or absolute consciousness according to the Śaṅkarites is merely a pure consciousness which is not mediated by the objects. Thus it is neither aware of itself nor of objects. Only such a consciousness can be said to be perfectly identical with being. Only this consciousness can be called a pure identity. Self-consciousness is not a pure identity but an identity-in-difference.

Sri Aurobindo does not use the word self-consciousness or self-awareness in the sense of Śaṅkara and the Śaṅkarites. Self-awareness or self-consciousness is, according to him, not necessarily mediated by an object. It is the very nature of existence. It does not have the awareness of itself through any process or operation of knowledge. Being is self-luminous and self-evident to itself. It does not stand in need of looking at itself in order to be aware of itself or of its existence. So self-awareness is the very nature of being or existence. It is a perfectly unconditioned principle. It is not conditioned or mediated by objects.

The identity of consciousness and being is not only revealed in the timeless self-concentration of the Absolute but is also revealed in the extension of space and time. Just as "spiritual Self-existence is intrinsically aware of its self, so it is intrinsically aware of all that is in its being: this is not by an act of knowledge formulated in a self-regard, a self-observation, but by the same inherent awareness; it is intrinsically all-conscious of all that is by the very fact that all is itself. Thus conscious of its timeless self-existence, the spirit, the Being is aware in the same way—intrinsically, absolutely, totally, without any need of a look or act of knowledge, because it is all—of Time-Existence and of all that is in Time. This is the essential awareness by identity; if applied to cosmic existence, it would mean an essential self-evident automatic consciousness of the universe by the Spirit because it is everything and everything is its being".[1] Thus the Absolute enjoys perfect identity of consciousness and being both in its timeless existence and in its extension of space and time. The Absolute is intrinsically aware of all as itself. It is not aware of all existences as objects but as itself. There is no distinction of subject and object at this stage. Knowledge at this stage is not an act or a process. It is pure intrinsic self-awareness inherent in the absolute Being. But the Absolute also admits within itself a subordinate movement of consciousness without changing or modifying its own eternal nature, "a subordinate and simultaneous awareness by inclusion and indwelling". It sees all existences in itself and itself in all existences. The Supermind is intrinsically aware of all existences as itself and at the same time is aware of them as within itself and itself in them. To quote again Sri Aurobindo's statement, "Brahman is in all things, all things are in Brahman, all things are Brahman," is the triple formula of the comprehensive Supermind, a single truth of self-manifestation in three aspects which it holds together and inseparably in its self-view as the fundamental knowledge from which it proceeds to the play of cosmos.[2]

Thus it is clear that the integral knowledge, according to Sri Aurobindo, is both relational and supra-relational. It bridges the gulf between the relational and the supra-relational consciousness. The Supermind has the intrinsic awareness of both the supra-relational and the relational aspects of the Absolute. Sri Aurobindo has found the way to reconcile the relational and the supra-relational knowledge in the principle of Supermind. Sri

1. *L.D.*, Vol. II, Part I, p. 305.
2. *L.D.*, Vol. I, p. 175.

Aurobindo approaches the problem of knowledge like all other problems, from the standpoint of higher reason or the logic of the Infinite. He shows that the relational and the non-relational or supra-relational knowledge appear as contradictory to each other only to our abstract reason which takes a narrow view of these terms and fails to comprehend their real significance. He shows that the non-relational or supra-relational knowledge does not negate relational knowledge but only exceeds its limitations. In the same way he shows that to say that knowledge is qualified does not mean that it exhausts the whole nature of knowledge. It is a real poise of knowledge. The Supermind may be said to be qualified unity. But here also in the primary poise of the Supermind, there is no difference between the One and the All. In Rāmānuja, the predicate always remains distinct from the subject though the former lies within the latter and forms an integral part of it. The individual souls remain always atomic in nature and though they are able to realise unity and fellowship with Brahman and attain its nature, yet they do not realise perfect identity with it. In the same way, *acit* always remains *acit*; it never enjoys perfect identity with Brahman. Thus though the predicate is not independent of the subject and does not lie outside it, yet it does not also enjoy absolute identity with the subject and retains its distinctness in the unity of the whole. But in Sri Aurobindo the predicate retains its individuality in the subject and forms an integral part of it and at the same time it enjoys perfect identity with the subject also. The individual souls retain their individuality in the Absolute and at the same time they enjoy, as we will show subsequently, their identity with the cosmos and the Transcendent. They are not eternally condemned to remain confined to their atomic status. So though the Absolute is qualified, yet its whole reality is not exhausted by this aspect. The Absolute is qualified and relational in nature and at the same time it transcends all relations. Knowledge is thus qualified as well as unqualified. It is a differentiated unity as well as an undifferentiated unity and at the same time it transcends both these aspects. So the undifferentiated unity and differentiated unity do not reject each other but they are the complementary aspects of knowledge. Both express the truth of the absolute knowledge in their own ways. The relational as well as the supra-relational knowledge form the complementary aspects of integral knowledge.

Sri Aurobindo does admit that the full nature of the absolute knowledge is not expressed in relations, yet he does not call relations false or unreal. Relations appear contradictory of the Absolute only when one looks at them from the standpoint of the finite reason which tries to judge them *a priori* on the basis of the principles of Formal Logic, namely, Identity and Contradiction, as we have discussed before. Though the full truth of the absolute knowledge is not revealed by relations, yet it is also not fully revealed by the non-relational or supra-relational knowledge. To say that the Absolute is simply pure consciousness, meaning thereby, that it is neither conscious of itself nor of the world is to get involved in an impossible situation. In that case the existence of the world will have no meaning for the Absolute and cannot be explained by it. Some principle like Māyā or Avidyā will have to be posited in order to explain it. But this is to involve oneself in a kind of dualism. The denial of the reality of the world from the ultimate standpoint does not save such a system from the charge of dualism. Moreover, an Advaitism which is established by denying the reality of one fundamental aspect of experience is merely abstract in nature. So the only way of establishing Advaitism on a sound foundation is to admit the reality of both the relational as well as the supra-relational aspects of Existence and reconcile them in the all-embracing unity of the Absolute as Sri Aurobindo does. The greatest achievement of Śaṅkara was to realise that the full and perfect nature of the Absolute cannot be revealed in and through relations. In this sense his system is undoubtedly superior, as we have maintained all along, to that of Rāmānuja, Hegel etc. Yet he was wrong in denying the reality of the relations, as we have shown above and in the preceding chapters, from the ontological or metaphysical standpoint. The greatest achievement of Sri Aurobindo is to realise that the Absolute is both relational and supra-relational in nature and at the same time it is beyond them both. It can be limited neither by our affirmations nor by our negations. Sri Aurobindo is fully justified in asserting that no category or no sum of categories can exhaust the nature of the Absolute. To say that the Absolute is simply relationless and devoid of all relations is also to confine the Absolute to the category of Being or pure consciousness. The integral view of the Absolute or the supreme Reality can be attained only by an integral knowledge and not by any partial source of knowledge. The supramental or integral knowledge bridges the gulf existing between reason and intuition and reconciles them in its own higher unity which has the intrinsic awareness of the relational as well as supra-relational knowledge. The higher unity of integral knowledge is not merely a dogmatic assumption of Sri Aurobindo but it can be conceived by reason, as we have shown above, if it gets rid of its abstract attitude. These higher truths as we have pointed out repeatedly can be understood and conceived only by our higher or synthetic reason and not by the abstract reason or the logic of the finite which is purely analytic in nature.

Now we proceed to give a critical estimate of Sri Aurobindo's conception of the individual soul.

(C) *Conception of the Individual Soul*

The merit of Sri Aurobindo's integral Advaitism is also seen in its solution of the problem of the individual soul. Śaṅkara regards the individual soul as identical with Brahman. The individuality, according to him, is nothing but the product of ignorance. We fail to realise the identity of Brahman and *Jīva* or the individual soul on account of ignorance. It is the Ātman or Brahman that appears as the individual soul or *Jīva* on account of its false identification with the psycho-physical organism. Thus the *Jīva*, according to Śaṅkara, is a complex of self and not-self. "The *Jīva* is subject-object, self and not-self, reality and appearance. It consists of the Ātman limited or individuated by the object. It is the Ātman in association with *ajñāna*."[1] *Avidyā* or logical knowledge, causes the sense of individuality of the empirical self, which is "alike deceiving and deceived". "The distinctive characteristic of the individual soul is its connection with *buddhi* or understanding, which endures as long as the state of *saṁsāra* is not terminated by perfect knowledge. The soul's connection with *buddhi* continues even after death. It can be broken only by the attainment of freedom".[2] The perfect identity of the individual soul and Brahman is realised on the attainment of freedom from ignorance. Thus it is clear that individuality, according to Śaṅkara, is merely the product of ignorance and it is cancelled on the attainment of liberation. Bhāskara

---

1. Radhakrishnan, *Indian Philosophy*, Vol. II, p. 596.
2. *Ibid.*, p. 596.

also regards the individual soul as one with Brahman, while its difference from Brahman is due to limitations or *upādhis*.[1] But he differs from Śaṅkara in regarding the *upādhis* as real. On the attainment of freedom from limitations or *upādhis*, the identity between the individual soul or *Jīva* and Brahman is finally realised. The individual soul, according to Rāmānuja, is a part or mode of God. It is regarded as real and atomic (*aṇu*) in size. On liberation the soul attains the nature of God, though not identity with him. The released soul becomes omniscient but it still remains atomic in size. It does not attain perfect identity with Brahman but enjoys unity and fellowship with him. Rāmānuja rightly holds, as we have stated in the preceding chapter, that it is egoity that is opposed to salvation and not individuality. But he is certainly not justified in denying the absolute identity of soul and Brahman. The views of Śaṅkara as well as Rāmānuja regarding the nature of the soul and its relation to Brahman seem to be partial and one-sided. Śaṅkara is right insofar as he maintains the absolute identity of *Jīva* or the individual soul and Brahman. But he is not justified in calling individuality the product of ignorance. Rāmānuja is right insofar as he maintains the reality of the individual souls but he is wrong in denying, as we have stated above, the absolute identity or oneness of the individual souls and Brahman. The reason of their taking a partial and one-sided view is that they make an approach to this problem through finite reason. The finite or abstract reason finds it self-contradictory to recognise the reality of the individual souls and at the same to assert their absolute identity or oneness with Brahman. Thus it is compelled to reject one of these views in order to escape the charge of self-contradiction. But Sri Aurobindo argues that we can assert the reality of the individual souls and at the same time assert their absolute oneness with Brahman without committing self-contradiction if we tackle this problem through the higher reason. The Self according to Sri Aurobindo is one in its being, yet it is capable in its very unity of cosmic differentiation and multiple individuality. It expresses itself, as we have seen in a preceding chapter, in three terms, the individual, the universal and the transcendent. The transcendent Self does not deny the truth of the individual and the universal

---

1. Cf. जीवपरयोश्च स्वाभाविकोऽभेद औपाधिकस्तु भेद: । (*Bhāskara-Bhāṣya* IV. 4.4)

aspects but only exceeds their limitations. The individual souls and cosmos are the powers of the transcendent Self. "The unity is its being—yes, but the cosmic differentiation and the multiple individuality are the power of its being which it is constantly displaying and which it is its delight and the nature of its consciousness to display. If then we arrive at unity with that, if we even become entirely and in every way that being, why should the power of its being be excised and why at all should we desire or labour to excise it? We should then only diminish the scope of our unity with it by an exclusive concentration accepting the Divine Being but not accepting our part in the power and consciousness and infinite delight of the Divine. It would in fact be the individual seeking peace and rest of union in a motionless identity, but rejecting delight and various joy of union in the nature and act and power of the Divine Existence. That is possible, but there is no necessity to uphold it as the ultimate aim of our being or as our ultimate perfection."[1] The soul, according to Sri Aurobindo, can enjoy unity with the Divine both in its essence and in its power. To become one with the Divine, to enjoy unity with it only in essence and not in its aspect of power is a partial and one-sided unity and not a perfect and integral unity. The integral and perfect unity of the soul with the Divine is possible only when the former identifies itself with the latter in its aspect of being as well as in its aspect of power, in its transcendent as well as in its universal and individual aspects. We do not forfeit perfect union with the Divine by enjoying unity with its cosmic and the individual aspects any more than the Divine forfeits his oneness by accepting them. "We have the perfect union in his being and can absorb ourselves in it at any time, but we have also this other differentiated unity and can emerge into it and act freely in it at any time without losing oneness; for we have merged the ego and are absolved from the excessive stresses of our mentality."[2] Nor are we required to reject differentiated unity and plunge ourselves into the absorption of an exclusive unity for obtaining peace and rest. For "we have the peace and rest by virtue of our unity with Him, even as the Divine possesses for ever His eternal calm in the midst of His eternal

---

1. *L.D.*, Vol. II, Part I, pp. 91-92.
2. *Ibid.*, p. 93.

action". The differentiation, Sri Aurobindo argues, has its Divine purpose: "it is a means of greater unity, not as in the egoistic life a means of divisions; for we enjoy by it our unity with our other selves and with God in all, which we exclude by our rejection of his multiple being. In either experience it is the Divine in the individual possessing and enjoying in one case the Divine in His pure unity or in the other the Divine in that and in the unity of the cosmos; it is not the absolute Divine recovering after having lost His unity. Certainly, we may prefer the absorption in a pure exclusive unity or a departure into a supra-cosmic transcendence, but there is in the spiritual truth of the Divine Existence no compelling reason why we should not participate in this large possession and bliss of His universal being which is the fulfilment of our individuality".[1]

Thus it is clear that the individual soul can realise itself as individual, universal and transcendent at one and the same time. The soul can enjoy its relations with other souls and with the cosmos but it does not fall from its essential unity with the Divine. It is our ego that is incapable of realising true unity with other souls, with the cosmos and the Transcendent and not the true individual soul. In Rāmānuja, as we have seen above, the soul on liberation attains the nature of God (Brahman) and enjoys fellowship with Him but it does not enjoy absolute identity with Him. In Śaṅkara, the soul enjoys perfect identity with Brahman on liberation but it is not able to enjoy fellowship with Him. But in Sri Aurobindo, the soul enjoys both absolute identity with Brahman as well as fellowship with Him. It enjoys the bliss of Brahman both in its undifferentiated unity and the differentiated unity. In Rāmānuja the soul is atomic in nature even after liberation. It develops in consciousness and power but not in its being. In Śaṅkara the individuality is regarded, as has been pointed out above, as the product of ignorance. It is cancelled when the ignorance is removed, Thus the individual soul is not given the status of reality in Śaṅkara's system. Brahman is incapable of manifesting itself as real individual souls according to Śaṅkara. But according to Sri Aurobindo, Brahman expresses itself eternally in the individual, the universal and the transcendent aspects. But this appears to our

---

1. *L.D.*, Vol. II, Part II, p. 93.

normal and abstract reason as self-contradictory. The reason is that our normal reason tries to interpret higher experiences in terms of the lower ones. As Sri Aurobindo puts it, "the whole difficulty and confusion into which the normal reason falls is that we are speaking of a higher and illimitable self-experience founded on divine infinite and yet are applying to it a language formed by this lower and limited experience which founds itself on finite appearances and the separative definitions by which we try to distinguish and classify the phenomena of the material universe. Thus we have to use the word individual and speak of the ego and the true individual, just as we speak sometimes of the apparent and the real Man. Evidentally all these words, man, apparent, real, individual, true, have to be taken in a very relative sense and with a full-awareness of their imperfection and inability to express the things that we mean".[1] "By individual," further observes Sri Aurobindo, "we mean normally something that separates itself from everything else and stands apart, though in reality there is no such thing anywhere in existence; it is a figment of our mental conceptions useful and necessary to express a partial and practical truth. But the difficulty is that the mind gets dominated by its words and forgets that the partial and practical truth becomes true truth only by its relation to others which seem to the reason to contradict it, and that taken by itself it contains a constant element of falsity. Thus, when we speak of an individual we mean ordinarily an individualisation of mental, vital, physical being separate from all other beings, incapable of unity with them by its individuality. If we go beyond these three terms of mind, life and body and speak of the soul or individual self, we still think of an individualised being separate from all others incapable of unity and inclusive mutuality, capable at most of a spiritual contact and soul-sympathy. It is, therefore necessary to insist that by the true individual we mean nothing of the kind, but a conscious power of being of the Eternal, always existing by unity, always capable of mutuality. It is that being which by self-knowledge enjoys liberation and immortality".[2] Our normal and abstract reason fails to grasp the essential significance of these higher experiences. We can understand the nature of the individual soul and its relationship with

---

1. *L.D.*, Vol. II, Part I, pp. 95-96.
2. *Ibid.*, p. 96.

the cosmos and the Divine only when we approach this problem through the higher reason which is not deluded by the magic of our ordinary words and concepts but takes a comprehensive and integral view of them. So we find that Sri Aurobindo is perfectly justified in maintaining the reality of the individual souls as well as their unity with the cosmos and the transcendent and he cannot be charged with indulging in self-contradiction. Thus it is clear that the integral Advaitism of Sri Aurobindo has made a fundamental contribution to the conception of the individual soul also as it has made, as we have pointed out above, to the theory of Reality and knowledge.

Now we proceed to make a critical estimate of Sri Aurobindo's Conception of Evolution and the Destiny of Man.

(D) Conception of Evolution and Destiny of Man

In the previous chapters we have made an elaborate study of Sri Aurobindo's conception of evolution and the destiny of man. We have seen that Sri Aurobindo admits a double process in evolution, the evolution of the individual soul as well as of the cosmos. Not only the individual soul but the cosmos also has to attain a higher or divine status. Nature also has to attain liberation along with the spirit. The destiny of man, according to Sri Aurobindo, can be fulfilled only when he attains not only the liberation of spirit but gets rid of all sorts of limitations and imperfections in the physical, vital and mental aspects of his personality also. A radical change in mental, vital and physical aspects of man's personality is necessary if he has to attain perfect integration of his personality. The liberation of spirit may enable man to enjoy perfect peace of mind and supreme bliss but it does not necessarily save his psychophysical organism from disease, pain, suffering, incapacity, etc. Only the descent of Supermind and Saccidānanda can effect perfect integration in man's personality and can enable man to enjoy perfect peace, bliss and immortality on this earth. The descent of Supermind in the course of evolution will take the cosmic process to a higher or divine status. This is, in our view, a special contribution of Sri Aurobindo to the theory of evolution and the destiny of man.

In this respect Sri Aurobindo's view, as we have stated in the preceding chapters on Evolution, differs from the Vedānta and other systems. Whereas Vedānta and other systems aim at the liberation of soul or spirit only, Sri Aurobindo aims at the liberation of the spirit as well as of nature. And this is possible, according to him, only when all the parts of our being are raised to a higher or divine status through the process of descent of the higher principles and their integration with the lower ones. The principle of integration, as we have pointed out in a preceding chapter, occupies a very important place in Sri Aurobindo's conception of evolution. "Evolution....does not mean the isolated raising of any principle to a higher level but an uplift and transformation of all the principles. If, therefore, a true uplift of human nature is to take place, this cannot be affected by raising only a part of our being to a higher level, detaching it from the lower parts, but the lower parts must be transformed in the light of the higher, leading to a complete change of all the parts of our being. If mind alone receives the higher light without being able to transmit it to matter as well as the vital principle, there cannot occur a general uplift of the whole universe." This explains why, in spite of the fact that so many individuals in different lands have obtained personal salvation by detaching themselves from mind, "life and matter there has been no transformation yet of the whole world into a higher status".[1] Sri Aurobindo aims at the liberation of the whole world by its transformation into a higher status—the divine status.

In this respect Sri Aurobindo's theory of evolution is superior to that of modern Western evolutionists who have taken their stand mainly on material, vital and mental principles. "A mechanical theory, a vitalistic theory and a mental theory of evolution," Dr. Varadachari rightly remarks, "are all that modern science has been able to arrive at, and the result is disappointing. The vitalistic theory surrenders something fundamental to the mechanical, and the mentalistic theory cannot explain the inward drive of the process of evolution".[2] Evolution, according to Sri Aurobindo, is ultimately spiritual in nature. It is the dynamic spiritual energy that is present in a latent form in the individual and the cosmos and is guiding the evolutionary process. It is Spirit that has manifested the cosmos through the process of self-concentration of its consciousness-force and it is this spiritual force which is leading the cosmic process

---

1. Dr. S.K. Maitra, *Studies in Sri Aurobindo's Philosophy*, p. 31.
2. Dr. K.C. Varadachari, *Divine Evolutionism*, Sri Aurobindo Mandir Annual, (1942), p. 16.

to a higher and higher status in order to enable it to receive the light, power and bliss of the Spirit. The mechanical, the vitalistic and the mental theories of evolution are according to Sri Aurobindo partial and one-sided in nature and they fail to grasp the real significance and express the full truth of the evolutionary process.

Sri Aurobindo is one with Bergson in rejecting the mechanical view of evolution. But he differs from Bergson in believing in teleology. "A manifestation of the greater powers of Existence till the whole being itself is manifest in the material world in the terms of a higher, a spiritual creation, may be considered as the teleology of the evolution."[1] "This teleology does not bring in any factor that does not belong to the totality, it proposes only the realisation of the totality in the part. There can be no objection to the admission of a teleological factor in a part movement of the universal totality, if the purpose—not a purpose in the human sense, but the urge of an intrinsic Truth necessity conscious in the will of the indwelling Spirit—is the perfect manifestation there of all the possibilities inherent in the total movement. All exists here no doubt, for the delight of existence, all is a game or Lila; but a game too carries within itself an object to be accomplished and without the fulfilment of that object would have no completeness of significance."[2] Thus Sri Aurobindo believes in the teleological factor in evolution. But this view of teleological factor in evolution differs from the ordinary view. The ordinary view of teleological evolution "puts forward narrow human ends, which, of course, it is impossible for philosophy to accept without degrading evolution to the level of a purely anthropomorphic theory. But the remedy for this lies not in abandoning all teleology but in substituting a higher for a lower teleology".[3] This higher teleology in Sri Aurobindo's view consists in the descent of the supermind and Saccidānanda in the world of matter, life and mind and the consequent transformation of these principles by the light and power of the Spirit.

It is necessary to consider here certain objections that may be raised against Sri Aurobindo's theory of evolution. Sri Aurobindo holds that there is not only an evolution through ignorance but an evolution through knowledge also. The process of evolution

1. *L.D.*, Vol. II, Part II, p. 661.
2. *Ibid.*, p. 661.
3. Dr. S.K. Maitra, *Studies in Sri Aurobindo's Philosophy*, p. 28.

does not come to an end after the supramental transformation. Whereas prior to the supramental transformation, the evolution takes place through ignorance, after supramental transformation, it continues through knowledge.

Now it may be said that the evolution from ignorance to knowledge is understandable, but the evolution through knowledge is difficult to understand. Evolution of a thing is indicative of its imperfection. It rises from a less perfect state to a more perfect state through the process of evolution. Ignorance represents the state of imperfection. So ignorance may get rid of its imperfections and turn into the principle of knowledge in the course of evolution. But the supramental principle has not even a trace of ignorance in it. So it is difficult to understand how there can be an evolution after supramental transformation. The triple principle of Saccidānanda, namely, bliss, consciousness and existence will surely manifest according to Sri Aurobindo after the supramental transformation has taken place. But it would be merely an expression and cannot strictly be called evolution. If the evolution of man continues even after he is transformed into a gnostic being, it will mean that he still suffers from some sort of imperfection and limitation and has not been able to reach the final goal. This will go against the view of the perfection of the gnostic personality. Man will not be able to reach the goal if it goes on receding further and further back forever. So it may be said that it is difficult to admit the evolution of the gnostic being on logical or rational grounds.

But a clear understanding of Sri Aurobindo's view makes it amply clear that the evolution through knowledge is perfectly conceivable. The emergence of the gnostic personality marks the liberation of the spirit and the body of the individual from the yoke of ignorance and inconscience but it does not effect a cessation of evolution through knowledge. The divine force now no longer has to work in a hidden and veiled manner in man. The supramental descent is thus marked by a decisive but long-prepared transition from an evolution in the Ignorance to an always progressive evolution in the Knowledge.[1] "It will not be," observes Sri Aurobindo, "a sudden revelation and effectuation of the absolute Supermind

---

1. *L.D.*, Vol. II, Part II, p. 821.

and the Supramental being as they are in their own plane, the swift apocalypse of a truth-conscious existence ever self-fulfilled and complete in self-knowledge; it will be the phenomenon of the supramental being descending into a world of evolutionary becoming and forming itself there, unfolding the powers of the gnosis within the terrestrial nature".[1] The supramental descent carries the individual finally from the realm of ignorance to that of knowledge. But the journey of the divine traveller does not come to an end after entering the gateway of the city of knowledge. Now new and vast vistas of spirit open themselves to him and he finds himself fully free to proceed further and further in the realm of joy, beauty and bliss, in the planes of Saccidānanda. Thus he is now able to enjoy in an endless manner the light, freedom, power and bliss of Saccidānanda. The gnostic Being is completely free from all ignorance and imperfection, but this does not rule out the possibility of his enjoying more and more the powers and bliss of the divine. There is an endless and unceasing flow of the powers and bliss of Saccidānanda in the gnostic personality just as there is an unceasing flow of the waters in the Gaṅgā, from the Himālayas. If a man takes a dip in the Gaṅgā, he becomes one with the holy river but his unity does not rule out the possibility of his swimming across the holy river or diving deeper and deeper into its bottom. In the same way the gnostic Being enjoys unity with the Divine or Saccidānanda but he can also dive deeper and deeper or soar higher and higher through the unending spheres of the Infinite. The goal of man's evolution or the destiny of man is attained when the supermind and the triple principle of Saccidānanda manifest themselves in his personality in an unveiled manner. But this unveiled revelation of the bliss and powers of Saccidānanda in the gnostic personality continues, as has been stated above, in an unceasing and endless manner. There can be no end to the realisation of the inexhaustible powers and the immeasurable bliss of Saccidānanda. Thus the perfection of the gnostic being does in no way exclude the possibility of his enjoying in ever new and infinitely variable aspects and in an endless manner the ineffable treasures and bliss of the Divine. Thus it is clear that the perfection

---

1. *L.D.*, Vol. II, Part II, p. 821.

of the gnostic Being is in no way incompatible with his further evolution in and through knowledge. On the other hand his very perfection enables him to participate in the eternal Līlā of the Divine and to enjoy it in infinite ways. It is not given to an ignorant and imperfect man to have even a distant glimpse of the Divine Līlā, not to speak of being a participant in the eternal and ever continuing and ever changing Divine Līlā.

So far we have dealt with the possibility of the evolution of the gnostic Being through knowledge. But along with the gnostic being there is the evolution of the cosmos also through knowledge after the descent of the Supermind. The sphere of knowledge is reached when there is the descent of the Supermind into earth-consciousness. But this does not immediately produce a total divinisation of the entire universe. As Sri Aurobindo puts it, "As we envisage it, it must manifest in a few first and then spread, but it is not likely to overpower the earth in a moment."[1] So evolution has to proceed through knowledge in order that there may be greater and greater revelation of the Divine consciousness, power and bliss in the entire universe. Prior to the descent of the supramental force in earth-consciousness, the cosmic evolution proceeds through igno- rance and after it, it proceeds through knowledge. Hence it is clear that there is no logical difficulty in conceiving the evolution of man and the cosmos through knowledge after the supramental descent.

But another objection may be raised here. Sri Aurobindo holds that the world-process is governed at present by the principles of inconscience and ignorance and after supramental descent it will be governed by the principle of knowledge. But he himself admits that the whole human race cannot rise in a block to the supramental status. If this is so, then the human race will be simultaneously governed by two principles, namely, ignorance and knowledge. The life of gnostic beings will be governed by the principle of knowledge and of the ordinary human beings by that of igno- rance. Even if at some future date the whole human race rises to the supramental status, even then the world as a whole cannot be said to be governed by the principle of knowledge, because there will be the animals and other living beings who will still carry on their shoulders the yoke of ignorance and there will be the world

---

1. *Letters of Sri Aurobindo*, First Series, p. 12.

418   THE INTEGRAL ADVAITISM OF SRI AUROBINDO

of pure matter which will have inconscience as its reigning principle. So the world as a whole will never have a chance to be governed and directed by the principle of knowledge. The principles of inconscience and ignorance cannot then be said to be ultimately transformed into that of knowledge. In that case the supramental descent will be able to raise merely the human race or a part of the human race to a higher status and not the whole of cosmos. The result will be that the rule of spirit will be limited only to a part of the cosmos and will not be applicable to the whole of it. And it will go against Sri Aurobindo's contention that the world-process will be governed by knowledge after the supramental descent.

This objection can also be removed by a clear appreciation of Sri Aurobindo's position. Sri Aurobindo holds the view that it is Spirit which is guiding and directing the course of cosmic evolution in a hidden and veiled manner. But after the supramental descent into earth-consciousness, the Spirit will be able to direct the evolutionary process consciously and in an unveiled manner. The effect of the Divine descent will not remain confined to the gnostic beings but will be felt in the whole of creation. The material, vital and mental principles of the cosmos will also be effected by the pressure and the impact of the supramental light and force; and this will give a new impetus to the evolutionary process. As Sri Aurobindo observes, "the presence of the liberated and now sovereign supramental light and force at the head of evolutionary nature might be expected to have its consequences in the whole evolution. An incidence, a decisive stress would affect the life of the lower evolutionary stages; something of the light, something of the force would penetrate downwards and awaken into a greater action the hidden Truth-Power everywhere in Nature. A dominant principle of harmony would impose itself on the life of ignorance; the discord, the blind seeking, the clash of struggle, the abnormal vicissitudes of exaggeration and depression and unsteady balance of the unseeing forces at work in their mixture and conflict would feel the influence and yield place to a more orderly pace and harmonic steps of the development of being, a more revealing arrangement of progressing life and consciousness, a better life order. A freer play of intuition and sympathy and understanding would enter into human life, a clear sense of the truth of self and things and a more enlightened dealing with the opportunities and difficulties of existence".[1] As he further observes, "Instead of a constant intermixed and confused struggle between the growth of Consciousness and the power of the Inconscience, between the forces of light and the forces of darkness, the evolution would become a graded progression from lesser light to greater light; in each stage of it the conscious beings belonging to that stage would respond to the inner Consciousness-Force and expand their own law of cosmic Nature towards a possibility of a higher degree of that Nature. This is at least a strong possibility and might be envisaged as the natural consequence of the direct action of supermind on the evolution. This intervention would not annul the evolutionary principle, for supermind has the power of withholding or keeping in reserve its force of knowledge as well as the power of bringing it into full or partial action; but it would harmonise, steady, facilitate, tranquillise and to a great extent hedonise the difficult and afflicted process of the evolutionary emergence."[2]

Thus Sri Aurobindo makes it amply clear that after the descent of Supermind into earth-consciousness, though the principles of matter, life and mind will be there and the evolution will continue through those stages, yet even there it will have the impact of the supramental light and power and will work under the principle of unity and harmony. Matter, life and mind will not be guided by the principles of inconscience and ignorance but by the principle of knowledge. If the presence of water, air and the sun 'has its undeniable influence in the evolution of animal, vegetable and mineral kingdom, there can be no gainsaying the fact that the presence of the supramental light and force is also sure to wield some effect on the cosmic evolution. Thus it is evident that the Supermind will direct the course of cosmic evolution after making a descent into the world and not any other principle, like inconscience and ignorance. Thus there is nothing wrong in admitting that the evolution will proceed through knowledge after the supramental descent and not through ignorance and inconscience. It is true that the ignorance and inconscience will not be abrogated all of a sudden and altogether by the descent of the supramental force but nevertheless they will henceforth

1. *L.D.*, Vol. II, p. 824.
2. *Ibid.*, pp. 824-25.

cease to guide and direct the course of cosmic evolution. As the beacon light does not dispel darkness from all the quarters of the sea, yet it gives an unfailing guidance to the ships to proceed safely onward to their destination, in the same way the supramental light and power may not be able to annihilate ignorance and inconscience all of a sudden and completely, yet it does not fail to give impetus and guidance to the evolutionary process in its ownard march to its desired destination. Thus it is clear that the presence of the principles of inconscience and ignorance will not entitle them to direct the course of cosmic evolution after the descent of the supermind. Hence there is no point in saying that the cosmos will be ruled by the principles of inconscience and ignorance also along with that of knowledge after the supramental descent.

Sri Aurobindo does not envisage the possibility of the cessation of evolution sooner or later from the Inconscience after the descent of Supermind and Saccidānanda into earth-consciousness. As he puts it, "A question might arise whether the gnostic reversal, the passage into a gnostic evolution and beyond it would not mean sooner or later the cessation of the evolution from the Inconscience, since the reason for that obscure beginning of things here would cease. This depends on the farther question whether the movement between the Superconscience and the Inconscience as the two poles of existence is an abiding law of the material manifestation or only a provisional circumstance. The latter supposition is difficult to accept because of the tremendous force of pervasiveness and durability with which the inconscient foundation has been laid for the whole material universe. Any complete reversal or elimination of the first evolutionary principle would mean the simultaneous manifestation of the secret involved consciousness in every part of this vast universal inconscience; a change in a particular line of Nature such as the earth-line could not have any such all-pervading effect: the manifestation in earth-nature has its own curve and the completion of that curve is all that we have to consider."[1] "Here this much might be hazarded," he further observes, "that in the lower triplicity the evolution here, though remaining the same in its degrees and stages, would be subjected

---

1. *L.D.*, Vol. II, Part II, pp. 877-78.

to the law of harmony, the law of unity in diversity and of diversity working out unity: it would be no longer an evolution through strife; it would become a harmonious development from stage to stage, from lesser to greater light, from lower type to higher type of the power and beauty of the self-unfolding existence. It would only be otherwise if for some reason the law of struggle and suffering still remained necessary for the working out of that mysterious possibility in the Infinite whose principle underlies the plunge into the Inconscience. But for the earth nature it would seem as if this necessity might be exhausted once the supramental gnosis had emerged from the Inconscience. A change would begin with its firm appearance; that change would be consummated when the supramental evolution became complete and rose into the greater fullness of supreme manifestation of the Existence-Consciousness-Delight, Sachchidananda".[1]

Sri Aurobindo regards the spiritual and the supramental evolution as a kind of logical necessity. It is true that it is not easy for human beings to believe in such a high destiny assigned to man and the evolutionary nature. Sri Aurobindo is fully aware of this difficulty. But he attributes this inability of the human being to the present limitation of his consciousness. "The descent of the Supramental," remarks Sri Aurobindo, "is an inevitable necessity in the logic of things and is therefore sure. It is because people do not understand what the Supermind is or realise the significance of the emergence of consciousness in a world of inconscient Matter that they are unable to realise this inevitability. I suppose a matter-of-fact observer, if there had been one at the time of the unrelieved reign of inanimate Matter in the earth's beginning, would have criticised any promise of the emergence of life in a world of dead earth and rock and mineral as an absurdity and a chimera; so too, afterwards he would have repeated this mistake and regarded the emergence of thought and reason in an animal world as an absurdity and a chimera. It is the same now with the appearance of Supermind in the stumbling mentality of this world of human consciousness and its reasoning ignorance".[2] Sri Aurobindo compares the present attitude of man in respect of his higher evolution

---

1. *L.D.*, Vol. II, Part II, p. 878.
2. *Letters*, First Series, p. 13.

with that of the Darwinian Ape. As he puts it, "we are in respect
to our possible higher evolution much in the position of the original
Ape of the Darwinian theory. It would have been impossible for
that Ape leading his instinctive arboreal life in primeval forests to
conceive that there would be one day an animal on the earth who
would use a new faculty called reason upon the materials of his
inner and outer existence, who would dominate by that power his
instincts and habits, change the circumstances of his physical life,
build for himself houses of stone, manipulate Nature's forces, sail
the seas, ride the air, develop codes of conduct, evolve conscious
methods for his mental and spiritual development. And if such a
conception had been possible for the Ape-mind, it would still have
been difficult for him to imagine that by any progress of Nature
or long effort of will and tendency he could develop into that
animal".[1] "His (man's) dream of God and Heaven," further remarks
Sri Aurobindo, "is really a dream of his own perfection; but he
finds the same difficulty in accepting its practical realisation here
for his ultimate aim as would the ancestral Ape if called upon to
believe in himself as the future Man. His imagination, his religious
aspirations may hold that end before him; but when his reason
asserts itself, rejecting imagination and transcendent intuition, he
puts it by as a brilliant superstition contrary to the hard facts of
the material universe. It becomes then only his inspiring vision of
the impossible. All that is possible is conditioned, limited and
precarious knowledge, happiness, power and good".[2]

Man is divine in essence. He has to become divine in actuality
also. He has realised divinity in his soul and spirit in the past. Now
he has to realise divinity in the dynamic aspect of his personality,
in mind, life and body also. His goal is not attained simply by the
realisation of divinity in the unchanging aspect of his being. He
will attain it only when he realises the divine fully in the changing
aspects of his being also. One cannot set a limit to the onward
march of man. The wonderful and miraculous progress of science
in the last few decades has turned many impossibilities into hard
realities. Science is also coming gradually to believe in the pos-
sibility of conquering even death. It has been the belief of the

1. *L.D.*, Vol. I, pp. 70-71
2. *Ibid.*, p. 71.

Yogic tradition of India that man can conquer death and attain bodily immortality by perfecting *Haṭha Yoga*. Human body has got certain potentialities in it which are not known as yet to medical science and if the secrets of these potentialities are properly discovered, then it is hoped that man may be able to conquer not only disease, suffering etc., but even death.[1] If such things were said a few decades back, they would have been simply hailed as senseless ramblings of superstitious minds. But man of today cannot afford to assume the complacent attitude of enlightened scepticism towards these things. Now if such possibilities are open to science, who knows what greater vistas of possibilities may open themselves to the ancient discoverer, the human spirit. So it is not reasonable for us to assume a pessimistic attitude with regard to the destiny of man or of the cosmos. We cannot cry halt to the progressive march of man. We are not entitled to tell him—thus far and no further.

A question may be raised here: supposing that the supramental evolution does not take place, will it not affect the integral Advaitism of Sri Aurobindo? We are definitely of the opinion that it cannot affect the integral Advaitism or integral Reality but it will certainly affect our realisation of the integral Reality. If the supramental evolution does not take place, then man will be able to have only a partial realisation of Reality and not an integral realisation of it. Moreover, in that case only spirit will be able to attain freedom from bondage and nature will have to suffer eternally under the wheel of necessity. The individuals here and there will be attaining salvation but the world will always remain a vale of tears. A few individual souls will be able to escape from the clutches of suffering, evil and ignorance but the multitude will be always crushed and pounded by them. The world in that case will always be governed by the undivine elements and not by the divine principle or law.

But though these consequences may follow from the failure of the cosmic process to attain the supramental and spiritual status in the course of evolution, yet they cannot affect the integral nature of Reality as such. It has been shown above and in the preceding chapters that there is no principle which is essentially opposed to the Absolute. The principles such as matter, life, mind, ignorance, evil etc. which are considered as opposed to the Absolute have

---

1. *Vide* Alexis Carrell, *Man: The Unknown*

been shown to be nothing else but the different forms and modes of the Absolute. So whether man and the cosmos rise to a higher or supramental status or not, by the descent of the Supermind, it cannot essentially affect the nature of the Absolute or Reality. The nature of Reality will remain the same whether man realises it or not. The integral knowledge inherent in the Absolute will not suffer any diminution if man fails to attain it. The Absolute is not dependent in any way on man either for existence or for knowledge. It is self-existent and self-conscious. Just as the Absolute of Śaṅkara and of Rāmānuja cannot be said to be affected if this man or that man or any man as such fails to know or realise it, in the same way the Absolute of Sri Aurobindo also will not be affected if man fails to realise its integral nature. But we cannot rule out, as we have stated above, the possibility of the supramental evolution and the attainment of gnostic being and consciousness by man.

Our discussion or treatment of Sri Aurobindo's system has made it amply clear that Sri Aurobindo has achieved admirable success in establishing his integral view of Reality or his integral Advaitism. The magnificent mansion of Sri Aurobindo's Integral Advaitism is built on the strong and sound foundations of higher reason or Logic of the Infinite and of integral knowledge. Sri Aurobindo has made a decisive contribution to Metaphysics, Logic and Epistemology by putting forward his conception of the integral Reality, of the Logic of the Infinite and of integral knowledge respectively, as we have shown in detail in the course of the present work. He has also made a significant and decisive contribution to the theory of evolution by indicating that the evolutionary process is being propelled by a spiritual and self-conscious divine energy and that it is destined to rise to a higher or divine status. His contribution to the theory of liberation lies in his showing that the destiny of man can be fully realised only when not only the spirit but even the physical, vital and mental aspects of man's personality attain freedom from all sorts of bondage, imperfection and limitation.

Sri Aurobindo lays great emphasis on the divinisation of life along with the realisation of spirit or Ātman. And this for the reason that he visualises the possibility and the necessity of the divine law, *Ṛta*, working freely and in an unfettered way in the realm of mind, life and matter. The spirit or the divine law has to guide the course of human life and the world in a conscious and direct manner instead of working in an indirect way from behind the veil of ignorance and inconscience. This aim has been partially fulfilled from time to time by the emergence of the immortal *Avatāras* or incarnations of the Divine and by the advent of the great saints and prophets in the world's history. But this is not enough. What is really required is the complete victory of Spirit over matter and the total divinisation of life which is the real aim of the individual and cosmic evolution. This will be possible only when the conscious force of the Divine makes a permanent descent into earth-consciousness and leads the human life and the cosmos from *imperfection to perfection*, from *darkness to light*, and from *death to immortality*.[1]

---

1. असतो मा सद्गमय, तमसो मा ज्योतिर्गमय, मृत्योर्मामृतं गमय । (*Bṛh.* 1.3.28)

SELECTED BIBLIOGRAPHY

SELECTED WORKS OF SRI AUROBINDO

The Life Divine, First Volume, Third Edition, 1947; Second Volume, Part I and II, Second Ed. 1944 (Ārya Publishing House, Calcutta).

On The Veda (Sri Aurobindo Ashram, Pondicherry, 1957).

Essays on The Gītā, First and Second Series (Ārya Publishing House, Calcutta, 1944-45).

On Yoga I: The Synthesis of Yoga (Sri Aurobindo Ashram, Pondicherry, 1956).

Savitri, Part I, II and III (Sri Aurobindo Ashram, Pondicherry, 1950-51).

Bases of Yoga (Ārya Publishing House, Calcutta, 1947).

The Human Cycle (Sri Aurobindo Library, New York, 1950).

The Ideal of Human Unity (Sri Aurobindo Library, 1950).

The Upanishads (Sri Aurobindo Ashram, Pondicherry, 1971).

The Mother (Sri Aurobindo Ashram, Pondicherry, 1946).

The Riddle of This World (Arya Publishing House, Calcutta, 1946).

Isha Upanishad, Translation and Comments by Sri Aurobindo (Ārya Publishing House, Calcutta, 1945).

Ayer, A.J., *Language, Truth and Logic* (Gollancy, London, 1964).

Belvalkar, S.K. (ed.), *The Brahma-Sūtras of Bādarāyaṇa with the Comment of Śaṅkarācārya* (Oriental Book Supplying Agency, Poona).

Belvalkar, S.K., and Ranade, R.D., *History of Indian Philosophy*, Vol. II (Bilvakunja Publishing House, Poona).

Bergson, Henri, *Creative Evolution* (New York, 1911).

Bhattacharyya, K.C., *Studies in Philosophy*, Vol. I, ed. by Gopināth Bhattacharyya (Progressive Publishers, Calcutta, 1958).

Blyth, John W., *A Modern Introduction to Logic* (Boston, 1957).

Bosanquet, Bernard, *Logic* (Oxford University Press, 1911).

Bradley, F.H., *Appearance and Reality* (Oxford University Press, London).

——*The Principles of Logic* (Oxford University Press).

Caird, Edward, *Hegel* (Blackwood's Philosophical Classics).

Candrakīrti, *Prasannapadā,* Commentary on the *Madhyamaka-śāstra* of Nāgārjuna, Ed. by P.L. Vaidya (The Mithila Institute, Darbhanga, 1960).

Chaudhary, Haridas, *Sri Aurobindo: The Prophet of Life Divine* (Sri Aurobindo Pathmandir, Calcutta, 1951).

——*The Philosophy of Integralism* (Sri Aurobindo Ashram, Pondicherry, 1967).

Clarke, W.N., *Outline of Christian Theology,* 1898.

Cohen and Nagel, *An Introduction to Logic and Scientific Method* (N.D. Allied Publishers).

Dasgupta, S.N., *A History of Indian Philosophy,* Vol. II (Cambridge University Press).

——*Indian Idealism* (Cambridge, 1933).

Dharmarāja Adhvarin, *Vedāntaparibhāṣā,* ed. by S.S. Suryanarayana Shastri (The Adyar Library, Adyar, 1942).

Hegel, *Logic,* Wallace's Translation (Oxford, the Clarendon Press, 1892).

——*Science of Logic,* Translated by W.H. Johnston and L.G. Struthers (George Allen, London).

——*Philosophy of Religion,* E.T. (1895).

Herbert Marcuse, *One-Dimensional Man* (Beacon Press, Boston, 1969).

Herbert Spencer, *First Principles,* 1862.

James Hastings (ed.), *Encyclopaedia of Religion and Ethics,* Vol. XII (Edinburgh, 1952).

James, William, *Varieties of Religious Experience* (1906)

Kant, Immanuel, *Critique of Pure Reason,* Max Müller's Translation (London, 1881).

——*Selections from Kant,* Watson's Translation.

Langley, G.H., *Sri Aurobindo* (London, Marlowe, 1949).

Mahadevan, T.M.P., *The Philosophy of Advaita* (Luzac and Company, London, 1938).

Maitra, S.K., *An Introduction to The Philosophy of Sri Aurobindo* (Sri Aurobindo Ashram, Pondicherry).

——Studies in Sri Aurobindo's Philosophy (Banaras Hindu University, 1945).

Mansel, Henry, Limits of Religious Thought (Bampton-Lectures).

Misra, R.S., Studies in Philosophy and Religion (Bhāratīya Vidyā Prakāśana, Varanasi, 1971).

Mookerjee, Satkari, The Buddhist Philosophy of Universal Flux (University of Calcutta, 1935).

Mukerji, A.C., The Nature of Self (The Indian Press Ltd., Allahabad, 1938).

Mure, An Introduction to Hegel (Oxford, the Clarendon Press, 1940).

Murti, T.R.V., The Central Philosophy of Buddhism (George Allen and Unwin Ltd., London, 1960).

Nāgārjuna, Madhyamakaśāstra, Ed. by P.L. Vaidya (The Mithila Institute, Darbhanga, 1960).

Pandey, K.C., Abhinavagupta: An Historical and Philosophical Study (Chowkhamba Sanskrit Series, Varanasi, 1935).

Patañjali, Yoga-Sūtra.

Paul Tillich, Systematic Theology, Vol. I (The University of Chicago Press, 1951).

Pitcher, George, The Philosophy of Wittgenstein (Prentice-Hall of India Private Ltd., New Delhi, 1972).

Radhakrishnan, S., (ed.), The Principal Upaniṣads (George Allen and Unwin Ltd., London).

——Indian Philosophy, Vol. I and II (George Allen and Unwin Ltd.).

——Eastern Religions and Western Thought (Oxford University Press).

——An Idealist View of Life (George Allen and Unwin Ltd., London).

Rāmānuja, Ācārya, Śārīrakamīmānsā-Bhāṣya—Gītā-Bhāṣya.

Ranade, R.D., A Constructive Survey of Upaniṣadic Philosophy (Oriental Book Agency, Poona).

Samuel, Alexander, Space, Time and Deity, Vol. II (Macmillan London, 1920).

Śaṅkarācārya, Brahmasūtraśāṅkarabhāṣya—Bhagavadgītā-Bhāṣya—Commentary On the Upaniṣads.

Shastri, A.B., Studies in Post-Śaṁkara Dialectics (University of Calcutta, 1936).

Sircar, M.N., The System of Vedāntic Thought and Culture—Comparative Studies in Vedāntism.

430   THE INTEGRAL ADVAITISM OF SRI AUROBINDO

Stace, W.T., *A Critical History of Greek Philosophy* (London, 1960).

Suzuki, *Outline of Mahāyāna Buddhism—Awakening of Faith.*

Tagore, R.N., *The Religion of Man* (George Allen and Unwin Ltd., 1958).

Theo-Stcherbatsky, *The Soul Theory of the Buddhists* (Bhāratīya Vidyā Prakāśana, Varanasi, 1970).

Trueblood, D.E., *Philosophy of Religion* (Harper Brothers, New York, 1957).

Urmson, J.O., *Philosophical Analysis* (Clarendon Press Oxford, 1956).

Vācaspati Miśra, *Sāṁkhyatattva Kaumudī—Bhāmati*, Nirṇaya Sāgara Edn.

Vyāsa, *Yoga-Bhāṣya*, Commentary on the *Yoga-Sūtra* of Patañjali.

Walter Kaufmann (ed.), *Existentialism from Dostoevsky to Sartre* (The World Publishing Company, New York).

Wittgenstein, L., *Tractatus Logico-Philosophicus* (London: Kegan Paul, 1922).

——*Philosophical Investigations* (New York: Macmillan, 1953).

Woodroffe, John, *The World as Power, Reality* (Madras).

Woodworth, Robert S., *Contemporary Schools of Psychology* (Methuen and Co. Ltd., London, 1949).

Zaehner, R.C., *Hinduism* (London, Oxford University Press, 1962).

——*Hindu Scriptures*, edited and translated by R.C. Zaehner (J.M. Dent and Sons Ltd., 1966).

INDEX

Absolute, Absolutism, Sri Aurobindo's integral view of Reality or, 15-22; as Existence, 115ff.; as Consciousness-Force, IV, 151ff.; as Bliss, V, 181ff.; as Supermind, VI, 201ff.; as unknowable, 127-28; as Indeterminability, 142-45; and the Logic of the Infinite, 29ff.; a critical estimate of Sri Aurobindo's view of, 391-400

Advaita, Advaitism, see under Śaṅkara and Integral Advaitism

Aitareya Upaniṣad, 156n.

Ajātivāda, 259

Alexander, S., 19, 382-84, his *Space, Time and Deity*, 383n.

Ānanda, see under V, Bliss

Ānandabodhācārya, 256

Anirvacanīya khyāti, 264

Aristotle, 46, 53, 54, 373

Aristotelian *nous*, 53

Arthur Avalon (ed.), *Principles of Tantra*, 172n.

Aruṇi, 116

Asatkāryavāda, 121

Aśvaghoṣa, 210

Ātman, 122-25, 161ff., 186; *see* under soul

Ātman-Māyā, 161-63

Atreya, B.L., his *The Philosophy of the Yoga-Vāsiṣṭha*, 185 n.

Aurobindo, Sri,
Meaning and significance of his Integral Advaitism, 3-6, *see* under Integral Advaitism; his criticism of materialism and idealism, 8-15; his integral view of Reality, 15-22, *see* under Absolute; his concept of integral knowledge, 22-27, *see* under integral knowledge; his con-

ception of the Logic of the Infinite, 29ff.; his solution of the problem of evil, 194-200ff.; his conception of ignorance, VII, 247ff.; his theory of mind, life and matter, VIII, 285ff.; his conception of evolution, *see* under evolution; his conception of rebirth, 343-50; his conception of the gnostic being, 366ff.

Ayer, A.J., 32-33, his *Language, Truth* and *Logic*, 33n.

Bādarāyaṇa, 219

Becoming, as ultimately real: Views of modern science. Hume, Bergson and Buddhists, 118-20; theories of, 120-22

Being, Absolute as existence or, 115ff.; negation of an impossibility, 124-25; as unknowable, 127ff.; existence or as indeterminability, 142-45

Bergson, 25, 113, 119; his view of intuition as the supreme source of knowledge, 139; his view of becoming as absolute reality, 119-20ff.; his conception of the unknowable 139; his rejection of the mechanical view of evolution, 414, his *An Introduction to Metaphysics*, 291 n.

Berkeley, 13

Bhagvad-gītā, 74n., 43n.

Bhāmatī, 216n.

Bhāskara, 25, 171, 212; his Bhāṣya, 212n., 437 n.; his view of intuition as the supreme source of knowledge, 25; his view of Brahman, 212; relationship of the individual soul with Brahman, 408.

bhūta-tathatā, 210

Bliss, Absolute as, 181ff.; cosmos manifested out of, and for, 182; psychic

the creative aspect of the absolute, 202-04; as a selective faculty of knowledge, 202; Integral Advaitism of Sri Aurobindo based on, 203; a link between the Absolute and the finite world, 228; holds a proper balance, between the one and the many; creates the world in accordance with the divine law, 231; as Truth-Consciousness or Real-Idea, 231-36; radically different from mind, 232; intervening grades between mind and, 232; Truth-Consciousness gives a precise meaning to the term, 232; order in the cosmos due to the presence of Truth-Consciousness within it, 233; meaning of Real-Idea, 234; the Vedic seers' conception of the, 235-36; gods as the powers and creation of, 235; as the upholder of the divine law, of Dharma, 236; the triple status of, 236ff.; ignorance does not exist in, 249; Evolution from mind to, 351ff; the supramental transformation, 366ff.

Suzuki, D.T., his *Awakening of Faith*, 210 n.; his *Outline of Mahāyāna Buddhism*, 214 n.

Śvetāśvatara Upaniṣad, 142 n.

synthetic judgments *a priori*, Kant's formulation of, 39 ff.; difference between analytic judgments and, 39; joint products of sensibility and reason; mark a fundamental change in the logical outlook, 40

Taittirīya Upaniṣad, 125 n., 126n.

Tantra, Tantras, 170, 173

Tantrāloka, 176n.

Tāntriks, Śākta, 170, 173

taṭastha lakṣaṇa, 209; and *svarūpa lakṣaṇa*, 209

Tathāgata, Nāgārjuna's view of, 211

Tattva-Pradīpikā, 254n.

Tattvoddyota, 211n.

Tautology, Tautologies, 31ff.; Laws of Identity and Excluded Middle as, 31;

Wittgenstein conceives propositions of Logic as, 31; necessary truths as, 31; not a picture of reality, 31

Theology, Henry Mansel's view of true, 135

Truth-function, Wittgenstein's view, 31; as tautologies and contradictions, 32

Truths, necessary and contingent, Leibniz's view, 39

Urmson, J.O., his *Philosophical Analysis*, 31n.

Vācaspati, dialectical criticism of the concept of change in the Absolute, 215 ff.; theory of Jīva or the individual soul as the support of nescience, 256; view of erroneous perception, 267

Vallabha, 321, 394

Varadachari, K.C., 5, 6n., 349n., 413n.

Vijñānavādins, 265

Vimuktātman, 254

Vivaraṇa School, 256

vyāvahārika satya and *prātibhāsika satya*, 265

Watson, his *Selections from Kant*, 42n.

Weber, Alfred, his *History of Philosophy*, 14n., 132n.

Will, Kant's view of moral, 132; autonomy of the, 132

William James, 226, his *Varieties of Religious Experience*, 226n.

Wittgenstein, 31; his view of the propositions of Logic, 31; tautologies and contradictions, 31, 32, 33

Woodroffe, Sir John, 171, his *The World as Power, Reality*, 171n.

Xenophanes, 335

Yājñavalkya, 173, 186

Yoga of Patañjali, 359

Yogācāra School, 13

Yoga-Māyā, 173

Yoga-Vāsiṣṭha, 185n.